D0857405

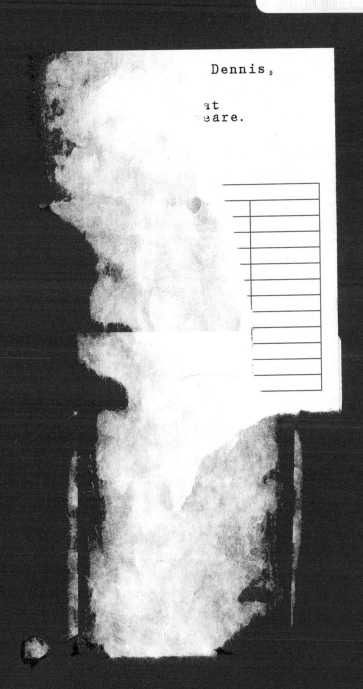

Dennis,

at
eare.

Shakespeare is widely recognized as the world's most popular playwright, yet most studies of the performance of his work concentrate on how the text has been played and what meanings have been conveyed through acting and interpretative directing. This book enlarges the notion of how the theatre creates meaning by investigating how the visual relates to Shakespeare on the stage. Dennis Kennedy demonstrates that much of audience reception is determined by the visual representation, which is normally more immediate and direct than the aural conveyance of a text.

The numerous and varied illustrations (172 in all, with 21 in full color) document and illuminate the commentary and constitute a valuable archive of pictorial resources for the study of Shakespeare and of twentieth-century theatre. They also clearly show the importance of the alternative traditions of Shakespearean performance outside of the English language, which are infrequently discussed by commentators.

Ranging widely over productions in Great Britain, Europe, Russia and North America, this book will appeal to those interested in Shakespeare, in the cultural uses of classic texts, in modern and postmodern theatre practice, in performance theory, and in the place of the visual in performance.

Dennis Kennedy is Professor of Theatre Arts at the University of Pittsburgh. His books from Cambridge University Press include *Granville Barker and the Dream of Theatre*, *Plays by Harley Granville Barker*, and a collection of essays entitled *Foreign Shakespeare*.

LOOKING AT SHAKESPEARE

Looking at Shakespeare

A VISUAL HISTORY OF
TWENTIETH-CENTURY
PERFORMANCE

DENNIS KENNEDY

CAMBRIDGE
UNIVERSITY PRESS

Published by the Press Syndicate of the University of Cambridge
The Pitt Building, Trumpington Street, Cambridge CB2 1RP
40 West 20th Street, New York, NY 10011–4211, USA
10 Stamford Road, Oakleigh, Melbourne 3166, Australia

First published 1993
Reprinted 1994

Printed in Great Britain at the University Press, Cambridge

A catalogue record for this book is available from the British Library

Library of Congress cataloguing in publication data

Kennedy, Dennis
Looking at Shakespeare: a visual history of twentieth-century performance /
Dennis Kennedy.
     p.   cm.
Includes bibliographical references and index.
ISBN 0 521 34655 X (hardback)
1. Shakespeare, William, 1564–1616 – Stage history – 1950 – Pictorial works.
2. Shakespeare, William, 1564–1616 – Stage history – 1800–1950 – Pictorial works.
3. Theatres – Stage-setting and scenery – History – 20th century – Pictorial
works. 4. Theatre – History – 20th century – Pictorial works. I. Title.
PR3100.K46 1993
792.9′5 – dc 20 92-19013 CIP

TAG

In memory of my father and mother
John and Gertrude Kennedy
something rich and strange

Contents

Color plates

Between pages 192 and 193.

Sources and credits

Cologne Theatre Museum (Institut für Theaterwissenschaft, Universität zu Köln): 1–3, 5, 12. *Play Pictorial* (London, 1912), courtesy University of Pittsburgh: 4. Austrian National Library, Vienna, courtesy Dr. Peter Pirchan: 6. Shakespeare Centre Library, Stratford-upon-Avon (England): 7–10, 13–17. Bibliothèque de l'Arsenal, Paris (copyright ARS, NY / ADAGP): 11. Gisela Scheidler: 18. Magnum Photos, Paris: 19–21.

Illustrations

Sources and credits

Shakespeare Centre Library, Stratford (England): 1–2, 4, 52–6, 60–1, 68–9, 76–7, 79–85, 113, 115–23, 141. The Longleat MS: 3. Theatre Museum, Victoria and Albert Museum, London: 5 (*Illustrated Times* 1856), 11. *Illustrated London News* Picture Library: 6 (*The Graphic* 1882), 22 (*ILN* 1901), 23–4 (*The Sketch* 1912). Cologne Theatre Museum (Institut für Theaterwissenschaft, Universität zu Köln): 7, 21, 29, 92–3. Deutsches Theater Museum, Munich: 8, 17, 129. Mander and Mitchenson Theatre Collection, London: 9, 64. *Le Petit Bleu* (Paris, 1898): 10. Craig, *The Art of the Theatre*: 12. Craig, *Towards a New Theatre*: 13. *Theatre and Art* (Moscow, 1912), courtesy Lawrence Senelick: 14. UCLA: 15. Alma Law archive: 16, 88–9. Austrian National Library, Vienna: 18–20, 31. Univ. of Michigan Library (Rare Books and Special Collections, Granville Barker promptbook): 25–7. *Le Théâtre* (Paris, 1914): 28. MacGowan and Jones, *Continental Stagecraft* (1947 redrawing by Jones, collection of Robert L. B. Tobin, San Antonio, Texas): 30. Academy of Arts (West) Berlin: 32–3. Dickinson, *The Theatre in a Changing Europe*: 34. Czech National Theatre archive, Prague: 35–40. Polish Theatre Museum, Warsaw: 41. National Academy of Sciences, Warsaw: 42–5, 86–7. Birmingham Shakespeare Library: 46–7, 57–9. Cave, *Terence Gray and the Cambridge Festival Theatre*, courtesy Chadwyck and Healey: 48–51. Jones, *Drawings for the Theatre*: 62–3. Library of Congress Federal Theatre Project Collection, George Mason University: 65. Billy Rose Theatre Collection, New York Public Library for the Performing Arts: 66–7. Stratford Festival archive (Canada): 70–3, 144. Harvard Theatre Collection: 74–5, 78, 90. Agence Enguerand, Paris: 91. Berliner Ensemble: 94–5. Deutsches Theater archive, Berlin: 96–8. Program, private collection: 108. Arena Stage, Washington: 112. Burgtheater, Vienna: 132–3. Bibliothèque Gaston Baty, Paris: 135. International Center for Theatrical Creations, Paris: 137–8. Guthrie Theatre, Minneapolis: 139. Royal National Theatre, London: 142. Hungarian Theatre Centre, Budapest: 147. Others acquired directly from the photographers identified in captions.

Preface

This is a book about the relationship between scenography and international Shakespeare performance in the modern and postmodern eras. My intention is two-fold: to investigate how the visual relates to Shakespeare on the stage and transmits meaning, and to attempt to understand some of the complex cultural uses of Shakespeare in the century. The project, which I explain in the first chapter, is intimidating in its material scope and philosophic implication, and would have been impossible without considerable help. A number of designers, directors, dramaturgs, and Shakespeare translators have volunteered their conversation and insight, and I offer particular thanks to Gerhard Blashe in Vienna, Maik Hamburger in Berlin, Adam Killian in Warsaw, Ming Cho Lee in New York, Milan Lukeš in Prague, and John Barton, Bob Crowley, Chris Dyer, Pamela Howard, and Timothy O'Brien in London. Over the past seven years and more I have profited greatly from the cooperation of a humbling array of scholars, including Denis Bablet, David Bradby, John Russell Brown, Jarka Burian, Richard Allen Cave, Krystyna Duniec, R. A. Foakes, Dominique Goy-Blanquet, Wolfgang Greisenegger, Alma Law, Patrice Pavis, Lawrence Senelick, Zdeněk Stříbrný, and J. L. Styan. Wilhelm Hortmann generously gave his hospitality, his memory of postwar German Shakespeare, and his help in acquiring some difficult illustrations.

The International Theatre Institute has been a highly valuable resource. Elizabeth Burdick of the New York office helped at an early stage through an impressive library relating to international scenography, and Martha Coigney was essential in arranging some extremely difficult research visits abroad. I must also thank ITI administrators in Europe, especially Gabrielle Heller in Paris, Malgorzata Majewska-Waraszkiewicz in Warsaw, Andrea Szabadné Suján in Budapest, and Eva Vítová in Prague. In a similar vein, much of the research into pictorial resources would have been impossible without the active assistance of archivists worldwide. I owe especial gratitude to Harris Balic of the Austrian National Library, Lisa Brandt of the Stratford (Canada) archive, Rita Engels of the Deutsches Theater archive in Berlin, Roswitha Flatz of the Cologne Theatre Museum, Heinrich Huesmann and Eckehart Nölle of the Munich Theatre Museum, H. Konecná and Jana Patocková of the Czech National Theatre archive in Prague, Martha Mahard (formerly) of the Harvard Theatre Collection, and Niky Rathbone of the Birmingham Shakespeare Library. Marian Pringle of the Shakespeare Centre Library in Stratford (England) has been unfailing in her generosity and archival assistance.

I have also received important material assistance. The University of Pittsburgh has made substantial contributions through the Office of Research, the Faculty of Arts and Sciences, the Department of Theatre Arts, and the Western European Studies Program. The National Endowment for the Humanities awarded me a Summer Stipend and a year-long Fellowship, which permitted extended research travel; then further awarded the book a publication subsidy which has paid for much of the high cost of the illustrations, especially of the color plates. Dependent as it is on so many pictures, the book would have been impossible without the active cooperation of Cambridge University Press, especially of Sarah Stanton, who first encouraged the project and maintained support through a long wait. I also wish to acknowledge the assistance of Julie Greenblatt of the New York branch; and of Chris Lyall Grant, most excellent subeditor.

My colleagues Attilio Favorini and Henry Heymann frequently lent their sensitivity about Shakespeare and design. Cary Mazer read some early chapters and made highly useful comments. Anthony Parise has proved his friendship yet again by carefully and graciously critiquing the entire manuscript; his labors have been invaluable. Bryn Bennett and Scott Vogel have been most efficient graduate research assistants; Scott Vogel has been equally so in preparing the index. Students at the University of Pittsburgh, in graduate seminars in European avant-garde theatre and in the history of Shakespeare performance, have influenced my thinking over the years, and I particularly thank John Barnes, Jay Scott Chipman, Gregg Dion, Ellen Kelson, David Kuhns, Frazer Lively, Erica Magnus, and Eugenia Popescu-Judetz. Ann Tyrrell Kennedy has supported me in ways too deep to catalogue, from helping when my languages failed (as they did too often) to reminding me by her presence of the reason for working.

Documentation and illustrations

References in the text and notes to scenographic archives (by city name) and to books (by author's name) point to the Selected References at the end. It would have been confusing, however, to register all my sources there, since many are highly specialized. Only works that are referred to frequently or that have general importance to the subject are so listed; the rest are given in full in the notes. Unless otherwise stated, the translations from foreign languages are my own; so are the mistakes. Quotations from Shakespeare come from *The Complete Works*, ed. Stanley Wells and Gary Taylor (Oxford, 1986).

The illustrations carry identifying captions: titles, dates, cities, artistic personnel, scenes depicted. The names of the director and of all the known designers are given only for the first illustration in a sequence dealing with the same production; but the photographer's name, when known, is given for each photograph. The sources of the illustrations can be found on pp. xii and xx. Every effort has been made to identify copyright holders of illustrations and to secure permission for their reproduction. I apologize if any infringements have occurred.

Abbreviations used in captions:

D   director
Des   designer (sets and costumes by same person or team)
S   set designer
C   costume designer
L   lighting designer
P   photographer

D. K.
University of Pittsburgh

1 | *Shakespeare and the visual*

Just before Shakespeare's birthday in 1978 the audience in his famous hometown looked at an unusual sight: a setting for *The Taming of the Shrew* that would have seemed proper in sixteenth-century Italy, taken almost directly from Serlio's example of the correct and decorous design for comedy. Spectators at the Royal Shakespeare Theatre had grown used to a nearly bare stage but here was a full illusionist picture, with a false proscenium framing a series of receding columns and arches, a colorful Renaissance view of Padua in perspective, built out of wing pieces and drop flats, with a painted landscape on a backcloth and a classical statue of lovers

1 *The Taming of the Shrew* 1978 Stratford. D: Michael Bogdanov. Des: Chris Dyer. L: Chris Ellis. P: Thomas F. Holte. The opening set, a witty parody of Serlio.

upstage center (illus. 1). This did not look like the usual work of Chris Dyer, nor the likely setting for a production by Michael Bogdanov, *enfant terrible* of British theatre; this looked, in fact, unlike anything seen at Stratford in the past quarter century.

But not for long. Before the play started, a drunk appeared in the audience in hot argument with a female attendant over the location of his seat. Shouting "I'm not having any bloody woman telling me what to do," he made his weaving way on to the stage, where he proceeded to attack the beautiful, proper set. He knocked over the columns, tipped over the baskets of fruit, tore down the front curtains, pulled apart the statue, as stagehands ran back and forth trying to stop him, simultaneously taking away the pieces he had demolished. This, it is fair to say, was a true deconstructive act. A flat fell on the drunk but he remained unscathed, its cutout window allowing him grace; another flat repeated the moment; yet still an occasional audience member failed to get the visual joke and went on the stage to help the crew

2 *The Taming of the Shrew* 1978 Stratford. P: Thomas F. Holte. The set after demolition: a metal scaffolding in front of the bare walls of the theatre. Here Kate and Petruchio (Paola Dionisotti and Jonathan Pryce) rested on the journey to his house, described by Grumio in 4.1, which was staged by their running up and down the steps and catwalks.

suppress the disruption. Even after wide press coverage some spectators, well into the run, recognizing neither Jonathan Pryce in the drunk nor the relevance of his sexist remarks, fled from the house. With the Renaissance set gone, those who remained now looked on the bare back and side walls of the stage, with an elaborate metal scaffolding in front (illus. 2) – a combination of San Quentin and Paddington Station, said one critic.[1] The drunk was soon identified as Christopher Sly; and, wrapped in the illusion of the Induction, later became Petruchio himself, making his first entrance on a motorcycle. The argumentative house attendant, Paola Dionisotti, reappeared as Kate. We were in Padua, yes, but clearly in 1978.

This production used scenography not only to establish environment and atmosphere but also to create a complicated theatrical signifier of its thematic approach. *The Taming of the Shrew* is not a play about fifteenth-century Italy, Bogdanov and Dyer implied, but about the more subtle sexism of the modern world; the hardness and brisk unsentimentality of the performance were established by the harsh materials and bare, imprisoned look of the set. Most productions use stage and costume design to comment on the play, as a guide to the interpretive treatment; this one, by showing us at the start a set that was subsequently rejected, added a view of what it might have been but deliberately was not. By the end, when Kate delivered her final speech without ironic inflections to the male characters assembled around a green baize gaming table, the lines had acquired a meaning opposite to their apparent one, and the men on stage (and some in the audience) cringed at her words. Thus the demolition of the *trompe l'oeil* scene at the start was also a demolition of the facile view of the play, that tendency of many productions to treat it as a delightful *commedia* romp, glossing over its jagged edges, ignoring its challenges for late twentieth-century society, avoiding the contradictions within the text itself. Most interesting of all, the strategy required the audience to deconstruct the visual text in their minds, for in order to understand the meaning of the production it was necessary to understand the oppositional meaning of the two sets. The scenography, therefore, was a visualization of Brecht's "Not...but" process: not then but now, not illusion but truth, not painted perspective but hard iron railings, not Serlio but Dyer. And, a traditionalist might add, not Shakespeare but Bogdanov.

What is the appropriate setting for Shakespeare's plays? Throughout the twentieth century that question has continually preoccupied artists concerned with their production, as well as audiences and critics who witness the results. That the question must be asked at all is significant, revealing

that the modern theatre does not know unconditionally how to dress actors
in classic plays or what physical environment to provide for them to move
in. In other words, for the past hundred years or so we have no longer
shared cultural convictions that would establish theatrical style. Instead the
century has offered a variety of answers, some primarily subjective, others
based on external events or fashions, that serve for a moment or a few years
and then become extinct. To say this is to say scarcely more than a
commonplace about the eclecticism and self-consciousness of twentieth-
century art. Yet the visual history of performance, which has been mostly
excluded from Shakespeare studies, rewards extended investigation because
of its intriguing relationship to the status and uses of Shakespeare, both in
the theatre and in the culture at large.

VISUAL CRITICISM

Visual fashions and gestural codes change swiftly, and are connected to
place as well as time. This probably has always been true, though the
extraordinary speed of communication in the modern world has greatly
accelerated the cycle of cultural dissemination, decay, and renewal. Popular
movies, television shows, and magazine advertisements only a few years old
often look false or artificial because they were created to reflect or elicit a
contemporary vogue, which, by definition, soon shifted. Similar cultural
variations occur among nations, races, or geographical groups; a commercial product, offered for sale worldwide, normally needs an entirely
different visual encoding in Bangladesh than in Japan. A theatrical event, as
the English term *production* implies, is also a cultural artifact and is subject to
the same external forces in the visual realm. Theatrical productions normally
have visual freshness because they have been manufactured for a highly
specific geographical and sociopolitical audience, and they rarely survive
long enough to look old-fashioned. When they are long-lived, they may well
need visual refreshening; eventually they will lose their significant
connections to the culture or the moment they invoke. This is a simple,
though incomplete, explanation of why classic plays seem to need theatrical
reinterpretation every ten or twenty years, and why the definitive Hamlet of
one generation will appear as an outmoded actor to the next. Peter Brook
reports that at Stratford he and Peter Hall determined that the maximum life
of a production was five years:

It is not only the hair-styles, costumes and make-ups that look dated. All the
different elements of staging – the shorthands of behaviour that stand for certain

emotions; gestures, gesticulations and tones of voice – are all fluctuating on an invisible stock exchange all the time ... A living theatre that thinks it can stand aloof from anything as trivial as fashion will wilt.   (Brook 1968: 16)

There is a clear relationship between what a production looks like and what its spectators accept as its statement and value. This seems obvious: the visual signs the performance generates are not only the guide to its social and cultural meaning but often constitute the meaning itself. Yet remarkably little attention has been paid to the connections between scenography and general performance style, or to the relationship between scenography and audience reception. Or rather, a great deal of attention is paid to these relationships by theatre artists in preparing a production, but critics after the fact have rarely studied how design might be used as a tool of commentary or investigated how to read it. Even less attention has been given to the historical meaning of visual reception; that is, to how the original audience read and understood the visual signifiers. Historians of the playhouse and of scene design tend to recount physical, technological, and aesthetic developments without giving much regard to the performance of specific playtexts for specific audiences. (There are exceptions of course; the groundbreaking work of Denis Bablet is particularly important.)

No doubt part of this reluctance derives from what is sometimes called the literary bias of theatre history, that tendency, natural enough to most writers, of relying on other written records – from the printed drama to newspaper reviews – when imagining the ephemeral moments of past performance. But there is perhaps a deeper anxiety in some minds about the visual, based on a fear that it can overcome the rational aspects of language and character with an appeal too direct and powerful to deny. The Greeks called the theatre a "seeing place," but from Aristotle on there has been a critical suspicion about the visual qualities of performance, despite the existence of a respectable amount of pictorial documentation. The "spectacle" or visual aspect of production, Aristotle held, can have "strong emotional effect but is the least artistic element, the least connected with the poetic art." His own literary bias is clear: "in fact the force of tragedy can be felt even without benefit of public performance and actors, while for the production of the visual effect the property man's art is even more decisive than that of the poet's."[2]

Aristotle's degrading of the visual had enormous effect on subsequent dramatic theory, especially in periods when questions about the theatre blurred into tenets of moral behavior. Certainly in England suspicion about the pictorial side of performance has run deep ever since the reign of James I; Ben Jonson established the prototypical antagonism between dramatist and designer in his bitter "Expostulation with Inigo Jones" over control of the production of court masques:

> And I have mett with those
> That doe cry up the Machine, and the Showes!
> The majesty of Juno in the Cloudes
> And peering forth of Iris in the Shrowdes!

A generation ago W. M. Merchant noted that the closing of the theatres "introduced an ambiguous visual approach to Shakespeare which has persisted to our own day" (20). On the one hand Restoration taste required elegant and expensive stage designs; on the other there was "a continuous line of hostile criticism" about scenery, that foreign importation, as in the prologue to Shadwell's *Squire of Alsatia* (1688):

> There came Machines, brought from a Neighbor Nation;
> Oh, how we suffer'd under Decoration!

The iconoclasm of Puritan religious reform in the seventeenth century led to a dramatic iconoclasm, in which the scripture of plays required protection from visual luxury, that vice of the Italian church and Italian theatre. Peter Hall has felt the same limitations well into the present. "The English suspect the visual delights of the theatre," he once wrote. "For centuries the drama has been studied as literature ... the play not only begins with the word, but it had better end with it as well; otherwise it is inferior, appealing more to the eye than the ear. The puritan distrust of emblems, of representation by symbol and artifice, is a recurrent national neurosis."[3]

But the visual is an essential part of the theatre, even when not particularly delightful or luxurious; what an audience sees is at least as important as what it hears. Shakespeare's rhetorical drama, so tied to a culture of speaking and listening, is nonetheless drama, and its mode of realization requires actors to move through an organized and lighted space. ("Organized" does not imply a decorated, but only a demarcated playing ground; and "lighted" does not imply an artificially illuminated, but only a visible one.) The narrative of a play in performance inescapably takes place in the realm of the seen. It is curious, to say the least, how often that simple fact has been neglected in Shakespeare studies, which have for the most part been rooted in linguistic analysis and have often demonstrated the distrust of emblem and artifice that Peter Hall speaks of. Some of the most important

Shakespearean scholars of the past have cared little for the theatre or have actively disliked it, and preferred to ignore the rather untidy visual messages it sends about the inconsistent value of the plays through history. From Charles Lamb to Cleanth Brooks and beyond, the dominant literary critics in English tended to treat Shakespeare's work as a special case, detached from its theatrical genesis and subsequent representation, of lasting interest chiefly because of its verbal power and philosophic applicability to the human condition.

Of course times have changed, both on the stage and in the study. Producers of Shakespeare are much more likely today to know something of current critical discourse, just as Shakespearean commentators are much more willing to admit the importance of the theatre to their intellectual enterprise. There is now, in fact, an unparalleled cooperation between the theatre and the academy and a growing body of publication that is interested in how production affects our understanding of the plays; a recent *festschrift* goes so far as to claim this discourse to be "the single most important tradition in contemporary Shakespeare studies."[4] Though capable of a wide variety of interpretation, in general usage the term "performance criticism" refers to commentary about aspects of performance that sheds light on the meaning of the plays. In other words, "stage-centered criticism," as it is also called, attempts to use the theatrical life of Shakespeare's plays to investigate their essential or authentic condition. Granville Barker's *Prefaces to Shakespeare* (written 1927–46, though his earliest formulations go back to 1912) is usually thought to be the progenitor of this line, and Barker's own position as a radical director of Shakespeare who retired from the theatre to become a reflective critic insured his patriarchal status: the great and true amphibian, he has long been admired by both theatre practitioners and academics. His approach has been elaborated and extended by a number of eminent Shakespeareans in the Anglo-American tradition, most notably by Muriel Bradbrook, Bernard Beckerman, John Russell Brown, and J. L. Styan, who have added enormously to our understanding.

But the very phrase "performance criticism," which is not often seen outside of Shakespeare studies, should alert us to a potential difficulty, for it implies a cohesive enterprise (criticism) about a unitary cultural activity (performance) and neither of these notions will withstand much scrutiny. First of all, to separate the consideration of Shakespeare's plays from the general movements of theatre history, as many performance critics do, is problematic. It may be convenient and may accord with the organization of the academy, but it would certainly be more historically comprehensive to stress Shakespeare's relationship to changing theatrical manners. There is little point in making the theatre central to an appreciation of Shakespeare if his work is then treated as if it existed in an etherium. Indeed the story of Shakespearean representation – whether in the theatre, in the transmission of the texts, or in the general iconic status of the writer's work in world culture – should forcibly remind us that the plays and their meanings have never managed to escape the marks of time.

Though the goal of performance criticism may be an unbiased perspective on the plays, in print it has often assumed an evangelical or moralistic tone about production. It is accepted practice for both journalists and scholars to condemn artistic realization of Shakespeare based upon their sense that an important aspect of the source has been violated; since such writers claim an unimpeachable and indelible authority, some of the most sophisticated critics of our time have been led into positions from which they feel obliged to defend Shakespeare against the uses the theatre has made of him. Not only do they privilege the written text above its performance, they also assume that standards or boundaries of interpretation must exist for its performance, usually determined by the critic's analysis of the playwright's objectives. Rooted in what can be called intentional hermeneutics, much of the tradition of writing about Shakespeare on the stage has been detached from any aesthetic investigation of what the stage does and why it does it. W. B. Worthen has noticed how some of this commentary reveals through its rhetoric a surprising distrust of the theatre, and "seems inexplicably isolated from the theoretical and methodological inquiries that might help to direct it."[5] In general, it has valued performance for what it teaches about the meaning of Shakespeare's linguistic text, which is assumed to be phenomenologically unaffected, durable.

Performance criticism of Shakespeare has been grounded in a different type of literary bias, the belief that the goal of theatrical activity is the authentic realization of playscripts. This is a misconception of long standing, attacked in recent years by a number of cultural historians, semioticians, and theatre artists.[6] Though a written drama is usually the foundation of a performance, the *sine qua non* of traditional theatre, it is far from being its sole or even primary rationale. A performance in a theatre, itself the result of extraordinary collaboration among a disparate group of artists coming together with successive series of audiences, has no single intention but rather a complex of vaguely related cultural objectives, ranging from declarations of high art or nationalist propaganda to the personal whim of an actor or the company's need to secure emergency funding. To put it another way, theatres produce scripts but the theatre is about more than scripts. For their part spectators have rarely arrived with the single-minded purpose of hearing a play; they come in addition to see an actress, a marvel of scenery, or each other. They assist at the spectacle as necessary receptors of, and as reciprocal generators of, a complicated and imperfectly comprehended set of signs. Their attitudes to the theatre building and the ludic space, their dress and manners, their own status in the audience, what they eat and drink at intermissions, whether they laugh or cry: all these and many more social strategies greatly affect the experience of what is so reductively called "playgoing." *King Lear*, the program says, but the adventure of performance says many things unrelated to the words which make up the text of the play.

If playgoing in general opens questions that go far beyond the consideration of playtexts, and beyond purely artistic concerns, concentrating attention on the visual aspects of performance returns us to aesthetic effect yet offers a way to investigate the non-literary manifestation of performance. Though normally based upon an idea or a vision engendered by the words of a play, stage, costume, and lighting design can easily disregard or transcend both the words and the notional setting, reminding us that though performance may seek as its goal the faithful transmittal of the dramatist's writing, it need not do so. We are also reminded that ideas about what constitutes fidelity are shifting; they may encompass a fidelity to the spirit of the play as understood at a given moment as well as a literal fidelity to the details of its fable. Even the briefest look at the history of Shakespeare staging will suggest how divergent visual approaches can be.

Bertolt Brecht, himself one of the great poets and playwrights of the century, exploited the practice of appropriation (*Aneignung*) of the classics for his own purposes, turning Shakespeare and other earlier dramatists into conveyers of new meanings for the present. While Brecht's practice seems extreme because it involved rewriting established texts, there is a sense in which every production of a play is an appropriation of its text, a seizing of its resources, whether the text has been translated into colloquial modern German or simply selected from available English editions. The regular practice by directors of cutting the plays, sometimes with ruthless tyranny, demonstrates how subject the text is to theatrical exploitation. How and why this occurs is of small literary consequence but of great cultural resonance, offering insights about the theatre as a social institution and about the place of classic plays in the world of the present. Because the lighting, settings, and costumes of a production establish its physical world in an incontrovertible manner, scenography is normally the most direct representation an audience receives of the performed meaning of the play – which is a separate matter from its literary meaning.

In brief, this book is about how the theatre has appropriated Shakespeare in the realm of the seen. Its method is to chronicle international scenography for the production of Shakespeare's plays in the twentieth century; its principal intent is to investigate how scenography may be used as a guide to the changes that have occurred in our understanding of Shakespeare and his place in the theatre. Some of my strategies rely on recent developments in theatre semiology; other are aligned with materialist interpretations of culture. These two methodologies are related in my approach because they both offer possibilities of understanding the cultural meanings of signs. Both also tend to suggest that the theatre event is larger than the artistic intentions that create it; since a performance is directed at an audience, what matters is not only the meanings the artists inscribe in their work – whether those meanings are political, social, or purely aesthetic – but also what meanings spectators actually receive.

While the study will incidentally (and roughly) recapitulate the general development of design in our time, its focus will be more specific. A number of important directors and designers unconnected with Shakespeare will have no place here, just as some visual movements pertinent to Shakespeare will assume more prominence than they would in a larger consideration. This is a huge subject, in some ways an intractable one, for Shakespeare has been almost everywhere in the century. The temptation to limit my focus has been great: by discussing only the tragedies, for example, or by selecting a few important plays as representatives, or by restricting attention to English-language productions. Despite the problems of size, however, only by seeing the subject whole is it possible to indicate its full significance and something of the importance of Shakespeare to the modern theatre.

I have naturally been forced to ignore many interesting and valuable productions in order to tell the main story. Three types of movements have been given paramount attention: those that clearly established a new visual vocabulary for Shakespeare that was exploited by subsequent designers and directors (like the work of Edward Gordon Craig, or the Peter Brook–Sally Jacobs *A Midsummer Night's Dream*); those that, while not innovative in themselves, were particularly successful in using design elements already established (like the many examples of Expressionism outside of Germany, or the elegant simplicity of Motley in England); and those that reflected a unique and powerful approach to performance, itself integrated into a visual conception, usually under the influence of a master director (like Granville Barker's productions, designed by Norman Wilkinson, or, more recently, Peter Stein's *As You Like It*, designed by Karl-Ernst Hermann).

Though they are central to its approach, this is not a book about designers. The position of theatre designers has always been slightly awkward, and it remains so today. They often have great scope to formulate or even dominate productions, yet they almost always work at the invitation of directors or producers, who hold the final power. Indeed, many important directors in the century have approached production from a visual standpoint, and often established the visual outlines of their work independently of its technical execution. Some of these directors, from Craig to Brook and Liviu Ciulei, have been accomplished designers themselves; others, like Granville Barker or John Barton, have merely made potent suggestions and left their designers free to draw in the details. At the same time there have been designers who have created new approaches and even new playing spaces: from Appia to Moiseiwitsch to Svoboda, a consequential area of performance has been controlled by the scenography. There is no single model. Design for Shakespeare is a collaborative process involving director, actors, a team of designers for sets, costumes, lighting, and properties (and occasionally a single scenographer for everything), as well as accidental or aesthetically incidental factors such as the shape of the ludic space, the look of the theatre building, and the clothing of spectators. If I occasionally suggest that the director is responsible for the visual elements of a production, it is simply because in the twentieth century the director has normally held more aesthetic authority than the designer or any of the other collaborators in the visual process.

Despite the over-rich scholarship on Shakespeare, no work like this has been attempted. There are general histories of scenography and general treatments of Shakespearean performance, but none that join the two. There are also a few illustrated accounts of Shakespeare in the theatre, the best of which is Robert Speaight's *Shakespeare on the Stage*; most of these books, however, use their pictures incidentally or uncritically. W. M. Merchant's *Shakespeare and the Artist*, which concentrates on the development of Shakespeare iconography over the centuries, is a confusing book yet a pointed predecessor. His major insight is that Shakespearean commentary has persistently ignored "visual criticism," which can be used as a creative supplement to standard "verbal criticism" (236). Though Merchant's interest is primarily in the visual responses British artists have made to reading and seeing the plays, and thus significantly different from mine, his work has formulated some of the questions I will deal with, particularly the notion that the visual provides a rich source of material for understanding the way the modern world has chosen to view the plays. From the middle of the nineteenth century the major revisions that have occurred in Shakespearean production have been associated with revisions of the visual. Surely it is time for that history to find its place.

SCENOGRAPHY AND PERFORMANCE

Scenery, scene painting, setting, décor, decoration, design, costume, dressing: many terms have appeared in English to describe what it is that constitutes the visual field of theatrical representation. Of all the terms available, *scenography* is the one with the largest and most useful application, encompassing stage and costume design, lighting, the arrangement of the acting ground, the movement of the actors within it, and anything else proper to a production that an audience sees, including the interior architecture of the playhouse surrounding the stage: all the ocular aspects of the ludic space. Scenography can profitably be thought of as a visual counterpart to text; while the spoken dialogue of the play creates the verbal sphere of the production, the scenography creates the visual. Scenography should remind us most vividly that the words of the play are insufficient for a thorough explication of performance. Semiotic theory, in particular, has insisted that performance must be viewed as separate from the words of the play to encompass a more comprehensive system of signifiers, which Marco de Marinis has called the "performance text" or "spectacle text."[7] The suffix *graph* helps to remind us of the ways in which scenography is a form of writing, a formulated code or language of the visual. In this light, scenography is also a text, and requires a separate reading.

The theatre leaves wide scope for visual interpretation of a script, a much wider scope than that granted to verbal interpretation. Even when the dramatist has conceived the scene precisely and realistically, the custom and convention of the theatre permit the director and designer great latitude in most nonverbal areas, from the groundplan to actor placement, from the physical environment to lighting. In "open" texts like Shakespeare's, with so little about scenic locale and physicality of character determined, those responsible for production must make elementary decisions about ocular matters long before they are able to offer a coherent performance. "This is Illyria, lady" – but whose Illyria, exactly, is this? Shakespeare may have needed nothing more than those words for a seacoast, but does that mean that nothing more than words will be appropriate in other times and other places? As Gordon Craig wrote (1923: 20), Shakespeare "also uses words to conjure up before us the people – their costumes – all. Are we to refuse to visualize all?... Either all words, or let all be visualized." Once Shakespeare's own theatrical codes were no longer readable (even in London this had happened by 1660), our ability to read his visual assumptions had also been seriously affected.

Directors and designers go to a great deal of trouble attempting to find appropriate visual counterparts for the world they hope to create, as conditioners and clues for the audience: where and when, class and circumstance, attitude and attribution, all can be suggested and commented upon by the scenography. The visual field of a production is a great and complicated signifying system that must be read by the spectators before they can make sense of the thing offered to them, the object *ostended* to them, to use Umberto Eco's phrase. In general, spectators decode the visual by two separate methods. The first, which requires little or no intellectual effort and is normally unconscious, is the kind of automatic deciphering that occurs when an actress sits and the audience understands that Ophelia sits, or when an actor wears a metal circle on his head and the audience understands that Claudius is the king. Because the scene on stage normally has a proximate relationship to the locale, period, and people it represents, scenography often is metonymic in nature. A medieval Danish costume for Gertrude places one set of codes in motion, a seventeenth-century English costume another; a fully detailed illusion of Elsinore speaks one language, a single throne another; but these codes require no special effort to read since they remain similar to the process of deciphering that we use in ordinary life, and are within the visual expectations western audiences customarily bring to *Hamlet*. Like the literary devices of metonymy and synecdoche, a metonymic design is based upon the contiguity of the presence on stage to the absence it represents. Much of the visual power of the theatre derives from the unexceptional but profoundly ambiguous proximity of the signifier and its meaning; in Peter Handke's wonderful phrase, theatre is "a brightness that pretends to be another brightness."[8]

The second method of audience decoding results from a more overtly metaphoric application of the visual, based, like metaphor and simile, on the similarity between the signifier and its reference. A metaphoric design on stage (it can also be called a symbolic design, just as a metonymic design can be called iconic) often requires the audience to think in order to comprehend.

This process can occur on many levels – engendered by heavily manipulated and highly conceptualized actions and visions, or by unintentional and unrepeatable actor accidents – but what makes sense out of the scene or events on stage is the tendency of audiences to impose a reading on them. To the audience there is no phenomenological difference between an action performed with great internal justification (Hamlet drops Yorick's skull because the director wishes to suggest the brittleness of life) and one merely aleatoric (Hamlet dropped Yorick's skull last night because it slipped from his hands). In both cases spectators will tend to seek a rationale and assign a meaning for the action, inside the larger narrative under construction on the stage and in their minds. (We assume that the deliberate action will provide a context that will justify itself, but there are many examples throughout theatre history where audiences have refused to read performance in the manner intended by the performers.) Spectators may or may not be willing to "accept" a half-nude Gertrude kissing her son on the mouth in the closet scene, but they will nonetheless tend to read the action, and attempt to construe significance. Similarly, setting *Hamlet* before a towering abstract monolith, playing *Richard III* on a giant staircase, or staging *The Winter's Tale* on a floor of green slime – these are scenographic encodings that demand effort to understand, and the further they move into the metaphoric realm the more effort they will require.

No visual element can have an absolute or fixed signification, since meaning depends upon shifting cultural perceptions. The major limitation of traditional (Saussurean) semiotics for the visual in general and the theatre in particular is in its tendency to overwork the linguistic model; that is, its tendency to assume that non-verbal signifiers have the same relative stability to their referents as words do. Some contemporary performances force this issue by placing images on stage that are consciously drained of conventional or stable meaning, denying or attempting to deny the authority or the value of symbol. In this postmodern movement, part of what Fredric Jameson calls "the waning of affect,"[9] the blank sign is at the extreme pole from the metonymic: a vision without meaning, a metaphor with one of its two elements absent. But if an image on stage looks like a sign, the habit of visual decoding is so strong that most viewers, especially of Shakespeare, will attempt to read a message from it, even if the message is that there is no message.

The metaphoric method of visual encoding reminds us powerfully of the place of the audience in theatrical activity, and of how dangerous to perception radical revisions of Shakespeare can be. Audiences are not homogeneous masses; they are made up of disparate individuals who can receive the details of performance in notably different ways. Yet spectators probably bring more preconceptions about how the play should look when they go to Shakespeare than they do to the work of any other dramatist. Directors and designers, seeking vital and contemporary interpretations, can never fully anticipate how a production will be read. The illustrative solutions they offer do not always succeed because miscues in perception are particularly widespread in the realm of the visual, bordering as it does on symbol and dream. Some visual concepts are too eccentric or solipsistic, and some are jammed with conflicting signals, so that disjunctions between text and reader are bound to occur. But blunders and failures, whether created by the performers' errors or by the spectators' limitations, should not blind us to the truth that all performance requires a "somewhere," an *ille*, that is seen, for fictive characters embodied by actors cannot exist apart from time and space. A *Hamlet* set in contemporary Berlin is a different play than one set in medieval Elsinore or in Elizabethan London, yet all three have legitimacy and even some Shakespearean authorization. To put it as simply as possible, how Hamlet is dressed reveals as much about the style and intention of the performance as anything he says, and may well influence a spectator more than Shakespeare's poetry.

This proposition is valid for theatre in general, I think, but Shakespeare gives us a unique opportunity to test and refine its usefulness. First, Shakespeare is the world's most produced playwright, regularly crossing national borders, allowing comparative study of performances on a scale not possible for any other dramatist or any grouping of plays along usual national or linguistic lines. Most students and even many specialists in literature and drama are unaware of how frequent and widespread performances of Shakespeare are, and how radically they can differ from one another. While the texts may be the same – though the texts are often altered, especially outside the Anglophone theatre – the productions certainly are not. "There is no Shakespearean tradition," Granville Barker wrote in 1912, proclaiming the director's freedom of interpretation, and looking at performances around the world in the twentieth century confirms his view.

Second, Shakespeare's plays present clear and exciting challenges for directors and designers to discover new and appropriate performance styles that illuminate the texts and yet ring true in a world almost totally transformed, both in and out of the theatre, since their composition. As Denis Bablet wrote (1965: 342), production of Shakespeare in the modern theatre has been "the occasion to rethink the principles of scenography." Shakespeare's rapid changes of locale, his alternation of exterior and interior scenes, his simultaneous presentation of multiple locations, his wide range of character types and classes, his use of supernatural and mythological figures, his combination of reality and fantasy, to cite only the most obvious examples, have provided the twentieth-century stage with its most consistent and extended set of visual problems. Sometimes the responses of directors and designers have been intentionally outrageous, like Terence Gray's *The Merchant of Venice* at the Cambridge Festival Theatre in 1932, with Shylock and Tubal fishing for lobsters in the Grand Canal; sometimes they have been brilliant but scenographically dubious, as when Ryndin's "iron curtain" set for Okhlopkov's *Hamlet* in Moscow in 1954 slowed the rhythm of the production ponderously while the great metal gates opened and closed. But since the beginning of the century visual solutions have often been responsible for reconsiderations of a play's value and effectiveness.

Third, and perhaps most important, for good or ill Shakespeare's plays constitute a common cultural inheritance for much of the world, an inheritance larger in scope and wider in appeal than any other canon of dramatic literature. As the Greek audience expected its tragic dramatists to reinterpret well-known myths, so our audiences expect – or allow – directors to reinterpret Shakespeare. Designers often take great liberties, including the liberty to redefine the meanings of the plays, and their work provides a fascinating index of changing responses to Shakespeare. To trace the visual history of Shakespeare in the twentieth century is to trace, at least in part, the outlines of our own aesthetic and cultural obsessions.

VISUAL RECORDS OF PERFORMANCE

The job of the theatre historian is to reimagine the moment of past performance and to contextualize it with a narrative about its social meaning. We work with imperfect tools and often without a clear blueprint. Considering the amount of information that is usually not known, the discipline at times seems closer to archaeology than to history. Performance is by definition instantaneous; like a vanished tribe it leaves behind traces that can be easily misread and too frequently cannot be read at all. Yet of the evidence that does survive, drawings, photographs, films, and videotapes are the most immediate, the most accessible; and of those elements of performance that pictures record, scenography is most capable of being accurately transmitted. What wouldn't we give for a single fuzzy black and white photo taken from a gallery of Shakespeare's own production of *Hamlet*? It would not tell us much about acting, but it would likely contain an enormous amount of information about staging, setting, costumes, playhouse, and spectators. Films and videotapes of stage performances (as opposed to cinematic recreations of playtexts) are still relatively few, but set and costume designs survive in great numbers – there are over 100,000 designs in the theatre collection of the Austrian National Library alone – and photographs of twentieth-century productions are legion.

Not all of these pictures are accessible, of course, and most of them are portraits of individual actors. When the pictures are reliable, however, and especially when they are action photographs showing costumed actors in relation to the scenic environment, we can approach them to learn something direct about performance style that is otherwise lost or extremely difficult to recapture. Taken with the standard evidence of theatre history, such as eyewitness accounts, memoirs, promptbooks, manifestos, and so on, we can begin to create a visual strategy for the study of production history. But before we go further it is necessary to consider the problems of documentation and of method.

Set and costume designs can be beautiful objects. Detached from their original purpose they can easily be considered works of art in themselves, hung on the walls of museums, admired for their color and form. Many theatre designers are masters of dynamic suggestion, and some of the best painters and sculptors of the modern age have in turn designed for the theatre: Bakst, Picasso, Dali. It is no wonder that some historians of scenography lean to reproducing designs rather than reproducing performance photographs; designs spotlight scenographers as artists, reveal their discrete and distinctive contributions, and make lovely books.[10] Designs also can convey through graphic techniques some elements of staging that are poorly captured on film, like full stage views, or effects of changing scenes, or the dimensionality of non-proscenium acting spaces. They have particular stature as costume records, where they can suggest characterization, indicate color and tailoring details, and even show fabric samples. More subtly, designs are superior whenever photo-technology interferes with the accuracy of the scene; before the development of fast-speed film, for example, photographers regularly relied on studio lamps to supplement or replace stage lights, and thus most production photos from early in the century do not show authentic lighting effects, a serious deficiency when considering Expressionist scenography, to cite one crucial instance.

But designs have their own disadvantage for performance history, and it is a major one: they are often not followed in production. Almost always created in advance (sometimes far in advance), they are visual notes of the scenographer's suggestions or intentions; frequently a production will depart from its design, prompted by practical circumstance or by aesthetic reconsiderations. As the American designer Robert Edmund Jones insisted, a design is "the promise of a completion, a promise that the actor later fulfills." To rely upon designs without corroborating evidence is to invite the documentary woe of the intentional fallacy, parallel to a military historian relying upon a general's battle plan alone for the truth about a campaign. We should also remember that graphic designs require skills in drawing or painting that are not necessarily relevant to a designer's main work, which is to create a three-dimensional acting area for the fictive world of the play. Designs on paper are useful and convenient but are actually holdovers from the age of painted scenery, attempting on a flat surface to create an illusion of extended space; "enchanting infidelities," Donald Oenslager calls them (12). In recent years many scenographers have preferred to work with three-dimensional set models in wood, cardboard, or plaster of Paris. Such maquettes are generally more serviceable for a director, who can move scaled figures around in them and visualize blocking and lighting effects; they have become the standard design method at the RSC. (Maquettes create an additional problem for the historian, however; since they are fragile and bulky, they rarely survive the life of the production.)

Drawings and paintings of production scenes made by artists after the fact are a different story, and constitute the largest part of the objective pictorial documentation of the theatre until after the First World War. Pictures made for the specific purpose of memorializing some aspect of production must be granted high status as visual evidence, but they also come at great cost: it is usually difficult and sometimes impossible to determine how much the artist has entered into the rendering, whether the scene has been improved or altered and for what purpose. Rarely do we have a record like that provided in *Continental Stagecraft*, a book written by Kenneth MacGowan and illustrated by R. E. Jones, a result of their theatre tour through Europe in 1922. Jones' sketches, as MacGowan notes (ix),

3   The Longleat Manuscript drawing of *Titus Andronicus*, *c.* 1595. Note the eclectic anachronism of the costumes as well as the formal staging of the characters.

give the actual visual quality of the best productions on the Continental stage far better than could photographs of settings and actors, which are usually flashlights innocent of the atmosphere produced by stage lighting, or the designs of the scenic artists, which are sometimes imperfectly realized and sometimes bettered in actual production.

Jones drew immediately after witnessing a performance for the specific purpose of recording it. This is not the usual case, and theatre historians have often been wary of pictures of theatres and productions, especially from earlier periods, having learned how unreliable they can be and how difficult they are to interpret. "The eye brings with it what it sees," wrote Allardyce Nicoll, discussing how audiences tend not to see certain conventionalized aspects of scenography, which in turn rarely show up in artists' renderings; the historian, he said, needs to preserve a "double vision" of what the audience saw and what it thought it saw.[11] We have only to recall the enormous controversies surrounding the de Witt drawing of the Swan Theatre to sympathize with this wariness.

Even more pertinent to the question of reliability is the sixteenth-century sketch of *Titus Andronicus* ascribed to Henry Peacham (illus. 3). Much has been made of implications of this picture for Elizabethan scenography: the eclecticism of the costumes, mixing Roman, Gothic, Elizabethan, and perhaps even Persian dress; the surprising emphasis on realistic properties; the black skin of the actor portraying Aaron; the graceful staging; the symbolic or stylized gestures. But is it an image of a production or simply the artist's illustration of the text which it accompanies? And if it was intended as a record of performance, how accurate can it be? Since it shows characters who are not at any time during the play on stage together in the attitudes depicted, it may be a generalized recollection, as R. A. Foakes suggests, "bringing together into a group separate sketches of individual actors made while watching a performance."[12] Thus the only contemporary picture of the staging of a scene by Shakespeare is fraught with difficulty and unanswerable questions. As a document it has authenticity without reliability.

Surprising as it may seem at first, the invention of the camera has not eliminated the difficulties of pictorial reliability. In the nineteenth century the word "photographic" was used to mean "naturalistic" and "truthful," but in the age of the consuming image we have become only too aware of how assiduously the camera can lie, especially when celebrity actors are its subjects. Unless a photographer has set out to document a production carefully and precisely, his or her pictures can present the same difficulty as set designs or scene drawings, despite the compelling power of their apparent veracity. Most theatre pictures have been made not for archives but for publicity, and the mission of the historian rarely coincides with the press agent's, at least in theory. Sometimes photographs show poses and blocking arrangements that differ markedly from the performance, even, in the name of convenience, introducing into a scene actors who have no legitimate business there – as if the Peacham sketch of *Titus*, with its "impossible" scene, had set the standard for Shakespeare iconography 400 years ago.

Since photographs are central to this book, the point deserves elaboration. When can we trust a theatre photo? Like drawings and designs, photographs are two-dimensional objects on paper that rely upon perspective to indicate depth of field and upon printed shadings to suggest objects and colors. Like any graphic representation, the meaning of photographs ultimately depends upon cultural signification. We have not always known how to read them, just as a remote tribesman today, seeing a black and white photo of himself for the first time, often cannot make sense out of its peculiar system of dots and spaces. As observers of photos we have learned certain responses that now come automatically to us; after 150 years of photography we tend to grant it an idealized status. Snapshots of our ancestors, for example, which are pictures of mechanically frozen time, are often accepted as deep and abiding emotional records in our personal histories, though they may represent moments that are false or completely undistinguished. I have a picture of my grandfather, whom I never knew, as a young man on a camping trip in the woods sometime about 1890; that picture is the most intimate access I have to him – even though no one in my family can remember the event or recall him going on other such trips in his life.

Just as family memory may be distorted by placing too much stress upon grandfather's enigmatic smile or Aunt Mary's floppy hat, so theatre history can be distorted by improperly emphasizing isolated moments that happen to have been recorded. We are ultimately at the mercy of two imponderables: the care the photographer has taken to be accurate, and the accident of the record's survival. An interesting case in point is provided by Angus McBean, who took photos of most of the important Shakespeare productions in England from about 1937 to about 1964, primarily at Stratford and at the Old Vic in London. McBean, who did some early work as a designer, achieved fame as an off-beat society photographer in the 1930s, particularly with doctored surrealist portraits of stars. He was a master of light and shadow, and some of his portraits of actors in character are extraordinarily beautiful and evocative, like the idealized publicity stills for Hollywood films; in fact, his pictures of Vivien Leigh in the late 1930s helped to get her the role of Scarlett O'Hara.[13] He was fond of closeups of stars in soft focus, yet he knew the Shakespeare plays well and strove to capture the individuality of the actor (illus. 4). He worked during the age of the posed photo call, when a half-day of rehearsal time was set aside for the photographer to record the production for the press. He used a large field camera mounted on a tripod throughout his career, even after most photographers had switched to the convenience and flexibility of the single-lens reflex camera, and the great majority of his pictures were taken on glass plates. He commonly brought 300 lbs of his own lighting equipment to the theatre.

These factors have almost certainly affected his reliability. A number of his proofsheets reveal the presence of studio lamps, indicating that some of the dramatic lighting effects in the pictures were created by the photographer. He knew the plays so well that he tended to direct actors in photo calls, disregarding the blocking of the production when he found his own arrangements more photogenic. One of his last assignments was the Peter O'Toole *Hamlet*, directed by Laurence Olivier as the first production of the new National Theatre at the Old Vic in 1963. Because of delays in the opening, McBean was forced to use a 35 millimeter camera and to shoot

4 *Titus Andronicus* 1955 Stratford. D: Peter Brook. Des: Brook with Michael
Northern, Desmond Heeley, and William Blezard. P: Angus McBean. Anthony
Quayle as Aaron, in one of McBean's classic theatre photographs. The character's
evil is submerged into the actor's exotic beauty, reflecting Quayle's treatment of the
role and Brook's method for the production, but much of what we are likely to read
from this photo has been created by the photographer.

during dress rehearsals – common practice in most theatres today, but disturbing to his normal sense of composition. "Alas never properly photographed," he wrote on an envelope containing the pictures.

Does this mean that the Angus McBean photographs are not to be trusted? Of course not. It does mean that care must be exercised in their use; the McBean case points out the general documentary difficulty of pictorial evidence. A photographer will often find room for improvement in a posed scene, if for no other reason than to return to it some of the life destroyed by the photo call. Common sense suggests a few guidelines for the historian. Photos taken from a distance and showing the relationship of actors to the setting are more likely to indicate actual performance conditions than posed closeups. (These are not always easy to obtain, however; Richard David [xv] complained in 1978 that contemporary theatre photography was more interested in "intimate action-pictures" than in "panoramas" of the stage.) A series of pictures, especially when taken at different times or by different photographers, will have authority as records that no single image can have. And, of course, relying on pictures alone, without the corroboration of other records, is to be avoided at all costs. Brecht said that a photo of the Krupp works tells us almost nothing about the organization; for that we need a history. As Susan Sontag comments (23), "only that which narrates can make us understand."

The last major difficulty of visual documentation relates not to the literal accuracy of drawings and photos but to their static character. One of the best books on theatre design, Fuerst and Hume's *Twentieth-Century Stage Decoration*, noted in 1929 the outlines of the problem:

It must be clear to every one, as it is to us, that the reproductions of photographs and designs for stage decorations are bound to be not only deceptive and inadequate, but often actually false. The mise en scène is a living organic whole in which the stage decoration plays its part, and no photograph and no design can ever give more than a hint of what that mise en scène, and more particularly its scenic environment, were like in actuality. (II:v)

This is a problem of design and performance history that only the dynamic records of film and videotape can solve, and then only imperfectly.[14] Clearly a snapshot of a three- or four-hour performance can never expect to convey more than a limited view of what the audience saw or how the isolated moment pertained to the complete visual experience. Just as performance requires time for its meaning to unfold, so does our history of it. Any moment a photo can show, even if it is an accurate moment, is necessarily a deception, for it is an image of time stopped. Photos, Sontag claims (23), cannot explain anything by themselves. That is why they "are inexhaustible invitations to deduction, speculation, and fantasy."

Despite their apparent veracity, then, photos need at least as much analysis as other historical documents, for they are just as prone to lie, or to seem complete when they can only be partial. In this work, as in most cultural history, the best defense against idiosyncratic conclusions remains multiplicity of evidence. Though limitations of space and cost prevent me from reproducing the full range of pictorial documentation for any production, I have made stringent efforts to compare photos and designs with one another (and with videos, when they are available) and have normally based my commentary on as many pictorial sources as possible. In some cases the pictures that best reveal scenographic style are not the best in photographic style; especially for productions from early in the century, I have occasionally been forced to reproduce poor quality photos for their documentary value. But even when all the shortcomings of pictorial verification are registered, the advantages of the method abide. No other path will provide the same immediate access to performance style.

2 | *Victorian pictures*

Shakespeare wrote for what is usually called architectural scenography: the theatre building itself provided the design for the production of his plays. Walls, doors, columns, recesses, upper galleries, the winch machine, the large open platform floor with trap space – these fixed but extremely versatile features of the Elizabethan playhouse formed the basis of the staging as well as the visual habitat. Scenography was far from plain, however; the structural elements of the stage may well have been decorated and the plays frequently relied upon actor-centered visual moments. Properties, for example, would achieve powerful signification as a result of their optical singularity, as Aaron's sword and Tamora's crown seem to have in the Peacham drawing (see illus. 3); and portable set pieces are often so crucial that they must have become luminous symbols of story and theme, like the throne in *Henry IV* or the bed in *Othello*. The lists in Henslowe's *Diary* suggest that companies kept a comprehensive properties cupboard, including three trees, two grassy mounds, two monuments, two steeples with bells, Phaeton's chariot, Hell-mouth, and a painted cloth representing the city of Rome. It has often been pointed out that in an age of great sartorial opulence much visual profit was realized from the rich costumes of Elizabethan companies, forcing further attention onto the actors. In a similar way discovery scenes, though rare in Shakespeare, hinge on moments of surprising visual authority, like the statue scene in *The Winter's Tale* or the chess game in *The Tempest*.

Though the most important scenographic development in European history had occurred in the mid-sixteenth century, the introduction of changeable scenes painted in perspective on flats, Renaissance stage design had practically no influence on the Elizabethan public theatres. Shakespeare was obviously aware of Italian scenery, at least after the Twelfth Night celebrations of 1604/5 when Inigo Jones delighted King James with it for Jonson's *The Masque of Blackness*; the sudden aristocratic taste for spectacle clearly influenced the writing in his last decade.[1] It is even possible that performances at court by the King's Men of *Macbeth*, *The Winter's Tale*, and *The Tempest* made some use of Italian devices. But when produced at the Globe, Shakespeare's final plays comfortably continued to rely on what was in essence a medieval scenography.

London was a new city when the theatres reopened in 1661 and William Davenant, who claimed to be Shakespeare's illegitimate son, had no apprehensions about providing painted scenery for Betterton in *Hamlet*. Samuel Pepys was present in August at Lincoln's Inn Fields to watch the first Shakespearean play ever produced on an Italian scenic stage, "done with Scenes very well," he thought (in Rosenfeld 40–1). It was a consequential evening. Davenant's discovery that an Elizabethan play, when adapted and revised, could be exploited in the new scenographic style set the course for future Shakespearean production. Though important aesthetic and technological changes occurred later, especially under Garrick with the Romantic, painterly designs of Philip De Loutherbourg, for the most part the visual story of Shakespeare for the next 250 years remained the story of illusionist sets and growing splendor. The Restoration tradition eventually provoked two distinct movements in the nineteenth century: pictorialism, which was the grandiose and logical culmination of Italian scene design; and Elizabethanism, which was a reaction against it. Despite their opposition, both were antiquarian movements. The first manufactured illustrative spectacles based on "accurate" renderings of the plays' historical periods; the second wished to return to the "authentic" performance conditions of the sixteenth-century public theatres. As the two developments form the immediate background for Shakespearean production in our own time, it will be helpful to review their scenographic propositions briefly.

PICTORIALISM

Victorian Shakespeare is an enormous topic, but its spectacular manifestation in the second half of the century is reasonably clear. Influenced by the growing interest in historical representation in painting and architecture, the stage saw the plays as opportunities for illustrating the past. When Charles Kean took over the Princess's Theatre in Oxford Street in London in 1850 he set out to produce Shakespeare with a detailed historical authenticity, which he defined solely in terms of the visual. Despite the efforts of Macready to restore portions of the original texts, and of Phelps to limit the number and splendor of the settings, Kean was content with cobbled versions of the texts but sent his designers off to Venice to reproduce St. Mark's Square accurately. His own passions for archaeology and education, so eminently Victorian, were granted complete indulgence; he cited sources in his playbills, flaunting his historical research, while his stage was filled with magnificent illusions of Athens or Rome.

The great flaw in Kean's antiquarianism, of course, was that it never considered whether accuracy of period and locale were in any sense relevant to a visual understanding of the plays. He substituted a literal, factual history for Shakespeare's metaphorical history, magnifying a cultural aspect of the age, the fascination with images. As Michael Booth has pointed out (in Foulkes 81), the nineteenth century was bombarded by unprecedented visual stimuli. From gaslight to the kaleidoscope, from the magic lantern to the diorama, from the illustrated newspaper to the camera itself, "this was a world saturated in pictures, and the dissemination of the pictorial image to a mass audience became and remained the most popular form of public entertainment." The images Kean put on the stage were simply reflections in the Victorian eye. He made a Shakespearean theatre that was, for the first time, self-conscious about its visual expression.

The Winter's Tale is a case in point. Since Bohemia does not have a seacoast, Kean reasoned, we must change the locale to a country that does. Bithynia is intriguing; there we can not only have a seacoast but lush oriental trappings as well, which will differ pleasantly from the restraint of classical Syracuse. So in 1856 the play became an exercise in contrasting visual splendors, a series of "*tableaux vivants* of the private and public life of the ancient Greeks," in Kean's own words (Merchant 211). These included interpolated dances by a *corps de ballet* and, for Perdita's sheepshearing, "at least three hundred persons engaged in this revel of organized confusion," according to the somewhat exaggerated account of Kean's biographer, J. W. Cole (Merchant 212). For Hermione's trial (3.2), placed outdoors in "the Theatre at Syracuse," Thomas Grieve set the main acting area off the centerline, suggesting great distance between Leontes on a raised throne up right and Hermione's litter on the floor down left (illus. 5). Solid set pieces (Leontes' platform, the wall behind Hermione) were integrated with flats to create the illusion of a colossal arena, with hundreds of spectators painted in perspective on the backdrop, supplementing the actors on the floor upstage center. Kean's relative success with this device must have derived from his general aesthetic: if the living actors are elements of a picture, what matter if painted figures swell the scene? They were ciphers to this great accompt. Every costume, painted or sewn, was authentically detailed, every prop

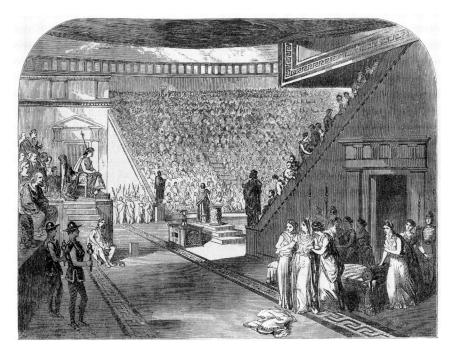

5   *The Winter's Tale* 1856 London. D: Charles Kean. Des: Thomas Grieve *et al.*
The trial scene in an artist's rendition for the *Illustrated News*, with rows of painted
spectators harmonizing with living actors. Charles Kean as Leontes (on throne)
looks across the stage at Mrs. Kean as Hermione, supported by two women. Period
has been created by visual information that is substantially redundant.

individually designed, creating numerous picturesque narratives inside the
larger dramatic narrative.

As a Victorian genre painting told a story by visual reference and a wealth
of the particular, so Kean asked the audience to read his scenes as metonymic
pictures that interpreted Shakespeare for the purpose of representing the
past. Some of his scenes, as Richard Foulkes has shown, should be
considered as living realizations of actual paintings known to his audiences.
Acting, naturally enough, suffered under the weight of wood, paint, and
canvas; Charles Kean was not his father Edmund, and perhaps he was only
compensating for his limitations when he disguised the plays in the heavy
garments of history. As the texts were cleaned of bawdy, "unauthentic," or
contradictory elements in order to rationalize the production, so the playing
style avoided emotional depth in favor of the sentimental or the merely
pretty. This was a limitation of major proportions, but it is unfair to
condemn it unconditionally, as so many Shakespearean commentators have

done. Nuance on the stage was not much admired anywhere at mid-century, and Kean was nothing if not of his time. He may have been, as Dennis Bartholomeusz insists (98), "a heroic victim to the pedantic heresy of fact," but his pictorial Shakespeare was a triumph of Victorian illustrative art.

Major scenographic developments, like those in architecture, often result from new technologies. The greatest scenographic advance in the theatre since the invention of changeable scenery occurred in the early nineteenth century, the introduction of gas lighting. Much more intense and controllable than candles, gaslight encouraged greater stage depth because performers could be seen from positions far removed from the footlamps. As the century progressed the action moved further away from the spectators, effectively dividing the stage and the auditorium into separate rooms, a movement that was complete when Henry Irving darkened the house. The apron tended to shrink in size, and actors could now play inside a scenic environment which depended less on the illusions of the painter and more on the illusions of the carpenter. If the scenographic revolution of the twentieth century was propelled by electricity, that of the nineteenth was fueled by coal gas. It depended on what Wolfgang Schivelbusch[2] has called "the industrialization of light."

Under Irving's guidance, gas became a major production element for Shakespeare. Irving was not only the leading actor of his generation, he was the theatre's first master lighting designer. He seized upon gaslight as a means of increasing the veracity of production while at the same time creating a fully dimensioned space for his own acting. He was not an innovator; when he took over the management of the Lyceum Theatre in 1878 it was already an old-fashioned house, and he steadfastly refused to work with electric light, which made its first appearance in theatres about that year. As his skill with gas increased, he relied more upon three-dimensional set pieces in the full depth of the stage. In 1853 Kean presented a canvas backdrop with Macbeth's castle as well as the effects of moonlight painted on; thirty-five years later Irving built a solid structure and created atmosphere with actual light. He sought not archaeological rectitude but a scenic environment that gave scope to Shakespeare's characters, or at least to the main character played by the manager. In order to build his structures, however, Irving also had to rely on frequent intermissions and bridging or "carpenter's scenes" – painted views on cloths that dropped from the flies just beyond the proscenium – so called because they hid the stagehands preparing the next big set. The illusion of time and place carefully established in the major scenes was constantly undercut by pauses and by

unseen but very audible hammers banging away upstage. The wedding in
Much Ado (1882), placed by William L. Telbin (the son of Kean's painter) in
the side chapel of a Sicilian cathedral,[3] was compared by contemporaries to
the splendors of the Princess's Theatre and clearly stole the show; but it
took fifteen minutes to set up.

Though at 44 he was too old for Romeo, and though lovers were never
in his line, Irving's production took his scenographic values to the extreme.
"*Hamlet* could be played anywhere on its acting merits," he said to Ellen
Terry, his Juliet. "It marches from situation to situation. But *Romeo and
Juliet* proceeds from picture to picture. Every line suggests a picture"
(quoted in Hughes 160). Irving's pictures cost him almost £10,000, a
fantastic sum, close to five times the expense of his spectacular *Merchant of
Venice*; there were eighteen solid sets, three designers, rich costumes, and
lighting so plastic that Juliet's bedroom had separate qualities for three
different times of day.

The great picture, however, was reserved for the end. As Alan Hughes
notes (165), the theatre of illusion is uncomfortable with the final scene of
the play because it begins outside the tomb and then moves inside. Much of
Romeo and Juliet works in a similar fashion, transferring location within a
scene in Elizabethan simultaneity. Irving's answer is indicative of the logic
of illusion: he made two sets, a churchyard for the duel with Paris and the
tomb itself for the finale. The first part ended after the death of Paris with
Romeo breaking open the door of Capulet's vault, showing a flight of steps
leading down. Then the curtain dropped and the spectators waited. When it
rose again they saw one of the most formidable accomplishments of pictorial
design yet created, Romeo now coming through the door he had broken
open, but far upstage, at the top of a massive flight of steps leading down to
Juliet's tomb (illus. 6). Through a set change Irving established a new
convention that would be used often with revolving stages and come into
its own with the cinema: he made the Realist scene appear spatially
discontinuous. The same actor is observed passing through a door from
both sides, not across the stage but up and down it, while the spectator
remains in place. Space itself is violated, common notions of location
denied, yet the audience looks on the scene credulously.

Down he came, then, dragging the body of Paris with him, down forty
steps or more of vertical stage space, through archways and over landings,
lit by the moonlight behind (coming of course from the churchyard he had
just left), literalizing Romeo's line, "I descend into the bed of death." Ellen
Terry tells us that line haunted Irving's conception of the scene, so that he

6 *Romeo and Juliet* 1882 London. D and L: Henry Irving. Des: Hawes Craven. The final scene, designed by William Telbin, in an artist's impression. Henry Irving as Romeo, Ellen Terry as Juliet. Paris lies dead on the floor, Friar Lawrence descends the steps with a lantern.

insisted "I must go *down* into the vault." Probably no single phrase of Shakespeare's has ever caused as much expense. After the deaths of the lovers the curtain closed again, and soon opened to reveal the entire set, stairs, platforms, floor, filled with the rustling but speechless nobility and citizenry of fair Verona, all bearing torches (Hughes 166). The ending focused not on the reconciliation of the two families but on the personal tragedy of the lovers. Irving's representation of horror and loss rendered the meaning of the play in purely scenographic terms, an extreme example of pictorial stagecraft where actors were valued exclusively as objects of the gaze.

The textual implications of solid scenery are as significant as the visual. Whereas earlier Shakespearean managers cut to fit an interpretation, Irving rearranged the script to fit the set. Except for four lines, all of the last scene after the deaths of the lovers was cut for the sake of that spectacular tableau (Hughes 166). Though Irving was hardly the lone surgeon in practice in London, it was this harsh result of his scenography that was seized upon by later detractors, like Shaw and Granville Barker, in their assault on his status as a Shakespearean interpreter. The pauses and the textual rearrangements meant to them that the rhythm of Shakespeare's plays had been destroyed for the sake of some questionable shows. Managers substituted technology for drama because they did not trust Shakespeare as a playwright; as late as 1909 Barker was blaming the "production-mongers" for making scenery into the protagonist of the play.[4] With the best of intentions Irving had built his own trap: he had created a beautiful, metonymic world on stage as foil to his subtle, psychological acting, but he wound up elevating the carpenter above the actor and the gasman above the poet.

Pictorialism was part of a large European concern with Realism in all the arts, and it is not surprising to find productions abroad, both in Europe and in North America, in much the same style.[5] In Germany especially, where Shakespeare had been one of the saints of early Romanticism, he had by mid-century been redefined as a spectacular dramatist. A chief example of the trend is Franz von Dingelstedt, whose adaptation of *The Winter's Tale* in 1859, the first performance of the play in Germany, was parallel to Kean's. By far the most important foreign Shakespearean in the period, however, was not a professional man of the theatre but the ruler of an insignificant duchy in Thuringa and cousin to Prince Albert. A committed historicist, Georg II of Saxe-Meiningen was a talented dilettante who used his unusual position to create an acting ensemble for the new drama and the classics. The company, directed by Georg with the substantial assistance and collaboration of Ludwig Chronegk, impressed audiences throughout Germany with an attention to authentic detail, fulsome energy, and mastery of crowd scenes. These were significant matters, but they were not new ones; while the effect of the company's work on the late nineteenth-century stage is undeniable, from a visual perspective the productions were simply an

7 *Julius Caesar* 1874 Berlin. D: Georg II of Saxe-Meiningen and Ludwig Chronegk. Des: Georg. Drawing of Forum scene by Johannes Kleinmichel (1879) after a sketch by Georg, based on his research in the Vatican. The set combines wing and solid pieces against a painted backdrop, in the manner of Charles Kean.

extension of the archaeological urge. Charles Kean sent his designers to Italy, Duke Georg sent himself. He always went, as John Osborne reveals (89), straight to the top; he got costume notions from the best contemporary sources and he copied his designs for the Roman Forum directly from sketches in the Vatican Museum. What is more, he made sure his audiences knew the historical provenance of the scenography: a note on the authenticity of the costumes went in the programs and he instructed Chronegk to provide news releases and handouts stating that "the *mise-en-scène* of *Julius Caesar* is the product of a visit by the Duke to Rome in 1869" (illus. 7).

Through European tours the Meininger extended their prestige widely, especially in a triumphant trip to London in 1881 where the management of the crowd in *Julius Caesar* was the subject of immoderate praise. The force of historicism was already passing, however, and they had less influence on English Shakespearean production than is sometimes claimed. Irving admired the troupe and invited them to the Lyceum but his work was not directly affected by them; the reverse is more likely the case, as Chronegk may have tried to emulate Irving's lighting in subsequent productions.

Steven DeHart[6] has shown that Georg's design for the final scene of *Romeo and Juliet* was directly copied from the published picture (illus. 6) of Irving's set.

In converting Shakespeare into readable pictures, historicism put a barrier before the action that was difficult to breach. Overwhelming spectators with "justified" scenography and a disciplined ensemble, the Meininger stood in danger of detaching the visual from its theatrical context, of making the set preeminent and the actors little more than moving scenery: Shakespeare as diorama. A hostile Viennese critic of the company, Ludwig Speidel, may have put the case best. Though a reactionary partisan of Dingelstedt's, his comments can be taken as a terse critique of pictorialism:

I want to enjoy a poem and they affront me with rich costumes and over-painted canvas; I want to revel in an artist's warm breath and they fling whole hordes of gesticulating, buzzing and shrieking extras at me; I want to be moved, edified, impressed, and instead they make me into a blinded, confused and confounded gaper.

ELIZABETHANISM

At the same time as pictorialism was establishing itself as the dominant mode of Shakespearean representation, an attack upon its premises began that would have wide results in the twentieth century. If Shakespeare wrote for an architectural scenography, the new argument went, would not his plays be more authentically performed if they were seen without historicist encrustations, in something like their original condition? It was a Romantic and somewhat naïve question: Romantic because it implied that a work's initial situation was privileged, and naïve because it assumed that the theatre would care to alter a commercially successful practice for the sake of stylistic experiment. That the primitive Elizabethan playhouse could instruct the progressive, technologically sophisticated Victorian stage seemed absurd to most practitioners. It has always been one of the chief virtues of the theatre that the moment rules. Earlier theatrical conditions, especially when accompanied by antiquarian or erudite motives, strike most audiences as deadly; the traditions of Shakespeare performance since 1661 reinforced the predilection for representations that agreed with current observance. But the simple logic of Elizabethanism saw an intrinsic relationship between the sceneless platform stage of Shakespeare's time and the swift rhythm of Shakespeare's plays, a rhythm that was damaged or destroyed by locating each new scene in a distinctive environment. The most radical implication of the movement was that a visual approach to Shakespeare should be derived, not from the taste of the time, but from attitudes inhering in the scripts themselves.

A growing number of English critics, spurred on by new bibliographic and physical discoveries relating to the plays, began in the second half of the century to suggest alternatives for the production of Shakespeare. Nonetheless it was in Germany that the first significant experiments in Elizabethan staging took place. This is not surprising: the English and American theatres were almost entirely commercial enterprises, whereas many theatres in the German-speaking lands retained ties to their courtly origins and received some form of aristocratic or state support. In England and America Shakespeare's value in the theatre was set by the willingness of middle-class audiences to buy tickets; in middle Europe his value could be set by the fiat of the theatre's Intendant.

One such Intendant was Karl Immermann, who capped his experiments in non-illusionist staging at the Düsseldorf Theater with a production of *Twelfth Night* in 1840. Since the performance was to take place not in a theatre but in a hall, Immermann was able to build the playing space to his own specifications; the result was the first stage constructed since the seventeenth century that consciously incorporated Elizabethan features. As Simon Williams (181) notes, it was not a historical replica but a workable hybrid that combined Elizabethan and Italian elements. Its principal innovation was an unlocalized platform which was used for public or exterior scenes, like Olivia's garden, the palace, or the street. Behind this was a decorated *scaenae frons* with two entrance doors and two archways which framed perspective scenery; the central area had walls and ceiling in perspective and provided a kind of inner stage for interior scenes, like Toby's midnight revels or Malvolio's imprisonment.

While Immermann's experiment was important, it is easy to make too much of it. The production was designed for the limited period of a festival, used amateur actors, and achieved a desirable but enforced intimacy in that the hall accommodated scarcely more than 200 spectators. Much more telling for the development of Elizabethanism was the creation of a "Shakespeare Stage" with extended life, at the Munich Residenztheater in 1889, almost fifty years later. In direct reaction to the pictoralism of the Meininger, Jocza Savits was commissioned to fashion a performing space that freed Shakespeare of the weight of scenery. Designed by Karl Lautenschläger (who would in 1896 build the first revolving stage in

Europe), the Munich solution began by covering the orchestra pit with an extensive forestage, projecting beyond the proscenium arch and suggesting an Elizabethan open platform. A set of steps led from the center of the forestage to the house. It was still an end-stage, of course, but one that began to attack the principles of illusion by placing the actors close to the audience and outside the realm of a localized scene; most future examples of Elizabethan staging inside a proscenium theatre would be based upon a similar plan. Some distance upstage a thick but false proscenium wall was placed, decorated in Romanesque style, its archway closed by a curtain. Here the new method made a curious compromise with the pictorial, for when opened the curtain revealed a perspective scene, usually painted on a backcloth, augmented on occasion by solid pieces. While the platform remained in full view, the false or second proscenium curtain was closed to change the vista beyond. Savits and Lautenschläger had reinvented the system of the Teatro Farnese: actors on a bare forestage were playing in front of illusionist, changeable scenery.

The first production on the new stage was *King Lear*, a play that cries out for non-illusionist treatment, and Savits attempted to find an Elizabethan rhythm for its many scene shifts.[7] The act curtain rose on Gloucester, Edmund, and Kent entering for their prose prologue; then the inner curtain opened to show Lear already in place on his throne, holding court. The daughters came through doors in the false proscenium, and then the entire court came down onto the open platform, the actors detaching themselves from the localization that the discovery tableau had established. At the end of the first scene the inner curtains closed briefly and then opened to find Edmund in an interior setting; but again the *illusionbühne* was momentary, for he moved to the forestage to speak his monologue close to the audience.

The picture we have of a heath scene (illus. 8) implies a very serviceable design, even if it is an impure one. The inner area, raised three steps above the main stage, was about 7.5 meters wide, large enough to present medium-sized scenes without cramping. In this example, at least, the platform appears to be used in a powerful way. The actors' placement far downstage, and the absence of any Realist representation immediately around them, suggest a surprising awareness of the virtues of the open stage. The acting evoked the environment; though backed by a scene the actors were not contained by it. The illusionist painting of the heath seems in some sense to be contradicted by the formal, baroque decoration of the false proscenium, the curtains, and the boxes, so that today the visual effect of the drawing is curiously unsettling – there is a disjunction between the two parts of the

8 *King Lear* 1889 Munich. D: Jocza Savits. Des: Karl Lautenschläger. The heath pictured in the inner area on the Munich Shakespeare Stage, with the open platform jutting well beyond the proscenium and over a portion of the orchestra pit.

playing space. The original audience, prepared to accept the vista upstage without thought, was confronted with a much more immediate, actor-centered event downstage. This *King Lear* was not unified, and was not authentically Elizabethan, but it nonetheless mapped out an alternative visual path.

Though Savits did not tour like the Meininger, his work had important international ramifications. One member of that original audience in Munich was an Englishman named William Poel. Though he "was not quite satisfied with the setting," he nonetheless felt it "the best cast and the most stimulating performance of the tragedy I have ever seen"; the only time, he wrote on another occasion, that he had witnessed "the whole play correctly rendered, with every character a vivid realization of the poet's conception." Poel had begun a lifetime of combat against pictorial Shakespeare in 1881, when he directed an amateur performance of the first quarto of *Hamlet* in London at St. George's Hall. Aside from the speed of delivery (the performance lasted just two hours), Poel's major innovations were visual: he discarded scenery and used Elizabethan dress. Savits had been conventional about costumes, setting *King Lear* in a vaguely Druidical period, but Poel would make no compromises with contemporary taste. From the start he wished to return Elizabethan plays to their original methods of performance, "so as to represent them as nearly as possible under the conditions existing at the time of their first production."[8] Poel was a crank, with the aggravating dedication of an evangelical madman. His notions of correctness were occasionally idiosyncratic, and he sometimes claimed discoveries in the name of faulty scholarship or as a consequence of his own fanatic hatred of the commercial theatre, but he followed his Elizabethan way with the absolute conviction of a great reformer.

A most important scholarly event occurred in this period, the discovery of the commonplace book of Aernout van Buchel in the library of the University of Utrecht. The manuscript contains a copy of a drawing of the Swan Theatre, made by van Buchel's fellow student, Johannes de Witt, on a visit to London about 1596. This famous sketch, published in 1888 by K. T. Gaedertz in his *Kenntnis der altenglischen Bühne*, forcibly modified Victorian notions about the appearance of the Elizabethan stage. The drawing indicated to most scholars that the Swan – and by implication, other theatres as well – was simpler and less decorated than hitherto supposed, and graphically demonstrated the size and thrust of the open playing platform. It gave new force to the argument against pictorialism and, together with the success of the Munich Shakespeare stage, led to Poel's first reconstructive performance. In 1893 he converted the interior of the Royalty Theatre in Soho into "as near a resemblance of the Old Fortune Playhouse as was possible in a roofed theatre," as he put it, for a production of *Measure for Measure*, a play that had been ignored by the actor-managers. The validity of the resemblance is highly questionable; *fin de siècle* ideas about Elizabethan playhouses, even after the publication of the Utrecht sketch, were unconsciously conditioned by Victorian theatres and theatre practice. Despite his purism Poel did not escape from these cultural habituations and occasionally marred his performances with covert modern intrusions, such as traverse curtains for scene alterations. As Cary Mazer has said, the Swan drawing was "a Rorschach, into which Victorian scholars projected their own theatrical needs and impressions" (60). But Poel's persistence was more important than his inaccuracy, for in the end his dry, antiquarian, amateurish experiments began to transform the look of Shakespeare.

For his *Measure for Measure* the stage was extended beyond the proscenium to create an open platform, while a high but narrow canopied structure

("Poel's four-poster," wags called it) filled up most of rest of the space
(illus. 9). Poel went to great lengths for a production with only four
performances, making his set into a period stage in the manner of Savits,
even continuing the decorations on the galleries out beyond the permanent
proscenium to cover the existing theatre boxes. The proscenium arch itself
was masked with simulated oak panelling that matched the canopy. The
Royalty stage was only 6.7 by 7.3 meters in size, and Poel's extension
measured just over 9 meters in width at the front.[9] Considering the effort
required to build the extra platform, it is surprising that the director then
chose to occupy so much of its small space with "Elizabethan" extras, seen
sitting in the photograph and staring at the camera, forcing the action into
cramped and uncomfortable quarters. Poel must have reasoned that this
onstage group was essential to recreating the feel of the Shakespearean
stage; the open platform, though designed in the sixteenth century for the
actor-as-character, in the nineteenth also needed the actor-as-audience.

J. L. Styan, in his influential book *The Shakespeare Revolution*, sees Poel's
general adventure as paramount in turning Shakespearean production

9 *Measure for Measure* 1893 London. D and S: William Poel. C: Jennie Moore.
Poel's first reconstruction of the Fortune, inside the Royalty Theatre. Poel as Angelo
sits center. The costumed gentlemen down left and right on the forestage, and the
ladies in the upper galleries, are acting as an "Elizabethan" audience.

towards the open stage, and finds this specific instance in 1893 of costumed gentlemen on the apron to be "the biggest step to date in seeking the non-illusory experience" (57). I doubt it. Though he wished to combat illusion Poel was unintentionally catering to it, using actors as part of a scenic presence the way Kean had done. Spectators in the house were not distracted from the play by manipulated historical pictures, it is true; they were free to imagine the scenic locale and to concentrate on the verse without visual prompting. But it can be argued that they were presented with a scenography as powerful as the most spectacular of Henry Irving's. Unlike Shakespeare's original audience, who read the architecture of the playhouse conventionally and therefore did not "see" it at all, Poel's spectators were confronted with a stage design that was as unfamiliar as it was undeniable. Since the audience in the house had not become Elizabethan, the scenery and costumes on the stage spoke the language of antiquarianism loudly and self-consciously. Had they been an active chorus, the gallants on stage might have worked against illusion; but they were primarily part of the visual field, treated like scenery rows, puffing clay pipes and strolling about during intervals. Far from distancing the event, they attenuated the visual shock of radical Shakespeare into the familiar sight of a costume party.

Poel founded the Elizabethan Stage Society in 1895 to put his experiments on a more regular footing, and his subsequent productions improved as he grew in experience and reputation. Both by necessity and design his work remained occasional, like that of other alternative dramatic organizations. But other "Sunday societies" like the Independent Theatre Society (1891) and the Stage Society (1899) made use of some of the best actors and directors in London on their days off, whereas Poel stuck to amateurs. This was partly by choice, for he knew that he could drill amateurs into the kind of performances he desired, and partly because many professional actors refused to work for him. Poel's limitations and contradictions were many, but the major drawback to his enterprise remained the quality of the acting. The first performance of the new ESS, *Twelfth Night* at Burlington Hall in 1895, reused the *Measure for Measure* stage, had new Elizabethan costumes, and music conducted by Arnold Dolmetsch; the program stated that it was "acted after the manner of Sixteenth Century." But to William Archer the virtues of the reconstruction were demolished by ruinous acting. His review noted that it would be fairer to say that the production was "staged (more or less) after the manner of the sixteenth century and acted after the manner of the Nineteenth Century Amateur." Poel seemed to care little about acting in the usual sense, and concentrated his attention on a musical arrangement of voices, orchestrating Viola as a mezzo, for example, Olivia as a contralto, Toby as a bass, Andrew as a falsetto.[10]

In the end it was not Poel's actual accomplishments that made his cause significant but rather his influence on other directors, like Granville Barker and Tyrone Guthrie, who succeeded precisely because they followed his intentions and not his practice. Barker said at the time of his own *Twelfth Night* in 1912, "I don't go as far as Mr Poel; I think his method is somewhat archaeological; there is somewhat too much of the Elizabethan letter, as contrasted with the Elizabethan spirit." Poel was a stubborn elitist, proclaiming by his actions that authentic Shakespeare could be appreciated by the right-minded. From a visual perspective it was Poel's remodeling of the stage architecture and apron that mattered. The use of Elizabethan costumes was a dead end; Mario Borsa commented in 1908 that if the Elizabethans made all periods contemporary the consequence today should be modern dress.[11] But not until after the First World War was Poel or any other major director prepared to take that extreme if logical step.

Further, Poel's remodeled stage, while undeniably influential, remained an iconic device: it was a metonym of the absent Elizabethan age. He rarely

10　*Measure for Measure* 1898 Paris. D: Aurélien Lugné-Poe. Des: R. Hista. Drawing by Flasschoen. Instead of Poel's onstage gallants, the audience at the Cirque d'Eté surrounds the actors.

managed to achieve the actor-audience rapport of Shakespeare's time that he admired and supposedly sought. As with the gallants on stage, what Poel recreated was not Elizabethan intimacy but an illusion of intimacy, "a picture of that rapport for a largely disengaged modern audience," in Mazer's discriminating expression (81). One of the first directors to rephrase Poel's academic insight into theatrical discovery was Aurélien Lugné-Poe, whose own visual sense had been exercised in early Symbolist productions. Lugné-Poe had seen Poel's *Two Gentlemen* at the Merchant Taylors' Hall in 1896, and two years later took the Cirque d'Eté in Paris for a production of *Measure for Measure* modeled on the methods of the ESS. His starting-point was the actor–audience relationship of the Swan drawing. In place of an antiquarian reconstruction, he put a booth stage with a balcony and three doors in the center of the circus ring and placed the audience in a large semicircle around it (illus. 10). The immediate effect of the production was negligible, and in later life Lugné-Poe spoke of it with skepticism (Bablet 1965: 356); the rhyming translation by L. Ménard was incomplete and "méchante," according to Jean Jacquot (40–1). Nevertheless Lugné-Poe got the speed as well as the intimacy of the Elizabethan stage. By departing from Poel's slavish notions of authenticity, in other words, he pointed to the permanent visual contribution of Elizabethanism. And his example, at the very end of the century, serves as a fitting reminder of the growing internationalism of Shakespeare performance.

3 | *The scenographic revolution*

At the dawn of the new century Shakespeare needed a new theatre. Illusionist pictorialism, though it staggered on until the war in ever more lavish guises, was aesthetically bankrupt. Its chief alternative, the architectural simplicity of Elizabethanism, began by promising much but soon was bogged down in amateurism and pedantry. What was needed was an entirely fresh approach, one that could revitalize the content of the plays by transforming the nature of their representation. It came as a result of the work of two Symbolist visionaries, theatre artists of a new and different mark, who in separate ways aimed to return the stage to its ancient condition and power: Adolphe Appia and Edward Gordon Craig. Their methods were innovative but notably simple; though neither was primarily a Shakespearean both had profound effects on Shakespearean production. What they achieved affected almost every facet of theatre and drama in the twentieth century, but the most revolutionary aspect of their contribution was in the realm of the visual.

The general reforms of Appia and Craig are so well known that it is only necessary here to point to their application to Shakespearean stage design. Working contemporaneously but separately, they were both motivated by the longing for a synesthetic integration of experience that had its origin in Wagner's notion of *Gesamtkunstwerk*. Appia, directly inspired by the cosmic mysteries of Wagner's music-dramas, was disgusted by their shoddy canvas-and-paint realizations. Wagner was an artistic prophet in most areas but the theatrical, for even his own productions at Bayreuth were limited by the same pictorialism that characterized the staging of Shakespeare. Appia saw a way to install the mythic power of Wagner's music into staging through evocative settings and light, and his great design achievement was to create psychological impressions of space. His objection to traditional stagecraft was fundamental: the actor's full dimensionality is weakened and contradicted by flat scenery. Rejecting the nineteenth-century desire to literalize the scene, Appia strove instead for optical harmonies established by

43

"sculptured light," a total scenography that used lighting as a companion to the musical score. Locale would no longer be an environment to contain the action but a visual extension of the character's inner state. For *Siegfried*, he wrote in 1900, it is not a scenic forest that is required but the feeling of a character who moves through time through a forest: "We shall no longer try to give the illusion of the forest, but the illusion of a man in the atmosphere of a forest."[1] His work was aided at this time by the practical experiments of Mariano Fortuny, who developed a system of diffused lighting that greatly enhanced the aura of mystery Appia sought. By installing a "sky-dome" (*Kuppelhorizont*) of colored silk above the stage, Fortuny was able to reflect electric light down on the scene in an even and natural manner that suggested the limitless arena of the Wagnerian universe.

Though the implications of Appia's psychic spaces were enormous, his actual designs for Wagner's misty supernaturalism were not often appropriate for Shakespeare. Of more direct influence was his discovery of the value of steps, most vividly realized in experiments at Emile Jaques-Dalcroze's Institute for Eurhythmics at Hellerau, near Dresden. In his Wagnerian designs Appia had already realized that the stage floor – which had for most of history been disguised or conventionalized by designers – was the key to a new vocabulary of space. As the physical link between the actor and the setting, the floor could be augmented by steps, slopes, and levels to form an aesthetic connection between the actor and the setting. (In practical terms at least he had been preceded here by Henry Irving and by the Meininger.) At Hellerau Appia discovered that banks of steps could be organized like music to create "rhythmic spaces" which physicalized time. The designer had become the actor's alter ego, creating an abstract visual representation of the character's inner state. Donald Oenslager (185) records that Appia, insisting on the kinesthetic basis of stage space, once warned a student, "design with your legs, not with your eyes."

CRAIG AND THE NEW STAGECRAFT

Edward Gordon Craig was also moved to scenic reformation through music. His innovations were first seen between 1900 and 1902 in limited performances of baroque opera, where as director and designer he discovered, like Appia, that the relationship between the actor and music was capable of visual expression. In productions for the Purcell Opera Society in London, Craig used lengthy rehearsals and the pliability of amateur performers to great advantage; he effectively coerced the performers into harmony with the scenography. Most of these productions occurred in non-theatrical spaces that required extreme simplicity of setting, which Craig soon learned to turn into an aesthetic virtue. His visual intention was to abandon the premises of Realism in order to free the spectator's imagination. This may sound a bit like Poel's agenda, but the two could not have been further apart. There would be no archaeology with Craig, or any appearance of scholarship; he announced in the program for his second production of *Dido and Aeneas* that he had "taken particular care to be entirely *incorrect* in all matters of detail" (Innes 41). Assuming all of the major responsibilities for production – direction, design, costumes, properties, lighting – he began to forge a modernist unity for theatrical performance.

When Laurence Housman's verse play *Bethlehem* was refused a license by the Lord Chamberlain in 1902 because of its biblical subject, Craig directed a private performance at the Imperial Institute. Using a method similar to that of his operas, he provided suggestive "decoration" instead of representative scenery; choreographic gesture and movement replaced optical locale. Few people had the chance to see the production but most who did were enthralled by the beauty of Craig's work, which had no parallel in London. It struck a sympathetic chord especially in the ears of the Symbolists, who found in Craig's theatre an echo of the evocative kingdom of *l'art pour l'art*. W. B. Yeats had already been won over by *Dido*, which he thought "created an ideal country where everything was possible, even speaking in verse or in music, or the expression of the whole of life in a dance." Ten years later Granville Barker would acknowledge that his own emancipation from pictorial scenery dated from seeing *Bethlehem*.[2] Not everyone was happy, however; Housman for one was thoroughly upset by Craig's cuts and constant demands for rewriting; in the end he called the production "a beautiful perversion" of his play (Innes 82). The expostulation between Ben Jonson and Inigo Jones was reoccurring. Already in 1902 the archetype of the twentieth-century designer-director saw poetic drama as a series of dynamic events for the eye: the theatre had become a visual art. It might be said that the theatre was primarily a visual art for Charles Kean and Henry Irving and Duke Georg as well, but their representations were rooted in dialogue, the conflicts expressed in language. For Craig the events on the platform were detached from speech; while language was not dismissed, the drama itself took place in the visual realm. Poetry, in the Craigian paradox, was to be expressed not verbally but visually.

In 1903 Ellen Terry gave her son control of a company at the Imperial Theatre for Ibsen's *The Vikings at Helgeland*. A good choice for Craig, it was an odd one for the grand lady of the Victorian stage, and few of her followers from the Lyceum cared to imagine her in Norse ice. The designs and some of the effects were exquisite, but for the first time Craig faced a professional company, under commercial pressure, with forceful acting traditions. No amateur pliability here, nor six months for rehearsals. His idea of the *Übermarionette*, the actor as a kind of superpuppet under the control of a designer-director, first expressed in 1906, probably owes much to the resistance his experimental methods now encountered. Things were even worse for the next production, *Much Ado About Nothing*, which for financial reasons had but two weeks of preparation. Besides heavy limitations on expenses for sets and costumes, Terry insisted on "the *old* play, and the *old* me in it" (Innes 98). She had originally played Beatrice opposite Irving in his 1882 production, a grand exercise in historical pictorialism mentioned in the previous chapter, and wanted none of Teddy's newfangled ideas to interfere with the success of her Shakespeare.

Craig was naturally unhappy, and probably had little control over the acting. He considered the entire production a vulgar travesty, "Bach's Passion interpreted by the Gaiety Chorus" (Innes 100), especially when the actors reverted to conventional comic mannerisms as the run continued. Most of the costumes were from stock. But under the severe economy the settings were elegant and evocative, and Shakespeare thus met what became known as the New Stagecraft for the first time, and in the only Shakespeare play directed by Craig in England. The church scene (illus. 11) offered a profound contradiction to Telbin's detailed cathedral for Irving: nothing but candles and a corridor of draperies. The ecclesiastical mood was created by colored shafts of light; "for truth and beauty combined, this dim scene is incomparably finer than any other attempt that has been made to suggest a cathedral on stage," said Max Beerbohm. "I went to see Much Adoodle-do yesterday evening," Shaw wrote to Terry. "As usual Ted has the best of it. I have never seen the church scene go before – didnt think it *could* go, in fact."[3] Count Kessler, who would soon become crucial in extending Craig's ideas, realized its visual merit:

While the Meiningen Company, and, in England, Beerbohm Tree, were making the stage into a branch of the Arts and Crafts Museum, piling up accurate historical detail, people found that Craig had used for Ibsen's *The Vikings* only curtains as background, and only such properties as were indispensable to the action; and in the church scene in *Much Ado About Nothing*, except for the curtains there was only

11 *Much Ado About Nothing* 1903 London. D and Des: Edward Gordon Craig. A woodblock print made by Craig of his preliminary design for the church scene (4.1). The perspective is reminiscent of Serlio, whom Craig much admired, but the "illusion" of depth comes from draped curtains.

one strong ray of sunlight, falling on the stage in a thousand colours through an invisible stained-glass window.[4]

Leonato's garden was equally simple, if more solid. In this case an elaborate wickerwork structure indicated formal topiary, arranged as three sides of a rectangle, creating a large open acting space; while more representational than the church, it was still in the realm of aesthetic fancy.

Craig's experience with the commercial theatre led him into an extremely early, histrionic retirement; with very few exceptions he would spend the rest of his life away from the active work of designing or directing plays. His rich effect on Shakespearean scenography was accomplished chiefly through his writing, his suggestive designs, and his general influence. He began a pattern of behavior that effectively insured he would not work in the professional theatre: he demanded total control over productions offered him, unlimited budgets, and huge fees. Convinced of his own genius, suspicious of theatre managers, and unwilling to compromise his ideals, he became a brilliant brooder.

So he began a series of publications that would disseminate his ideas worldwide, perhaps more effectively and more lastingly than localized performances could have done. The most important of these was *The Mask*, a journal issued occasionally from 1908 to 1929. The first, however, was *The Art of the Theatre*, published as a pamphlet in separate English and German editions in 1905; the German version had an introduction by Count Kessler. It was much expanded as *On the Art of the Theatre* in 1911 and included some impressive suggestions for Shakespeare, scenographic proposals without specific productions to hand. The Calpurnia scene (2.2) in *Julius Caesar*, for example, is conveyed in one design by monumental walls right and left with a low roof and colonnade up center; in another, Macbeth's "Tomorrow and tomorrow" soliloquy (5.5) is placed in front of abstract monoliths, solid on one side, arranged in gigantic steps on the other, dwarfing his figure. In a dissimilar vein, the Forum for *Caesar* reveals something of Craig's nineteenth-century influences with its massed citizens sketched on a backcloth. But the assembled Romans are barely more than brush strokes, visually closer to the clouds above them than to the main characters (illus. 12). Though the scene feels expansive and open, the design has rejected the Meininger method entirely, taking the emphasis off the crowd and placing it on the silent conspirators.

"Steps, a fine theme," he wrote on a picture of stairs in the Vatican (Innes 106). In architecture banks of steps can have great visual and kinetic power, both indoors and out, because they unite function with emblem. As we walk up or down them in daily life, stairs can unexpectedly evoke desires for corporeal and spiritual elevation or fears of falling and loss. Telbin's massive stairway leading down to the tomb in Irving's *Romeo* began to suggest, albeit in a pictorial way, how a designer might transfer that architectural power to the theatre (see illus. 6). Craig's plan for *Caesar* brings to mind some of Appia's early work, like the 1896 designs for *Tristan und Isolde* and *Parsifal*, where levels have atmospheric function yet are integrated into the representation of locale. In other words, the steps are double agents here: they are abstract and metaphoric (they form a barrier, they elevate Antony,

12 Craig's 1905 design for *Julius Caesar* (3.2). Mark Antony is in the middle distance
at the top of a rostrum, leaning toward the crowd and away from the audience. The
conspirators are downstage. The accent, Craig wrote in his own caption, is not on
Antony's oration, but on the split he causes between the two groups; placing the
conspirators in the foreground means that "silence can be felt."

they isolate the conspirators) while at the same time they are literal and metonymic (they appear to be of marble, they signify the Roman Forum). Craig began to experiment with stairways as settings complete in themselves with his 1905 series entitled "The Steps" (published in *Towards a New Theatre* in 1913), in which a repeated monumental structure tells an ethereal story in four acts or "moods" by means of lighting changes and actor disposition. This was drama as Craig dreamed of it, universal, timeless, wordless, the narrative engineered by the visual alone. Many of these drawings, however, seem highly impractical, apparently requiring a proscenium about 25 meters high. It was this inclination that led Lee Simonson (337) to dismiss Craig's designs as "the irresponsible improvisations of a romantic water-colorist."

Hamlet was almost an obsession for Craig from the time he played the role in 1896 (wearing Irving's costume), and led to one of the most curious and unlikely collaborations of the young century. Aware of the limitations and growing obsolescence of his own brand of Naturalism, Stanislavsky carried on a series of half-hearted and mostly unsuccessful flirtations with the new movement; Isadora Duncan, who had begun a passionate affair with Craig in 1904, suggested that he was just the man to produce Shakespeare for the Moscow Art Theatre. Chronically short of funds and sensing an opportunity for total artistic control, Craig agreed in 1908 to design and stage *Hamlet*. That was about as far as agreement went, however; from the first consultations differences between the two directors over the nature and purpose of the production began to affect the outcome. Craig traveled to Moscow a number of times; the idea was that he would provide the "concept," the designs, and the outline for the direction, which Stanislavsky or his assistant director, L. A. Sulerzhitsky, would execute in day-to-day rehearsals. The story, told in full by Laurence Senelick, is a tale on both sides of misunderstandings, childish affronts, and imagined treacheries, coupled with the usual Craigian demands, delays, and damnations. At one point Stanislavsky became seriously ill, postponing work for about a year. In the end neither he nor his house designers were in sympathy with Craig's methods and the result was inevitably compromised. The production, finally mounted in 1911/12, was much abused by Craig but it nonetheless secured the international reputation of the theatre and provided the single major demonstration of his ideas for Shakespeare.

The starting-point was Craig's notion that *Hamlet* is a monodrama, that the universe of the play should be shown through the eyes of the central character. One of the finest of Craig's preliminary designs, made about 1910,

13 Craig's early sketch for the second scene of *Hamlet*, with the languorous figure of the prince on the left side in the foreground, as if dreaming up the court. The strict verticals of the setting and of the royal figures are in notable contrast to Hamlet's horizontal posture. The entire court seems to be wrapped in the King's cape.

is a graphic realization of the concept (illus. 13). Hamlet lounges like an aesthete, shadowy and diffident, while Claudius establishes his authority over the court. "You see the stage divided by a barrier," Craig wrote in his own caption to the picture in *Towards a New Theatre* (81). "On the one side sits Hamlet, fallen, as it were, into a dream, on the other side you see his dream. You see it, as it were, through the mind's eye of Hamlet." The other characters are therefore figments, significant only as they relate to the protagonist and his dream; "the king speaks as if he were an automaton." Obviously this is a limited view of the play, popular with *fin de siècle* Symbolists, effectively transforming it into a Romantic parable about a sensitive artist-prince at odds with his surroundings and alienated from action. During rehearsals in Moscow there were continual difficulties over acting and performance technique that stemmed from the interpretive slant, Stanislavsky demanding more Chekhovian realism, Craig pushing for stylization.

If monodrama is the central idea in this design, the central scenic device is also apparent. Craig's famous screens, seen in the picture placed flat against the upstage wall, were his major innovation in setting. As he envisioned them, they were a dynamic and living element, arranged in new shapes and angles to reflect the shifting emotional content of Hamlet's mind as well as to solve the practical problems of shifting the twenty scenes of the play. The screens would provide a fluid space, constantly changing with the dramatic locale yet remaining abstract and suggestive. With them, Craig wrote in his journal (Innes 141), "we pass from one scene to another without a break of any kind, and when the change has come we are not conscious of any disharmony between the new scene and that which is past." As Cubism reevaluated the composition of the visual world, Craig's "scene with a mobile face" (as he called it later, Craig 1923: 19) reevaluated the nature of the theatre.[5] There may not have been any conscious influence, but Craig's system was a dynamic application of some of the recent discoveries of Cubism. Though Craig never wished to abandon perspective, the screens broke scenography down to first principles, then rebuilt the stage space in a modernist, geometrical rendering of its component parts.

Basically the screens were simply flats: monochrome canvas was stretched on wooden frames, which were hinged together to be self-supporting. Though Craig experimented with other covering materials, it was not their construction but their application that was original. Because they could be aligned in many configurations they provided a technique of simulating architectural or abstract lithic structures out of supplies and methods common to any theatre in Europe or the Americas. In Moscow they were built taller and heavier than those Craig had made in London, which made them less stable and more difficult to move. Craig wanted them to be shifted in full view by costumed stagehands in the Japanese manner, but Stanislavsky, reverting to his Naturalist aesthetic, expected the curtain to close after each scene to hide the changes. Circumstances took charge; at the final dress rehearsal the screens were somehow dislodged and came crashing to the floor. In a famous passage in *My Life in Art* (521), Stanislavsky described the "crack of breaking wooden frames, the sound of ripping canvas, and then the formless mass of broken and torn screens all over the

14 *Hamlet* 1911/12 Moscow. D: E. G. Craig and K. S. Stanislavsky. S: Craig. C: Craig and K. N. Sapunov. The first scene, showing the Ghost and the soldiers amid the screens, here suggesting battlements. The Cubist arrangement is more apparent in this contemporary sketch by A. Lyubimov than in the models or photos, though the height of the screens has been exaggerated. In reality the proscenium arch of the MAT would have cut across the verticals about two-thirds of the way up.

stage." (Craig was not present at the accident and was never told about it, so when the autobiography first appeared in 1923 he vehemently insisted the story was a lie and later threatened to sue Stanislavsky.) With the opening a few hours away, the screens were hastily repaired and weighted with ballast to prevent further disaster; but this insured that the curtain would be used and that scene changes would be much slower.

Considering the difficulties encountered in the three years of preparations, the production achieved more visual unity than might be expected. The first scene, for example, was a startling application of the screens, implying castle walls in broken perspective with the soldiers half lost in the shadows between them (illus. 14). At times the Ghost "was altogether unseen," wrote Stanislavsky (518), "then he appeared again in the halftone of the light of a projector. His long cloak dragged behind him." The second scene, elaborate and precise, effectively underlined the monodramatic concept; everything until the exit of the court was Hamlet's nightmare. The screens were covered with gilt paper, and the royal pair were installed above the court as in illustration 13, in long golden mantles. As Stanislavsky (514) described it,

The King and Queen sat on a high throne in golden and brocaded costumes, among the golden walls of the throne room, and from their shoulders there spread downwards a cloak of golden porphyry, widening until it occupied the entire width of the stage and fell into the trap. In this tremendous cloak there were cut holes through which appeared a great number of courtiers' heads, looking upward at the throne. The whole scene resembled a golden sea with golden waves.

The entire feudal order was represented symbolically, wrapped in a vast garment of gold. Actually the effect was accomplished not with a single piece of cloth but with capes on the individual courtiers, and it was necessary for the actors to remain motionless for most of the scene; although this was physically demanding, it increased the nightmare mood. "Though yet of Hamlet our dear brother's death" was spoken, as Craig wanted, as if the King "were an automaton." At his words "Come away," the court remained in position while a black tulle curtain fell in front of it like a fog between Hamlet and his bad dream.

Craig complained bitterly about the changes made to his costume designs, as obsessed with treachery as Hamlet, and in the end K. N. Sapunov, one of the MAT designers, was given credit for them in the program. No doubt there was legitimate cause for his concern, though the photo we have of Claudius and Gertrude reveals a stylized pose in heavily stylized costumes (illus. 15) in keeping with Craig's preliminary sketch. The screens were also used more or less according to plan, despite the slow changes. In the Mousetrap scene, one of the highlights of the production, the back line of screens was pulled out so that the full depth of the stage was exposed. The King and Queen sat far upstage on a high throne, in an echo of their first appearance, while Hamlet prompted the Players downstage, up to his waist in a long narrow trap. Simple pieces were added for some scenes, like a rectangular canopied bed on a stepped platform for the Queen's closet or two stone monuments in the graveyard, but the screens carried the preponderance of the visual burden.

Their potency was most apparent in the final scene, recorded in the only production photograph that shows the scenography clearly (illus. 16). The contrast between the horizontal body of Hamlet and the rising lines of the

15 *Hamlet* 1911/12 Moscow. N. O. Massalitinov and Olga Knipper as Claudius and Gertrude in their golden crowns and capes.

other actors and of the screens recalls the parallel contrast in the second scene, Hamlet again stage right, dreaming in death the entrance of Fortinbras as he dreamed in life the vision of the court. The central panel of screens was removed to disclose the waving spears of his army. (This waving was much ridiculed in the Moscow press; it seemed too comic and literal-minded for such a symbolic moment.) Fortinbras stared down at the dead dreamer, "like an Archangel," according to Stanislavsky (517), a golden cross on his tunic and a nimbus shield behind him. The soldiers filled the stage, lowering their white banners on the body, "showing only the dead and happy face of the great cleanser of the earth who had at last found the secrets of life on earth in the arms of death."

In general terms the performance was either a flawed success or a brilliant failure, depending on the point of view. Privately Craig castigated the debasement of his conception, publicly he made profit from its apparent fulfillment. A few international reports were ecstatic, seeing Craig as the savior of the theatre and the production as a high water-mark of art. The MAT was practically unknown in London prior to a glowing notice in *The Times* by Terence Philip, who thought the production "a completely

16   *Hamlet* 1911/12 Moscow. Final tableau: the thrusting verticals of the screens, the spears, the flags, and the huge sword contrast to the prone bodies. V. I. Kachalov as Hamlet on the steps, I. N. Bersenev as Fortinbras above him.

realized success" of Craig's theories; some other responses were equally effusive. (They are summarized in Senelick 174–83.) The Moscow papers were less enthusiastic. Though most acknowledged V. I. Kachalov's triumph as the Prince, there was only qualified praise for the direction and design.

The basic problem with the production was a conflict in style between the playing and the scenography. What else would we expect when the champion of the interior actor met the advocate of the *Übermarionette*? Craig reached for an art of suggestion – *la totalité expressive* is Denis Bablet's phrase – in which the actor was larger than his body, a unit of a cosmic design: the scenic actor, he might be called. Stanislavsky stressed instead the human dimension, the actor's fleshiness; the success of his theories needs no comment, and they have dominated acting and writing for both the theatre and film in the twentieth century. The expostulation in Moscow provides us with a paradigm, in question form, about how to produce Shakespeare: play the characters or play the themes? Should the tragedies, especially, be used as vehicles for investigating the oddity and durability and suffering of the creatures who inhabit this world, or should they be used as channels for conveying the spiritual orbit that encircles those creatures? And in the theatre are the two necessarily at odds? Craig's scenographic work unveiled the necessity of the question, which is still very much alive, because he saw Shakespeare neither as cultural icon nor as commercial property but as an artist of extremity. Craig often wrote that Shakespeare's plays were too great to be staged; like Charles Lamb he thought of them as mystical compilations that could be fully exhibited only in the mind. The responsibility of the theatre artist who attempted them was to suggest to the eye the forces that lay just beyond sight. The Soviet director Grigori Kozintsev, whose films of *Hamlet* and *King Lear* have been influential in our time, sensed that this was Craig's primary contribution. "Craig was the first to insist," he wrote in his production log,[6] "that Shakespeare's tragedies are concerned not only with human passions and the relationships between the main characters in the plays, but first and foremost with the conflict of some sort of mighty visual powers."

REINHARDT AND HIS DESIGNERS

Craig's reforms were effectively ignored in England in the first decade of the century. In Germany, however, they found a receptive soil, if not a completely full harvest. With the work of Jocza Savits and Karl

Lautenschläger continuing in Munich, and the tendency to simplicity spreading elsewhere, the German theatres were much more willing than English ones to consider a new approach to Shakespeare. Craig's influence dates from December of 1904, when an exhibition of his work was mounted at Friedmann and Weber's gallery in Berlin. The catalogue contained a long introduction by Harry Kessler, a knowledgeable and liberal patron of the arts dedicated to the new movement and fully assured that Craig would be the salvation of the stage; he later commissioned Craig designs for his well-known Cranach Press edition of *Hamlet*. Count Kessler introduced the designer to the new lessee of the Deutsches Theater, Max Reinhardt, who was overwhelmed by the exhibition and engaged Craig to design four productions. Craig actually began work on Shaw's *Caesar and Cleopatra* and made notations for *King Lear*; of course he demanded total artistic control, which Reinhardt was not about to grant, and the arrangement soon collapsed. Nonetheless it was their meeting that convinced Reinhardt of the lasting value of stylization.[7] The real story of the twentieth-century visual approach to Shakespeare begins here.

But Reinhardt's approach to the theatre was not, as the Germans say, *Craigische*; whatever effect or influence Craig had on his designers, Reinhardt himself worshipped a different god, and his work on Shakespeare shows this clearly. Far and away his favorite playwright, Reinhardt turned to Shakespeare for most of his life, directing twenty-two of the plays for something like 3,000 performances.[8] In a Shakespeare festival in 1913 and 1914, he produced ten of the plays at the Deutsches Theater – partly as a propaganda effort aimed at showing the capacity of the German nation to rise above national differences where art was concerned. Productions of *A Midsummer Night's Dream*, which he staged numerous times between 1905 and 1939, seen in cities as diverse as Budapest, Stockholm, and Los Angeles, can give us a capsule history of his approach.

His first *Dream* was designed by Gustav Knina with spectacular woodland settings, using a forest of thick tree trunks, realistic branches, and a carpet of grassy moss in the manner of Beerbohm Tree (illus. 17). The revolving stage of the Neues Theater in Berlin made the rhythm rapid and fluid, but the sets were fully detailed. When Reinhardt produced it at Georg Fuchs' Künstlertheater in Munich in 1909, the spare facilities of the shallow "relief" stage (itself influenced by Savits) enforced a minimalist setting. In place of a deluxe forest Karl Walser set four naked trees, a few simulated branches, and a plain green cloth on the floor. But Reinhardt disapproved of the spatial limitations of the Künstlertheater (he called it "the little kiddie

Scene aus „Ein Sommernachtstraum"

17 *A Midsummer Night's Dream* 1905 Berlin. D: Max Reinhardt. S: Gustav Knina.
C: Karl Walser. Puck (Gertrud Eysoldt) leads the lovers through the real trees of the
woodland, on the revolve at the Neues Theater.

coffin"), and the simplification did not continue. Ernst Stern redesigned the
play for the Deutsches Theater in 1913, making the forest its scenic essence
and its aesthetic rationale; the huge revolve there encouraged the spectacular
mode. Eighteen meters in diameter and extending into the wings and almost
to the edge of the apron, it permitted a wondrously swift flow of scenes; no
longer need the text be chopped up to accommodate the carpenter, no
longer need the audience wait for the next built-up set. In solving the great
dilemma of nineteenth-century pictorialism, however, Reinhardt's revolve
fostered the same visual aesthetic: theatre technology again provoked
fastidious over-production. By the time of the famous outdoor performances, like those in the Boboli Gardens in Florence and in a huge
meadow in Oxford in 1933, Reinhardt was exploiting the natural environment in an extravagant, cinematic manner – in fact anticipating his
own film version made for Hollywood in 1935. "Real grass and cardboard
actors," Karl Kraus concluded.[9]

And yet Reinhardt came closer than any director of his era to effecting a
coherent visual reform for Shakespeare, chiefly because of his collaboration
with some of the best designers of the new movement. One result was that
his productions often had a sophisticated and contemporary look, as in

Edvard Munch's work for *Ghosts* in 1906 or Stern's Expressionist designs for Sorge's *The Beggar* in 1917. It is clear that the director often controlled the visual approach himself; Reinhardt normally wrote his detailed *Regiebuch* before design consultations, and these director's scripts, as Stern noticed, were "studded with stage sketches and scenes."[10] The designer's contributions, in other words, were controlled by the director's evolving tastes.

The case of Emil Orlik is representative. Already in tune with post-impressionism, he spent a year in Japan in 1900 learning woodcut techniques and studying Kabuki theatre. These influences strongly affected his art when he returned to Vienna and Berlin, yet his first assignment for Reinhardt, an illusionist *Merchant of Venice* of 1905, bore no resemblance to his own style. Though Orlik is sometimes credited with the complete design, in fact his contribution was limited to the costumes; the pictorial environment was made by a Berlin scenery company, doubtless following the instructions of the director.[11] After Reinhardt's contact with Craig, however, the new look began to appear in Shakespeare at the Deutsches Theater. Orlik saw the Craig designs and adapted the methods. While the pictorial *Merchant* was on stage he made beautiful gouaches for a much simplified version of *The Winter's Tale*, which would open in September of 1906 with Agnes Sorma as Hermione. Now encouraged by Reinhardt to follow his own visual sense for a fanciful script, Orlik provided what may have been the first application of Craig's ideas to Shakespeare production. "He has swallowed Craig," Arthur Hopkins said of Reinhardt, "but he has digested him."

The stylization of the setting is immediately apparent in the design for the front of the palace (color pl. 1), where the towering vertical lines above the actors, emphasized by the asymmetrical recesses in the walls, are similar to Craig's early drawings. The simple curtain closing the doorway was Orlik's signature for the production, its motif picked up in interior settings and in the costumes, often in green and gold. This design was widely reproduced and influenced scenographers in many countries.[12] Leontes' court was even more impressive in its simplicity, constructed of patterned curtains and minimal set pieces (color pl. 2). Orlik's interest in Japanese woodcuts can be detected here in the colors and in the geometrical patterns on the curtains. The set photos reveal that Reinhardt followed both of these designs in production – exactly in the first case, with the elimination of the red carpet in the second.

When the play moved to Bohemia, however, Japanese austerity was abandoned for an exuberant, childlike fantasy. The Chorus' speech provided an image for the transition: Time was a young girl with golden hair and a

floral head-wreath, carrying a staff. Regardless of Shakespeare's geographic confusion, Bohemia was taken literally in the costuming, with Perdita and her friends in multi-colored Czech peasant dresses and Polixenes as a Tartar chieftain. Orlik, who was born in Prague, may have been remembering fairytale books of his own Bohemian boyhood for his festive set, with its maypole in the foreground and pennants on the distant hill (color pl. 3). Craig would have demanded a method of uniting the visual effect of Bohemia with the first half of the play, but Reinhardt wanted a strong contrast to the Sicilia scenes and did not hesitate to mix styles in order to achieve it.

Sicilia had not been all simplicity in any event, though that is how most historians record it. Certainly Orlik's designs are admirably frugal and suggestive but when we look at what Reinhardt actually put on stage a different picture appears; particularly at the crisis point of the play he could no more resist visual overstatement than he could with *A Midsummer Night's Dream*. We have already seen how the trial scene was subjected to spectacular treatment in the nineteenth century. Illustration 18, a production shot of the moment when Paulina returns to inform the court of Hermione's

18 *The Winter's Tale* 1906 Berlin. D: Max Reinhardt. Des: Emil Orlik. P: H. L. Held. The end of Hermione's trial scene (3.2), showing the full stage set with massed chorus. Freidrich Kayssler as Leontes is slumped in the throne to the left of the photo, Max Schütz as Antigonus is center with Paulina (Hedwig Wangel, on her knees).

death, is a clear demonstration of the need to go beyond a designer's sketches and even beyond set photos when discussing the visual effect of performance. Here the green curtains were drawn back to show the entire depth of the stage, from the checkerboard apron to the stepped platform to the white plaster cyclorama (a recent modification of the Fortuny *horizont* lighting system) at the rear. From the standpoint of scenery alone Orlik's restrained plan had been realized: the few set pieces were chiefly cubes, the slanted proscenium uprights lent a noble frame, and the actors, placed relatively close to the audience, accented the open playing space in an Elizabethan manner. The dominant element, however, was not the décor but a vast group of dark-clad priests, five or six rows deep, more than a hundred extras crowding upstage in perspective format. They acted as witnesses to the downstage event, an organized chorus like the citizens in the Meininger *Julius Caesar*, their reactions a powerful visual counterpart to the human drama before them, their very presence signifying a reliance on the dazzling. While maintaining Craigian simplicity in the set, in other words, Reinhardt made a spectacle out of the bodies of actors in the same way that Kean and Dingelstedt had done half a century before.

A second early production deserves consideration as a further experiment with symbolic scenography on the commercial Berlin stage. *King Lear* was the one Shakespeare play that Reinhardt had asked Craig to design, and, according to L. M. Newman, Craig made notations for "a curtain setting with steps and blocks, which made no use of revolve or cyclorama. A painted, gradated backcloth was to be modelled by shafts of limelight, while ground-rows and cut cloths were employed for the outdoor scenes." Newman holds that Carl Czeschka, who eventually designed the production, leaned on Craig's ideas though with considerably less lightness and grace.[13] Reinhardt wanted a stark look in high relief to underline the violence and cruelty of the script, and Czeschka gave him strong geometric patterns, often in black and white. The production, which opened at the Deutsches Theater in September of 1908, used a stylization more pronounced than that of *The Winter's Tale*, as in the formidable curtain setting for the first scene (illus. 19). Geometrical simplicity had been exaggerated in the extreme, as if a mad king had decorated his own council chamber.

Exteriors were more representational. The façade of Gloucester's castle was monumental and functional like a Greek *skene*, but also indicated a sense of particular locale. On the heath an isolated tree stump protruding from a groundcloth and a few scattered rocks led to the hovel; the stage then revolved to expose the inside of a rough, thatched hut with wooden beams

19 *King Lear* 1908 Berlin. D: Max Reinhardt. Des: Carl Czeschka. A violent
mixture of patterned panels of cloth signaled barbarity.

and benches. Czeschka's costumes conveyed an elegant barbarity, especially
in the contrast between the black squares on Regan's cape and the triangles
on Edmund's, or in the heavy contrast between Lear and the Fool (illus. 20).
Lear's costume, in gold, black, yellow, and red (according to Czeschka's
design, in Cologne), was like a ritual garment from some primitive realm of
cruelty and pain.

Despite the symbolic examples of *Winter's Tale* and *Lear*, the revolve was
really the determining design factor for most of Reinhardt's Shakespeare.
For *The Tempest* in 1915 the large stage at the Volksbühne, which Reinhardt
had acquired as his third Berlin theatre, became the opportunity for further
mechanical exploitation. It was equipped with a drum stage, which meant
that as well as turning the floor could be raised or lowered up to 2 meters.
As Ernst Stern himself explains:

When it sank away out of sight it left a cavity about 60 feet across, and over this
cavity our ship rolled and swayed splendidly on a lively sea. And when in the middle
of the tempest Gonzalo exclaims, "Now would I give a thousand furlongs of sea for
an acre of barren ground" ... the ship disappeared in a thick cloud and our island

20 *King Lear* 1908 Berlin. The violent patterns continued in costumes.
(a) Hilma Schlüter as Regan, Oscar Beregi as Edmund.

(b) Alexander Moissi as the Fool, Albert Bassermann as Lear.

rose from the depths. Its gentle, regular undulations were covered with strangely shaped brown and yellow rocks and unreal reddish vegetation of cactus type.[14]

Stern made a large isometric drawing of the scene, showing Ariel on top of a rock in a spotlight and other characters reveling amid the palm trees and hillocks. The drum revolve, lowered below the stage floor, made it appear as if the island was protruding from the sea.

Earlier I suggested that Reinhardt's reliance on the revolve encouraged a speeded-up variant of nineteenth-century pictorialism; this scenographic revanche, which might also be called a movement towards the cinematic, revealed itself further in the outdoor productions, in huge spectacles like *The Miracle*, in enlarged drama at the Grosses Schauspielhaus after the war (which included *Hamlet* and *Julius Caesar*), and in urban environmental productions like Hofmannsthal's *Jedermann* at the Salzburg Festival. His contribution to Shakespearean design lay chiefly in adapting some of Craig's visual vocabulary to a more earthly, pragmatic cause. Craig felt for the rest of his life that Reinhardt had stolen his thoughts; in an early number of *The Mask* he wrote that Reinhardt's *Winter's Tale*, *Twelfth Night* (1907), and *Salome* (1908) were the first imitations of his designs, and, as Newman puts it, until 1957 he continued to inflict "a long drawn-out revenge upon the director, stigmatizing him in print as an unoriginal, tasteless, and stingy firm."

But while Craig nursed his wounded genius, Reinhardt got on with the job, little concerned with Craig's wounds or the coarsening of Craig's concepts. Above all Reinhardt was a showman; even with Ibsen's Naturalist plays or the emotionally supercharged Expressionist drama it was the show that interested him, the "magical, complete world" he could make on the stage. He admitted the limitation of his approach, and something of its failure regarding Shakespeare, in an interview in 1916:

I had gone far in the direction the Meininger had taken. I aspired towards the completion of decor. I engaged painters with famous names for my stage to make the illusion almost complete for the audience. With that I achieved a quite opposite effect. People came to see real trees on my stage; that was a novelty that impressed them more than the art we had to offer.[15]

One might be tempted to comment that if you put real trees on your stage, you are asking people to look at them as real trees and not as art. The director applied his semiosis in a confusing way, for extreme examples of Naturalism in the theatre begin to look artificial. Real trees, taken out of nature and placed in a representation of nature, only point to the incomplete identification of signifier and signified. Despite his openness to the workable aspects of the New Stagecraft, Reinhardt was in many ways still fighting the battles of the nineteenth century.

Yet it would be incorrect to suggest that his Shakespeare was retrograde. The director's attention to the demands of the particular play, and his remarkable rapport with actors, insured that much of his work was revelatory and moving. Some of the best productions were visually adventurous, and still seem advanced in both plans and photographs. *Macbeth*, which Stern designed in an Expressionist manner in 1916, used symbolic color, a disturbing chiaroscuro, and massive shapes in the set pieces to overshadow human figures.[16] Reinhardt's first *Hamlet*, which opened at the Künstlertheater in Munich in June 1909 and moved to Berlin in October, was another example of linear contrasts. Fritz Erler's design was strongly indebted to Craig: the battlements, for example, were dark narrow pillars upstage, while the Ghost in a flowing shroud pointed horizontally into the wings. The same careful composition of actors and set was apparent in the final scene when Hamlet was carried off, stiff-legged and completely horizontal, raised by soldiers above their heads (illus. 21). Fortinbras stood in front of his company, their tall spears raised vertically. Though the

21 *Hamlet* 1909 Berlin. D: Max Reinhardt. Des: Fritz Erler. P: J. Fuchs.
A Craigian contrast of verticals and horizontals, anticipating the Moscow production. Alexander Moissi as Hamlet, Jakob Feldhammer as Fortinbras.

Schluss-Scene aus „Hamlet" (Deutsches Theater).

banners and the overdressed throne indicate the usual Reinhardt fussiness, the general visual effect seems profoundly simple. It is also remarkably similar to the final moment of the Craig–Stanislavsky *Hamlet* of 1911 shown in illustration 16 above. Interestingly enough Stanislavsky saw Reinhardt's production in early 1911 (Senelick 124); though he did not like it, except for the acting of Albert Bassermann, then playing the lead, who is to say what effect the scene may have had on him? It would be irony of some strength if Reinhardt's scenography, itself a debasement of Craig's reforms, in turn had affected Craig's own production.

POST-IMPRESSIONISM: GRANVILLE BARKER AND WILKINSON

In Edwardian London Shakespeare for the most part lived in extravagant reproductions of pictorialism. Herbert Beerbohm Tree, whose performances at Her or His Majesty's Theatre set the standard for the age, was an astute cultural businessman who had judged the temper of the time well: his upholstered, ornate Shakespeare was the vehicle for excessive and conspicuous display, the Weird Sisters flying on wires like Peter Pan, a huge type of Meininger crowd filling the stage for *Caesar*. As Ralph Berry has noted,[17] Tree's famous *Midsummer Night's Dream* (1900), with its live rabbits running in the wood, actually belongs to the same genre as Walt Disney. For Tree's production of *Twelfth Night*, Hawes Craven copied Olivia's garden from a picture in *Country Life* (Speaight 125), complete with trees, topiary, working fountains, and a huge flight of grassy steps (illus. 22). These were not Appia steps or Craig steps – like everything else beyond the first few risers they were painted on. Cary Mazer (46–7) has shown, by means of a production photograph of the same set, how shallow and lifeless the landscape actually appeared. The fact that the illusion was accepted so readily, and that reporting artists drew it after the fact as convincingly as in this picture from the *Illustrated London News*, demonstrates that the chief nineteenth-century visual convention was still strong among audiences of the regular theatres. Indeed, a sketch included in the souvenir program placed Malvolio far up on the fourth terrace, almost at the top of the picture, though even the most confounded gaper could easily have seen that he could not stand on the backdrop.

Most visual styles go into some form of baroque excess before they disappear. While Tree blithely exploited the scenic devices of fifty years, the convention was nonetheless breaking down rapidly. Craig (1913: 18) found

22 *Twelfth Night* 1901 London. D: Herbert Beerbohm Tree. Des: Hawes Craven.
Tree as Malvolio, Maud Jefferies as Olivia, at Her Majesty's Theatre. Craven's design
was originally copied from a picture in *Country Life*; the artist here has reversed the
process and made the stage set look like nature.

Craven's design laughable, of course, but he was hardly a solo voice. The reformers of the stage, led in the nineties by Shaw, had been complaining for nearly a generation about the sorry state of Shakespeare, and in the first decade of the new century even some of the London papers began to notice with embarrassment that English production of the national dramatist was lagging behind that on the continent. For all its nostalgic delights, the Edwardian age was a period of deep social uncertainty. Prompted partly by a rising fear of a German invasion, isolationism in politics and traditionalism in art became admired characteristics in official circles. Since most of the new movements were foreign it remained easy to dismiss them as intruders, especially when they seemed to challenge political or social assumptions along with artistic ones. In the midst of the hard confusions offered across the Channel, Beerbohm Tree's Shakespeare seemed like a comfortable overstuffed armchair from Victoria's reign.

But England could not resist the European wind forever, and "in or about December, 1910" – while Tree's spectacle of *Henry VIII* was playing at His Majesty's, invincible in its commitment to the old scenography – "human character changed." Virginia Woolf[18] was referring to the cultural differences between Edwardian and Georgian fiction, but her date for the change coincided with the first post-impressionist exhibition in London, which opened at the Grafton Galleries in November of that year; entitled "Manet and the Post-Impressionists," it included many works by Gauguin and Cézanne. Though all three of the main artists represented were dead, and though the exhibition would seem very tame in light of the recent Cubist paintings of Braque and Picasso, it marked a major penetration by the new forces into the island kingdom. And visually things did not stop there. In the summer of 1911 Diaghilev shocked London with Nijinsky and the exorbitant, painterly designs of Léon Bakst for *Le Spectre de la Rose* and *Schéhérazade*; Reinhardt brought *Sumurun* to the Coliseum and created *The Miracle* at Olympia that same year, then staged *Oedipus* at Covent Garden in January of the next. These were productions on a scale and with a scenic mastery never before seen in England. If human character did not actually change, it is possible that the human eye did.

It was Harley Granville Barker who realized that if Shakespeare was to have a revitalized presentation in London it would have to be under a new order, something like the subsidized system that operated in Germany. Barker's remarkable three seasons at the Court Theatre (1904–7), in which he altered the face of production in London and introduced significant new dramatists, were made possible only by extreme economy and limited production. As soon as he tried to extend the enterprise into the West End on a larger scale, it failed financially. The high rents of London theatres made large houses and long runs prerequisites to success; they in turn meant capitulation to the box-office and the dictatorship of majority taste. When an enlightened aristocrat offered a small subsidy for Shakespeare, Barker leapt at the chance. His production of *The Winter's Tale*, which opened at the Savoy Theatre in September of 1912, opened a new territory for the eye.

Suddenly and almost without warning, it was all present, all or almost all of the ingredients for a new Shakespeare that reformers in England had been crying for: the full text of a rarely seen and difficult play, performed swiftly and without pauses for set changes and with only one interval, the verse spoken briskly and with intelligence, the acting subtle and psychologically charged, the actors playing together and not deferring to a star, the direction attending to small matters as well as large, the stage modified into a semblance of Elizabethan openness, the lighting direct and bright, and the design – well, to read some of the critics one would have thought that Barker had broken open Shakespeare's tomb in Stratford and rattled his interréd bones. "Mr Granville Barker, in a distressful striving after the artistic, has achieved that mingling of discordant, ill-related elements, that impossible jangling of different keys, which can never be far removed from vulgarity." So said *The Athenaeum*. "Granville Barker has been to Berlin," wrote his friend, J. T. Grein, "and, as some travellers who write a book on a country after a week in a boarding house, has, for our benefit, Reinhardtised Shakespeare." "Scenic Discords," said the *Daily Mail*: "a triumphant vindication of existing methods." As for the costumes, they "range from Layard's Nineveh to the Nice carnival"; some courtiers "look like Highlanders dipped in ink"; Paulina is "dressed as a Salvation Army lass of the nth century."[19]

What is interesting about the reactions of the hostile critics, and some of the friendly ones as well, is how often they focused on the visual: Barker's innovations were many but it was the look of his production that was most disturbing. No one had seen an authoritative performance of Shakespeare quite like this before, and the commentators had to struggle for points of reference. What his designers had done was to create a new scenic vocabulary in order to express an exemplary or classical attitude to performance. The basic aim was to place the text in primary position, to treat Shakespeare as a serious dramatist who knew what he was doing. Barker's objection to the "production-mongers" was that they substituted scenery for drama, canvas for human conflict. His audacious reforms all spoke the same message, that

23 *The Winter's Tale* 1912 London. D: Harley Granville Barker. S: Norman Wilkinson. C: Albert Rothenstein. Lillah McCarthy makes her entrance as Hermione amid white and gold at the Savoy Theatre.

the old way could not be trusted any longer. "To invent a new hieroglyphic language of scenery, that, in a phrase, is the problem," Barker wrote a little later, expressing succinctly the problem as felt by Appia, Craig, and Reinhardt as well.

The remodeled stage was the key to the approach and was used for all three of Barker's Shakespeare productions at the Savoy. It followed the three-tiered pattern already well established on the continent: a raised level upstage, a mainstage area in front of that extending to the proscenium, and two steps lower a curved forestage built out over the first rows of seats, about 3.5 meters in depth, projecting into the house. The footlights of necessity were removed and illumination for the forestage came from recently developed "torpedo" lamps mounted in view of the audience on the dress circle. The flexibility of the modifications permitted a rapid external pace, as the stage depth could be cut off or enlarged quickly for a new scene with dropcloths at different points, and the upper level could be used as an Elizabethan discovery space. For Sicilia, Norman Wilkinson designed a winter-white world trimmed in gold that moved the play away from specific time and place into the realm of fantasy and romance. This set, indicating Leontes' palace (illus. 23) and serving for the trial scene as well, plainly leaned toward the metaphoric. It was a white gleam that reflected brilliant light in order to set off Albert Rothenstein's eclectic costumes. The art critic of *The Observer*, reviewing the production specifically from a visual perspective, held that the color contrasts, in "the most vivid hues of magenta, lemon yellow, emerald green, scarlet," were not distracting and actually assisted the action and the speed of the verse; "immeasurably finer than anything that Professor Reinhardt, that clever adapter of English ideas, has given us."[20] Barker wrote in a brief note on the production that the Sicilian costumes were based on the paintings of Giulio Romano ("that rare Italian master," Paulina calls him in the play) using "Renaissance-classic, that is, classic dress as Shakespeare saw it."

For the sheepshearing festival a different setting was placed upstage, a metonymic thatched cottage against a green cloth. Two lines of wattle fencing were in the middle area. "Bohemia is pure Warwickshire," Barker wrote in his note, and some of the costumes here were Elizabethan in style, with huge peasant hats. For all the other scenes of the play in both Bohemia and Sicilia, curtains served as backdrops. Even the finale, with its mysterious moment of a statue coming to life, a moment that seems made for the theatre of illusion, was played far downstage on the extended apron, in bright frontal light, before a dropcloth reminiscent of Orlik's designs (illus. 24). The curtains were made of rich fabrics and hung in generous folds. Most were geometric in pattern, though a few suggested locale: the seacoast scene, for example, used a white cloth with abstracted windswept trees painted on. It appears that seven separate drops were used, four backcloths, and a white act curtain.[21] Thus, with the exception of the shepherd's cottage, the production relied on devices of Craigian simplicity.

Critics rushed to point this out, as well as to charge German plagiarism. Barker had been to Berlin in 1910 to watch rehearsals of Reinhardt's *Oedipus*; some of the new lighting techniques, as well as the remodeled stage, had been seen in Reinhardt's version of that play in London. (In fact, Barker had adapted the staging for his own production of *Iphigenia in Tauris* in March of 1912.) He also saw Reinhardt's *Dream* and *The Comedy of Errors* in Berlin. Not that it much matters. Barker himself put the matter in perspective in a light-hearted letter to the *Daily Mail* about *The Winter's Tale*: "It is ten years and more since I made that remark to and of Mr Gordon Craig, that he was an excellent man to steal from. Mr. Craig shortly emigrated ... and the German-speaking theatres shortly began to give point to my mild epigram." He went on to admit his indebtedness, especially to *Bethlehem*, which "destroyed for me once and for all any illusion I may have had as to the necessity of surrounding every performance of a play with the stuffy, fussy, thick-bedaubed canvas which we are accustomed to call stage scenery." He also gladly acknowledged his debt to William Poel, "who taught me how swift and passionate a thing, how beautiful in its variety, Elizabethan blank verse might be." He objected, however, to the habit of unmasking progenitors instead of viewing the work with fresh eyes:

All we ask in return of the critics and the public is to be allowed to make that trial upon their open minds and natural taste, not upon their artificially stimulated prejudices. There is no Shakespearean tradition. At most we can deduce from a few

24   *The Winter's Tale* 1912 London. The statue scene in a non-illusionist curtain setting. The patterns on the dropcloth recall those used for Reinhardt's production in 1906. Eclectic costumes on Lillah McCarthy as Hermione, Esmé Beringer as Paulina, Henry Ainley as Leontes, Cathleen Nesbit as Perdita (kneeling), Charles Graham as Polixenes.

scraps of knowledge what Elizabethan methods were … We have the text to guide us, half a dozen stage directions, and that is all. I abide by the text and the demands of the text, and beyond that I claim freedom.[22]

Perhaps Barker would have been more accurate if he had said there are many Shakespearean traditions, but his point is a crucial one: there has never been a practice of Shakespearean representation that remained vital for more than a generation or so. This *Winter's Tale* was the first English production of Shakespeare that consciously intended to shock its audience out of visual complacency, and the shock was great. "Yes, there is no other word for it," said Walkley, "save the word that in popular usage denotes a special kind of artistic assault on conventionalism: it is Post-Impressionist Shakespeare." However synthetic Barker's scenographic approach may have been, his object was to find a new visual mode that would astonish the twentieth century.

But the sight he provided also reflected the sixteenth. Barker had been affected by Poel ever since he played Richard II for him at age 22 in 1899; he wrote Reinhardt that Poel taught "more about the staging of Shakespeare and the spirit of playing in it, I think, than anyone else in Europe." The remodeled stage at the Savoy was designed to emphasize the actor–audience relationship in an Elizabethan manner, giving point to the rapid and intimate speech; the bright frontal illumination was intended to suggest the daylight of the Globe. The two directors were nonetheless traveling different roads. Shakespeare for Barker was a popular dramatist, one who had to be brought alive for the audience at all costs. He knew that antiquarian productions were doomed to remain experiments: "We shall not save our souls by being Elizabethan … it is asking too much of an audience to come to the theatre so historically-sensed as that."[23]

The best example of the rage to vitality was his *Twelfth Night*, which opened on 15 November, using the same stage architecture but a more thoroughly integrated and symbolic design. The familiarity of the play made it easier for audiences to accept the visual method, and the freshness of the comic acting insured a degree of success denied to *The Winter's Tale*. This time Norman Wilkinson designed the entire production, relying chiefly on dropcloths to achieve an uninterrupted flow of action, sometimes raising or lowering them while a scene was in progress. Orsino's palace was nothing but a yellow and black curtain in triangular patterns (illus. 25) reminiscent of Czeschka's approach to *King Lear*. Olivia's garden was the only full stage set; formalized and overly symmetrical, it was a manifest critique of the lush

25 *Twelfth Night* 1912 London. D: Harley Granville Barker. Des: Norman Wilkinson. P: *Daily Mirror* Studios. Orsino's court, seen here for "Come away, death" (2.4); the costumes combine a Persian flair with geometric shapes. Arthur Wontner as the Duke (on throne), Lillah McCarthy as Viola, Hayden Coffin as Feste.

illusion of Hawes Craven's set for Tree. No grassy steps here or pictures of topiary, only architectural components and hard geometrical shapes, an exercise in Cubist geometry (color pl. 4). The box trees of the script were represented by two Futurist space needles, conveying a strange sense of artificiality to an exterior scene, prefiguring the Constructivism of the 1920s. There was also something naïve or primitivist about the set, especially about the colors, and many critics compared it to confectionery or to a child's Noah's Ark.

The third production in Barker's series, also designed by Wilkinson, was *A Midsummer Night's Dream* in February of 1914. No play of Shakespeare's came into the new century with more Victorian encrustations, from grassy bowers to Mendelssohn's music, from gossamer wings to Bottom's comic business. Barker dispensed with all of that, seeking a fresh aspect in general production and an entirely unexplored visual model. Whereas Reinhardt centered his presentation on a revolving replication of the wood (complete with Mendelssohn accompaniment), Barker found the essence of the play in the fairies. It is typical that his optical starting point would not be the environment but the characters. Dispensing with any conventional notion of dragonflies and tulle, he made the fairies so surprising that he forced the audience into a distanced reception, and most commentators referred immediately to the disturbing effect: ormolu fairies from an antique clock, they were called, Cambodian idols, painted graven images, golden figures from an Indian temple. They were gold from head to foot, in gold and bronze-gold costumes, headdresses, and shoes, with gold-leaf makeup on their faces and hands. Some had hair or beards of curved gold buckram like wood shavings, others carried a book, a scroll, a scimitar, all of gold. "They must not be too startling," Barker cautioned. "But one wishes people weren't so easily startled."[24]

Their first entrance (2.1) showed the intention clearly. To banish the misty shadows of nineteenth-century elves Wilkinson brought out the courts of Oberon and Titania on the midstage and forestage before a stylized drop and in white frontal light (illus. 26). Thirty-one fairies, only four of them children, are seen in this picture of a highly conventionalized forest, the golden woodland punctuated by Titania's mauve train and by Puck in flaming scarlet. For the major scenes in the wood some concessions to atmosphere were made, both in lighting and in the set. Wilkinson provided a green (but not grassy) mound center stage for Titania's bower, in relief against a semicircle of stylized forest curtains (illus. 27). A dimmer light set the mood; some color was added from above the stage, but the main source was still the white torpedo lamps from the dress circle and the scene itself was never far upstage.

In these three productions Barker and Wilkinson synthesized the reforming modes of stagecraft that had appeared since 1890. Poel's notions of acting space, Craig's simplicity in curtains and in architectural shapes, Reinhardt's lighting, Orlik's geometric restraint, and Bakst's extravagant coloration – all of these visual forces were blended together to make a new Shakespearean style. To them must be added the general effect of a Europe busy with revolutionary manifestos about the purpose of art. Most of these forces can be called modernist, and all of them reacted against the inflated propensities of nineteenth-century pictorialism. For Barker the orotund delivery of the actor-managers was the vocal equivalent of their upholstered sets; both denied the value of Shakespeare's verse and both required thorough renovation. Metaphoric scenography was the key not just to visual reform but to a complete rethinking of the nature of Shakespearean production.

26   *A Midsummer Night's Dream* 1914 London. D: Harley Granville Barker. Des: Norman Wilkinson. Ill met by moonlight: Christine Silver and Dennis Neilson-Terry as Titania and Oberon. A posed photograph at the Savoy Theatre showing the painted forest dropcloth at the proscenium line and Puck (Donald Calthrop) lying on the steps and forestage extension. A proscenium entrance made out of a stage box is partially visible at the right of the picture.

Barker's major principle as a director was an insistence on the primacy of the playwright: he thought of himself as an interpreter, a guide to actors and audience through the rough terrain of Shakespeare's texts. When he retired from active theatre work after the war and became a critic, he kept the same intention. His famous *Prefaces to Shakespeare* were the reflective counterpart of his directing; like Craig in his later designs and publications, Barker imparted his gifts away from the day-to-day business of the stage. Unlike Craig, however, Barker was cautious about the visual, insisting in his writing that design should not distract from the action or become an element independent of the overall performance. A designer must treat a play according to his own understanding, he wrote in 1930, but if he finds himself "competing with the actors, the sole interpreters Shakespeare has licensed, then it is he that is the intruder, and he must retire."[25]

Whether he followed this elegant ideal in 1912 and 1914 is open to question. Norman Wilkinson's scenography was often outlandish in the eyes of contemporary spectators, suggesting that it diverted attention from the play as a whole. The closeness of the actors, the bright light,

27 *A Midsummer Night's Dream* 1914 London. Titania with her court. The painted curtains fell in such heavy folds that the forest pictures appeared almost abstract; the wreath above the mound was dotted with glowing fairy lights.

Rothenstein's costumes for *The Winter's Tale*, the futurist set and colors of *Twelfth Night*, the fairies in *Dream*, these were systematic shocks to an audience accustomed to a much less intrusive visual field. Many spectators found that the new scenography did exactly what Barker had condemned about the old: it interposed itself between the play and its reception. That the problem might have been with an unadventurous public, as often charged by commentators like Shaw, is really beside the point; audiences are what they are and, though they can be trained, they cannot be remade overnight. Half-hearted reformations rarely succeed, of course, and Barker knew he had to risk offense and alienation in educating London to a novel mode of representation. His achievement with Shakespeare was much larger than his visual success, involving rehabilitated approaches to the text, to verse speaking, and to acting as well. But the fact that scenography was the acknowledged framework for Barker's radical Shakespeare is a powerful reminder that for the audience the visual is not only an essential element of performance, it is often the primary one.

4 | *Styles of politics*

The scenographic harvest of the first years of the century was principally aesthetic. Symbolism in general retreated from social and political questions to dwell abstractly in art; neither Appia nor Craig attempted to affect or comment upon specific conditions on the earth. For them the great drama of the past was universal because it applied to an unchanging human situation, evoking and reflecting certain psychological and spiritual truths that rewarded study and theatrical reproduction. The works of Wagner or Shakespeare, in other words, were treasure-houses to be valued because of their beauty and comprehensive veracity. Though there are proto-fascist slants to some of their designs and writings, and though Craig admired Mussolini (until he met him), these were tendencies they shared with many early modernists who were often politically naïve and attracted to the fascist promise of a better, more democratic world. For the most part the discoveries of the New Stagecraft, and the Shakespearean realizations of them before the First World War by Reinhardt and Granville Barker, were notably apolitical.

This was also the case in Paris, where occasional applications of the new look began to appear. André Antoine had presented the first complete version of a Shakespeare play in France in 1904, a *King Lear* with restrained acting and rapid scene changes; though the rhythm was fast and the décor (by Lucien Jusseaume) simplified, the general effect was painterly and pictorial. His *Coriolanus* in 1909, designed by Paquereau, reduced settings even further but again relied upon the principles of illusion. Firmin Gémier acted in a number of the plays before and after the war, most notably in a *Hamlet* produced with Lugné-Poe at the Théâtre Antoine in 1913. This was memorable for an architectural set by Jean Variot which used an open playing space in front of a wall with a large recessed arch in the center. Costumes were in period but place was established by simple furniture and changeable dropcloths behind the archway, which could also serve as an inner locale, reminiscent more of Savits' Shakespeare stage than of Poel or Barker.[1]

The major French example of the aesthetic approach was openly inspired by Barker's example. As Jean Jacquot says, it was no accident that Jacques Copeau chose *Twelfth Night* and *The Winter's Tale* as his only Shakespearean productions: he was won over not only by Barker's scenography but also by the balanced ensemble playing and the fresh comic approach to Toby, Andrew, and Malvolio. Copeau began his experiments in 1913 with Heywood's *A Woman Killed with Kindness* on an almost bare stage, the décor limited to a few items required by the action or the actors; the proscenium arch at the Vieux-Colombier was even masked to hide its gilded plasterwork (the arch would be removed entirely in 1919). *Twelfth Night* was the final offering of the first season in May of 1914, and immediately became one of those rare productions that assume almost mythical proportions, no doubt helped in memory by Copeau's retirement from directing soon after the war. Copeau himself later recalled the set as chiefly composed of an empty forestage, a pink drop cutting off the rest of the space for Orsino's palace, a yellow one for exterior scenes. Behind the drop line was Olivia's palace, a single locale for inside and out: a cube, a bench, a one-step platform, a central recess, and two artificial shrubs (illus. 28). White curtains framed the scene.

When Barker saw the revival in 1921, he admired it greatly, more than most English productions of Shakespeare. Though he valued the forestage and the simplified Elizabethan structure, he thought that Copeau had not sufficiently clarified locations nor adequately distinguished between the "opposing masses" of Orsino's court and Olivia's household. He also thought that the costumes, designed by the Englishman Duncan Grant, were a serious mistake in that they ignored Olivia's mourning and made Malvolio into a lifeless figure of fun. Barker was chiefly impressed with the extraordinary acting of Suzanne Bing as Viola and with the democratic mix of workers, students, foreigners, and literary people in the audience. Despite his reservations, he considered this *Twelfth Night* a model for what Shakespeare performance in England lacked.[2]

Copeau showed the production in New York in 1917 during his company's sojourn at the Garrick Theatre, and a redesigned version was performed in Paris each year in the early twenties. (Louis Jouvet's unit setting of a rear stairway and recessed inner stage was used for *The Winter's Tale* in 1920 as well, though to less enthusiastic response.) But the outbreak

28 *Twelfth Night* 1914 Paris. D: Jacques Copeau. S and L: Louis Jouvet. C:
Duncan Grant. The upstage area at the Vieux-Colombier in a drastically reduced
variation of Granville Barker's set; note how Norman Wilkinson's Futurist box trees
have shrunk to potted plants. Suzanne Bing as Viola is on the left of the picture.

of war, which closed the Vieux-Colombier in Paris, ended Barker's dream of
a national theatre in London, and seemed to make Shakespeare an
irrelevancy in his own land, had a very different effect elsewhere.
Unprecedented slaughter, the dislocation of the old order, and the
breakdown of traditional moral values, which brought political turmoil and
revolution to so much of middle and eastern Europe, also brought extreme
artistic experimentation and a reevaluation of the classics. Withdrawn
aestheticism was no longer an appropriate response to the art of the past;
suddenly Shakespeare had a new meaning, which derived from the uses the
present might find in him. At the same time, Craig's vision of a monumental
and mystical theatre underwent a fanatical sea-change.

EXPRESSIONISM: JESSNER AND PIRCHAN

The most immediate and most lasting visual result of the war appeared in Germany. Expressionism, which began as a movement in painting early in the century, had soon influenced poetry and especially drama. Loudly objecting to the paternalism of the Wilhelminean empire, "Ich-drama" was a version of the outrage of the adolescent son against his father – Expressionists were unregenerately male – proclaiming and often screaming against generalized inhumanity and personal repression. The anguished cry of the oppressed hero demanded a scenography of distortion, a subjective extension of his terrifying inner state. (Expressionism leaned towards the optics of the cinema; in fact, it was through German films like Robert Wiene's *The Cabinet of Dr. Caligari* of 1919 that its international influence became greatest, and their techniques are still relied upon today for the horror film, which retains elements of the Expressionist vision.) In the regular theatres Reinhardt had led the way in finding a design and directing style useful for this drama as early as 1906; as we have seen, Ernst Stern began to apply certain Expressionist mannerisms to Shakespeare during the war, especially to *Macbeth* in 1916.

Expressionism's strident rejection of Realism made it especially congenial to young artist-rebels of the time. Wilhelm Worringer's book *Abstraktion und Einfühlung* (Abstraction and Empathy, Munich, 1908) gave a theoretical context to the movement; Worringer claimed that realism and abstraction were opposing forces in history and could be seen as guides to the nature of a culture. His reproach of Realism as a celebration of the political status quo was hauntingly appropriate to a Germany in torment, and his notions were seized upon by Expressionists as justification for excessive visual deformity. So Paul Klee wrote in his diary in 1915, "the more terrible this world (as it is today), the more abstract our art, while a happy world produces art of the here-and-now" (in Patterson 50).

The scenography developed for Expressionist drama was based upon an exaggeration of Craig's idea that visual elements should be limited to those which reflect the essence of the play. As Bablet notes (1977: 77), "since the designer did not want to depict a *real* world, he did not visualize a *real* place"; the dramatic text suggested visions, not a representative locale. Though Expressionist drama is dynamic, its structure is melodramatic and moves towards tableaux, like the crucifixion of the Cashier at the end of Georg Kaiser's *From Morn to Midnight*; in production its scenography often existed to support the protagonist in static outbursts of pain or despair. But in addition to their tendency to distort the scene, designers also found that the spatial discoveries of Appia and Craig could be exploited further, and often made an entire visual expression out of a single potent symbol in a rhythmically organized space. It was this second aspect of Expressionist scenography that directly affected production of Shakespeare, particularly in the designs of Emil Pirchan.

Leopold Jessner's appointment in 1919 as Intendant of the newly created Staatstheater in Berlin was openly political. After the war and the revolution this former Prussian Royal Theatre was remade into a democratic, state-supported institution by the socialist government of the province. Jessner – a republican, a member of the Social Democrat Party, and a Jew – was selected, at the special recommendation of the Actors' Union, to bring a new vision of humanity to the very boards that had supported the culture of the *Kaiserreich*. But Jessner was not captivated by the wilder, shrieking side of Expressionism. His own program was a clever remodeling of *Bildung*, the long-standing German tradition that classics have educational value and that the theatre is a moral force, and he had no hesitations about appropriating the drama of the past for present purposes. He wrote later that the poet's work is nothing but raw material for the director, who must split apart – today we might say deconstruct – the play and make a new ordering of its elements in staging. In another article he insisted that "basically there are neither classic nor modern authors. From the point of view of the theatre the poet belongs to no generation. ... Shakespeare, Schiller, Wedekind must be thought of as the representatives of this generation as much as the youngest writers." Jessner inaugurated his reign with a revisionist production of Schiller's *Wilhelm Tell* that vehemently attacked the illiberality of the old monarchy and prompted one of the noisiest outbursts in the modern theatre. Pirchan's setting was a massive application of Craig's abstractionism, with a central stairway leading to two high, dark curtains upstage with the sky beyond, the mountain tops mere triangles of gray, a perception of the play diametrically opposed to its pictorial conventions so familiar to German audiences.[3]

Richard III in November of 1920 tested this method further and provided the chief and most influential example of Expressionist Shakespeare. Pirchan's design disdained historical evocation in favor of symbol: the constant sight of an upstage gray-green wall dominated and enclosed the action. In front of this was another wall half its height, with an archway in the center and a narrow walkway above. This architectural simplicity was easily adaptable to Elizabethan methods, particularly in the prayerbook

29 *Richard III* 1920 Berlin. D: Leopold Jessner. Des: Emil Pirchan. "And see, a book of prayer in his hand" (3.7): Fritz Kortner as Richard above in the center, Rudolf Forster as Buckingham below. Buckingham's posture and gesture here echoed the distorted physicality of Richard in other scenes, and the shadows heightened the Expressionist quality.

scene with Richard above on the castle wall and the citizens below (illus. 29). The photo shows the stone-like texture of the walls as well as the projected shadows of the characters on them, a common element of Expressionist staging. Jessner used the device to great effect after the wooing of Lady Anne (1.2) when Richard mocks the light:

> Shine out, fair sun, till I have bought a glass,
> That I may see my shadow as I pass.

The scene had been gradually darkening but now a spot from the prompter's box suddenly cast Richard's shadow hugely against the wall, a violent silhouette of the lust for power (illus. 30). A similar moment occurred soon after, when Clarence sat upstage in prison (1.4) in a triangular patch of light while the monstrous shadows of the two murderers appeared on the walls surrounding him. Bablet has written that Jessner used the wall as a symbol of "the terror that reigns over England";[4] in these and other scenes he used light not to illustrate the action but as an emphatic interpretive signal, making "ruptures" between characters.

30 *Richard III* 1920 Berlin. Robert Edmond Jones' eyewitness sketch of Gloucester's projected shadow in 1.2, which indicates the effect better than any of the available photographs.

Jessner saved his trademark for the second half of the play. When the curtain rose after the intermission, the audience saw a gigantic flight of steps rising from the proscenium line to the lower wall in narrowing sections, effectively occupying the playing space (illus. 31). Like Appia's design for *Orfeo ed Euridice* at Hellerau (which Jessner saw in 1913), Pirchan had made a staircase into the entire setting. In an interpolated scene (prior to 4.2) Richard ascended the steps slowly for his coronation. Nearly everything was in red: the steps, the King's robe, the lines of subordinates who flanked him. At the top "the red of the steps was linked to the red of the sky by the crimson of Richard's gown," Patterson explains, "as though an electric charge of evil had leapt the gap between heaven and earth." A contemporary critic, Alfred Polgar, said that "it is as though the sky itself provides a bloody reflection of Richard's atrocities."[5] Pirchan's design for the scene (color pl. 5), showing the violence of this strategy of color, is the best evidence that the scenography carried much of the burden of the production. The audience gazed at a world that was discernibly changed by Richard's presence, a world where evil had become a visible force. Jessner was the first major director of the century to realize that the power of Shakespeare's plays

31 *Richard III* 1920 Berlin. A photo of *Jessnertreppen*. The prompter's box with a powerful light mounted to it is at the lower center of picture.

could be intensified by deliberately limiting their thematic concerns. This was *Motivtheater*, as he called it, where incidentals – including the "incidentals" of character development, psychological ambiguity, and narrative complexity – were discarded for the sake of the central motif, which was essentially intellectual. The action on stage, he wrote, was "der abstrakte Schauplatz mythischer Begebenheiten": the abstract scene of mythic events.

Acting had to become abstract as well. In place of the swelling human movement of Reinhardt or some of his Expressionist colleagues, Jessner positioned groups with "the stiffness and symmetry of primitive effigies," Polgar said; "they strove for the effect of relief." Alfred Kerr thought the ensemble often looked "like figures out of a chronicle." Jessner was achieving the effects Craig had desired with *Übermarionetten*: his "staircase directing"[6] privileged the visual qualities of the actor and reined in individuality.

For Fritz Kortner as Richard, however, this was no limitation. Kortner's intense, ecstatic portrayal, with flaring eyes and maniacal gestures, was well suited to the obstructions and levels of *Jessnertreppen*; in his memoirs Kortner went so far as to claim credit for the idea of mounting the play on the staircase. His walk was an extension of a man's broken stride on the stairs, his postures the twisted misgivings of a caricature. Critics compared him to a monster, a toad, a swollen spider, a body in despair. A famous photograph (illus. 32) provides one type of example, with Richard pulling the strings of Buckingham, who seems to be wrapped in a straitjacket, both actors exhibiting the expressive qualities of silent film melodrama. The picture seems posed and may not reflect a moment from the production literally, but we are probably justified in reading its signals about gestural acting. On a larger scale, the end of the battle scene allowed Kortner full exploitation of the steps. "A horse, a horse, my kingdom for a horse," that difficult line so prone to evoke laughter, was spoken offstage just before he appeared at the top of the wall, shirtless, his crown under his arm "like a decapitated head," in the words of Herbert Ihering.[7] He then hopped down the staircase, step by step, astride his sword as if he were simultaneously impaled by it and riding the missing horse. Richmond's army, four soldiers all in white, killed him at the bottom with stylized blows that never actually struck him.

The stagecraft was eminently emblematic and equally obvious: as he mounted the steps in red glory for his coronation, so he fell into the arms of white retribution, a compelling prefiguration of Jan Kott's image of the history plays as a "grand mechanism." As a malevolent figure who hacked

32 *Richard III* 1920 Berlin. Kortner's Svengali fingers above Forster.

his way to the throne, Kortner's Richard was a condemnation of German dictators, whether of royal blood like the deposed Kaiser or of common stock like the leader to come, a notion that was not lost on the hyper-political Berlin audience of 1920. Kenneth MacGowan condemned this lack of subtlety:

Jessner appears to worship the obvious, to believe that the theatre is a place of A. B. C. impressions and reactions. He is daring enough in his technique but not in his ideas. He flings out symbols right and left, but they are the symbols of the primer. He directs in words of one syllable. ... Richard begins the play in black against a black curtain ... Richmond ends it in white against a white curtain ... This is symbolism in baby-talk, presentational production in kindergarten terms.

(MacGowan and Jones 142)

It is a charge that still stings. But for all its reductionist tendencies, Jessner's humorless production had the virtue of absolute clarity, admirably supported by Pirchan's metaphoric scenography.

Though giant staircases acquired Jessner's name and soon appeared everywhere in Europe, his other Shakespeare productions modified their use severely. For *Othello* in the next season, Pirchan provided a series of five concentric platforms isolated at center stage. These gradients were steps, of course, but instead of dominating the space they tended to focus attention on the action. The cyclorama showed a different color for each scene, ranging from black to hot orange to blue to red, and lighting tended to pick out individual actors in down spots. Othello's arrival in Cyprus was played against a huge sail and a swirling black sky as backdrop; a small flight of seven steps led from the ship to the crowd below (color pl. 6).

The major visual symbol of the production was the bed, placed directly on the center platform and draped with expansive white curtains. A white stand for the lamp, the white gowns of the actors, the white bedclothes, all were designed to contrast to Othello's black face. The murder of Desdemona was clearly planned as the visual center of Jessner's interpretation; an action photograph (illus. 33) reproduces Pirchan's design in almost every detail, including the postures of the actors. The Expressionists tended to see *Othello* as a play about uncontrollable, animalist urges, and the elegant scenography of this production set off Kortner's anarchist power. In this case Pirchan's fragmentary or incomplete settings reflected a fragmented view of life; they were metonyms of a world in decomposition.

Macbeth at the Staatstheater in 1922 was not as exciting visually, despite an ecstatic performance from Kortner. Walter Reimann relied on what had by

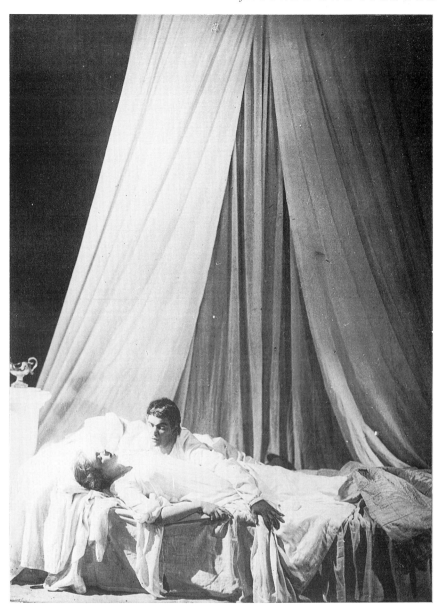

33 *Othello* 1921 Berlin. D: Leopold Jessner. Des: Emil Pirchan. Kortner as Othello, Johanna Hofer as Desdemona. Monumental draperies replaced the monumental staircase of *Richard III*.

then become fairly conventional platforms, steps, and bridges; the Expressionist tone came from painted Gothic vaulting, like spiders' webs. As the force of Expressionism wound down Jessner took a break from Shakespeare, then mounted an openly political, modern-dress *Hamlet* in 1926, designed by Caspar Neher as a play about militarism and power. The costumes were Wilhelminean, a uniform with shoulder brushes and breastplate for the King, opera glasses and an ostrich fan for Gertrude; for the Mousetrap scene the royal pair stood in a box in a rococo theatre, recreated on stage. Kortner played Hamlet as a modern rebel caught in the spiral of power and rot in Denmark, appearing in one scene in an oilskin cape and sailor's hat, smoking a pipe, an obvious incongruity at the Imperial Prussian court. As the political climate in Germany worsened, Jessner stuck to his objective analysis of the classics as contemporary works. His *King John* in 1929, also designed by Neher, presented the protagonist as a lonely child, lost in the world of might. In one scene Rudolf Forster as John, blond hair over his eyes, wrapped in white loose cloak, sat lonely on an enormous throne on a raised platform, an outsized stand with huge candles next to him. In his hand was a baton with the German eagle.

Neher used metonymic visual devices that isolated and reduced the protagonists, showing them as dreamers hopelessly mismatched in the harsh game of *Realpolitik*. The productions departed from the scenography of Expressionism but not from its major theme of the sensitive individual crushed by the mindless machine of authority. The visual brightness that Granville Barker and Copeau gave to Shakespeare was in productions of the comedies; it is not surprising that Jessner selected the darker plays, those with an affinity in theme or atmosphere to the nightmare of Expressionism. "The greatest dramatists are always dead," Barker said in 1910, objecting to Reinhardt's approach to the classics; "if a producer of plays, climbing the ladder of his own genius, gets to think that his ideas about Hamlet, Faust, and the Agamemnon overtop those of Shakespeare, Goethe, and Aeschylus, there is no one with absolute authority to say him nay."[8] That statement, despite its apparently objective and timeless appeal for textual integrity, was as much a product of the serene world of *la belle époque* as Jessner's *Richard III* was of a world that had harrowed hell. In his portrayal of Shakespearean characters caught in the steel jaws of power Jessner might have been portraying himself: his anti-monarchist *Hamlet* created a storm in the provincial assembly and the National Socialists kept up the attack. In Germany an absolute authority to say nay had arrived, and after the 1930 elections, a few months after *King John*, he was forced to resign as director of the Staatstheater. He went into exile in 1933; most of his colleagues and collaborators, from Reinhardt and Kortner to Kaiser and Brecht, would soon follow. Berlin, the center of European arts in the 1920s, packed up and moved to Los Angeles.

CONSTRUCTIVISM AND THE UNIT SET

The machine which crushed and humbled Expressionist man was to be the apotheosis of Soviet man and woman. In the optimistic early days of the new Russia, desperate to transform a feudal economy into an industrial worker-state, the machine assumed the status of a great social force, the model not only of the new person but of the new order itself. In the theatre its employment is most obviously associated with Meyerhold, whose system of actor training called Biomechanics, in direct opposition to the internalized Naturalism of Stanislavsky, was developed to give performers the flexibility and strength of engineered mechanisms. Like Expressionism, Constructivism discovered that its revised view of humanity required a revised scenography; thus the machine, and machine-like devices, became central to the visual portrayal. The levels, steps, and ramps of Appia and Craig were transformed from objectifications of dramatic forces into pure machines for acting: platforms with their structures exposed, scaffolding proclaiming its proletarian utility, ramps in spirals like factory chutes: nothing representational and nothing merely aesthetic.

Classic drama had little place in that Soviet dawn and Shakespeare had none at all for Meyerhold, who was one of the few major directors of the century to ignore him; from his high place in the cultural administration after the Revolution he severely criticized the "academic" theatres of Stanislavsky and Alexander Tairov for their archaic repertoire.[9] Yet the one important Shakespearean production of the time that made use of Constructivist design was Tairov's, a *Romeo and Juliet* in 1921 that blended the new Soviet style with prewar aestheticism. Tairov founded the Moscow Kamerny (or Chamber) Theatre in 1914; he also sought a method opposed to Stanislavsky's, but whereas Meyerhold leaned to the democratic techniques of the circus Tairov's approach was based on the more refined expression of ballet and *commedia dell'arte*.

In his book *Notes of a Director*, published in the year of *Romeo*, Tairov set forth a program for a theatre based on disciplined performance and stylized communication. He denied the place of literature in the theatre, insisting that "faithful interpretation" of a play was not the director's function but rather the creation of an autonomous *"new work of art to be valued in and of itself."* It was in pantomime that he found the key: the figures of Pierrot, Pierrette, and Harlequin, deprived of the crutch of speech, must be exemplified by actors who can command the same control over their bodies that musicians have over their instruments. "Action should be transferred to a plane of the most intense emotion," he wrote, where the normal gestures and "conventionalized informative actions" of realistic drama would not be needed and even words would become irrelevant, replaced by "emotional gesture." "For in moments of maximum emotional strain, *silence* sets in. ... The pantomime is a production of such scope, such spiritual revelation that *words die*, and in their stead genuine scenic *action* is born ... "[10]

Because *Romeo and Juliet* exhibits such clear marks of the early Elizabethan stage, it has been particularly prone to scenographic revision. The variety of locales and their uses – marketplace, street, ballroom, garden, friar's cell, bedroom, churchyard, funeral vault – have forced subsequent productions to make difficult decisions about performance style. Some locations change within a scene, the first orchard scene being a good example, or Capulet's ball where Romeo and friends arrive outside then enter the house without a textual break. We have already noted that insistence on illusion caused Henry Irving to build eighteen separate sets, including two massive ones to handle the double locale of the finale. Reinhardt went to the revolve, especially in Stern's design for the long-lived 1914 production, which gave speed as well as verisimilar and multiple settings, using technology to replace simultaneity. Indeed the history of scenography for *Romeo and Juliet* is a pocket guide to changing attitudes about Shakespearean representation.

Tairov strenuously avoided the carpenter's solution, and avoided as well a return to Elizabethanism. The production exemplified many of the principles in *Notes of a Director*; Tairov called the play a "tragic sketch," and started with the idea that it needed an architectural setting parallel to its structure. His brilliant designer, Alexandra Exter, one of the leaders of the Russian avant-garde, was trained as a painter in Paris; for *Romeo*, however, she created an architectural unit set that permitted uninterrupted action on assorted levels. Seven different acting stations were "rhythmically calculated to represent the numerous obstacles in the path of the lovers," as Nick Worrall (37) puts it. Romeo and Juliet, played as strong, healthy people, worked out their fates athletically and in a vortex, the design suggesting a falling motion, leading to death at the center of the main stage floor (illus. 34). The stage space had been attacked vertically, broken into parts not only by steps but also by platforms, ramps, hidden landings, and pinnacles.

34 *Romeo and Juliet* 1921 Moscow. D: Alexander Tairov. Des: Alexandra Exter. The death of Tybalt at the Kamerny Theatre, a Cubist unit design with Constructivist acting stations.

Exter was flexible enough to include some elements suggestive of bridges, balconies, and portals, but the basic visual effect was Cubist. The set was inlaid with mirrors (later replaced by tinfoil) that glittered in the swirling action, reflecting and distorting movement. Sometimes the stage "was almost obliterated in the swirl of capes," Worrall says, "as the set became swamped by a constantly ebbing and flowing tide of figures dressed in sumptuously brilliant colours reminiscent of a Renaissance painting." Exter's costumes, though eminently wearable, were dynamic exhibits of color and form. Cubist designers tended to make actors into two-dimensional pictures, painting color on their bodies and clothes, or tended to make actors into Cubo-Futurist sculptures as Exter's friend and mentor Picasso did for *Parade* in 1917. Exter achieved something different and much more theatrical, an application of Cubist principles that assisted characterization and acting. But this was still designer's theatre with a vengeance, and naturally enough many critics thought that Shakespeare had been "suffocated."

Romeo and Juliet is a highly visual piece. Its Elizabethan characteristics, however, keep its visuals simple and actor-centered: a boy and a girl separated by height and space, a duel, the girl faking death, corpses in a tomb. The overlaid complexity of Exter's design seems unnecessarily busy, but at root it was an attempt to apply modernist methods to the specific challenges of – theatrically speaking – an obsolete dramaturgy. Shakespeare's simultaneity, a medieval device surviving in a modified Tudor form, was already becoming archaic when the play was written and poses serious problems for modern representation. This is not because it requires an audience to rely upon imagination, but because it seems to put stress on locale (the ambience of a street or a tomb, for example), while at the same time playing fast and loose with the habitations it evokes.

The unit set, combining abstract levels with suggestions of place, which subsequently became a standard design motif in the twentieth century, applied the inventions of the New Stagecraft to the dilemma of Shakespearean place. As usual it was Craig who initiated the notion, with designs he made for generic scenes in permanent sets, and one impressive multipurpose drawing of a unit setting for *Hamlet* and *Macbeth* in which steps, levels, and archways are severe but serviceable, capable of a variety of lighting effects and moods (reproduced in Innes 107). Instead of Elizabethan formality, which derived from a playhouse architecture that preceded and influenced literary composition, the unit set is, *a posteriori*, a conceived site extracted from the dramatic and emotional requirements of the script. It suggests locale without insisting upon it. Constructivist scenography aimed at providing a single *assemblage*, revealed from the moment the spectators entered the auditorium, that was a functional and rhythmic structure in which to act the play. To this Tairov added a persistent concern for sets and costumes that were beautiful objects in themselves. Whatever the distractions of Exter's *Romeo*, she offered the first major example of a Shakespearean design that provided an abundance of acting stations within an aesthetically controlled permanent environment.

SYNTHESIS IN CENTRAL EUROPE

The countries of central and eastern Europe were under some form of imperial domination until after the war, severely restricting the development of theatre traditions separate from those of Vienna or Berlin or St. Petersburg. In the second half of the nineteenth century Shakespeare was viewed as a Romantic, revolutionary writer, as he had been in the German lands earlier – at various times the Czarist censor banned the plays in Warsaw because they contained too many incidents of rebellion – and the

35 *Hamlet* 1926 Prague. D: Karel Hugo Hilar. Des: Vlastislav Hofman. P: Karel Vána. Leopolda Dostalova as Gertrude, Eduard Kohout as Hamlet at the National Theatre, in an unusual staging of 1.2. The symmetrical arrangement of the white screens sets off Hamlet and the Expressionist double throne and candelabra.

first extended translation projects in Czech, Hungarian, and Polish were connected with the rise of an indigenous national drama. The independence granted by the Treaty of Versailles was seized by theatre artists as an unprecedented opportunity to apply avant-garde methods to the new nationalist stages, and in the years between the wars Shakespeare would become an important force in this larger movement.

Stage design has always been taken seriously east of the Elbe and nowhere is this more apparent than in Prague, architecturally one of the most beautiful cities in Europe, where the tradition of scenographers as major artists continues to this day. After the war Karel Hugo Hilar, head of drama at the National Theatre from 1921 to 1935, directed Shakespearean performances that matched any of those elsewhere in Europe. His chief collaborator was Vlastislav Hofman, an eclectic and wide-ranging designer with "an amazing ability to assimilate different styles" (Bablet 1977: 148), who often combined Expressionist and Constructivist elements under a Craigian masterplan. Their production of *Hamlet* in 1926 is representative of

36   *Hamlet* 1926 Prague. P: Karel Váńa. Polonius (Sara Ravilov) with Gertrude
(3.4). The same central platform was used with a different arrangement of the
screens, here with the two kings' portraits attached.

their best work. It was particularly noteworthy for the use of changeable
screens and high chiaroscuro which conveyed the feeling of events taking
shape out of darkness (illus. 35). Edward Kohout played Hamlet as a frail
youth with "sensitive longing" even in his passion, a clear image of the
postwar generation and its rejection of the world of its fathers.[11] The screens
were shifted easily, as Craig had desired for his own production in Moscow,
and Hofman was able to suggest different locations by simple, fragmentary
additions. Three screens were set in descending height for Gertrude's closet,
and the arras was simply thrown over a partially exposed frame (illus. 36).

   Almost every scene contained a different type of large candlestick, a
phallic presence indicating Hilar's Freudian approach to the play. Costumes
also proposed a contemporary reading, deliberately crossing periods to
combine a very modern look for Gertrude with a Renaissance exuberance
for the courtiers and a timeless style for Hamlet. The graveyard was set in
front of a freestanding façade of a church, whose rose windows were
nothing but circular cutouts showing the black beyond. For the final scene
six screens were arranged in a semicircle upstage, making a larger acting

space and echoing the effect of the opening; even there, however, actors were kept to a minimum number and the illuminated areas stood out against a dead black backdrop, throwing events into high relief. The most visually impressive use of the screens added texture to their surface and to that of a tall obelisk behind the throne (illus. 37).

Hofman's other designs included interesting work on the history plays. For *Henry IV* in 1930, directed by Karel Dostal, he defined three horizontal playing areas by separate backdrops in symbolic colors. *Richard III* in 1934, directed by Jan Bor, had similarities to *Hamlet*; the designs again used large candles and isolated set pieces, but in place of the screens Hofman relied upon three-quarter height traverse curtains to effect scene changes.[12]. Other designers were also at work on Shakespeare, including Václav Gottlieb, Alois Wachsmann, and Antonín Heythum, who would later collaborate with Piscator. But the most important of the Czech scenographers of the 1930s was František Tröster; with him the tendency toward the massive in Craig and the Expressionists reached literally colossal proportions. At the same time he isolated components of a scene until they became surreal. For

37   *Hamlet* 1926 Prague. P: Karel Váňa. Claudius and Gertrude in front of Hofman's textured screens and phallic needle.

Beethoven's *Fidelio* (1936) a huge toppled column and ruined temple filled much of the stage; for Cocteau's *The Knights of the Round Table* (1937) chess pieces and optically distorting reflections made the set look like a game in a house of mirrors.

Tröster's Shakespearean designs for the director Jiří Frejka followed from this pattern. Frejka used the term "hyperbolic realism" to describe their work, and it seems appropriate for *As You Like It* in 1937 where giant chestnut leaves and their echoing projections filled the higher planes of the stage. Fragmentary branches and leaves became something of a design cliché for the comedies at the RSC in the 1960s and 1970s; in this and other ways Tröster anticipated later currents by a generation. For *Romeo and Juliet* in 1938 vertical monoliths at the wings and rear enclosed the actors in a dark prison, broken in some scenes by circular windows showing the sky. The best example of his Surrealism was *Julius Caesar* in 1936, where the megalomania of the play, so frighteningly appropriate to the time, was incarnated by absurdly monumental statuary. For Caesar's progress in the first act the scene was a wildly tilted pedestal, looking as if it would tumble to the ground at any moment, with the legs of an equestrian statue extending

38 *Julius Caesar* 1936 Prague. D: Jiří Frejka. Des: František Tröster. P: A. Paul. Surreal colossus at the National Theatre.

39 *Julius Caesar* 1936 Prague. P: A. Paul. A dominating Caesar (Václav Vydra) in front of his image at the Capitol. The stage floor at the right of the picture rose steeply on a ramp.

40   *Julius Caesar* 1936 Prague. Tröster's design for the murder of Cinna at the end of act 3.

up out of sight into the darkness of the flies (illus. 38). Cassius' cynical reference was rendered visually by the citizens passing under the pedestal:

> Why, man, he doth bestride the narrow world
> Like a Colossus, and we petty men
> Walk under his huge legs, and peep about
> To find ourselves dishonourable graves.

At the Capitol this was transformed into a titanic head of the emperor on an upright pedestal, the whole rising about 5 meters above the floor, itself set at disturbing angles. As the statue towered over everything, Caesar in the flesh towered over the other actors; in one of Tröster's drawings he appears to be part of his intimidating icon, his arm raised high in salute. The head of the statue was built in quadrants (the joints are visible in this photograph, illus. 39), implying the decomposition of the state and of his reign.

In a Europe hurtling toward another confrontation the ambiguous political implications of *Julius Caesar* were especially resonant: a dictator is slain for liberal motives but chaos and war ensue. After Caesar's murder the set collapsed, again indicating in ocular terms the disintegration of Rome. The colossal head split open on the floor, and the stage was littered with

41 *Romeo and Juliet* 1931 Warsaw. D: Arnold Szyfman. Des: Karol Frycz. Friar Lawrence's cell at the Polish Theatre, in a late example of international Expressionism.

Surrealist broken columns (illus. 40). It was as if the threatened war had arrived not in the Roman Empire but in Prague. The production was received enthusiastically and marked the high point of the collaboration between the designer and director, but its results were personally disastrous. To call attention to the menace of imperial governance and possibility of revolt in Czechoslovakia in 1936 was a dangerous action, and both were soon under attack from the right-wing press. After the Munich Accords in September of 1938, which put an end to the Czechoslovak state as well as to experimentation in its theatre, Tröster was cut off from work with Frejka until after the war.

Further east in Poland Shakespeare had even more importance. Much of it is traceable to the lasting magnetism of Stanisław Wyspiański (1868–1907), poet, playwright, painter, designer, and director, who anticipated many of the reforms of Appia and Craig, and whom Craig thought the only complete man of the theatre in history. A neoromantic visionary, Wyspiański longed for a democratic, "immense" theatre "with great and empty spaces," where word and action would combine with the visual in a mighty spectacle of nationalist and personal liberation. His essay on *Hamlet*, which has similarities to Craig's monodramatic view of the play, has been extremely influential on Polish theatre of the twentieth century, and led to an important production by Arnold Szyfman in 1922, designed in Craigian style by Karol Frycz. Szyfman founded the first modern private theatre in Warsaw permitted by the Czarist authorities, the Polish Theatre (Teatr Polski, opened 1913), a large building with a very deep stage appropriate for Wyspiański's ideals. After independence in 1918 it flowered, becoming "a veritable window upon Europe"[13] in regard to the new theatrical styles. Szyfman's production of *Romeo and Juliet* in 1931, also designed by Frycz, is one example out of many of a sophisticated adaptation of Expressionism (illus. 41). The Polish Theatre profited much by the presence of its dynamic and restless literary director, Leon Schiller. Though not well known in the west, Schiller became one of the century's major theatre artists; his Shakespearean productions, reaping the harvest of Wyspiański, have left indelible marks on the visual history of performance.

Schiller was a close friend and open disciple of Craig and wrote about Wyspiański and other Polish subjects in *The Mask*, but his work was a synthesis of the most important European forces between the wars. His acute visual sense led him into close association with each of "the big four" Polish designers, Frycz, Andrzej Pronaszko (and occasionally his brother Zbigniew), Wincenty Drabik, and Władysław Daszewski. In 1924 he founded the Boguslawski Theatre in Warsaw, intending it as a people's stage with a strong socialist agenda. Many of the plays he presented were concerned with the plight of the European proletariat, but he refused to make concessions to the usual notions of mass taste and his repertoire included Wyspiański as well as Shakespeare. Soon joined by Andrzej Pronaszko, Schiller sought a performance style that was advanced in the extreme and rooted in the visual; treating the verbal text as an opportunity for theatrical exploitation, he forced what Władysław Zawistowski called in 1937 "a very strong intrusion of the theatre between the dramatist and the spectator."

At first his productions had a Cubo-Futurist look, recalling Wilkinson and Exter. *The Winter's Tale* in 1924 was designed by Pronaszko in an abstract and painterly mode, the characters treated as part of the visual field, submerged in an antirealist and slightly distorted formalism (illus. 42). "Boldly articulated," Bablet (1977: 143) says of Pronaszko's work, though in this case perhaps too heavily outlined as well; in some photographs the characters seem practically indistinguishable from the abstract backdrops.[14] For *As You Like It* in 1925, Drabik continued the motif of geometric costumes and metaphoric settings: the Duke's court was conveyed by

42   *The Winter's Tale* 1924 Warsaw. D: Leon Schiller. Des: Andrzej Pronaszko.
Swirling Cubist Bohemia.

upward swirling lines of color and Constructivist steps, two locales in the
Forest of Arden by somewhat threatening Expressionist fragments of trees.

The combination of politics and audacious experimentation brought a
harsh reaction from the conservative press. Schiller's financial management
proved less than perfect and the Boguslawski Theatre, soon in debt and tax
trouble, was closed by the municipal authorities after only two years of
operation. Thereafter he directed often in provincial cities (especially in
Łódź, where his Shakespearean work culminated in a production of *The
Tempest* in 1947, discussed in chapter 7). In Warsaw he returned to the
Polski, where he devoted himself to large-scale versions of Polish Romantic
drama and of Shakespeare in the mid-1930s. In tune with general European
trends he began to turn away from pure stylization towards a simpler, more
objective manner, but the most interesting of these productions, both
intellectually and visually, retained his social and aesthetic passion: *Julius
Caesar* in 1928, designed by the Pronaszko brothers.

Though the scenography did not impose Tröster's Surrealist landscape,
Schiller's social context was more direct. He drew upon the long tradition
in Russia and eastern Europe of skirting censorship by using classic texts as

coded messages about the present, a tradition that has continued to this day. United and independent for the first time in centuries, Poland after the war was dominated by the military hero Marshal Josef Pilsudski, who had defeated the Red Army in 1920 and had engineered peace and a constitution the following year. Though now admired for preserving the nation, Pilsudski maintained order in an extremely contentious political arena by questionable means. Faced with the growing popularity of the Communists, he organized a coup in May 1926 and thereafter ruled the country by veiled military dictatorship, often crushing his opponents with harsh measures. Like Hindenburg in Germany, he relied upon the army and the conservative nobility for support; though he held no public office after 1930, he continued to govern until his death five years later.

Schiller was a Communist, and saw the ambiguity in his country's case; he responded by presenting an intriguing variant of Shakespeare's play. In Kazimierz Junosza-Stepowski he provided a Caesar who was manifestly ambivalent: a man to be admired and loathed, clever in his policies and stupid in their execution, blessed with good counsel and cursed in its observance. Schiller thought Junosza's psychological acting created a

43 *Julius Caesar* 1928 Warsaw. D: Leon Schiller. Des: Andrzej and Zbigniew Pronaszko. "The game of the crowd" (1.3) at the Polish Theatre. Expressionist lighting and pantomime movement used to convey the storm.

"down to earth, anti-aesthetic pathos,"[15] but he made him a paragon of the aristocrat, always rising above the crowd, and the application to Polish conditions was unmistakable. It was not an "equation" production, where characters or events in the text are made to stand for their modern equivalents – for one thing, there was no Brutus powerful enough to oppose Pilsudski's Caesar – but it was nonetheless highly political. The visual effect underlined this by depending almost entirely upon lighting and the crowd, borrowing the methods Schiller had developed for the "immense" dramas of Wyspiański and Adam Mickiewicz. Most exterior scenes were set in a large architectural unit with an arched bridge and tall uprights upstage center, a staircase stage right, and high panels left. Massed extras filled the space for an interpolated scene the night before Caesar's death (illus. 43), their white arms illuminated and their gestures miming the storm. Schiller passed over the Meininger tradition of making the crowd a sum of individuals; instead he treated it as a moving mass, a communal expression of natural and social forces, extending and softening the geometrical setting. From Jessner he took the side lighting and the substantial steps, from Meyerhold the anti-illusionist use of actors' bodies.

44 *Julius Caesar* 1928 Warsaw. Jerzy Leszczynśki as Mark Antony enraging the crowd.

The Forum orations pushed the acting further in the direction of the visual, with arms and heads and an occasional white garment intermingling with the cubic volume of the stage and the vertical planes of the columns and steps (illus. 44).

Schiller referred to these massed scenes as "the game of the crowd," implying, it seems, that cunning and cynical politicians play the people to achieve or maintain power. The most striking of the massed moments, however, were the battle scenes at Philippi. With nothing but abstract rocks and a cyclorama behind a bare stage, armies decided the future of Rome in a chaos of spears (illus. 45). Here the masterful combination of lighting, projections, actors, levels, and props gave the audience one of the most memorable sights of Shakespeare in the century. The spectacle still seems impressive in this picture: but it was a spectacle rooted in a social approach to the play, not grafted on purely for visual excitement.

Theatre is supreme among the arts in its ability to straddle time, to suspend past and present in an instantaneous alliance that confers emotion and meaning to both. In making *Julius Caesar* a morality play about Pilsudski's Poland, Schiller claimed Shakespeare as a contemporary a generation before Jan Kott: the plain at Philippi might be the Battle of Riga

45 *Julius Caesar* 1928 Warsaw. The battle at Philippi in pools of light, spears and their shadows intermingling like a painting by Uccello.

or any battle to come where men die for noble causes not their own. What Kozintsev said of Craig, that he saw Shakespeare as concerned with "the conflict of some sort of mighty visual powers," Craig's disciple Schiller staged in Warsaw, transforming aesthetic vision into political testimony, climaxing in a kinesthesis of lance and shadow.

BIRMINGHAM AND CAMBRIDGE

The experimentation of the 1920s had much smaller results in the Anglo-Saxon world, where audiences and producers tended to be protective of Shakespeare's official cultural status and defensive regarding his poetry, which led them to be conservative about visual representation. Despite the shining example of Granville Barker on both sides of the Atlantic (his *Dream* played in New York in 1915), the general approach remained closer to Tree than to Craig. Of course neither England nor America directly suffered the political and social cataclysms that provoked a revision of Shakespeare's iconic position in Europe, and it is not surprising that the new look arrived in London and New York more slowly and with more deliberation, as we shall shortly see. Organization and financing were also relevant: the majority of theatres in central and eastern Europe, whether state-controlled or private, operated on a repertory system, as they still do today. The large expense and large cast of a Shakespeare production can be more readily justified when spread over extended time, playing occasionally with a company already under a stable contract, than in the commercial theatre where everything must be gambled in the hope of a long run. By diligent programming Reinhardt could keep his *Winter's Tale* in repertory for eleven years; Barker had to close his after six weeks.

Significantly, the major visual contributions to English Shakespeare production in the 1920s came from two regional theatres, insulated from the high costs and restrictive practices of London, each supported by the personal drive and private fortune of a dedicated reformer. The better known of these is the Birmingham Repertory Company, founded by Barry Jackson in 1911 and operating in "the first purpose-built repertory theatre in the country" (Rowell and Jackson 50) from 1913, one of very few major theatres to have been started and run by an accomplished designer. Jackson was not a political creature like Jessner or Schiller; he belongs in this chapter by virtue of his social orientation and his willingness to experiment. His attitude to Shakespeare production, the logical extension of the Elizabethanism of William Poel, proceeded from his observation that period costumes and "poetic" vocal delivery were artificial barriers between the play and the spectator. To eliminate those barriers it was necessary to eliminate the entire tradition that continued to dominate Shakespeare performance in Great Britain. His method was simple: set the plays in the present and act them like Chekhov or Noel Coward.

Jackson was not the first to produce Shakespeare in modern dress; there were a few minor examples before the war, and in 1920 Stern designed *Hamlet* for Reinhardt's Grosses Schauspielhaus in unobtrusive contemporary clothes. But Birmingham's *Cymbeline* in 1923 was the first to call attention to the device in a blatant way, putting Iachimo in evening dress for the wager, the court in military uniforms, and the disguised Imogen in knickerbockers and cap. It was for this production that critics invented the catch phrase "Shakespeare in plus-fours" (Trewin 95). Jackson thought the local success sufficient to warrant trying the experiment with *Hamlet* in London, and in 1925 his director, H. K. Ayliff, staged it as a modern play with Colin Keith-Johnston as a very modern, distressed young prince; Ivor Brown thought his performance, "with its gabbling cynical world-hatred and its fiery mood of relentless raillery, was a perfect expression of a shell-shocked world" (in Styan 147). It rapidly became known worldwide and remains today a seminal production.

Though there were many scoffers, Jackson's motives were perfectly sincere, and his program note was an eloquent appeal to take the performance seriously. The object, he said, was to make Shakespeare accessible to the ordinary playgoer, to strip the veil between the man on the street and the author's intention; "this modern production is not an irreverent joke."[16] An interview in *The Observer* emphasized his democratic ideal: "we have never succeeded in getting hold of the people for Shakespeare. ... Our effort at the Kingsway is aimed at making the people of England believe to-day that the plays of Shakespeare are really good stuff – the right thing." That the setting was not a gimmick is attested by the treatment of the opening; aware that the first sight of the costumes would cause laughter, Ayliff played it in dim shadow, the figures almost indistinguishable. The second scene, in bright light, was therefore the shocker, with formal evening dress, monocles, medals from the war, cigarettes, butlers, "the bobbed-hair Queen" (*Observer*), and Hamlet himself in a shabby dinner jacket and soft shirt.

Paul Shelving's design placed the court in a semblance of Ruritania but emphasized contemporaneity with every cut of the clothes. The physical environments were modern as well; though they tended to the austere and the architectural, with low platforms and gradients and a generally open

46 *Hamlet* 1925 London. D: H. J. Ayliff. Des: Paul Shelving. P: Lenare. Barry
Jackson's Birmingham Rep in modern dress at the Kingsway Theatre. Colin Keith-
Johnston as Hamlet, in plus-fours and white shirt, in the final scene. Robert Holmes
(Laertes) is at the left, Guy Vivian (Osric, in naval dress) stands on the sofa in the
center.

playing space, they went almost unnoticed by commentators. Attention was
naturally focused on the costumes, which carried the major visual
signification (illus. 46). "Hamlet Dons Plus Fours to Kill Laertes in Oxford
Bags," read one photo caption; "Ophelia's madness is damaged by the
inescapable shortness of Ophelia's skirt," said *The Times*. For most
spectators this was a violent wrenching of the context of the play, not as
optically disturbing as Norman Wilkinson's treatment but in other ways
equally challenging. If Barker and Wilkinson forced the audience to
reconsider the scenographic tradition by stylized dislocation, Ayliff and
Shelving were forcing a reconsideration of the entire conventional structure
that supported Shakespearean interpretation in England. The comfortable
familiarity of a classic is seriously threatened when it is presented as if it were
just written; *Hamlet* was no longer a safe play. "Something, however, had
to be done to rouse the people from their apathy about Shakespeare,"
Jackson said.

 Despite the visual shock the production was welcomed by audiences and
critics. "Here was not an addition of obscurity, but an opening out of fresh

light upon the play," *The Times* concluded. "The deepest *Hamlet* I have ever seen," wrote Hubert Griffith in *The Observer*. Jackson must have struck just the right moment and just the right play, for his experiment was rapidly imitated. Widely reported in the American and German press, Jackson's version prompted within six months a modern-dress *Hamlet* with Basil Sidney in New York, one with Alexander Moissi at the Deutsches Volkstheater in Vienna, and another with Ernst Deutsch at the Thalia Theater in Hamburg. Jessner's version followed in 1926. In 1927 the Shuberts invited Ayliff to direct *The Taming of the Shrew* in New York, which he restaged for Jackson in London the following year. That play encouraged a travesty approach at odds with Jackson's original intention: Kate in bobbed hair and short green taffeta dress, Petruchio in goggles and golfing cap while driving to Padua, the car's wheels whirling "madly and behind them bizarre scenery flew by."[17] In New York Grumio was a modern cowboy, in London a black-shirted fascist.

But the differing methods of *Hamlet* and *Shrew* were not automatically applicable to the entire canon, and Birmingham's next London production, *Macbeth* in 1928, was disastrously received. Shelving transferred the battlefields of Europe directly to the heath. The army uniforms, machine guns, and noises of exploding shells confused many spectators when they tried to make literal sense of the setting: how could a story about the First World War be taking place in Scotland? (See illus. 47.) *Hamlet* succeeded partly because it was fixed in time but reasonably vague in place, suggesting that these enacted events could happen anywhere. *Macbeth*, on the other hand, insisted on a strict localization and lost its universality; the characters seemed to be in a modern thriller.[18] The fashionably low-key acting – Eric Maturin, who played Macbeth, had never seen a performance of the play, and Lady Macbeth (Mary Merrall) took a stiff whiskey before "That which hath made them drunk hath made me bold" (Trewin 110–11) – this time appeared self-conscious. Ayliff's burlesque treatment of *Shrew* perhaps affected his attitude to *Macbeth*, for he seemed to be striving for clever, superficial associations rather than significant relationships. According to the promptbook, for example, Duncan's arrival at Inverness (1.6), that classic moment of dramatic irony and foreshadowing, was announced by "3 hoots" of a motorhorn.

The Jackson productions outlined much of the subsequent grammar of Shakespearean modern dress. They also pointed to its inconsistencies, chief among them being the contradiction between contemporary manners and Elizabethan diction. "A joke's a joke," Granville Barker concluded of the

47 *Macbeth* 1928 London. D: H. J. Ayliff. Des: Paul Shelving. Birnam Wood arrives in the uniforms of the First World War, at the Court Theatre. Laurence Olivier as Malcolm salutes above the body of Macbeth (Eric Maturin).

Hamlet; "and, our medicine taken, it can go back to its cupboard till next time."[19] Whatever the truth of that critique, the example of *Hamlet* nonetheless proved luminous, and probably had more effect on twentieth-century international performance than any other British production between the wars. Suddenly it seemed possible to open Shakespeare to the latest cultural or theatrical vogue, to gain interpretive profit from deliberately faddish representation.

Though Jackson's Shakespeare achieved fame through occasional London performances, it is important to stress that his theatre thrived precisely because it was not stationed in the capital. This was equally true for the other advanced regional company of the period in England, Terence Gray's Cambridge Festival Theatre. Jackson's significance to our story lies in the exemplary status of his modern-dress productions, Gray's from his being a sensitive receptor of messages from Europe. There is scant precedent for him in the history of the theatre. An Egyptologist with a private fortune, he had no professional contact with the stage; yet he started the CFT in 1926 with his own money specifically to reform English production. He was, as Rowell and Jackson note (60), "in the most creditable sense of the terms, an amateur and a dilettante." Greatly influenced by Craig and Appia, he was convinced that the theatre must turn away entirely from what he called "the old game of illusion, glamour and all the rest of the nineteenth century hocus pocus and bamboozle." He rejected all forms of Realism and even engaged his cousin, Ninette de Valois, to choreograph actors' movement in balletic style. What he wanted was an overt "theatre theatrical," and to get it he removed the proscenium from the Theatre Royal, Barnwell, installed a small revolve and the latest continental lighting system, and built the first permanent curved cyclorama in England, even raising the roof to accommodate its height of 12 meters. Steps connected the apron to the auditorium, tying the audience to the event. The alterations made the building into an unitary shell like Copeau's Vieux-Colombier, an excellent space for Shakespeare. "The theatre as-it-is often incurs the scorn of the intelligent," he wrote in his program-journal, *The Festival Theatre Review*. "Why? Because much of it is based on infantile make-believe. When it discards all that and becomes a work of art pure and simple, the intelligent will come back to the theatre and take it seriously."[20]

Gray chose Cambridge because of the university and then pursued its population in high style; his attention to audience development marks him most clearly as a reformer. The auditorium was one of the most comfortable in England and other amenities were unmatched anywhere: the best restaurant in town, with excellent wines priced inexpensively, buses to and from the theatre, cast lists that could be read in the darkened auditorium (they were made of dark waxed paper with transparent lettering that was legible when held up against the stage light). After 1931 it was Gray's policy that any audience member could see a production a second time free of charge, providing space was available. "You are welcome to smoke," the program announced. "The supreme desire of the Management is to see you enjoying yourself." The enjoyment, however, had to be on Gray's terms. Viniculture was another of his passions and in order to enlighten undergraduates he refused to sell beer and spirits in the restaurant and printed little essays about wine on the menus. His productions were equally educational, with much longer essays, as if each season were a course in the European avant-garde, an example of what the commercial theatre ("the trade theatre," he called it) could never accomplish. The schedule even coincided with the eight-week university terms.

But the productions certainly were not dry. Gray was the very opposite of an academic director; though Appia and Craig lay behind much of his thought, his immediate influences were the most extreme practitioners in Europe, Jessner for his approach to classic texts, Meyerhold for his approach to design. Gray was concerned with production, not with plays; his repertoire excluded new scripts almost entirely and the playwright, whether classic or contemporary, had no advocate at his court. His interest in Shakespeare, therefore, was the interest of an outright appropriator. He carried the interpretive load of postwar Europe to Cambridge, though without much of its political weight.

His first Shakespearean production was something of an homage to Jessner and Pirchan, a *Richard III* of 1928. Gray designed the theatre's chief scenic innovation himself, what Rosenfeld (183) calls "a hollow box system" of twenty-four light-weight cubes, drums, and cylinders in varying sizes that could be arranged in many combinations to signify mountains, forest, or abstract architectural forms, useful for any number of plays. They were colored according to shape, the cubes a pale blue or gray, the cylinders terracotta. For *Richard* cubes were arranged on the turntable in conjunction with steps to provide a versatile sequence of playing spaces (illus. 48). The spiral gradients provided a pliable structure even when stationary; for example, as Buckingham primed the Mayor on the forestage (3.7) the audience also saw Gloucester on the steps disguising two of his henchmen as bishops. For his entrance aloft between them, the stage rotated slowly into the position in the second drawing. Basically this was a Constructivist method, combining the unit set with the mechanics of the revolve, another attempt to recreate the flexibility of the Elizabethan stage by modernist

48 *Richard III* 1928 Cambridge. D and Des: Terence Gray. L: C. Harold Ridge. Gray's design for the "hollow box system," seen in two positions for 3.7 on the turntable.

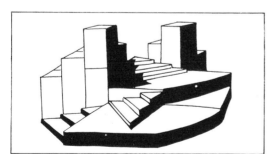

means. The tendency towards minimalism operated in the textual treatment as well. Gray pared the play down to essentials, performing only the major scenes and some necessary connective material. Similarly, he omitted most properties, which he thought hindered dramatic action: Richard was crowned in mime and signed his name with gesture. Costumes were designed for their individual expressiveness or their suitability to character and did not attempt to represent any period. Like Jessner, Gray sought not a mirror of real life but an abstract scene of mythic events.

And like Jessner he sought emotional power through Expressionist lighting. Gray's lighting collaborator was C. Harold Ridge, a first-rate designer and technician whose book became the standard text on the subject in England. Ridge explains that for this production no general illumination was provided; instead he relied upon focused spots, often one at a time, "the characters in conflict at the moment alone being picked out from the surrounding darkness." Middle blue and violet tints gave a hard light that brought out the primary colors in the costumes and emphasized "the atmosphere of plotting and deeds of darkness."[21] Ridge accented frightening shadows in the same manner as Jessner, as in illustration 49. For Richard's death the lighting was at its most effective. Four spears, the only physical props used in the entire performance, were held by Richmond's soldiers in the light, while the bloody dog was almost in shadow (illus. 50).

49   *Richard III* 1928 Cambridge. P: Scott and Wilkinson. The ghosts scene (5.3) at the Cambridge Festival Theatre, with huge projected shadows.

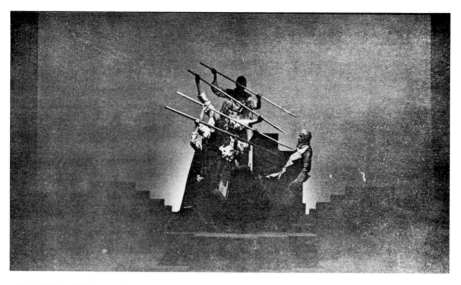

50 *Richard III* 1928 Cambridge. P: Scott and Wilkinson. Ridge's lighting forcing attention on the spears.

Gray was joined the next season by Doria Paston, an artist well in tune with his mission, whose design for *Romeo and Juliet* was one of the major visual accomplishments of the Cambridge Festival Theatre. At first sight it must have seemed outlandish, with flamenco costumes and a spirit inspired by the films of Rudolph Valentino, but the unit set was actually more Elizabethan than most Shakespearean productions of the time. Paston's starting point was the problem of locations, which was solved by simultaneous staging. The houses of Capulet and Montague were facing each other downstage, the one with a spitting cat, the other with a snarling dog painted on the front door. Two further doorways upstage indicated the palace of the Prince; the Friar's cell and Juliet's balcony were on the revolve (illus. 51). Thus the separate locales were medieval mansions, lighting bringing them into prominence as required, and the brightly colored design as a whole looked like an illuminated manuscript. Scenes were played continuously, and the colored blocks used for furniture center stage were changed in full view of the audience. Gray eliminated props and, even more radically, functionary characters; the Apothecary, for example, did not appear (his lines were spoken by a prompter offstage), and Romeo took his poison from an invisible phial.

Norman Marshall worked for a time as a director at the theatre and found a basic flaw in Gray's leadership: unable to accept compromise or criticism, he surrounded himself "too often with third-rate people. ... He required disciples rather than collaborators."[22] Interestingly, these were characteristics of William Poel as well, and in both cases resulted in uneven companies of actors. Gray received an inordinate amount of abuse from the press, only some of it justified, and as time went on he reacted with more and more outrageous productions. Frankly bored with *The Merchant of Venice* he took the bizarre recourse of signifying his boredom: Portia delivered the mercy speech listlessly while the court yawned and the Duke played with a Yo-Yo, Shylock and Tubal angled for lobsters in the Grand Canal (to bait fish withal?). Of course there are no lobsters in Venice and Orthodox Jews do not eat shellfish; was this insensitive ignorance on Gray's part or character comment? Probably the latter, since in the final scene Shylock, dirty, greasy, the object of ridicule, returned playing a barrel organ.

Other examples of Gray's willful eccentricity anticipated future travesty treatments of Shakespeare. In 1928 Rosalind was a Boy Scout and Celia a Girl Guide in a black and white Arden, everyone in silver wigs. The characters in *Henry VIII* (1931) were dressed as figures from a deck of playing cards, Henry as the King of Hearts, Wolsey as the Ace of Diamonds, and the courtiers as plain cards whose suits indicated their loyalties. In 1933 Toby and Andrew were on roller skates.

51 *Romeo and Juliet* 1929 Cambridge. D: Terence Gray. Des: Doria Paston. L: C. Harold Ridge. P: Scott and Wilkinson. Medieval mansions, flamenco costumes, flying birds: the unit set in the opening tableau.

Gray tried to extend his operations with links to the Oxford Playhouse and to the Gate Theatre in London, but was frustrated in both cases. He resigned in June 1933, a month after his *Twelfth Night* opened, claiming he had said all he wanted to say: he became a wine-grower in France, and after 1939 bred horses in Ireland, and never worked in the theatre again. Nor is he well remembered today, although he is still growing grapes in Monaco. But his contributions to the visual aspects of production, together with those of Doria Paston and Harold Ridge, were substantial. Despite the arrogance of his method, he was sincerely dedicated to advancing the theatre and to taking the audience along with him; in the deepest sense he was a social artist. The CFT brought European scenography to England for the first time on a regular basis. For Shakespeare it demonstrated the value of the unit set, of robust lighting effects, and of costuming removed from period and literalization, all of which would become fundamental to future developments. Gray's influence on subsequent designers and directors was indirect; he was more an index than an epitome. Yet his extended example has a permanent place in the history of English Shakespearean performance.

5 | *The stuffed stag and the new look*

In 1919 Nigel Playfair directed *As You Like It* at Stratford-upon-Avon in an uncut version that abandoned the traditional look for costumes and sets designed after medieval tapestries and illuminated manuscripts. Arden was rendered with pieces of colored cardboard on netting, using shocking hues of scarlet and lemon, lime-green and pink. Audiences, unprepared for a revision of the leafy illusionism of the greenwood tree, reacted in horror; Playfair reports that he was treated as a "national criminal" at his hotel, other guests turning their backs or walking out of the room when he entered. The cast was openly disdained on the streets of Shakespeare's birthplace. But the greatest opprobrium was reserved for the designer, Claud Lovat Fraser, demonstrating again the power of the visual. A woman, unable to control her outrage, publicly shook her fist in his face. "Young man," she said, "how dare you meddle with our Shakespeare?"[1]

As its name announced, the Shakespeare Memorial Theatre was intended not so much as a place of performance as a monument to the Immortal Memory. Completed in 1879, just three years after the Bayreuth Festival, the Stratford building was the first theatre in history specifically dedicated to the work of a single playwright. Its early life was ignoble. For its first forty years the governors effectively rented it to visiting companies for an annual festival coinciding with the Shakespeare birthday celebrations, and it was not until after the Second World War that it fully overcame the geographical isolation and fierce parochialism that had maintained it as a minor institution. From the start it was under the paternalistic care of the Flower family, owners of a Stratford brewery; Archibald Flower (known locally as Sir Archie), the chairman of the governors from 1903 to 1944, was the chief advocate of its shoddy work, insisting upon low budgets, low salaries, and ridiculously short rehearsal periods, even when the SMT had achieved unparalleled financial security. But the theatre's root difficulty as a producer of Shakespeare was a distrust of the modern, whether in acting, in-

120

terpretation, or in design, in favor of an unexamined reliance upon nineteenth-century stage traditions and local color.

The stuffed stag is the best example: Stratford legend has it that young Shakespeare was caught poaching deer in Sir Thomas Lucy's park, so in making a museum for the writer a descendant of Lucy's putative herd was shot and stuffed for display. Inaugurating the building in 1879, Barry Sullivan had borrowed this stag for *As You Like It*, carried into Arden racked on a pole, and it had dutifully reappeared in every performance of the play at Stratford thereafter, many of them directed by Frank Benson, a total of some twenty-four productions. Though the stag had no necessary connection to the play its entrance was an expected event, a sign that theatrical orthodoxy ruled, a ritual fulfillment of Stratford's claim upon Shakespeare. By 1919 it was moth-eaten and very tired, yet since the play had not been performed for four years it was a longed-for sight. The real problem with Playfair's *As You Like It* for Stratford spectators was visual but did not lay in the medieval design (which critics called Cubist); rather it lay in Playfair's adamant refusal to use the stuffed stag. The festival had been disrupted, a tradition of forty years violated.

That same year the first permanent director of the theatre was appointed, William Bridges-Adams, whose attempts to breathe life into Shakespeare were sincere and would have succeeded under a more benevolent financial administration. He realized quickly that the local attitude to the SMT had to change; "my choice lay, so to speak," he wrote, "between Ye Olde Oake Shakespeare Bunne Shoppe and Bayreuth."[2] A sensitive designer himself, he began to use semi-permanent settings with atmospheric lighting, reflecting some of the advances of the continent; by alternating short scenes in front of traverse curtains with full-stage sets he was able to get speed of performance and yet literalize the major scenes according to custom. But Sir Archie got it into his head that Bridges-Adams was too interested in the look of the stage and regularly refused to authorize expenditures that would enhance production. In fact, the director held a balanced view about the importance of design and began his work at Stratford by stressing the primacy of the word: he offered nearly complete texts, a practice which led Ben Greet to call him "Unabridges-Adams." (The name has stuck, though later he commonly made merciless cuts.)

The major administrative problem at the SMT, however, was a nineteenth-century notion about the value of rehearsal. In his first year the director was required to prepare six plays in four weeks, and the situation did not significantly improve in the future. Under such conditions it became routine to rely upon old Stratford hands and old Stratford productions as the basis for a new season. The theatre's historian, Sally Beauman (159–60), has shown that Bridges-Adams and his successor, Ben Iden Payne, worked from old promptbooks when remounting a play, fossilizing the performance texts, conceptions, characterizations, and the basic scenography. The limitations of the building, which were severe, added to the difficulty of finding new vitality for Shakespeare in it; its disadvantages had been so openly discussed that when it burned down in 1926 both Sir Archie and Bridges-Adams joked that they had airtight alibis. But the fire caused further problems in that performances had to be moved to a converted cinema until a new building was ready in 1932. The result was that very few productions in the 1920s at the SMT were noteworthy for any reason, and not a single one was visually remarkable. The Shakespeare Memorial Theatre had become a memorial to mediocrity.

In London the story was not very different. The major outlet for Shakespeare in the early part of the century was an unlikely venue near Waterloo Station, rechristened the Royal Victoria Coffee Music Hall in 1880 by its new owner, Emma Cons. "Coffee" meant temperance; Miss Cons, a right-thinking humanitarian with a touch of William Morris socialism, was dedicated to bringing wholesome, uplifting, affordable entertainment to the working classes south of the river, who affectionately called the place the Old Vic. In 1895 she was joined by her niece Lilian Baylis, who guided the theatre morally and financially from Miss Cons' death in 1912 until her own in 1937, a reign approximate to Sir Archie's at Stratford. These "philanthropic God-fearing women," as Harcourt Williams called them,[3] set an unusual tone for the theatre that proclaimed itself between the wars as "The Home of Shakespeare and Opera in English." Lilian Baylis' combination of Victorian idealism and absolute trust in God had an overwhelming effect on the house and the work that was performed there. Extremely limited finances and a prejudice against elaboration justified one another; the result was a Shakespearean stage with a distrust of the visual and an emphasis on traditional literary values. Whereas in Stratford the SMT tendered Shakespeare as a monument to England, in London the Old Vic presented the plays as an austere, evangelical alternative to lasciviousness and drink.

William Poel was frequently mentioned as the inspiration for Old Vic Shakespeare, but it was Poel's contempt for luxury that was influential rather than his radical Elizabethanism. An uncluttered production style has clear advantages for a theatre on a low budget; Bridges-Adams noted that "when in 1919 the price of canvas soared from tenpence a yard to four shillings there was an economic as well as an aesthetic case for the simplified settings which are almost universal today."[4] The Old Vic, however, was not interested in rethinking the texts or in theoretical exploration of performance but simply in a method of production that would accommodate many plays in a season without debilitating expense. Its general scenography was reminiscent of that in Victorian provincial theatres where stock flats and costumes would be adapted to new uses: the productions were not so much designed as outfitted.

The major accomplishment of Baylis' early years was the showing of every play in the First Folio, a task no theatre had ever undertaken before. Presented between 1914 and 1923, directed mainly by Ben Greet and Robert Atkins, this mammoth undertaking was simultaneous with the final elevation of Shakespeare into England's national writer in the academy and in popular culture. Producing all of the plays is the theatrical parallel to publishing a complete edition, where each text has at least the appearance of equal worth. Prior to the Old Vic project script selection for Shakespeare operated as it did for most dramatists; the most popular or most accessible works got staged regularly, the others infrequently or not at all. Now the value of the canon as a whole had been raised so that any play, the Old Vic implied, was commendable because it was written by Shakespeare.

Thus at a time when experimentation with Shakespeare was at its height on the continent, the two principal theatres in England devoted to his works retreated into institutionalized reverence. The design achievements of the early century, from Craig to Stern, from Pirchan to Hofman, and their importation by Barry Jackson and Terence Gray, were defied. Even more pointedly, the breakthroughs of Norman Wilkinson for Granville Barker's Savoy productions were passed over as if they had not occurred. Nor did either theatre offer a significant visual alternative.

BRIDGES-ADAMS AND KOMISARJEVSKY

Despite the retrograde traditions of Stratford, Bridges-Adams was in an unparalleled position for Shakespearean leadership in the late 1920s. Through a highly successful American campaign, more than enough money had been raised after the fire for the SMT to build a new theatre and to endow an acting company on a permanent basis. With the advice of Granville Barker, Bridges-Adams drew up the specifications for the theatre himself; he wanted a flexible playing space suitable for Elizabethan as well as pictorial staging. The young architect, Elizabeth Scott, selected in a national competition, was a modernist intent on making a functional and an unfussy statement. Even Sir Archie had been convinced that the prestige of Stratford required that the new SMT should be equipped as well as possible, and traveled with his director and the architect to see the best theatres in Europe.

Things went wrong from the start. The contest adjudicators, fearing that the architectural specifications would be too restrictive, had silently loosened them; thus Scott's plans did not incorporate many elementary ludic features and Bridges-Adams was forced to modify what should have been the unshakable essence of the building. "What we eventually got," he wrote much later, "when the architects, pressure-groups, quacks and empirics had finished with us, was the theatre, of all theatres in England, in which it is hardest to make an audience laugh or cry." The proscenium arch was too small (about 9 meters wide by 6.5 meters high), the apron too narrow, and the fan-shaped auditorium separated from the stage by an orchestra pit. The proscenium was extended towards the audience by a series of three additional frames, each angled outwards at 45 degrees against the side walls and lintel, creating a funnel-shaped visual entrance to the stage, which seemed to recede into the distance. The result, as Beauman (113) says, was "a tunnel effect" with the audience "looking through a narrow opening at a great stage some 40 feet deep." The many subsequent remodelings of the building, which stands today as the home of the Royal Shakespeare Company, have been rather desperate attempts to alter an intractable playing space. Backstage the disasters multiplied: no rehearsal rooms or workshops or greenroom, too few dressing-rooms, and a great deal of up-to-date stage equipment that refused to work.

The two *Henry IV* plays were selected for the opening on 23 April 1932, in matinee and evening performances, directed and designed by Bridges-Adams himself. But the rush of preparing the building, the director's uncertain health, and the usual shortage of rehearsal time added up to acute disappointment: the performance was uninspired, the actors difficult to hear, the expensive lighting system an initial failure, and the scenography an uncomfortable mix of the old and the new. London critics, enticed to Stratford for the opening, were almost unanimous in condemnation. Some left at the interval and few bothered to stay for the second part in the evening. Thus the impressive production of *A Midsummer Night's Dream* four days later, which achieved some of the excitement denied to the first night of the theatre, got little press attention. Norman Wilkinson, a governor of the SMT since 1919, returned as a designer of Shakespeare with the play that had been the high point of his collaboration with Barker before the war. The set designs were so successful that – in a continuation of the SMT's policies – they were reused in modifications as late as 1938. The production treated the play as an Elizabethan epithalamium, emphasizing its proto-masque qualities and setting it in London rather than Athens. The opening drop was a painted curtain with a representation of a palace façade, and the interior for the first scene continued the motif.

Wilkinson came into his own with the wood, where he provided a useful, atmospheric set. Avoiding the extreme stylization of his work with Barker, this forest of darkly painted trees on a backdrop was nonetheless naïve or childlike, while a mound stage right supported a three-dimensional tree trunk (illus. 52). The trunk was moved to suggest different parts of the wood, sometimes pulled by fairies (played by children) with tinsel cords. Puck was dressed in scarlet, as in Barker's production, but this was not a formalized, golden fairyland; it was a moonlit nocturne with the ambience

52   *A Midsummer Night's Dream* 1932 Stratford. D and L: William Bridges-Adams. Des: Norman Wilkinson. P: Claude A. Harris. Dorothy Francis as Titania, Roy Byford as Bottom. Bridges-Adams' lighting brought out the characters while Wilkinson's dark wood remained in shadow.

of silver dust. Fabia Drake, who played Hermia, wrote that "it was a midnight wood, of midnight blue, streaked here and there with the silver of moonlight; the fairies, dressed in the same midnight-blue and silver, *disappeared* when they stood against the treetrunks."[5] The moonlight effects were achieved by Bridges-Adams' delicate lighting, which was focused on the characters rather than the set; the dark backdrops absorbed the light and made the scene mysterious. Bridges-Adams did not like the "hygienic whiteness" and "egalitarian brilliance" of Barker's Savoy Shakespeare, which came from horizontal front lighting which bounced off the set. His inclination was to the romance of Irving's gaslight; he relied on side lights and down spots mounted behind the proscenium, and, though he had the most modern lighting system in England, on occasion reverted to Victorian limelights for special effects.

The mixture of the older Stratford methods with the new look was continued in *Coriolanus* the next season. Aware of the topicality of a play concerned with popular elections and military threats – Hitler had been appointed Chancellor just three months before the opening – Bridges-Adams nonetheless felt himself to be a "custodian of the eternal values" and steadfastly avoided political overtones in his production. He thought it "shockingly improper" when a theatre artist "turns his stage into a platform and takes sides in the temporal issues that divide us."[6] Nothing shows the retreat of British Shakespeare from the external conditions of the world more clearly than the decision of the director of the official Shakespeare theatre to treat *Coriolanus*, in 1933, as "a very simple play, dependent mainly on sincerity and drive." Later that same year a production at the Comédie Française was read by audiences as an attack on the socialist government, and demonstrations from the left and right disrupted the performances night after night, causing their eventual cancellation. But British audiences, neither attuned to find messages in classic drama nor encouraged to see them by the SMT performance, remained aloof from the contemporary applications of Shakespeare's most insistently political play. The director ostensibly strove for a balanced view, but he had managed to make the play "very simple" by substantially cutting the political speeches and some of the minor political arguments. Visually he followed the same pattern. The costumes might have come any time in the past fifty years, said the *Birmingham Post* (25 April), but the setting was a grand classical staircase clearly indebted to Jessner and Pirchan (illus. 53). Like Reinhardt before him, Bridges-Adams was using scenographic techniques derived from German political theatre for a resolutely apolitical statement – though his

53 *Coriolanus* 1933 Stratford. D, Des, and L: William Bridges-Adams. The triumphal entrance of Coriolanus (played by Anew McMaster) in a design by Bridges-Adams. The crowd (mostly local supers) was used in the tradition of the Meininger and of Tree, while the architectural setting at last brought Craig and Pirchan to Stratford. (Drawing recreated by Bridges-Adams for an Arts Council exhibition in 1947, from "rough sketches and notes on the backs of old envelopes.")

very resistance to the partisan content of *Coriolanus* can be read as a conservative political act.

Perhaps the most significant accomplishment of Bridges-Adams' fifteen years at Stratford lay not in his own productions but in his hospitality to another designer-director whose work at last established a new visual approach to Shakespeare in the British theatre. After resisting outsiders for years, Sir Archie was persuaded to invite Theodore (Fyodor) Komisarjevsky to stage *The Merchant of Venice* in the first season of the new theatre. Despite an irreverent approach and a total of five rehearsals, it was a grand success with Stratford audiences, and thereafter Sir Archie welcomed him as good news for the box-office. Komisarjevsky's early career in St. Petersburg and Moscow was centered on "synthetic" theatre, a Craigian notion of total performance where words were equal in importance to movement, song, and the general visual effect. Some of his designs, like a *Lohengrin* for the Moscow Soviet Opera in 1918, show clear influences of Constructivism. He emigrated to England in 1919 and, out of necessity, made a new reputation as a director of Chekhov and realist Russian plays for small theatres and the

Stage Society. Prior to the Stratford assignment he had only one contact
with Shakespeare, a *King Lear* for the Oxford University Drama Society in
1927. He was an outsider to British Shakespeare in every sense.

At age 50 Komisarjevsky could hardly be considered an *enfant terrible*, yet
that is the role he actively played for the next seven years at Stratford. His
Merchant began by treating the play as Reinhardt had done, as a carnival
event, but Komisarjevsky's set, designed in collaboration with Lesley
Blanch, sought not a recreation of Venice and Belmont so much as fanciful
celebration of theatricality. Delighted by the possibilities of the new stage
machinery, which the SMT technicians finally mastered, he set the tone with
a tipsy revision of a pictorial Rialto (illus. 54). Venice split apart to make
Belmont, the Lion sliding stage right, the Bridge of Sighs stage left, Portia's
room rising on an elevator from beneath the floor. For the suitors' scenes
Belmont rose further, creating a platform above and a curtained discovery
area below for the caskets. The trial was played in an abstract space in front
of the cyclorama, watched by Venetian noblemen painted on a jagged flat
placed to the left; the Duke tended to nod off, and Antonio, unconcerned
about the outcome, referred to a little mirror kept on a chain around his

54 *The Merchant of Venice* 1932 Stratford. D: Theodore Komisarjevsky. S:
Komisarjevsky and Lesley Blanch. C: Lesley Blanch. P: Ernest Daniels. A leaning
Lion of St. Mark stuck improbably in the midst of bridges.

neck.[7] This was a jester's cartoon world, and the performance style was in key with the scenography. A *commedia* prelude began the action: black and white pierrots dancing to Bach's Toccata and Fugue in D Minor were forced off by a Harlequin who turned out to be Launcelot Gobbo. Old Gobbo was costumed as Pantaloon, Morocco was a blackface minstrel. Randle Ayrton countered Irving's sentimental usage of the Jew wronged, still the active tradition in England; he was a Shylock intent on revenge alone, whose removal was welcomed so that the play might rush on to love and closure.

The next season brought a *Macbeth* that carried some of the feeling of Soviet Constructivism into a metaphoric structure of burnished aluminum with curved screens, scroll work, and turning staircases. Though it had the initial appearance of a unit set, its sections could be moved so that the action occurred in an adjustable abstract architecture, suggesting by turns a castle exterior, an interior, or the open plain. The performance was not much admired by the critics, yet it was a memorable design, and eclectic visual references to the First World War brought further profit.[8] When Bridges-Adams resigned from the SMT in 1934, Komisarjevsky lost his champion but was nonetheless invited back the next year for *The Merry Wives of Windsor*, which he treated as a Viennese operetta. The turning-point in his work at Stratford came in 1936, when he mounted *King Lear* with Randle Ayrton in the lead. This time there were few scoffers at the method, and few complaints about interpretive license, for Ayrton's performance was commanding, the scenography masterful, and the production an integrated whole.

Ayrton had played Lear in Komisarjevsky's production for OUDS, and tackled the role again for Bridges-Adams in 1931 and 1932, which helps to explain how Komisarjevsky could stage this version in only six rehearsals. Ayrton was a monumental Lear, still possessing strength and courage in the first scene; his division of the kingdom occurred not as senile folly but rather with "the coolness of a man making a settlement to escape death duties," said *The Scotsman*.[9] Komisarjevsky publicly stated that he wished to emphasize the acting and to avoid the charge of visual impertinence (Beauman 147), thus his simple design removed the play from Celtic conventions but imposed no eccentric stamp. The unit set was, Gordon Crosse wrote (97), "a huge flight of steps occupying the whole stage, which successfully gave the impression of a single titanic action." The director thus created an example of Jessner's "abstract scene of mythic events," though he built a significant modification into the Pirchan model for tragedy: the sections of these steps were placed at different angles and

55 *King Lear* 1936 Stratford. D and Des: Theodore Komisarjevsky. P: Ernest Daniels. *Jessnertreppen* at the SMT for 1.1, opening with a barbaric trumpet blast with the full court on stage (the preliminary prose dialogue among Gloucester, Kent, and Edmund was cut). The costumes appear hieratic but not fixed in time. Rosalind Iden as Cordelia (sitting, at top), Randle Ayrton as Lear, Geoffrey Wilkinson as the Fool, Buena Bent as Regan, Barbara Couper as Goneril.

interrupted by platforms. When the entire set was visible, as in the opening scene, the gradients offered multiple acting levels as well as a hierarchical picture of a world struggling to maintain its order (illus. 55). Sometimes the actors literally struggled; in order to fit the set under the low proscenium, the steps were constructed so narrowly that to mount them actors were forced to go on tiptoe or sideways.

Smaller scenes were played in narrow pools of light, occupying a single platform or a few of the steps. This was the method of Tairov and of Gray, isolating acting areas on a permanent set by light so that short scenes would flow swiftly; it is now so common that we scarcely give it a second thought. Throughout Komisarjevsky established emotional levels with lighting as well. The play of light upon the cyclorama provided the chief visual variety, changing color from dun to pale blue to blood red, and providing, *The Times* reported, "a powerful reinforcement of the acting." T. C. Kemp was equally impressed with the visual effects, especially in the final scene. The

56 *The Comedy of Errors* 1938 Stratford. D and Des: Theodore Komisarjevsky. P: Ernest Daniels. A scene with Doctor Pinch (C. Rivers Gadsby, arms outstretched). Throughout the performance the tower clock would strike the wrong hour and the hands would race to catch up.

light faded slowly in the sky, he wrote, and the darkness moved slowly down the steps:

Line by line the motionless soldiers fade from view: the light lingers for a moment on the dead Lear and Cordelia. Finally they, too, dissolve into the gloom; the rolling drums die away, and the curtain slowly descends on the darkened stage.[10]

This was staircase directing at its best, where the levels were both obstacles to naturalistic movement and opportunities for symbolic grouping. Komisarjevsky demonstrated to Stratford that the modern visual approach to production, far from being inconsistent with traditional notions of Shakespearean tragedy, was a supple interpretive strategy.

Despite the success of *King Lear* it was with the lighter comedies that Komisarjevsky made his most popular contribution. His *Comedy of Errors* is perhaps the best example, a play ripe in 1938 for illustrative transformation. It got a treatment worthy of a great visual director, integrating the styles of the fairytale and *commedia* into what Trewin (179) calls "an operatic, balletic diversion." Illustration 56 shows much of the disturbing nature of the production. The toy-like set, with its skewed perspective and unsettling combination of three-dimensional units with flat houses, carried the production into that area of farce where real human problems are indistinguishable from supercharged absurdities. Ralph Berry notes that in the photographs the stage seems to have "a haunting, almost hallucinogenic quality. … There is some deep law of visual dynamics illustrated here," a law relating to "the quintessentially dreamlike nature of the action for those experiencing it."[11] The costumes, ranging from comic variations of Elizabethan farthingales to United States Navy uniforms, were dislocating examples of that dream world.

Komisarjevsky greatly loosened the notion of period, moving away from any strict image of temporal unity; he saw no need to be either logical or literal in the visual field. The Victorian pictorial approach demanded historically justified scenography, putting the action in the past tense; Poel demanded a recreation of Elizabethan methods (in practice, chiefly by Elizabethan costumes), making the action overtly fictive and putting it in Shakespeare's time; Barry Jackson proposed universality proceeding from the present. Those three presumptions about Shakespearean setting – the period play, the Elizabethan play, and the modern play – were the active traditions in the 1930s, each with its fanatically partisan adherents. Komisarjevsky brought a fourth alternative, leaning strongly to the metaphoric, for he denied that a production required a consistent visual reference based on time and place. In his own way he reactivated Granville Barker's visual approach, where the scenography was deliberately intended to remove the plays from specific locale in order to emphasize the aesthetic and fanciful.

Berry is right to point out that Komisarjevsky's work anticipated British treatments of Shakespeare in the 1960s and 1970s. The fluid use of stage space and of time period, reliance upon lighting to provide a swift flow of scenes, entrusting visual metaphor to erect a context for interpretation, all have become part of the common vocabulary of postwar Shakespeare. It is, however, equally important to note that his productions gathered many of the vital European movements of the early part of the century, especially those from central and eastern Europe, that had their theoretical foundation in Craig. Komisarjevsky was the first director of Shakespeare in the English mainstream theatre to insist that his ideas were as important as the words of the play, and to insist that acting style follow from the visual concept. His foreign birth meant that he was never fully accepted as a Shakespearean but perhaps also gave him a freedom denied to English directors between the wars. Terence Gray met a degree of opposition far greater than Komisarjevsky did and had much less effect on the subsequent bearing of Shakespeare as a result. "Komis," he was usually called in England – a diminutive that made him accessible but still retained a portion of his essential otherness, like the visiting clown at the feast.

MOTLEY

The conservative approach to Shakespeare that generally held sway in England between the wars was based on the notion that the plays did not need exceptional attention, either with regard to text or mise en scène, in order to be competently staged. Much of the reason for this widespread belief is to be found in the close relationship that English-speaking actors, directors, and audiences have felt since the eighteenth century to the language of the plays. Shakespeare's poetry is undeniably one of the major achievements of human history, but the reverence accorded it has sometimes had curious effects in the Anglophone theatre. In foreign-language productions there is normally an awareness that the dialogue has encountered at least two stages of alteration in its journey from the source writer: that brought by translation, and that brought by fashioning the translated words into performance scripts. The linguistic accessibility of translations is relevant; many are contemporary, and the oldest of them in regular use today in any country, the Schlegel–Tieck versions, were published between 1797 and 1833. Thus even the "classic" German translation is immeasurably closer to the language spoken on the street in Zurich or Vienna or Berlin than Shakespeare's language is to that of London or New York or Melbourne.

On the English-speaking stage the archaism and cultural status of the spoken text naturally grants it greater importance than in another language, and has led to a frequent opinion that an audience should be permitted to hear it directly, to experience the play unmediated. No one who has worked in the theatre at any time in history could possibly believe that drama can be presented without mediation; from the first moment of play selection the written text (itself of course already mediated by scribes, editors, and printers) goes through a lengthy series of handlings by directors, designers, dramaturgs, actors, and publicity agents before it is enacted – at which point it must still cross the minefield of signified meaning to be mediated by the minds of disparate members of an audience. Nor does the mediation cease there, for the audience in response and reviewers in print transmit some of the understood meaning back to the actors, who in future performances work with a knowledge of how the production has been accepted and interpreted. But since much of this process is invisible to the public a production can, if it wishes, maintain the illusion of direct access to Shakespeare, and this seems to have been the general attitude in England between the wars. Reacting against the excesses of the Victorian theatre, and reinforced by the reforming zeal of Poel and Barker (their writings more than their actual practice), many actors and directors sought an ideal Shakespeare in the unencumbered word.

The results, as we have seen, were the standard productions in Stratford and London in plain style, uncertain of their status as representations. Eventually an English compromise appeared, a middle way between the continental revisions of Komisarjevsky and the dowdy curtain settings of the Old Vic. The director who prompted the change was John Gielgud, whose own sense of the visual rejected somber aridity; greatly influenced by Barker, he was a protector of the spoken text but no slave to tradition, whether old or new. In his early productions in the 1930s he wanted an elegant look that supported the acting and did not interfere with the words. He found his ideal designer in a team of three young women – Elizabeth Montgomery, and the sisters Audrey and Margaret Harris – who collectively called themselves Motley. Their work with Shakespeare continued regularly in Britain and North America into the 1960s, and may have been the most influential until the formation of the RSC. It certainly was the most characteristically English in its practicality and restraint.

The occasion that made Gielgud's reputation as a director, and established the Motley style for the next three decades, was the famous *Romeo and Juliet* of 1935, an Old Vic production at the New Theatre. Most of the attention at the time was naturally focused on the acting. Peggy Ashcroft made her reputation overnight as Juliet, Edith Evans consolidated hers as the Nurse, and Gielgud and Laurence Olivier, opposite in style and in competition as classical actors, greatly impressed London as Mercutio and Romeo, then astounded the same audiences by switching roles after six weeks. Using a complete text, the production gained power from combining Gielgud's superb, somewhat ethereal vocal music with Olivier's harsher, more modern speech. Without question it was the most important rendition of the play anywhere in the first half of the century. Barker wrote to Gielgud that it was "by far the best bit of Shakespeare I'd seen in years."[12]

Gielgud had actually directed the play before for OUDS, using both Ashcroft and Motley, but he was not satisfied with the Oxford triple-arched unit set, and looked for a more flexible design. Shakespeare's tragedies often

57 *Romeo and Juliet* 1935 London. D: John Gielgud. Des: Motley. Laurence Olivier and Peggy Ashcroft in the farewell scene on the elevated bedroom, with the balcony tower higher up.

seem centered on an irreducible physical element, like the bed in *Othello* or the daggers in *Macbeth*, standing as both a symbol and a prop; the balcony in *Romeo* is certainly in this category and Motley regarded it as "the main thing that sets off how you think about the play." While desiring a non-intrusive and flexible set, Gielgud yet revealed the habit of the time in wanting to suggest a locale for each scene. Ashley Dukes explained it this way: "If, says the young director to himself, we cannot stand in the midst of our spectators and speak to them as the Elizabethan actors spoke, at least we will not allow any actual complications of a scenic nature to stand between us" (Levenson 56, 49).

The Motley solution was to use two sets of diagonal black curtains running to a permanent central tower or penthouse for the balcony, which divided the stage for scene changes. While the tower remained fixed, the other scenery, like Friar Lawrence's cell, slid in and out behind closed curtains. A platform served as Juliet's bedroom, signifying by furniture and patterned hangings an interior room separate from the balcony (illus. 57); Gielgud was convinced that the Elizabethan convention of multiple locales in the same stage space "would hardly be accepted by a modern audience." Thus after the lovers awoke (3.5) Romeo left the bedroom by mounting five steps to the top of the tower for his farewell, then climbed down from the balcony. The flexibility of the setting is clearly seen by comparing

58 *Romeo and Juliet* 1935 London. The central tower used as a house to suggest the street below. Glen Byam Shaw as Benvolio, Gielgud as Mercutio, Olivier as Romeo, and Edith Evans as the Nurse in 2.4.

59 *Romeo and Juliet* 1935 London. The central tower masked by colorful hangings to create Capulet's ball. The two archways were pushed on for this scene. Ashcroft at the left, Olivier down center.

illustrations 58 and 59, where the treatment of the tower is indicative of the production's visual variety.

The general style was based on Botticelli and Carpaccio, especially in the colors and cuts of the clothes. Costumes were used to establish mood as well as period; Romeo was in sober grays and blues when he first appeared in his melancholy state, but in banishment his costume, a blood-red velvet tunic, became emblematic of his desperation. The most important aspect of the scenography, however, was how Motley achieved simplicity and elegance through economical means. The open metal-work of the balcony, the slender pillars and arches, the restrained decorative features, all of which became characteristic features of Motley designs, gave a lightness and visual austerity that centered the performance in the verse. Many of the reviewers commented on both the quality of the speech and the effectiveness of the setting in supporting it. *The Times* (18 Oct. 1935) noted the swiftness resulting from scene shifters working on one segment of the stage while actors worked on another; James Agate in *The Sunday Times* (20 Oct.) was impressed with "the spirit of the place and time," though he objected to placing scenes in such small sections of the stage ("the action seemed to take place not so much in Verona as in a corner of it"). This was not scenic

60 *Twelfth Night* 1939 Stratford. D: Irene Hentschel. Des: Motley. P: Ernest
Daniels. Victorian parasols for grief; the metal trellis-work is visible behind the
actors. John Laurie as Malvolio, Lesley Brook as Olivia (center), Betty Hardy
as Maria.

innovation, but it was successful because the stage images were swift,
dynamic, and unmettlesome.

Motley's introduction to Stratford came at the invitation of Irene
Hentschel, herself the first woman to direct there, for a production of
Twelfth Night in 1939. The setting was an elegant but thoroughly artificial
garden, established principally by a wrought-iron, trellised arbor upstage
left with three plants suspended from the top. The costumes were early
Victorian, especially for Olivia's mourning household; the men were
dressed in a lighter Regency mode (illus. 60). This was one of the earliest
productions at the SMT to choose an identifiable period that was neither
that of the play's fictional time nor Elizabethan. Such a strategy is
theoretically similar to that of modern dress, but requires spectators to draw
upon their own historical sense, to take into Shakespeare's play their shared
cultural attitudes regarding an intervening age. Motley offered here a vision
of moony Illyria overlaid with a cramped Victorian sensibility, suggesting
a materialist view of *Twelfth Night*; Lesley Brook disturbed the critics by

playing Olivia as "a spoilt young heiress rather than the conventionally mature and sympathetic heroine" (Beauman 159).

But in general Motley's work tried not to insinuate itself between the spectator and the play. The vast majority of Motley designs at Stratford (some sixteen separate productions over the next twenty years), in London, New York, and at the American Shakespeare Festival in Connecticut, were conservative about period, restrained about costume, and adaptable about set. The Gielgud *Romeo and Juliet* prototype proved successful: a basic unit setting, with an open playing space downstage, would be altered by the addition of easily shifted pieces, often dropped in from the flies. The trellis in wood or metal was the Motley signature; almost as common was the use of colored silks draped from above.

Another *Romeo and Juliet*, directed by Glen Byam Shaw at Stratford in 1954, shows the development of many of these features. The open floor was prominent, with a compass pattern painted on the center platform, reflected

61 *Romeo and Juliet* 1954 Stratford. D: Glen Byam Shaw. Des: Motley. P: Angus McBean. Period costumes, flown silks, trellis patterns, and a large open center space, all characteristic of Motley designs. Keith Michell as Tybalt (on steps to left), Zena Walker as Juliet (center), Laurence Harvey as Romeo (on steps to right).

by the curve of a bridge running across the stage (illus. 61). Mantua was constituted by dropping a solid flat with arched windows in front of the bridge; for the tomb the bridge was removed, a curved stairway descended from the upper level, and metal bars sealed off the lower space upstage. The design endorsed the youth of the protagonists, accenting speed and graceful passion. It was a long way from Irving's massive settings for the same play; it showed the influence of a half-century of experiment with light-weight materials and symbolic suggestions; and yet it followed the intrinsic custom of pictorialism in offering illustrative outlines for changing locales. The Motleys were inventors but not pioneers; their ultimate importance lies not in revisualizing Shakespeare but in consolidating approaches already established into a practical and repeatable method. They demonstrated that Shakespearean scenography could be elegant, beautiful, inexpensive, yet remain a resolute ally to the spoken text.

R. E. JONES AND ORSON WELLES

The institutionalized support provided by the SMT, the Old Vic, and regional companies like those in Birmingham and Cambridge may have been small by the standards of the great subsidized theatres of central Europe and the Soviet Union, but it was nonetheless significant for the artists who worked in England between the wars. It provided a degree of continuity and of vision that was almost entirely lacking in North America, where the economics of the theatre persevered along nineteenth-century capitalist lines and programming was determined by the marketplace. Under such conditions Shakespeare was never likely to be a prominent part of the New York commercial stage; and the few institutional ventures that arose in the period, like the Provincetown Players, the Theatre Guild, and the Group Theatre, attended to modern plays.

Designers, accustomed even today to working freelance, are particularly vulnerable to the harsh rigors of trade. They rarely achieve the repute of actors, and have little recourse for employment when invitations from directors or producers do not arrive. At the turn of the century in New York they were hardly recognized as separate from carpenters, tailors, or scene painters, yet this rugged environment produced one of the greatest designers of the modern age, Robert Edmond Jones. From his first professional engagement, Anatole France's *The Man Who Married a Dumb Wife* for Granville Barker in 1915, Jones conducted the New Stagecraft to the new world. Greatly influenced by Craig, he brought to his work the very qualities that Craig lacked, a craftsman's attention to the details of construction, a practical concern for realization, and a delight in actors. He was particularly associated with the plays of Eugene O'Neill, from *Anna Christie* in 1921 to *The Iceman Cometh* in 1946; his work in 1924 for *The Emperor Jones* and for *Desire Under the Elms* may have been the most influential designs in the history of the American theatre.

Shakespeare was crucial in helping Jones to establish his reputation and his style. *Richard III*, designed for Arthur Hopkins and with John Barrymore in the title role, combined realized locales with Expressionist techniques, yet it opened in March of 1920, nine months before Jessner's production in Berlin. Barrymore ordered copper and black armor so heavy and authentic that he injured himself every time he fell in it, but Jones provided variations on a unit set that accented mood. The best example is a horrifying gibbet at the top of stairs for the penultimate scene ("my kingdom for a horse") that contextualized Richard's death with the murders he has caused (illus. 62).

Expressionist attributes were the dominant motifs for *Macbeth* a year later, with Lionel Barrymore and Julia Archer. Though the acting was unsure, for Stark Young this design was "the most profoundly creative décor that I have ever seen in the theatre."[13] The visual premise was established in the first scene, with powerful beams of light descending from three huge masks

62 *Richard III* 1920 New York. D: Arthur Hopkins. Des: Robert Edmond Jones. Expressionist applications onto a pictorial setting for 5.4. Plymouth Theatre.

63 *Macbeth* 1921 New York. D: Arthur Hopkins. Des: R.E. Jones. The appearance of Banquo (3.4) in Jones' design. The Witches' masks above the stage were a continuing reminder of supernatural evil.

suspended above the stage; the Witches wore similar triangular masks. The ogive figure was carried through the production: in the letter scene (1.5), for example, Lady Macbeth stood in a triangle arch made from a freestanding screen, with other triangles in other screens behind her; the masks remained visible on high for most scenes. The abstract arches, as Bablet says (1977: 243), suggested "the world as seen through the tormented minds of the protagonists." Jones' understanding of light marked him as a designer involved with the final stage effect, the plastic moment of the actor occupying space, more in the tradition of Appia than of Craig. In an important essay he wrote that drama is not an "engine" but "a living organism"; a designer needs to understand that light is "a part of that livingness." The banquet scene design shows him at his best, where the dimensionality of the actor is a major part of the harsh vision of candlelight and spotlight (illus. 63). Reflecting on this work, Jones said he wished "to carry the audience into that other region where the ideal play takes place" and "to find the simplest, broadest, grandest way to take the audience there, and to keep them there."

Jones' most widely admired Shakespearean setting was for John Barrymore's *Hamlet*, also directed by Hopkins, seen in New York in 1922. Despite his vocal limitations Barrymore was for many viewers the Hamlet of a generation; few had any doubts whatsoever about the design. Young thought it "princely, austere, and monumental"; James Agate wrote that the London transfer in 1925 was "the most beautiful thing I have ever seen on the stage" (Speaight 168). Craig's designs for the *St. Matthew Passion* lay behind it, along with Pirchan's work which Jones had seen on his European tour with Kenneth MacGowan. Speed and monumentality were again achieved by variations on a permanent set, this time dominated by a large high arch reaching towards the flies (illus. 64). Light was the key to mood and to action; some of its expressiveness is captured in this photograph, where the play of shadows deepens the conception of the lonely prince yet simultaneously provokes a starker, postwar challenge to that same Romantic image.

Jones could have become a major designer for Shakespeare but his inclinations, and those of the New York theatre, took him in other directions. He brought to his work, whether for Shakespeare or O'Neill, a supreme interest in serving the playwright and the actor; despite his visual innovations he thought of himself as an interpreter, as the Motleys did. At the absolute opposite extreme was the other American of the period whose work on Shakespeare had profound visual results. Orson Welles, actor, director, writer, producer, radio personality, filmmaker, universal celebrity, thought himself responsible chiefly to his own vision. He dealt with Shakespeare, especially in his heady days as world *wunderkind*, as raw material to be mined for social profit and lusty entertainment; as Richard France says, Welles transformed Shakespeare into "a spectacle of thrills and sudden shocks."[14] His results, often outlandish and reductionist, had wide effects on subsequent performance. In an idiosyncratic and off-balanced way he was as influential as any Anglo-American director of Shakespeare between the wars, including Komisarjevsky and Tyrone Guthrie.

The Works Progress Administration, one of Roosevelt's most inspired responses to the Depression, was designed to create work in socially useful projects, from building bridges to painting murals on post office walls. The WPA Negro Theatre Project, headed almost by chance by John Houseman, had as its goal the employment of as many African-American actors as possible. Until very recently many citizens of the United States have resisted government support of the arts, often fiercely, and thus the Project, combining racially sensitive activity with public subsidy, was automatically

64 *Hamlet* 1925 London (originally 1922 New York). D: Arthur Hopkins. Des: R. E. Jones. John Barrymore on the open playing space with a Craigian monument behind him. Curtains closed off the archway for Ophelia's mad scene; a figured curtain at the proscenium line was used for front scenes like 3.2. Haymarket Theatre.

imbued with political overtones. The enterprise was fraught from the beginning with conflicting agendas; Harlem had suffered severe economic distress, which led to riots in 1935, continued endemic suspicion of the white world, and a generalized distrust of government agencies fueled by the Communist Party whenever possible. When Welles was invited to direct a classic play in a Harlem theatre and decided, in response to a stimulating suggestion from his wife, to set *Macbeth* in nineteenth-century Haiti using an all-black cast, the political elements became paramount.

As far as I have been able to discover, this was the first major production of Shakespeare in English to select a locale for the action that was overtly foreign to the spirit of play. It was also, according to Houseman, "the first full-scale, professional Negro Shakespearean production in theatrical history."[15] Once the setting had been chosen, both the conception and the visual rendering were predetermined. The treatment of the script, characteristic of Welles' cinematic methods, followed as well: it was drastically reduced in length and severely reduced in scope, becoming a sensational melodrama about inescapable evil. Macbeth's character and career were based on Henri Christophe, "the Negro king of Haiti," who killed himself when his cruelty prompted a popular revolt. Taking visual and auditory cues from *The Emperor Jones*, Welles placed Macbeth's castle amid a frighteningly massive jungle and accompanied the action by drumbeats played by Africans recently arrived from the Gold Coast. The first two scenes were cut entirely, so that the opening showed Macbeth and Banquo flogging through dense vegetation to come upon a circle of voodoo celebrants – not three witches but an entire chorus – led by a male Hecate, who set the play in motion at the end of the scene with "Peace! The charm's wound up." The main setting then appeared for Lady Macbeth's letter soliloquy (1.5), eliminating Duncan's victory and the execution of Cawdor, making a strong connection between the witches and Macbeth's rapid rise.

The design by Nat Karson was established by a detailed model Welles built himself. It was serviceable but not particularly distinctive; the visual liveliness resulted directly from the costumes and locale (illus. 65). Directoire uniforms were in pale blue, scarlet and gold; Macbeth was in canary yellow and emerald green, with high riding-boots. This European gloss, accented by Virgil Thomson's arrangement of Josef Lanner waltzes for the court, stood in extravagant contrast to the voodoo costumes, the febrile greenery of the jungle, and the drums. Brooks Atkinson's review in the *New York Times* (15 April 1936), though supercilious and a little racist, caught the flavor:

65 *Macbeth* 1936 New York. D: Orson Welles. Des: Nat Karson. L: Abe Feder.
The voodoo *Macbeth*, final scene. Malcolm (Wardell Saunders) is on the throne
at the base of Macbeth's castle, while Macduff (Maurice Ellis) is at the top of the
tower. The voodoo witches hold Macbeth's impaled head aloft. Lafayette Theatre.

ship the witches into the rank and fever-stricken jungles of Haiti ... beat the voodoo
drums, stuff a gleaming naked witch doctor into the cauldron, hold up Negro masks
in the baleful light – and there you have a witches' scene that is logical and stunning
and a triumph of theatre art.

Much of the excitement came from anticipation in Harlem of an unusual
performance event, one that employed about 130 residents and was taken
seriously by sections of the dominant culture. In one sense it is strange that
the black community took to the production so thoroughly, ensuring full
houses for ten weeks at the Lafayette Theatre and prompting a small
Broadway success and a national tour. Despite its unique nature, this

Macbeth exhibited some of the patronizing attitudes that black leaders had been denouncing: it was organized and planned by whites, treated derisively by some white critics, and attended by the liberal white bourgeois come slumming to Harlem. It was directed by a 20-year-old white boy who even played Macbeth in blackface for a week in Indianapolis when the lead actor became ill. More to the point, Welles' retelling of the story was hardly complementary to African-American culture, since his Haiti, run by an evil king, was thoroughly under the mastery of evil African magic. Emphasizing the supernatural in this way meant eliminating the possibility of progressive change from Shakespeare's tragedy. At the end Malcolm was legitimized by the voodoo chant of "All hail, Malcolm," followed by frantic drumming and sudden silence as Hecate stepped forward to repeat the anthem "Peace! The charm's wound up." Welles provided a pessimistic *da capo* ending, diametric to a Marxist reading, the cycle of evil beginning again with a fresh victim, hopelessly repeating ignorance and oppression – and in a black context.

What then were the Harlem audiences seeing when they admired the "Voodoo *Macbeth*"? The eye carries its own meaning, it seems, for Welles' revised theme finally did not matter, nor the somewhat arrogant circumstances of production. What mattered was the powerful novelty of a disenfranchised race appropriating the exemplary English dramatist. It wasn't so much Shakespeare's play that affected spectators, in other words, it was the realization that Shakespeare had been naturalized. The voodoo overtones were valued for their ability to exclude whites, for their suggestion of a power specific to blacks. One black critic cautioned whites to stay away entirely: "They could hardly be considered a sympathetic audience for what was being revealed. ... We therefore warn downtown visitors that this play is purely for Harlem consumption."[16] Indeed rumors of actual magic were rife. The Africans, who were tribal priests, had ritually sacrificed five black goats in the theatre at night for the drum skins. Upset by a reactionary and abusive review from Percy Hammond in the *Herald Tribune*, they had done voodoo on him; he was struck by pneumonia and died a few days after the opening.

Jack Carter, the impressive actor who initially played Macbeth, had blue eyes and did not look like a man of color; he was raised in a French château (his mother was a member of the original Floradora Sextet) and unaware of his racial origin or the "race problem" until he came to America in his teens. To an objective eye, this Macbeth was a white man. Harlem spectators saw him as black, however, because of their knowledge of his history and their opportunity to requisition the play. Thus the most powerful image of the production, an accomplished black professional actor playing one of Shakespeare's most famous white heroes, was not really visual at all.

Without doubt the harsh external events of 1936 added to the timeliness of the event. Before the opening, newspapers and newsreels had been dominated by the shocking images of nearly naked Ethiopian tribesmen fleeing before Mussolini's modern war machines, and thus fascism and its racial policies were very present for African-American audiences at the WPA *Macbeth*. The next year Welles focused more directly on European conditions with his famous *Julius Caesar* for the Mercury Theatre, a production much simpler in style and scope but more compelling in its visual metaphors. As we have seen, Schiller's political production in Warsaw in 1928 and Tröster's surrealist vision in Prague in 1936 established a new reference for the play; visually both of those productions worked by overlaying the modern fascist meaning on top of the ancient Roman setting. Welles took the motif one step further by making the time contemporary. When he struck Mussolini's image onto Shakespeare's Caesar he revised the play's commonly accepted value in the English-speaking world.

As *Macbeth* was reduced to a fable about the evil king of an evil island, *Julius Caesar* was condensed into a melodrama about the failure of liberalism caught between despotism and mob hysteria: *Death of a Dictator* was the subtitle. It was the moral character of Brutus that Welles found central, "the classical picture of the eternal, impotent, ineffectual, fumbling liberal," he wrote. "He's the bourgeois intellectual, who, under a modern dictatorship would be the first to be put up against a wall and shot."[17] To effect this restricted view of the protagonist he cut vast areas of the text, including Caesar's ghost and almost all of act 5, concentrating on the scenes with Caesar, Brutus, and the citizens of Rome. Most surprisingly he even omitted the moment of Brutus' suicide, jumping from his words "Hence! I will follow" in the last scene directly to Antony's "This was the noblest Roman of them all," providing a connection only with lights and music. Welles thus reduced the play to a fast-paced collage of striking images, 109 minutes in length. The stage was mostly bare and the costumes were modern, aspects which Welles claimed as Elizabethan. But theoretical recourse to the conditions of Shakespeare's stage was a common expedient for directors in the period and should not be taken too seriously. Though he avoided pictorialism and certainly accented swiftness, there was little about the performance that was Elizabethan in any sense; Welles relied not so much upon the actor on the open platform as he did upon directorial invention and brilliantly creative lighting. Even more than *Macbeth*, this was a cinematic production.

Caesar was played by Joseph Holland, who had an arresting resemblance to Mussolini, a fact much noticed by the press. His costume was military, as were those of most of the main characters; though without insignia, the allusion was clearly to contemporary Italy and Germany. The setting by Samuel Leve, consisting of simple platforms and steps, made the acting space flexible and irregular, but its most important feature was the exposed back wall of the stage, textured like brick and colored blood red. Against this actors would be picked out by directional light which manipulated mood and cast the production in the chiaroscuro of Nuremberg (illus. 66). Jean Rosenthal, at the beginning of a great career as a lighting designer, remembered Welles' instructions for "a very simple look based on the Nazi

66 *Julius Caesar* 1937 New York. D: Orson Welles. Des: Samuel Leve. L: Jean Rosenthal. P: Lucas Pritchard. Mercury Theatre production with the bare back wall and slanted lighting effect. Caesar (Joseph Holland) stands in Mussolini posture in 1.2, which was Welles' opening scene; Publius (Joseph Cotten) and Antony (George Coulouris) to the left.

67   *Julius Caesar* 1937 New York. The "Nuremberg" effect with up-lights and Expressionist shadows. George Coulouris as Antony addressing the crowd.

rallies at Nuremberg," the chief effect coming from up-lights placed in the floor.[18] With banners and flags draped behind Antony, the funeral scene was given an unmistakable reference, drawing upon one of the most powerful images of the century, one that haunts the world still (illus. 67).

Despite the intrusive scenography, Welles was not offering political testimony. Caesar was a fascist dictator, the mob an unthinking beast, and Brutus a pitiable failure: since Octavius was cut entirely, these unacceptable alternatives led only to Antony, little more than an eloquent opportunist, whose fascist associations with Caesar brought the action full cycle, in the same way that Hecate closed the voodoo *Macbeth*. As one New York newspaper put it, "Brutus' tragedy – the tragedy of liberals in fascist lands – is that he is outwitted by the Archdemagog Antony and loses his life." Welles' talent was not intellectual analysis but showmanship, and his *Julius Caesar* played upon the audience's generic fear of fascism in the same way as *Macbeth* exploited the black audience's need for cultural identity.

The best example of the production's use of the fascist mentality was in the scene with Cinna the poet. Little more than thirty lines in Shakespeare, Welles expanded it into the highlight of the production with inventions, borrowings from *Coriolanus*, and an offstage echoing chant. ("Come. Kill. Ho. Slay.") Norman Lloyd played Cinna as a bewildered street poet, his pockets stuffed with verses that he handed out to prove his identity, impotent against the hatred that Antony had unleashed. Sidney Whipple recorded that around Cinna "is a small ring of light, and in the shadows an ever-tightening, pincer-like mass movement," then suddenly "the jaws of the mob come together on him and he is swallowed up and rushed into black oblivion,"[19] gone like the nameless, unnumbered victims of der Führer or il Duce. In moments such as this Welles was as far from the marmoreal habits of the SMT or the Old Vic as he was from Victorian pictorialism. He had transfigured Shakespeare's play into a set of dangerous and swift images for a dangerous and swiftly changing time.

6 | *Reinventing the stage*

The most important development in Shakespearean scenography of the modern age occurred in mid-century and far from England, in a small town in Canada with no connection to Shakespeare save for the accident of its name. Until the creation of the Stratford Shakespearean Festival in Ontario the Elizabethan stage movement had been more notable for its failures than its successes. In England the architectural example of Poel had been debilitating and, with the notable exception of Barker's productions at the Savoy, attempts to modify existing Victorian theatres to accommodate an open stage had been marked by an acute awareness of the limitations of the enterprise. The proscenium theatre, which developed historically for opera and other musical spectacles, tends to force actors and audience into two separate rooms, separated by two barriers, by what Tyrone Guthrie called "a barrier of fire, which is the footlights, then a barrier of space called the orchestra."[1] It is nearly impossible to insert a thrust stage of any meaningful size into a rectangular auditorium without major alterations to the interior of the building. This restriction led Poel, never in a position to build his own theatre, to perform in unconventional spaces like lecture halls, and in one notable case, for his production of *Twelfth Night* in 1897, in the hall of the Middle Temple in London, the supposed site of its first performance.

Though there was no money for building an open stage in England, there had been no lack of ideas. Barker had led the theoretical fight for a national theatre in London, operating on repertory principles and performing the classics and the best modern works. Since Shakespeare and the Greeks would play an important role in such a venture, he argued forcefully in 1922 for a building with two theatres, one of which would be a flexible open stage, "a platform with footlights abolished and suitable entrances for Elizabethan plays," that could also convert "part of the stalls into an arena for a Greek chorus," and that even would allow performances in daylight. Settings for Shakespeare should be simple, and the auditorium arranged in a horseshoe shape so that spectators never quite lose sight of each other:

"the relations of the spectators among themselves are part of their united good relations to the play."[2]

When Shakespearean theatres were built between the wars, however, they were all seriously affected by antiquarianism. Nugent Monck, who had worked with Poel, built a small Elizabethan theatre in Norwich, the Maddermarket, where he staged reconstructed performances of small interest and smaller effect. A number of working models of the Fortune or the Globe were built in academic settings, especially in America, with questionable degrees of accuracy; and full-scale outdoor theatres were constructed in both Ashland, Oregon, and San Diego in 1935. Their Elizabethan tiring-house façades had "Ye Olde Oake Shakespeare Bunne Shoppe" inscribed within the architecture. The San Diego version was designed as a monument and did not begin to house productions regularly until 1949. Old Globe nostalgia, it seemed, was far from dead.

GUTHRIE AND MOISEIWITSCH

Tyrone Guthrie built a solid reputation as a Shakespearean interpreter between the wars, as well as a reputation for irreverence and showmanship, but his work in England made him increasingly restless about the limitations of the picture frame. At the Old Vic, where he directed sixteen Shakespeare plays between 1933 and 1939, a permanent setting by Welles Coates provided a modern architectural look and an enlarged forestage provided more intimacy, but they did little to alleviate the dominance of the proscenium between them. Guthrie brought young film stars to Shakespeare, including Charles Laughton and Laurence Olivier, and often managed to wrest enough money from Lilian Baylis to escape the usual Old Vic tattiness. Poel and Barker were his acknowledged authorities but there was no consistent visual style. A coronation year *Henry V* in 1937, for example, with Olivier and Jessica Tandy, was done with hanging banners and fanciful medieval costumes, and had considerable influence on Olivier's wartime film. *A Midsummer Night's Dream*, on the other hand, opened on Boxing Day the same year, designed by Oliver Messel as a rampant Victorian reminiscence – a pastiche of painted gauzes, flying fairies, Mendelssohn's music, and dancers trained in the Romantic manner by Ninette de Valois – in every way the opposite of Barker at the Savoy. Visually the most arresting of the Guthrie Old Vic productions was Alec Guinness' *Hamlet* of 1938, a vision of an Edwardian formal court threatened by modern military power, recalling Jessner's production of 1926. Roger

Furse gave the Ghost full European battle dress, complete with greatcoat, boots, metal helmet and front pack; the women were in long gowns; Ophelia's funeral was marked by dripping umbrellas and wet slickers over court costumes.

But it was Olivier's famous Oedipal *Hamlet* of the previous year that accidentally set Guthrie's course towards the open stage. The Old Vic company had traveled to Denmark for a performance in the courtyard of Elsinore Castle; a half-hour before the elegant opening night rain was coming down in what Guthrie called "bellropes," and a hasty removal to the ballroom of a hotel seemed preferable to cancellation. The story has been told often: the improvised thrust stage, the improvised blocking, and the proximity to the audience made the play fresh and unforgettable beyond the experience of any of the participants. The director himself understood that much of the excitement was the result of actors and spectators simply pulling together to surmount adversity. But he also saw that the enforced intimacy had a benefit for Shakespeare that was "more logical, satisfactory and effective" (Guthrie 190–2) than the arrangement of a proscenium theatre.

Guthrie's first real chance to use an Elizabethan design came in 1948 and not with Shakespeare. For the second Edinburgh Festival he had been asked to present a classic Scottish play and had chosen David Lyndsay's *Aine Satire of the Thrie Estaites*, an early sixteenth-century morality of little distinction, selected chiefly because "scene after scene seemed absolutely unplayable on the proscenium stage, almost meaningless in terms of 'dramatic illusion'" (Guthrie 306). Tanya Moiseiwitsch, an English designer he had worked with two or three times before, covered the center of the Assembly Hall of the Church of Scotland with a thrust stage: a narrow acting space on a platform was backed by a structure with an upper level and curtained recesses below. Surprisingly this unknown script became the hit of the festival. Guthrie had no doubt that the configuration was the chief cause of the immense triumph; seated around three sides of the stage, the audience, he wrote, "focused upon the actors in the brightly lit acting area, but the background was of the dimly lit rows of people similarly focused on the actors" (311). The event, in other words, was marked not by the usual standards of theatrical success but by the conspicuously shared activity of player and playgoer. Illusion – at least pictorial illusion as normally understood – was gone, and something more valuable had been gained: the spectator became "a participant in a ritual."

Without question the intensity of the audience experience at such a performance is increased by the temporary nature of the event, as it had been for the Elsinore *Hamlet*. The commercial theatre presents plays as consumable commodities, repeatable night after night for as long as the appetite lasts; it is "culinary theatre," in Brecht's deathless phrase. Festival theatre, from the music drama of ancient Athens to the music drama of modern Bayreuth, signifies instead the allure of the seasonal, emphasizing the particularity of live performance by limiting the opportunity for viewing. The commercial urban theatre, competing for time and attention in a dense economy, may be more suited to the architecture of the proscenium: the events on stage, framed by intense illumination and the separating arch, are more clearly distinct from the audience, more clearly purchased entertainment like movies or television, those mechanically reproduced events which are, theoretically at least, endlessly reproducible. Festival theatre, which has historically tended to gather spectators in patterns based on the circle, normally wishes to accent the shared texture of our lives in a temporally limited environment, bringing a disparate population together in a special place. There is of course a vast cultural difference between an ancient festival that has grown over centuries out of a religious belief, like that of Athens or of the medieval cathedral cities, and a modern one which has been manufactured to celebrate the artistic accomplishments of Shakespeare or Mozart. The first type creates new works to validate or question the shared assumptions of the population; the second commodifies the classics as a form of self-justification. But ultimately the distinction may be less important than the fact that both types encourage mutuality between actors and audience.

After the Edinburgh venture Guthrie and Moiseiwitsch were faced with the same difficulty that most Elizabethanists had faced before them, the problem of edifice. In 1949 they worked at Stratford for a production of *Henry VIII*, with Anthony Quayle in the title role, that attempted to take advantage of what they had learned about the open stage. The set was a frank compromise, integrating an Elizabethan stage with the picture frame tradition. An apron extension, 4.5 meters deep, was thrust into the pit of the SMT. On the regular stage a gallery and inner stage were built to one side, surrounded by multilevel acting spaces, a variety of entrances, changeable units, and swirling banners (illus. 68). It was a set to move in, and move quickly in – an almost complete text was taken at Guthrie's characteristic rapid pace. Detailed, richly colored costumes accented the reality and vitality of the play's fiction, with the shape and tones of Holbein; Michael Langham called it "a teeming, sweaty vision of a period of history."[3]

68 *Henry VIII* 1949 Stratford. D: Tyrone Guthrie. Des: Tanya Moiseiwitsch. P:
Angus McBean. The trial scene: Anthony Quayle as Henry on throne at left, Diana
Wynyard as Katherine in the dock, Harry Andrews as Wolsey at right. A grand
spectacle placed inside a mock-Elizabethan form, with actors placed in a large circle
surrounding the Queen. Note the amount of visual redundancy used to create the
sense of period, similar to Kean's method.

While Guthrie was busy elsewhere, Moiseiwitsch worked with Quayle
for the Festival of Britain production of the *Richard II* tetralogy, the first
time the plays had been seen together at the SMT since Frank Benson's
performances in 1905. She designed a unit set for the cycle that was flexible
and useful but that continued to demonstrate the irreducible dilemma of the
proscenium theatre for Shakespeare. A raised pavilion in the center had a
deep inner area and an upper level; a platform for the tavern was stage left,
and the throne, the first thing to be lit for each play, remained on stage right
continually (Leiter 575–7). In *Henry V* the basic structure was covered by a
circular tent for the English camp scenes, and sumptuous period costumes
changed the rough visual quality. The most notable feature of the design,
however, was the attempt to disguise the proscenium with billowing
curtains at the top and sides of the arch (illus. 69). While these hangings
muffled the edges of the picture frame, they did nothing to alter the receding
perspective placed on the stage proper. Seventy years of Elizabethan

69 *Richard II* 1951 Stratford. D: Anthony Quayle. Des: Tanya Moiseiwitsch (assisted by Alix Stone). P: Keith Ball. A unit set for four history plays. Rough-hewn timbers and a basic Elizabethan configuration were inserted inside the proscenium, which was softened by the flown hangings.

experiment had given designers great insight into the requirements of a remodeled Shakespearean stage but, for all her good intentions, in essential ways Moiseiwitsch's unit set in 1951 was little different from Poel's "four-poster" set for *Measure for Measure* in 1893. Both were pictures of an Elizabethan stage rather than the thing itself.

THE OTHER STRATFORD

"Will you come to Canada and give advice? We want to start a Shakespeare festival in Stratford, Ontario." So went the telephone call that changed the shape of the Shakespearean theatre. It was Tom Patterson on the line, a Canadian journalist who had been captivated by opera in Italy and theatre in England during the war and wanted to bring something of equal quality to his hometown. Guthrie went, advised, and within a year had presented two plays in a tent theatre designed by Moiseiwitsch that incorporated most of the workable features of the Elizabethan stage.

The international success that the Stratford Festival has achieved since

1953 tends to obscure the excessive uncertainty of its beginning. Guthrie's enthusiasm and impetuosity combined well with the naivety of the local organizers; what would have been treated as impossible in a more sophisticated or established theatrical environment seemed achievable and right in Ontario. The financial setbacks, construction delays, and the dangers of the tent in high wind have become part of the mythos of the place and of theatre history. But above all, Guthrie and Moiseiwitsch made two elementary architectural decisions that determined the values of the Festival. The first was that while the stage would conform "to the conventions of the Elizabethan theatre in practicalities, it should not present a pseudo-Elizabethan appearance. We were determined to eschew *Ye Olde*."[4] The second related to the auditorium, where the seating arrangement was indebted more to ancient Epidauros than to any theatre in sixteenth- or seventeenth-century London. The acting space was placed directly in the middle of the tent, with the audience arranged in a 220 degree arc around it, looking down at the platform. The stage was literally as well as figuratively the center of Guthrie's Shakespeare project.

The organizers at first wanted to perform outdoors, which Guthrie discouraged. As there was no suitable building in Stratford and no time or money to construct a new one, a tent was the interim result. It was an extremely fortuitous convenience, for it allowed Moiseiwitsch to concentrate on the essential fixture of theatre architecture, the shape of the stage and its orientation to the audience. The tent also allowed room for experiment; since the permanent theatre was not started for another three years, there would be opportunity to correct mistakes, unlike the disastrous case of the SMT. The original stage of 1953 (illus. 70) set the course for the enterprise. Though the wall unit at the rear of the stage would undergo modifications, it has always been treated functionally rather than decoratively – a set of plain wooden panels with doors, windows, and stairs. The stage balcony has also been altered, especially in the number of columns that support it, but today it is approximate to the original conception and still looks a bit like the prow of a ship. The permanent house added a second bank of 858 seats in a balcony, which permitted a capacity of 2,258. That would be a huge number in an end-stage theatre, acceptable for grand opera but out of keeping with modern notions of acting for drama. At Stratford, however, the extended semicircle insured that no seat would be farther than 20 meters from the stage. In a witty bow to its origin, the exterior roof of the new building was designed to suggest a tent.

Thus Guthrie and Moiseiwitsch thought the open stage virtuous not for

70   The tent being raised for the first time over the stage, Stratford, Ontario, 27
June 1953. Stage designed by Tanya Moiseiwitsch in collaboration with Tyrone
Guthrie. The seating was in a single bank of 220 degrees, and two vomitoria
came through the house for actors' entrances. Despite subsequent changes to
the backdrop, the polygonal open stage has remained unaltered, approximately
9 by 11 meters in size, and the basic shape of the auditorium has been maintained.
P: Peter Smith.

Poel's reasons but for Granville Barker's. It was the bare platform that
mattered, not Tudor trappings; even more, the surrounding, non-illusory
awareness of the spectators mattered. There was never any thought of
replicating the conditions of the Globe in lighting, seating, or decoration.
Though the Elizabethan stage was its official model, in theory and in
construction the scheme reached back to theatre experiments of the early
century: Appia at Hellerau, Reinhardt at the Grosses Schauspielhaus,

Copeau at the Vieux-Colombier. All were architectural attempts to create what Richard and Helen Leacroft (141) call the "spiritual unity of actors and audience," privileging the human ludic relationship over solely aesthetic considerations. Staging and design for Shakespeare would follow from an architectural principle. Since the actors were more or less in the middle of the audience, and since there would be no scenic point of view shared by all spectators, color and visual variety would come primarily from costumes, accessories, and hand props. The other Stratford would of necessity require an actor-centered scenography.

For the opening season in 1953 Guthrie chose a company of Canadian actors led by two imported stars, Alec Guinness and Irene Worth. *Richard III* put Guinness center stage in a piece with a "strong thread of melodrama," as Guthrie wrote (320), while *All's Well That Ends Well* emphasized the ensemble and contrasted significantly in tone. Moreover, the program showed off the Stratford theatre in contrasting visual ways, using rich period costumes for the first play and modern dress for the second. Guinness' fame insured the necessary level of attention, especially from the New York critics, though his performances were not exceptional. He was a handsome, considered, psychological Richard, with one drooping eye and a contorted walk, not quite in keeping with Guthrie's large-scale, ritualistic treatment of the play. The director and designer made use of every opportunity of the new stage they could think of, clearly breaking in the machine. The citizens stormed on aloft; soldiers ran up through the vomitoria, shocking the spectators within touching distance; Richard wooed Lady Anne in the light of tapers accompanying Henry VI's corpse. In a magnificent scene the ghosts haunting Richard the night before the battle (5.3) appeared one by one from traps in the platform. The coronation was the climax of the visual experiment, with giant crosses and rich costumes making a grand show, yet on a human scale and in the round. Moiseiwitsch's master touch of actor-centered spectacle was Richard's dark red velvet robe, which trailed some 8 meters behind him (illus. 71).

All's Well was contemporary in setting, dominated by the cool black and white of morning coats and evening tails at the King's court. Formal dress for men is less specific in overtone than workday clothing, and thus tends not to force the play into the here and now; but the military uniforms, tropical Royal Army khaki and black berets, pointedly took their reference from the Second World War. The women in the court wore vivid ball-gowns; Helena distinctly stood out from the others, first in white as she chose her husband (illus. 72), then in an impressive yellow gown in the final scene. The swirl and movement of both productions, which excited audiences and was noted often by critics, came from Guthrie's blocking. He discovered immediately that at Stratford it would be necessary for actors to shift positions often, both to open their faces to different sections of the house and to prevent one actor from masking another for more than a few moments. Guthrie's productions tended to be dancelike whenever a small group or a larger crowd was on stage, striving to make a virtue out of the necessity imposed by the 220 degree seating. They often had a restless quality, acceptable and even desirable in many comic or ceremonial scenes but occasionally distracting in the quiet or intense moments that occur regularly in Shakespeare.

As a director Guthrie was criticized throughout his career for a tendency to the frivolous. He was rarely superficial but, like Reinhardt, he could easily

71 *Richard III* 1953 Stratford, Ontario. D: Tyrone Guthrie. Des: Tanya Moiseiwitsch. P: Peter Smith. The opening production in the Festival tent. Alec Guinness mounts the throne in the coronation scene, in a dress rehearsal. Note the movie cameraman in action at the lower left of the picture.

become more interested in the showy aspects of production than in the deeper underpinnings of the play. Respect for the Shakespearean text, which was the source of his desire for the open stage, did not imply for him conventional fidelity. The best and the worst of his visual habits were seen in *The Taming of the Shrew* in the second season, which was treated as a wild-west medicine show at the turn of the century. Its eclectic costumes and manners derived from vaudeville pranks and pratfalls, the general effect being dependent on fast-paced comic routines. To Guthrie the script was a farce, nothing more. The characters in the Induction wore mackintoshes and hunting boots and carried modern rifles; Sly, a dirty American hobo, remained on stage to watch the antics of the strolling players, which included a cancan by Edwardian chambermaids performed to hoedown music (Leiter 668). Kate and Petruchio fell obviously in love at first sight, so that even the central action became a kind of game, a form of loveplay

72 *All's Well That Ends Well* 1953 Stratford, Ontario. D: Tyrone Guthrie. Des: Tanya Moiseiwitsch. P: Peter Smith. Alec Guinness as the King of France and Irene Worth as Helena in the "ballroom" scene (2.3), in the Festival tent. The actor placement here is indicative of Guthrie's circular staging.

73 *The Taming of the Shrew* 1954 Stratford, Ontario. D: Tyrone Guthrie. Des: Tanya Moiseiwitsch. P: Peter Smith. William Needles (Petruchio) whoops it up in the Festival tent.

postponing an inevitable end. William Needles, a hesitant and unlikely Petruchio in cowpoke gear and black hornrims, arrived on a vaudeville horse, the jeans and sneakers of its two-man team visible underneath (illus. 73).

The contributions of Guthrie and Moiseiwitsch to stage architecture are obvious and undeniable. The Tyrone Guthrie Theatre in Minneapolis, which they built together in 1963, used the same spatial concepts and profited by their Canadian experience. The modified open stages of the Chichester Festival Theatre (1962) and the Sheffield Crucible Theatre (1971) were constructed under their direct influence; the Olivier stage at the National in London (1976), and the series of remodelings of the Royal Shakespeare Theatre from 1960 onwards, were also made with the Ontario image in mind. In the United States, where a movement to arena staging was already underway, Guthrie's example affected a number of buildings in the 1960s, from New York to Los Angeles. Most of these theatres were designed to focus on classic drama, with the works of Shakespeare important or even central to the enterprise; more modern plays, the thinking ran, even those written for the proscenium, would profit from the increased audience involvement. Whether the Guthrie model works for all scripts and all styles is open to question. Certainly some directors and designers have felt otherwise, even with Shakespeare, as we will see in the last chapter; and many actors in Ontario have found it difficult to engage the entire house from any position other than at the base of the thrust.

Yet in reinventing the stage for Shakespeare, Guthrie and Moiseiwitsch also made a significant contribution to general scenographic usage. Building on the example of Motley, Moiseiwitsch's simple sets, colorful costumes, actor-controlled props, and sculpted light created a visual dimension that was interested more in the player than in the scene. Instead of an environment for fictive illusion she made a dynamic space for overt performance. Lacking the shared visual frame of the proscenium, the audience at the Canadian Stratford is invited to consider the play rather than be swept away by it. As Berners Jackson wrote, the spectators are part of the environment of the performance, watching "an elaborate make-believe, cunningly constructed and assiduously pursued, that, without pretending to be reality, interprets and illuminates reality."[5] The sight of others engaged in the same act of watching, replicating the viewers' contemporary manners and clothes, thoroughly conditions the visual experience. Modern dress on stage, or eclectic stylization, or a setting wrenched into a different period – none of these strategies seems especially eccentric, since the dominant visual idiom is established by the open stage architecture itself. The designer's work there is not to sculpt or paint a world for the play but to outline a site for costumed actors to move in.

PETER BROOK AND THE IMAGE

The second major visual influence on postwar Shakespearean performance was based on a notion of the text similar to Guthrie's, but grew out of modernism rather than Elizabethanism. Peter Brook has made it his life-long business to apply innovative and avant-garde methods to the mainstream theatres, asking his audiences to rethink classic plays in terms of contemporary life and transcendent images. In this regard he has followed central and eastern European traditions with Shakespeare more than those of Britain. While some commentators have condemned his work as an extreme example of the excesses of director's theatre, his Shakespeare productions at Stratford in Warwickshire have had undeniable impact on subsequent critical and theatrical observance.

Unlike many of his colleagues, Brook has frequently explained his premises and his intentions with great conviction and clarity. An early essay, "Style in Shakespearean Production," argued for the freedom of the director to redraw Shakespeare according to the demands of the modern world, insisting that only by reinterpretation can we hope to achieve fidelity to the imaginative jurisdiction of the text. Whatever eternal qualities Shakespeare's plays may possess, Brook insisted that in the theatre the time is always now:

When Garrick played *Romeo and Juliet* in knee-breeches, he was *right*; when Kean staged *The Winter's Tale* with a hundred Persian pot-carriers, he was *right*; when Tree staged Shakespeare with all the resources of His Majesty's, he was *right*; when Craig staged his reaction to this he was *right* too. Each was justified in its own time; each would be outrageous out of it. A production is only correct at the moment of its correctness, and only good at the moment of its success.[6]

The Empty Space, Brook's much-read manifesto, describes how "the Deadly Theatre" continually oppressed English production of Shakespeare by taking the opposite view, especially at the SMT:

When I first went to Stratford in 1945 every conceivable value was buried in deadly sentimentality and complacent worthiness – a traditionalism approved largely by town, scholar and press. It needed the boldness of a very extraordinary old gentleman, Sir Barry Jackson, to throw all this out of the window and so make a true search for values possible once more. (46)

A true search for values: that sums up Brook's notion of the obligation of the director. He believes in the existence of values in drama, and believes that they inhere in the text; and he passionately believes in the importance of searching.

In 1944 Sir Archie was succeeded on the Board of Governors of the SMT by his son Fordham Flower, who soon set about dismantling the Victorian traditions that had ruled since 1879. Fordham's organizational reforms, which ultimately permitted the creation of the RSC under Peter Hall, led him to appoint Barry Jackson as director after the war, with a brief to revitalize the moribund conditions of the theatre. Peter Brook, then twenty years old and fresh from Oxford, came along; his *Love's Labour's Lost* opened in April of 1946 with the almost unknown Paul Scofield as Don Armado. Speaight (242) tells us that Brook had recently seen the play in Paris, "in a translation where echoes of Marivaux and Musset, and even an

74 *Love's Labour's Lost* 1946 Stratford. D: Peter Brook. Des: Reginald Leefe. P: Angus McBean. Valerie Taylor as the Princess and Ruth Lodge as Rosaline (on steps) in Brook's "Watteauesque" version at the SMT. Note the *commedia* clown on the steps, a mute figure in whiteface who accompanied the Princess.

epigram from Voltaire on the lips of Moth, seemed in no way out of place." Advancing this idea into the realm of the visual, Brook based his production on Watteau's paintings, especially *The Age of Gold*, because he found the melancholy of their "autumn springtime" transferable to the tone of the play (Brook 1987: 11). The style of Watteau's dresses, Brook wrote in his essay on Shakespearean production, "with its broad, undecorated expanses of billowing satin seemed the ideal visual correlative of the essential sweet-sad mood of this play." In a sense he offered a prototype of what would become his general method: since the Euphuistic foundation of the play has little or no meaning for a modern audience, the director searched for a scenographic equivalent, a "visual correlative," that would cut across the centuries. Some of that quality appears rather pictorial in the photographs, especially in the garden scene (illus. 74), where the new image for the play still relied on the old methods of wing pieces and cutout teaser curtains.

Brook's *Romeo and Juliet* in 1947 was another matter, and was vigorously attacked for its perverse reading and "obtrusive" scenery.[7] Noting the negative reactions, Trewin (205) adds that it "would not have been strange in 1964." Brook went a long way in refining his approach, focusing more

75 *Romeo and Juliet* 1947 Stratford. D: Peter Brook. Des: Rolf Gérard. P: Angus McBean. The Prince (Robert Harris) in the first scene, in the middle of sandcastle set. The octagon shape extended well beyond the proscenium. Much of the visual power came from hot lights on the bare floor and cyclorama.

clearly on a central idea expressed visually. He saw the play chiefly in terms of "mad blood" and "hot days," just as Franco Zeffirelli would a generation later, so Rolf Gérard's scenography was founded in the textual images of Verona as hot, dusty, and mad. The main set was an octagon surrounded by very small crenelated towers and walls like sand castles, in front and at the rear of the stage, which suggested a toy theatre or a fairytale kingdom (illus. 75). The floor was a sand-red cloth and, together with the estranging boundary towers, made the stage blaze with heat and light. Other settings were very simple – a flown canopy, a white wall for the balcony, a high platform at the top of an open marble stairway for Juliet's bedroom. Gérard's minimalism achieved a sense of dislocation and a concentration on the lovers' story, but did so experimentally. The original plan used much greater detail; Brook has written that he and the designer started throwing out scenery at the dress rehearsal until "gradually we came down to an empty orange arena, a few sticks – and the wings were full of elaborate and expensive discarded units." This is a powerfully effective method, though not one calculated to make the management happy.

"For me, the theatre always begins with an image," Brook wrote in the same source. "If I find this image through the design, I know how to continue with the production. If I go into rehearsal with a nagging sense

that the set is not right, I know that I will never find my way out again."[8]
It is clear that he began his directing career believing the theatre to be an
iconographic art. In 1974 he explicitly noted that when he was young he
thought the job of the director was to have a vision of the play and to
"express" it, in the same way that a film director "shows his pictures to the
world." Brook's notions about the visual are so central to postwar
Shakespeare that they deserve extended quotation:

I had a set of images in mind which I wanted to bring to life, just like making a film.
So *Love's Labour's Lost* was a very visual, very romantic set of stage pictures. And
I remember that from then all the way through to *Measure for Measure* my conviction
was that the director's job, having found an affinity between himself and play, was
to find the images that he believed in and through them make the play live for a
contemporary audience. In an image-conscious time, I believed that designing and
directing to be inseparable. A good industrial designer has to sense just what the
shapes are for a particular moment, and therefore he produces the right car body,
and so on. In exactly the same way I understood that a director studies deeply, is as
in tune with the play as he can be, but that his real work is the making of a new set
of images for it.   (Brook 1987: 78)

Designing and directing were indeed inseparable for most of his
productions. Like Craig or Leon Schiller, Brook insured that the look of his
Shakespeare radiated the interpretive stance, sometimes extending his
authority to the execution of the image as well as its conception. "In human
terms, my closest relationships have been with designers," he once
admitted; "nothing makes me happier than to take a piece of cardboard and
begin to fold and tear it into a set myself."[9] His productions at the SMT and
in London with John Gielgud in the major roles – including *Measure for
Measure* in 1950, *The Winter's Tale* in 1951, and *The Tempest* in 1957 – fall into
this category, where the "resuscitation" of the play progressed from
making a new set of images for it.

Titus Andronicus in 1955 capped Brook's work with undervalued texts,
and marked the start of scholarly and theatrical interest in a play which had
never before been seen at Stratford. Brook designed a structure of plain
wood panels mounted in monumental fashion, its square pillars capable of
different positions for new scenes (illus. 76). Laurence Olivier's performance
was the most remarkable aspect of the production, investing Titus with
tragic dignity and power, bringing him close to Lear, but in terms of image
it was the stylization of violence that was notable. Brook composed *musique
concrète* that supported the clash of primitive forces and, like his scenography,
rendered it abstract. He was convinced that a realistic portrayal of the blood-

76 *Titus Andronicus* 1955 Stratford. D: Peter Brook. Des: Brook with Michael
Northen, Desmond Heeley, and William Blezard. P: Angus McBean. The final
moment, with Anthony Quayle as Aaron at the Thyestian feast. Lucius and Marcus
(Michael Denison and Alan Webb) in an inset above; Laurence Olivier (Titus),
Vivien Leigh (Lavinia), Maxine Audley (Tamora), and Frank Thring (Saturnius)
dead at the table.

77 *Titus Andronicus* 1955 Stratford. P: Angus McBean. Brook's stylized horror:
Vivien Leigh as Lavinia after the rape (2.4).

and-guts action would underline the melodrama so that a modern audience
could not take the play seriously – in its production at the Old Vic in 1923,
the first in Britain since the eighteenth century, the unremitting murders
provoked nothing but laughter.

He devised a method that conveyed the physical horrors by elegant and
even beautiful estrangements. Anthony Quayle's portrayal of Aaron (see
illus. 4) provided one indication, but the chief example was the unforgettable
apparition of Lavinia after her rape and mutilation, in front of an abstract
forest, with scarlet and white streamers flowing from her mouth and wrists
(illus. 77). Brook here used a visual metaphor to effect a heightened dramatic
moment the way a lovely operatic aria might be used to convey a character's
pain; Lavinia's entrance was accompanied by harp music. The costumes,
severely limited in color, gradually moved towards the universal red of dried
blood. The immediacy of the terror was greatly reduced, and thus it can be
argued that the play's essence was not fully conveyed, but Brook's almost
Asian symbolism welcomed the audience into its unfamiliar spirit,
transforming it into a piece of visual and performative virtuosity. As he told
Sally Beauman (224), "*Titus Andronicus* was a *show*; it descended in an

unbroken line from the work of Komisarjevsky." Kenneth Tynan wrote in 1954, "we are living at the end of the era of the word: soon the quicker responses of the eye may be officially paramount. Brook … is the prophet of that unborn time, when to show images will be more than to tell in phrases."[10]

The concern with image reached its climax a few years later in Brook's most controversial work. *Titus* had toured in Europe in 1957; there it "touched audiences directly," he wrote, "because we had tapped in it a ritual of bloodshed which was recognized as true" (Brook 1968: 47). In Warsaw it was seen by the critic Jan Kott, who read the production as a reflection of the postwar absurdist world. "*Titus Andronicus* has revealed to me a Shakespeare I dreamed of but have never before seen on the stage," Kott wrote.[11] His notice was reprinted in some editions of *Shakespeare Our Contemporary*; more importantly, that book contains an essay entitled "King Lear or Endgame," which Brook read in French early in 1962 while discussing with its author a developing concept for *Lear*. Kott situates Shakespeare's tragedy in the entropic universe of Samuel Beckett, a metaphorical and theatrical place made up of absences. In *Endgame* (first produced in Paris in 1957) disintegration and closure are most significant, thematically and visually; "there are no more sugar plums," in Clov's icy litany, no more bicycle wheels, pain killers, coffins, no more people. Kott found in this denuded world an appropriate moral landscape for *Lear*, which itself is made to stand as *theatrum mundi*:

> When we are born, we cry that we are come
> To this great stage of fools.

Though he doesn't say so, Kott actually uses as his model for the comparison of Shakespeare to Beckett the Christian iconography of hell. Much of what appears as chaos in *Lear* can be read according to the remorseless logic of pain, found in European culture since the twelfth century in the extensive literature and art of damnation.[12] Beckett's emphasis on torture, on the absolute cohesion of a closed system, deriving from the war and from the postwar conditions of Europe, becomes in Kott's essay a meditation on the ironies and unfathomable cruelties in Shakespeare's play: Nagg and Nell as flies to their wanton boy. As Brook wrote a few years later, "Kott is undoubtedly the only writer on Elizabethan matters who assumes without question that every one of his readers will at some point or other have been woken by the police in the middle of the night" (Brook 1987: 44).

To achieve this vision Brook severely limited *King Lear*'s sprawling implications, achieving intensity by restricted focus. His cuts are well known and much discussed. The Gentleman's report on Cordelia's sorrow (4.3), Lear's passionate happiness in "He that parts us shall bring a brand from heaven / And fire us hence like foxes" (5.3), Edmund's repenting his order for the execution of the King and his daughter ("some good I mean to do, / Despite of mine own nature") – all had to go. Following the Folio, Brook omitted the dialogue of the two servants who sympathize with Gloucester after his blinding, and agree to help him: but, most notoriously, the director left them onstage, brought the house lights up as the audience was preparing for intermission, then had the servants push and shove the old man as he bumped into them, finally leaving him to grope off alone, smelling his way to Dover. From Nahum Tate to A. C. Bradley the blinding of Gloucester was thought problematic at best; "an act too horrid to be endured in dramatick exhibition," said Dr Johnson. Lilian Baylis concurred, and insisted that intermission at the Old Vic always take place before the blinding scene, so that the squeamish could remain in the coffee bar until it was over.[13] Shakespearean representation had traveled a long way by 1962, to reach the point where the horror of *King Lear* was no longer considered optional, or gratuitous.

Brook designed the production himself, accenting minimalist symbol that derived from Beckett: "*Lear* for me is the prime example of the Theatre of the Absurd, from which everything in good modern drama has been drawn." Whereas a bad play needs decoration to disguise its poverty, "with *Lear*, on the contrary, one has to withdraw everything possible" (Brook 1987: 89). Kott reports that whenever they discussed the play Brook had "his hands on a design of the set. For Peter the production was first of all to be planned in the set."[14] He began by designing a unit set in rusty iron with complicated bridges and stairways. "One night, I realized that this wonderful toy was absolutely useless" (12), so out it went. While not completely bare, the stage that remained was made into a signifier of emptiness. Only essential props, hewn from rough wood and metal, stood in front of the huge flats that dominated the background. Placed at 45 degree angles to the proscenium, one displayed a rectangle, the other a trestle figure that looked a little like a Chinese ideogram. Trewin (248) called them "tall, coarse-textured, off-white screens" against which "various rusted metal shapes" were positioned; "at the last we were left with an empty stage and the rigour of the tragedy." Charles Marowitz, who acted as Brook's assistant, noted that the design intended to suggest a world in a "constant state of decomposition"; the costumes, mostly of leather, were "textured to

78   *King Lear* 1962 Stratford. D and Des: Peter Brook (C in collaboration with
Kegan Smith). P: Angus McBean. Albany (Peter Jeffrey) and Goneril (Irene Worth)
amid the wreckage of 1.4, with one of the screens behind them.

suggest long and hard wear." After Lear's knights spent their anger in
Albany's palace, the upturned tables and implements prefigured the larger
disintegration about to occur (illus. 78). Kott thought that Brook's major
achievement was "the disintegration of the stage plateau. By the end of the
performance the surface of the stage had been eroded as after an
earthquake."

For the storm scenes Brook lowered three rusty thunder sheets from the
flies, which manufactured storm noises before the audience's gaze. They
distanced the storm because of their blatant artificiality, yet brought its
representation on stage powerfully: the actors crouched before them, and
were driven across the stage by their terrifying vibrations. The sounds of the
storm, in other words, became visible, became part of the scenography; the
physical presence of the thunder sheets made the storm more "real" than
recorded noises. Brook looked for essences in the costumes as well; they did
not make a temporal statement, focusing instead on defining character. Lear,
for example, began in a rich robe which was designed solely to distinguish
him as king; later he changed to leather and boots, and on the heath was in
rags (illus. 79). Brook believed that the clarity of the production was the

79 *King Lear* 1962 Stratford. P: Gordon Goode. The Beckettian meeting at Dover (4.6). Paul Scofield as Lear, Alan Webb as Gloucester, Brian Murray as Edgar.

result of restricting fully detailed costumes to the eight or nine major characters, "the number one can normally focus on in a modern play," and giving the rest undistinguished clothes. When thirty or forty actors are dressed in an elaborate manner in Shakespeare, "the eye is blurred and the plot becomes hard to follow" (Brook 1987: 90).

It is typical of Brook to assume a relationship between the eye and the plot. Speaking of why he designed *Lear* himself, he noted the danger of relying on another artist to solve visual problems when the director is still struggling to find the spirit of the play. "If you are doing it yourself, it means that over a long period of time your imagery and your staging evolve together" (Brook 1987: 91). In this case the evolution created a production visually eclectic and morally neutral, halfway between barbarism and the richness suggested by the play's language. Sympathy and especially sentiment were set aside to investigate an image of the implacable universe. Paul Scofield strove for the man behind the emblem, and gave an angry, unheroic portrayal; in the first act, at least, it was as easy to see Goneril's point of view as her father's. "Instead of assuming that Lear is right, and therefore pitiable, we are forced to make judgments – to decide between his claims and those of his kin," Tynan wrote in *The Observer* (11 Nov. 1962). Like Beckett, then, Brook used a metaphoric procedure to convey the most painful reality. It was a misanthropic vision, and curiously uncommitted in its politics, yet intensely relevant to postwar Europe where the nightmares of the absurd continued to be enacted and where, through Jan Kott, the vision had its source. On a tour to the United States, Brook thought that the production did not connect with audiences more remote from its themes of absence and loss (Brook 1968: 21–3); it had been vastly different in eastern Europe, and "the best performances lay between Budapest and Moscow."

JOHN BURY AND PETER HALL

Aside from Brook's work, the SMT in the 1950s was in transition. Under the direction of Anthony Quayle and Glen Byam Shaw the accent was on stars, beautiful production, and the theme of universal order. There were a number of notable performances, especially from Olivier, Gielgud, and Ralph Richardson, but the look of things was glossy, perfectly suited for the photographs of Angus McBean. It would have been impossible to predict Brook's *Lear* from Shaw's production in 1959, with Charles Laughton in the lead, designed by Motley in a most graceful, delicate, and purified manner. In general British theatre was luxuriating in postwar excess rather than postwar angst, prompted by an insular school of designers that included Rex Whistler, Cecil Beaton, and Oliver Messel, all of whom firmly rejected modernism.[15] Mariano Andreu's pictorial designs for Gielgud's *Much Ado*, which opened at the SMT in 1949 and was revived in London and on tour for the next decade, are good examples from the Shakespeare stage. Excess tempted modernist designers as well; it became febrile in the work of Loudon Sainthill, whose overripe fantasies were displayed in *The Tempest* in 1951 (illus. 80). Using outcrops that looked like dripped sand castles, the scenography was busy in the extreme, halfway between Surrealism and a Jacobean masque.

Though Peter Hall would preside over a transformation of Shakespearean production at Stratford, much of his early work there was with Lila de Nobili, an Italian painter who was part of the same neoromantic tradition. Their 1957 *Cymbeline* treated the play as a fairytale of misty shapes; the scenery may lie heavily on stage, said *The Times* (3 July 1957), but is intended "to create a haze of colour in the mind" so that "the wildest of romantic tales will appear true." They worked together for *Twelfth Night* the following year, set at the court of Charles II, where Nobili used burnished

80   *The Tempest* 1951 Stratford. D: Michael Benthall. Des: Loudon Sainthill. P: Angus McBean. Alan Badel as Ariel in 4.3, amid surreal excess.

russets and golds to accent the melancholy strain. *A Midsummer Night's Dream* of 1959, with Laughton as Bottom, made intelligent use of a unit set of a Jacobean double staircase (color pl. 7). Again Nobili relied on a limited palette of earth tones and flowers, accented by rushes on the floor. Photographic projections of trees became the backdrop for the scenes in the wood, and the "inner stage" served as Titania's bower. The director stressed that the entire play was a wedding gift, and the set implied that its performance was occurring in the great hall of a nobleman.

The same year Olivier gave a mighty performance in Hall's *Coriolanus*, in an intriguing unit set by the Russian-American Boris Aronson, his first Shakespearean design, which began to suggest the future course for the theatre. Aronson had studied with Alexandra Exter in Moscow and had assisted her in designing *Romeo and Juliet* for Tairov in 1921.[16] His unit set for *Coriolanus* seemed made of metal and stone, suggesting a powerful culture just rising from primitivism: "bodeful and semi-Incaic splendour," said Alan Pryce-Jones. A doorway above resembled the gates of a city, and a second one below, with metal teeth at the joint, might have opened onto the bowels of the earth (illus. 81). In an unforgettable moment, Olivier fell from the top platform to his death, only to be caught at the last second by the ankles, dangling upside down like Mussolini. The set pushed the action forward; as Stanley Wells notes (11), the production was an early attempt on Hall's part to break the barrier of the proscenium arch.

In 1960 and 1961 Hall reorganized the Shakespeare Memorial Theatre as the Royal Shakespeare Company, renamed the building the Royal Shakespeare Theatre, and began to establish a permanent core of actors, directors, and designers to produce Shakespeare for the contemporary age. The title for the enterprise was a calculated contradiction: exchanging the memorial foundation for monarchical patronage may not have been the clearest indicator of Hall's new attitude for Shakespeare. (As a wit once remarked to Hall, the name has "everything in it except God.") The acquisition of the Aldwych Theatre was crucial to Hall's plan, not only to give the company an outlet in London but also to cross-fertilize its classic work with modern plays. This is a well-known story, told in detail by David Addenbrooke and by Sally Beauman, and needs no repetition here; it becomes important in the

81 *Coriolanus* 1959 Stratford. D: Peter Hall. Des: Boris Aronson. P: Angus McBean. Mary Ure and Edith Evans as Virgilia and Volumnia greet the conquering hero (Laurence Olivier).

visual context with the arrival of John Bury in 1962, and the subsequent creation of an RSC "house style."

Bury had been the designer for Joan Littlewood's Theatre Workshop in Stratford East in London, operating in ways vastly different from the commercial theatre or the SMT. With highly restricted budgets and no storage space, sets were built on the stage, production by production, out of extremely cheap or scavenged resources. *Richard II* in 1955, for example, with stark lines and only fourteen actors, deliberately contrasted to Michael Benthall's lavish production at the Old Vic of the same year. Littlewood strove to find "the hatred and cruelty of the period" and Bury's set emphasized "fear and oppression" by using raw, unpolished materials.[17] Bury was one of the first important British scenographers without formal training in art or design. In place of the painterly approach of Messel or Nobili, he sought to make an environment with a direct theatrical purpose – not an evocative space with beautiful costumes but a hard-edged scene with visceral appeal. This was "selective realism," as it is often called, which stressed the relationship between physical materials and the theme of the play as established by the director. Through Bury the third major visual movement of postwar Anglo-American Shakespeare – after the open stage movement and the modernist attention to image – made its appearance at Stratford: the influence of Bertolt Brecht.

The year 1956 was a turning-point in British theatre not only because of John Osborne's *Look Back in Anger*, the play that marked the beginning of a loose movement that would affront bourgeois society and the bourgeois theatre by stressing social ugliness and unrest. The visit of the Berliner Ensemble to London in August, the very month of Brecht's death, was much more significant visually, revealing that the prized clarity of expression of the company was partly dependent upon – especially when performing in a foreign country – an economical approach to design. (It was also significant organizationally, since Hall modeled the RSC upon its structure.) Abandoning purely aesthetic considerations and conventional notions of period consistency, designers like Caspar Neher and Karl von Appen strove to make the actor central and to provide statements about the character's social status. Limited optical resources achieved a concentration of purpose, forcing the audience to attend to the economic and political overtones of the action, matters that the British approach to production, especially for Shakespeare, normally glossed over or obscured.

Peter Hall needed a major artistic accomplishment to define the style and purpose of the RSC, and decided on the unprecedented task of mounting the two history cycles over two seasons as the theatre's contribution to the quadricentennial of Shakespeare's birth. The first cycle opened in July 1963, a redaction by John Barton of four plays into three, which he called *Henry VI*, *Edward IV*, and *Richard III*. The overall title was *The Wars of the Roses*. Barton cut about half of the total text and added some 1,400 lines of mock-Elizabethan verse as connective, tightening the political argument of the unfamiliar works.[18] The second cycle, the four plays of the Henriad treated in a less savage textual manner, opened in April of 1964. Thematically Hall was influenced by Kott's essay on the histories, "The Kings," while the visual and performance styles were influenced by the proletarian manner of the Berliner Ensemble.

Bury evoked what Kott calls the "Grand Mechanism" of history chiefly by materials made of metal, adding their heavy weights and resonating sounds to the iron-cold heart of the early history plays. Metal seemed everywhere, in broadswords, in costumes, in the furniture, on the walls and floor (illus. 82). The whole cycle, Peter Hall has written recently, "revolved around steel – its texture and its brightness and its capacity to rust."[19] Bury said that "we wanted an image rather than a naturalistic surrounding ... we were trying to make a world; a dangerous world, a terrible world . . ." (Addenbrooke 126). By using treated plastics and sheet metals for hand props and small furniture, however, the design suggested heaviness while allowing actors to carry and move many units without interference from stagehands or blackouts. Interior scenes were often dominated by a huge council table, made of iron, its solidity mocking transitory human power: the table reappeared for the three plays of the first cycle, though the characters sitting at it changed regularly, as if they were playing a macabre party game (color pl. 8). Trewin wrote (*Birmingham Post* 18 July 1963) that "all is stern, metallic, and ringing. The stage is wide and bare, a sounding-board for fierce words and fierce deeds."

The general set for all the plays was capable of quick changes but basically was "two huge iron-clad doors which slice into or grip the action like the cruel jaws of a vice," said Phillip Hope-Wallace (*Guardian* 18 July 1963). Bury called it "the great steel cage of war"; its movable wings, reducing the size of the upstage area, suggested a claustrophobic world (illus. 83). Like periaktoi, the walls could pivot as well as slide along a curved track, easily altering the face of the stage: the English court was tightly enclosed, the countryside was shown by shifting the walls outward and adding bare trees, France was indicated by reversing them to reveal copper sides.

The flexibility of the design allowed the walls to be partly opened, as they

82 *3 Henry VI (Edward IV)* 1963 Stratford. D: Peter Hall with John Barton
and Frank Evans. Des: John Bury with Ann Curtis. David Warner as Henry VI,
Donald Sinden as York (on throne), Brewster Mason as Warwick, in the opening scene
of the second play of *The Wars of the Roses*. Note the metallic costumes, throne,
and weapons.

were for Henry V's funeral in the first scene of the cycle, his empty throne
upstage setting the emotional quality visually. When closed, the metal jaws
forced the action forward; thus the two factors most characteristic of
Guthrie's work in Ontario, speed and intimacy, were imported into a
proscenium setting. This was possible because Hall had redesigned the stage
in 1960 by adding a steep rake and pushing the apron out more than 4 meters
into the auditorium (Addenbrooke 44). The stage floor, now seen by the
entire audience because of the rake, was given varied treatments, from metal
to bare planks to painted designs. Bury has written that the floor at Stratford
is the most important element of design (in Rosenfeld 193), and it has
become customary at the RSC to use the floor and lights to establish the
basic emotional coloration for production.

   The playing style of *The Wars of the Roses* was thoroughly in keeping with
the visual qualities, accenting robust, unstylized acting in a manner indebted
to Brecht. David Warner, then only 22, was central to the project as Henry

VI and as Richard II; his unrhetorical speech and naïve polity seemed to connect the plays directly to Hall's announced intention of remaking Shakespeare. Peggy Ashcroft gave one of her finest performances as Queen Margaret; though she was 56, far too old to be the child-king's wife, she played the early scenes with a youthfulness to match Warner's, then gradually became a stern matriarchal figure haunting the court of Richard III. She was "a royal Mother Courage," wrote Robert Potter, "an ineffable sexual goddess of a thousand disguises."[20] The pervasive violence of the scripts was treated realistically and often gruesomely: Clifford's corpse was decapitated on stage, Clarence was noisily drowned in malmsey on stage, the heads of Richard of Gloucester's victims were stuck on pikes, swordplay was athletic and dangerous. The clank and the spark of metal, along with the sweat and the grunts of the actors, conveyed a thoroughly anti-romantic view of the middle ages.

The ambience of period, normally considered one of the chief attractions of the histories, concerned Hall and Bury less than narrative clarity and

83 *Henry IV* 1964 Stratford. D: Peter Hall with John Barton and Clifford Williams. Des: John Bury with Ann Curtis. P: Gordon Goode. Set model for both parts of *Henry IV*, showing Bolingbroke's room. The metal-clad walls provided the basic set for both cycles.

contemporary relevance. In a lecture entitled "Against Falsehood," Bury said that he wanted "to take the fancy-dress out of costumes"; he strove "to remain true to the period in silhouette" and used other techniques to "reduce the historical identity down to essentials." Thus, like Brook's *Lear*, which anticipated some of Bury's attention to texture and metal, and like the Berliner Ensemble's productions of Brecht's own history plays, the violent world on stage presented an estranged view of the present.

BROOK'S DREAM, JACOBS' BOX

From its beginning the Royal Shakespeare Company was under the artistic and administrative control of men whose sensibilities were formed at Cambridge University. Peter Hall, John Barton, Trevor Nunn, all read English literature at Cambridge; Hall and Nunn particularly were taken by the teaching and the literary methods of F. R. Leavis. There is an irony here, since Leavis hated the theatre, but his rigorous analysis of literary texts and insistence on the power of literature to change human lives had a profound effect on the RSC style.[21] For many of the directors of the new regime at Stratford, the conceptualizing of the plays, the intellectual examination from which productions would grow, was based in a detailed study of the language and literary images of the text. The director had become, in one sense at least, a literary critic, whose job was to explain the meaning of the play, first to actors and then to audiences. The actor on the (more or less) bare platform became the visual symbol of the RSC method, but the authority of the actor, especially the authority of the star actor, had been decentered. At the chief and most influential Shakespearean company in the world, it was the director who ruled.

Peter Brook, one of the leaders of the company since its foundation, was certainly a major architect of the director's authority; nonetheless he disagreed with many of Hall's early aims, especially those that emphasized expansion and growth (see Beauman 241). His own interest was in forming a small group of actors to work intensely on projects with a lengthy, developmental rehearsal period, unaffected by the pressures of commerce or production deadlines. He accomplished this under the auspices of the RSC in the "Theatre of Cruelty" seasons in London, which began in 1964 with scenes from Jean Genet's *The Screens*, included his seminal production of Peter Weiss' *Marat/Sade*, and culminated with a Vietnam piece called *US* in 1966 – work of great fame and power that linked certain Brechtian elements with the ideas of Artaud and the rehearsal techniques of Jerzy Grotowski.

Some of these methods were applied to Shakespeare in an adaptation of *The Tempest* produced in Paris and at the Roundhouse in 1968. It was obvious that Brook was attending to a different and much more insistent drummer than the other directors of the company, as he moved toward founding a multicultural troupe of actors in Paris in 1971. On the road there he applied his recent discoveries to a version of *A Midsummer Night's Dream* that became the most influential Shakespearean production of the postwar period; after Reinhardt's various mountings of the same play, perhaps the most influential of the century.

Sally Jacobs, who had designed the Theatre of Cruelty project, used a three-walled unit inside the edges of the proscenium, a structure that reminded many viewers of a squash court or a gymnasium and that immediately established an unconventional, non-illusionist context. It was a startling and insistent sight for a play about mystery and illusion: a catwalk at the top, and ladders for access, made the set appear to be a small bright theatre mounted inside the larger theatre, a space for the demonstration of overt performance (color pl. 9). Self-conscious, virtuoso playing is most familiar to us in the circus, and Brook acknowledged this intention when he said that the company "turned to the art of the circus and the acrobat because they both make purely theatrical statements. We've worked through a language of acrobatics to find a new approach to a magic that we know cannot be reached by 19th century conventions."[22]

The basic object was to cancel any suggestions of the Victorian or balletic tradition, which, despite the efforts of Norman Wilkinson and Granville Barker, still claimed its partisans; nonetheless it is a little strange to find an avant-garde director speaking so resoundingly against a pictorial tradition long out of date. The reason may be that Brook was reacting against his own earlier methods that centered performance on the director's image. As he said in 1974,

my view has changed, evolved, through a growing awareness that the overall unifying image was much less than the play itself. And eventually, as I worked more and more outside proscenium theatres and in forms of theatre where the overall image proved to be less and less necessary and important, it became clear that a play of Shakespeare, and therefore a production of Shakespeare, could go far beyond the unity that one man's imagination could give, beyond that of the director and designer.

(Brook 1987: 78–9)

He began work on his *Dream*, therefore, not with a defining ocular premise but with a company of actors – just as Peter Quince does. The eight weeks of rehearsals were to allow for the gradual development of a style; through games, exercises, and study he hoped to let the play work on the actors instead of forcing them into a predetermined intellectual pattern. "You must act as a medium for the words," Brook told John Kane, who played Puck. "If you consciously colour them, you are wasting your time. The words must be able to colour you."[23]

In keeping with this ensemble approach, Jacobs replaced the sentimental fairyland with a vigorous scenography that drew its reference from the world of virtuoso performance. "These modern theatres with their electric lights, switchboards and revolving stages are all well enough but what is really needed is a great white box." So Granville Barker spoke of his own production (Kennedy 1985: 166), and fifty-five years later Jacobs seemed to take him literally. As seen in color plate 9, the fairies at the top of the walls of her white box watched the mechanicals rehearse in the wood. But there were no scenic elements here to reproduce or imply a forest; Brook and Jacobs transferred the magic of a supernatural place and of supernatural beings directly to the bodies of the actors, which is to say that the production relied not on the scenic tricks of the theatre but on the athletic tricks of the performer (color pl. 10). Puck's magic flower was a spinning plate, handed to Oberon on a pole; the fairies often descended on trapezes as a signifier of their invisibility, swinging above the mortals (illus. 84).

A number of production elements stressed specialist performance skills or called to mind circus motifs: the overt athleticism of the acting, especially of the lovers; the doubling of Alan Howard as Oberon and Theseus, of Sara Kestelman as Titania and Hippolyta, of John Kane as Philostrate and Puck, and of Philip Locke as Egeus and Quince, all of whom occasionally changed character in view of the audience; the onstage musicians and the singing of some verses as operatic arias; and the clown-like nose and ears for Bottom-as-ass (illus. 85). Costumes, brilliant but simple satins, derived from those of Chinese acrobats. There was often a sense that the action might spill out into the audience, if only by the sheer energy of the playing, and in a famous maneuver at the end, Puck's line "Give me your hands, if we be friends" was taken literally, as the cast ran throughout the house to shake hands with the audience. It was an all-encompassing moment, uniting the play, the performers, and the spectators.

What Jacobs provided, then, was a simple but semiologically rich environment in which the transformations wrought by love could be investigated inside a visual metaphor that liberated performance. Unlike many of the imitations that followed, the design did not establish a simile

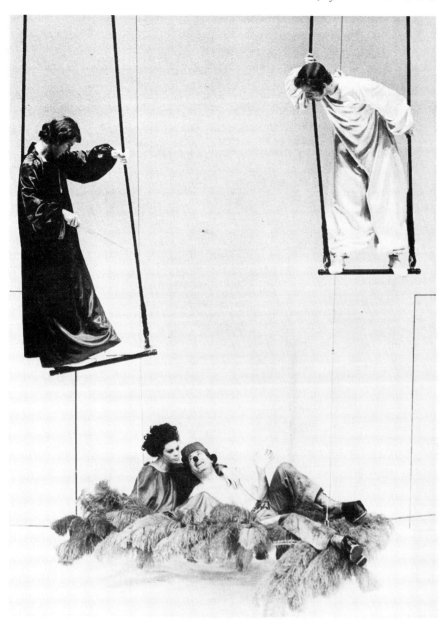

84 *A Midsummer Night's Dream* 1970 Stratford. D: Peter Brook. Des: Sally Jacobs.
P: David Farrell. Alan Howard as Oberon and John Kane as Puck on trapezes,
above Sara Kestelman as Titania and David Waller as Bottom. The ostrich-feather
bed is Titania's "bower," which was suspended from wires and could be raised
and flipped. The outlines of two doors in the upstage wall are partly visible under
the trapezes.

85   *A Midsummer Night's Dream* 1970 Stratford. P: David Farrell. The "wedding"
of Bottom (David Waller) and Titania (Sara Kestelman) in 3.1. One fairy provides a
stiff-arm phallus for Bottom while others drop petals and confetti from the catwalk.
Mendelssohn's wedding march for the fifth act, so closely associated with Victorian
productions of the play, was used here as ironic counterpoint.

between the play and the circus;[24] the secret of the white box was its emptiness, its power to call forth the imagination, not its ability to invoke a specific set of cultural responses. In this sense, at least, the design bore resemblances to the Guthrie–Moiseiwitsch open stage. Brook's production, however, was eminently portable and achieved unprecedented fame: objections that the vigorous acting and design obscured Shakespeare's words and altered his intention were usually drowned by ovations across Europe, America, and as far away from Stratford as Sydney and Tokyo. There were a number of reasons for its popularity, of course, but certainly a major one was its new scenographic vocabulary. Brook and Jacobs had redefined the relationship of Shakespearean production to the visual; happily, some of that relationship is preserved in the photographs, which convey a portion of its innovation, endurance, and dramatic probity.

7 | *The liberation of Europe*

The three most powerful images of the twentieth century, I think, are all connected to the Second World War and became known through dissemination on film: pictures of the Nuremberg rallies, of the stacked emaciated corpses from Hitler's death camps, and of the atomic devastation of Hiroshima and Nagasaki. That these images still color our sleep demonstrates how searing the war was for the consciousness of the age. Most people alive today were born after 1945, yet almost everyone, at least in the industrialized world, has seen or will see some photographic version of those sights and be affected by them. With them the eye lost an essential part of its innocence, and is not likely to regain it.

Shakespeare too has lost some innocence since that war, and the generally darker interpretations given to the plays is at least partly the result of the darker time we have lived in. The productions of the histories and tragedies at Stratford in the early 1960s revealed an awareness of *Realpolitik* and the ironies of history not usually associated with British understanding of Shakespeare. In Europe, strategies for reviewing Shakespeare derived much more forcefully from the war and from the great ideological tension between fascism and socialism which marked the first half of the century. Freed from the Nazi threat, theatres from Moscow to Milan were freed from conventional thinking and conventional scenography. For Shakespeare, the new or rebuilt European theatres created a visual renaissance that was unprecedented and that has not been matched in the Anglo-American tradition – at least partly because European directors and designers felt little of the responsibility to Shakespeare's text that has, naturally enough, restrained most productions in English in the century. The growth in international travel and in production touring after the war meant that new developments had broader and more rapid effect outside their countries of origin; thus a survey of the visual principles of postwar European Shakespeare should be less concerned with national and linguistic boundaries.

SOCIALIST RECONCILIATION AND DISCORD

We can begin in Poland, the country most directly in the crossfire of the war, hot and cold. Leon Schiller's political use of Shakespeare was renewed in a notable production of *The Tempest* for the Shakespeare Festival in Łódź in 1947, which carried his earlier concerns into the brave new socialist world he had dreamed of in the twenties. Designed by Władysław Daszewski, it was "conceived as an intellectual morality play about the triumph of reason over the forces of nature,"[1] in which human and spiritual conflict was resolved in magnanimity and love. Much of the effect came from a simplified staging that drew upon medieval, Renaissance, and modern scenography. The chief devices were emblematic: two levels, one for spirits and one for humans; Prospero's cell stage right and Caliban's cave stage left, "good" and "evil" aligned as in the fifteenth-century moralities; tree trunks and hanging branches with huge leaves. Behind the action was a convention-alized Elizabethan map of an island and ships, the words "Totus Mundus Histrionem Agit" printed at the top.

The play began with Prospero in front of the map, speaking as prologue his lines from the fourth act (illus. 86):

> Our revels now are ended. These our actors,
> As I foretold you, were all spirits...

He then climbed to the upper level as a drop descended, decorated with Zodiacal signs and with a large circle cut out – a keyhole through which the audience viewed the first scene. Prospero pointed to a ship on the map and the storm began (illus. 87). The transplanted prologue and the magic circle framed the tempest as Prospero's artifice, and suggested a tension in his character between the creator and the colonist. This was accented by Karol Adwentowicz's performance, a serious, glowering magus in beard and Spanish black, whose actions against Caliban and the royal party sometimes appeared excessive. Schiller, encouraged by Stalinist cultural policies to moderate his avant-garde methods, was determined to reconcile the elite artist with the masses, represented by Caliban. But if Caliban was a proletarian rebel against Prospero's power, he was an awkward symbol for the people, for he was still in thrall to the forces of bestiality and unreason. In 1938, for a production in Yiddish at the Jewish Theatre in Łódź, Schiller wrote a final scene in which Prospero apologized to his slave; in 1947 the characters played a similar action in pantomime, ending with Caliban bowing to Prospero, who gently set his hand on Caliban's head. Despite its intention, this tacked-on resolution was more likely to reveal the contradictions in the text than Shakespeare's own ending. Schiller treated the play, in Edward Csató's words, as "a discourse about the nature of power,"[2] but seemed unwilling to admit to the full implications of Prospero's use of power. Like Daszewski's design, the production mixed Renaissance and modern ideas without actually unifying them. Schiller's *Tempest*, a bridge between the revolutionary socialism of the prewar period and the institutionalized socialism of a people's Poland, was a visually resourceful production struggling to find a center.

The case was very different in Moscow in 1954 with one of the most problematic productions from the socialist world, Nikolai Okhlopkov's "Iron Curtain" *Hamlet*. Here the object was not political accommodation but the transformation of Shakespeare into a critique of Stalinist policy. *Hamlet*, always a favorite play in Russia, was usually given an overly Romantic interpretation, stressing languorous and self-obsessive inaction. But Stalin had banned it during the war, its political allusions too sensitive for a supreme dictator and its hero too tentative for the nation's militant

86   *The Tempest* 1947 Łódź. D: Leon Schiller. Des: Władysław Daszewski. Karol Adwentowicz as Prospero in the interpolated prologue, in front of the map and the narrow upper platform. A massive tree branch is silhouetted in front of the map.

cause, and only after Stalin's death in 1953 was it again permitted. Okhlopkov, often called Meyerhold's artistic heir, frankly abducted the play to serve as a comment on the recent past. Hamlet is a rebel against the "cold embraces of this prison" of Denmark, the director wrote. "A tragic fate awaits those prisoners who keep aloof from the struggle and bide their time, while the army of murderers is growing and growing. Tragic, too, is the fate of those who answer blow for blow too early or too late." Since Claudius cannot stop the forces of history, the militant humanist Hamlet has the future on his side; "beyond his death, beyond his personal defeat, lies the historic victory of humanism."[3] Thus the production sought to provide an historicist understanding of tragedy while at the same time criticizing the strongman tactics of Soviet Communism.

Vadim Ryndin, Okhlopkov's usual designer at the Mayakovsky Theatre, made prison the visual metaphor for the production, relying upon static and often colossal spectacle. "Elsinore is presented as a sort of Viking dungeon," said Norris Houghton. The major design component was a pair

87 *The Tempest* 1947 Łódź. The cutout drop in front of a bi-level stage; the map is partly obscured (1.1). Spirits on the upper level with the mariners (the only time humans appeared above), Ariel below with the noblemen. Though angled, the upper platform remained steady and the actors mimed the movements of the storm.

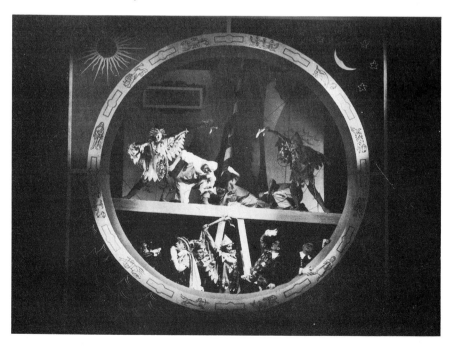

88 *Hamlet* 1954 Moscow. D: Nikolai Okhlopkov. Des: V. F. Ryndin. The Murder of Gonzago in the "Iron Curtain" *Hamlet*, with the units of the massive gates used as boxes.

of vast metal gates or castle doors, bolted and heraldically decorated, that could slide forward and back, could open in sections, or could swing fully apart in the center. They might be an impenetrable wall of the palace, an interior setting, or a peep-show aperture, but always a constraint or an interdiction. Massive objects sometimes appeared behind them: giant columns for the closet scene, capped with fingers of fire (strips of red cloth blown upwards by hidden fans), or a huge Viking ship drifting across the stage for Hamlet's voyage to England. The chapel scene took place with the inner doors of this great iron curtain partially open, revealing Claudius at the foot of a huge crucifix far upstage, a scene reminiscent of Craig's Moscow production or of Hofman's design in Prague in 1926. The most interesting use of the gates was in the play scene when their individual sections were transformed into theatre boxes, with the royal couple and courtiers watching the players on the main stage floor (illus. 88). When Laertes returned seeking vengeance, a second grate or portcullis was lowered at the proscenium line, preventing him and the populace from breaking into the palace.

The iron curtain was an ingenious solution for Okhlopkov's reading of the play, yet the design as a whole was ponderous and over-literal. The chief difficulty was in pace: altering the configuration of the gates a few times in

Plates

1 *The Winter's Tale* 1906
Berlin. D: Max Reinhardt.
Des: Emil Orlik. "Before
the Palace," a design for the
Deutsches Theater showing
Craig's influence in the
geometrical patterns and
in the massive walls.

2 *The Winter's Tale* 1906
Berlin. Orlik's "Japanese"
design for the interior of
the palace.

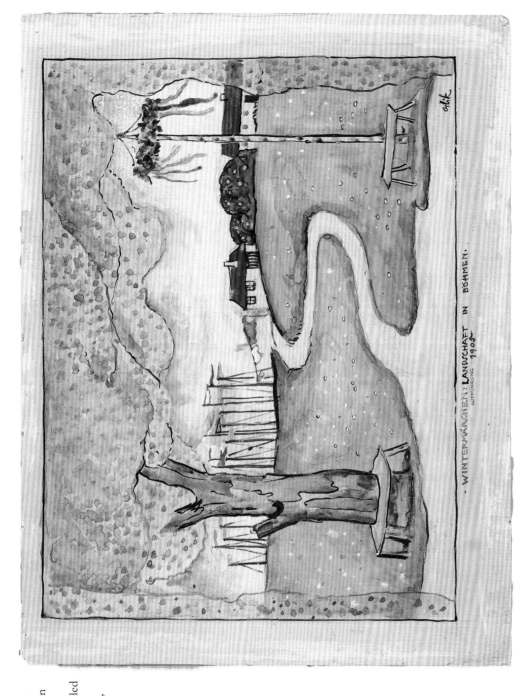

· WINTERMÄRCHEN: LANDSCHAFT IN BÖHMEN.
AUFFÜHRUNG 1905

3 *The Winter's Tale* 1906
Berlin. Childlike Bohemian
exuberance in contrast to
Sicilian restraint. Orlik titled
this watercolor sketch
"Landscape in Bohemia."

4 *Twelfth Night* 1912
London. D: Harley
Granville Barker. Des:
Norman Wilkinson. Lillah
McCarthy as Viola-Cesario
in front of the Futurist
garden. Another gold bench and
box tree needle were balanced
on the opposite side of the
stage.

5 *Richard III* 1920 Berlin.
D: Leopold Jessner.
Des: Emil Pirchan. Pirchan's
design for the coronation
scene (just before 4.2),
showing the red steps
crossing into the red sky by
means of Richard's robe.

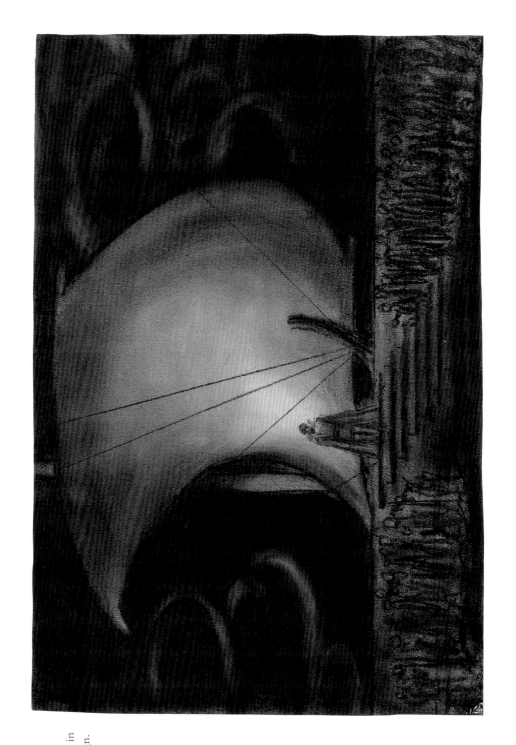

6 *Othello* 1921 Berlin.
D: Leopold Jessner. Des:
Emil Pirchan. The arrival in
Cyprus, in Pirchan's design.

7 *A Midsummer Night's Dream* 1959 Stratford. D: Peter Hall. Des: Lila de Nobili with Jean Marie Simon. L: Michael Northen. P: Thomas F. Holte. The opening scene on a Jacobean unit set.

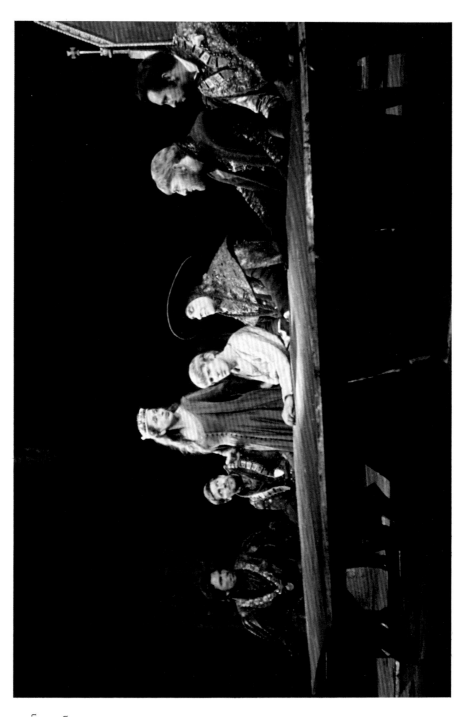

8 *Henry VI* 1963
Stratford. D: Peter Hall with John Barton and Frank Evans. Des: John Bury with Ann Curtis. P: Thomas F. Holte. Peggy Ashcroft as Queen Margaret with the King's council around the iron table, used as a symbol of power in *The Wars of the Roses*. David Warner as Henry VI is in white. Note the textured metal and leather on the costumes. (This photo is of the 1964 revival.)

9 *A Midsummer Night's
Dream* 1970 Stratford.
D: Peter Brook. Des: Sally
Jacobs. P: Thomas F. Holte.
The mechanicals rehearsing
in the wood (3.1), showing
the full set with fairies at
the top.

10 *A Midsummer Night's Dream* 1970 Stratford. P: Thomas F. Holte. Oberon (Alan Howard) puts Titania (Sara Kestelman) asleep with his wand (2.2), while Puck (John Kane) watches.

11 *Henry IV* 1957 Lyon.
D: Roger Planchon.
Des: René Allio. Allio's
design for the histories,
showing the thrust stage at
Villeurbanne and the
medieval pictogram maps of
England. The small models,
used to present locales,
indicate "London" (at left)
and "a street" (at right).

12 *Henry V* 1961 Vienna.
D: Leopold Lindtberg.
S: Teo Otto. C: Ploberger.
Otto's design for the English
camp at the Burgtheater,
with fires under tattered
canopies.

13 *Richard II* 1973
Stratford. D: John Barton.
Des: Timothy O'Brien and
Tazeena Firth. L: David
Hersey. P: Thomas F. Holte.
Richard Pasco as King
Richard watches the lists at
Coventry from a litter
upstage (1.3). Denis Holmes
as Mowbray on blue hobby-
horse, Ian Richardson as
Bolingbroke on red horse,
Richard Mayes as Lord
Marshall in center.

14 *Henry V* 1975 Stratford. D: Terry Hands. Des: Farrah. L: Stewart Leviton. P: Thomas F. Holte. The Southampton scene (2.2), with the heraldic canopy aloft and the English dressed for war. Alan Howard as Henry, sword drawn, is at the right of the picture.

15 *Henry V* 1975 Stratford. P: Thomas F. Holte. In France the canopy was lowered to establish a muddy battlefield; note the guy wires still attached, creating mounds out of the cloth. Montjoy (Oliver Ford-Davies) demands ransom from Henry (3.6). The costumes of the French and English, now of the same period, nonetheless provided a contrast similar to that of the tennis balls scene (illus. 120).

16 *Macbeth* 1976 Stratford.
D: Trevor Nunn.
Des: John Napier.
L: Leo Leibovici. P: Thomas
F. Holte. A rare picture
showing the extremely close
relationship of the spectators
at The Other Place to the
action. In an interpolated
scene before 1.2, Duncan
(Griffith Jones, all in white)
prayed, while Macbeth (Ian
McKellen) held his garment.
The witches crouched inside
the circle, and other actors
watched from crates just
beyond its magic line.

17   *As You Like It* 1977
Stratford. D: Trevor Nunn.
Des: John Napier. L: John
Watts. P: Thomas F. Holte.
Operatic conclusion to an
operatic version, as Hymen
appeared in two-dimensional
clouds.

18 *Hamlet* 1977 Bochum.
D: Peter Zadek.
S: Zadek and Peter Pabst. C: Pabst. P: Gisela Scheidler. Gertrude (Eva Mattes) displays inner character by outward means, her hands on Hamlet (Ulrich Wildgruber, kneeling). Claudius (Hermann Lause) is in a scarlet doublet, while the Ghost observes through a mirror frame at rear of picture. The anarchy of styles is apparent in the general costuming, and the open factory space in Hamm is visible in the background. The chairs were for spectators (this photo was taken at a daylight dress rehearsal).

19 *Richard II* 1981 Paris. D.: Ariane Mnouchkine. S: Guy-Claude François. C: Jean-Claude Barriera and Nathalie Thomas. L.: Jean-Noël Cordier. P: Martine Franck. Théâtre du Soleil actors as a pseudo-Japanese court. Cyrille Bosc as Bolingbroke to the left, Georges Bigot as Richard in white at the center (2.1). Note the formal mingling of Elizabethan costumes with Samurai dress, the mats on the floor, and the Asian use of billowing cloth to establish the general design motifs.

20 *Richard II* 1981 Paris. P: Martine Franck. The deposed King (Georges Bigot) in a prison of poles, in loincloth and Kabuki whiteface, attacked by Samurai murderers in 5.5.

21 *1 Henry IV* 1984 Paris.
D: Ariane Mnouchkine.
S: Guy-Claude François.
C: Jean-Claude Barriera
and Nathalie Thomas.
L: Jean-Noël Cordier.
P: Martine Franck. Prince
Hal (Georges Bigot) saves
his father (John Arnold)
from Douglas (Maurice
Durozier) in 5.4. Note the
mask on King Henry, and
the red yarn from the mouth
of Douglas to indicate blood.

each act swallowed up many minutes, in the wasteful manner of nineteenth-century pictoralism. The often frantic internal rhythm of individual scenes was frequently retarded by the scenographic concept. Similarly, placing scenes far upstage (the chapel, the closet) deprived them of their intimacy and much of their dramatic power. Some foreign commentators found the general effect exciting but a little tasteless: Ossia Trilling thought that Tchaikovsky's music, used as in a Hollywood film, showed a "monumental insensitivity to Shakespeare's text"; Faubion Bowers felt that "an air of fussiness pervades the entire production, both in the individual acting and in the overall direction."[4] Despite its political resonance, it was a *Hamlet* at odds with itself.

Not so with Yuri Lyubimov's production in 1971 at the Taganka Theatre, an event of major political and theatrical importance in Moscow, which played in repertory until the early death of Vladimir Vysotsky in 1980. Vysotsky, a greatly popular actor and protest singer, was the center of the interpretation; as the American journalist Hedrick Smith put it, he was "no self-doubting prince but an enraged young man struggling against an evil ruler in an evil time (King Claudius as Stalin?)."[5] This Hamlet's function was to oppose the despotic present and instruct others how to overcome it. As if to make the resistant reading of the play paramount, he began the evening, dressed in turtleneck and slacks, playing his well-known guitar and reciting Pasternak's poem "Hamlet" from *Dr. Zhivago*, a novel which the audience had not been allowed to read, while two gravediggers, unmistakable as Russian peasants, shoveled through a pile of real earth in front of him, extracting skulls. The guitar, the singer, the graveyard: an archetypal image of protest. Pasternak's translation, already acknowledged as a dissident text, was the backbone of Lyubimov's "broken montage" method, in which he laminated disconnected moments of poetry, song, and action onto Shakespeare's play.

The chief scenic device provided by David Borovsky was again a curtain: not the iron gates of Ryndin's design, nor the flexible screens of Craig's aestheticism, but a heavily textured drop suspended from a pivot and track system that allowed it to move up and down stage, across from right to left, and pivot diagonally as well. Coarsely crocheted from wool and hemp, it was both cinematic and highly practical, capable of dividing the stage quickly into sections for different scenes and responsive to changes in lighting color and intensity (illus. 89). It was at various moments a wall, a screen, a net, the arras, a shawl for Ophelia, even the royal throne.

It could be controlled by the performers, but it could also operate mechanically, as if on its own, and became a symbol of the hidden forces beyond the characters' power, threatening at any moment to sweep offenders into the open dirt grave. After Vysotsky's prologue, for example, the entire cast was on stage as the curtain made its appearance, rushing across the cast, forcing the actors to fall or be swallowed up in its rough embrace, clearing the space for the first scene with the Ghost. It favored political authority:

89 *Hamlet* 1971 Moscow. D: Yuri Lyubimov. Des: David Borovsky. L: K. Panshin. The inhuman curtain surrounds Hamlet (Vladimir Vysotsky), standing with Rosencrantz and Guildenstern (I. Dikhovichnyi and Aleksandr Vilkin).

Polonius hid behind it, and it mysteriously supported Claudius and Gertrude when they sat on it or leaned against it. As Margaret Croyden wrote of a performance at Belgrade (*New York Times* 31 Oct. 1976), "Throughout, that curtain hangs and moves like a giant monster, dominating the action, setting the pace, and holding within its folds the symbols and tools of power – black armbands, swords, goblets, thrones edged with knives." It controlled the performance, establishing rhythm and sometimes even drowning out the actors as it rushed along its track. At the end it swept up the corpses left on the stage, in the same way it had knocked down the actors at the beginning, indifferent to human life and death. The final moment was particularly horrifying, the curtain moving toward the audience in the fading light, "as though to destroy it too."

Until Lyubimov's exile in 1984 the Taganka was allowed to operate as an unofficial safety valve of theatrical dissent, practicing an extremely delicate alchemy that transformed playtexts into objects of social contention, but that stopped short of the uncoded denunciation that would awaken the wrath of the regime. In other words, in a land where Shakespeare was licensed but new plays attacking the status quo were not, Lyubimov's trick was to make a *Hamlet* that looked like a new play to the audience but could still claim the protection of an established classic to officials. Borovsky's curtain – anonymous, sinister, and implacable, threatening and eventually obliterating the melancholy, rather folksy protests of Vysotsky's Hamlet – was a signifier of constraint even more potent than the iron iconostasis of Okhlopkov's version in 1954. It was a rare example of a simple scenographic device that was both practical and perfectly aligned with theme and performance style.

THE DIRECTOR'S LENS

In western Europe the approach to Shakespeare operated on different and less political principles, especially for the first decade or so after the war. Exhausted by years of fighting, spectators often looked for an escape from the deprivations of the present, and the visual responses offered were frequently based on shopworn ideas and prewar nostalgia. This was most evident in Italy, where the traditions of monumental presentation of opera were strong, and where the visual authority of the director had been fortified by the success of the new Italian cinema. Luchino Visconti's film work was gritty and low-key, but his work with Shakespeare was spectacular and very costly: the films showed the poverty and the harsh reality, and, using the same actors (like Vittorio Gassman, Ruggero Ruggeri, and Marcello Mastroianni), the theatre showed the fantasy. Visconti's *As You Like It* in 1948 at the Teatro Eliseo in Rome, for example, toyed with the idea of escape from urban cares in Surrealist fashion. Designed by Salvador Dali, and tied to an exhibit of Dali's paintings, the production offered a vision of the court framed by golden elephants on long, stick legs; Arden was signified by a huge single apple inside a box, painted on a backdrop. Reliant upon song and dance as much as the riotous color of Dali's dreams, it became "one of the strangest performances of Shakespeare that the present age has seen," wrote Mario Praz.[6] *Troilus and Cressida* was treated in a similar way the next year in Visconti's outdoor production. Franco Zeffirelli, who had supervised the set construction for *As You Like It*, spent an amazing sum to transform the Boboli Gardens in Florence into a walled Troy, all in white, accessible only by drawbridge. The costumes (by Maria de Matteis), the horses, what Praz called "the circus-like pageantry" – all were intended to help the audience abandon cares by delighting the eye in an uncritical and culinary spirit. This may have been a socially useful escapism, but the choice of *Troilus* for such an expenditure a few years after the war, with the country lying in ruins, now seems almost perverse.

Zeffirelli's own productions of opera and plays continued the lavish scenographic methods, eventually transferring them to film as well. His best-known work with Shakespeare was the 1960 *Romeo and Juliet* at the Old Vic in London, where his own designs achieved the illusion of a hot and dusty Verona by lighting and pictorial set pieces. One of the most popular productions of the time, it was established visually by operatic *verismo*, just when such an approach was finally being abandoned for Shakespeare at Stratford and elsewhere. Peter D. Hall's costumes and Nina Rota's music followed the traditions of Hollywood epic movies, inscribing sentimental Romanticism into a sensory evocation of period. Like Reinhardt before him, Zeffirelli took these performance ideas back to their "source" when he staged the play in Italian in the Roman Theatre in Verona in 1964. The accent of the Old Vic production on youth was intensified, for the actors playing Romeo and Juliet were appearing on stage for the first time. The real city of Verona assisted the stage fiction, as church bells blended into the onstage cries of vendors, and old buildings beyond the theatre blended into the set (illus. 90). Zeffirelli's interest was in the cinematic creation of locale, in order to create a corresponding immediacy for the love story; his well-known film version (1968) realized this ideal with location shots and three-dimensional film sets. Both on film and on stage this was a nineteenth-century Shakespeare manufactured with twentieth-century technology.

Film directors elsewhere had similar trouble fastening onto Shakespeare's potential in the postwar theatre. In Sweden Ingmar Bergman directed *Macbeth* three times (1940, 1944, and 1948) as demonstrations in visualizing the evil within, almost as exercises for his masterful films of the succeeding decades. The last version used a permanent set on two levels, designed by Carl-Johan Ström, that overhung the proscenium of the Gothenburg City Theatre with a huge, gnarled tree. The witches climbed in it; four hanged men dangled from it in the hellish scenes. During the banquet their bodies were replaced with carcasses of roasted oxen. Ström's design and Bergman's direction implied that evil is always with us, oppressing and informing our lives; unfortunately this concept directly clashed with the interpretation of the actor Anders Ek, a committed socialist, who wished to stress that Macbeth's fall from grace was the result of historical forces connected to the

90 *Romeo and Juliet* 1965 Florence. D and S: Franco Zeffirelli. C: Peter D. Hall. A late example of locale pictorialism, in a street scene in the outdoor production which originated in Verona in 1964 (this photo is from the Maggio Musicale tour in Florence).

decay of feudalism.[7] It was a minor example of one of the major dissensions of postwar Shakespearean representation, the conflict between seeing the tragedies and histories as expressions of anguished souls and seeing them as social resources for communal polity.

In France it was not new film devices but old stage traditions that affected the production of Shakespeare. "The poetic atmosphere of his art which rises towards suprareality and ideal forms," said Jean-Louis Barrault, "is cruelly dispelled by the cold light of our severely rationalized language."[8] Whatever the truth of that sentiment, it is undeniable that the grandiloquent, official style of performing the classics in France has often prevented the deep responses to Shakespeare characteristic of the more Romantic habits of central and eastern Europe. Between the wars a number of important productions were mounted, especially by Gaston Baty and Charles Dullin, but few were of international importance visually. Perhaps the most distinctive were those of Georges Pitoëff and his wife Ludmilla, French-Russians who worked with Copeau before forming their own company. Pitoëff's *Macbeth* (Geneva, 1921) used an abstract design, punctuated by light, that abhorred the literal; it was nothing, he said, but "the plastic expression of the plane on which the whole of *Macbeth* occurs." *Romeo and Juliet*, which Pitoëff designed in 1922 but did not produce until 1937 in Paris, showed some of the vortex influence of Exter's design for Tairov combined with the shadows and foreshortening of Expressionism.

After the war, production of Shakespeare followed the two major trends of the French theatre, decentralization into the provinces and expansion into districts of working-class audiences, trends that became cultural policies for successive governments. Jean Vilar was a leader in these movements, founding both the Avignon Festival and the Théâtre National Populaire in Chaillot; his most important work with Shakespeare was *Richard II*, which he directed and in which he played the title role for a number of years. It was first performed outdoors in the Court of Honor of the Papal Palace at Avignon in September 1947. The spare style had been influenced by Copeau, and contrasted sharply to the Italian outdoor spectacles; it was nonetheless monumental in scale, performed on a vast open stage in front of the fourteenth-century backdrop, and for 3,000 spectators (illus. 91). Brilliant banners and costumes with geometric patterns flared out against the dark-brown stone walls, visible far from the stage, and Vilar's pools of light made characters appear and disappear from the surrounding darkness.[9] The production transferred well to the vast space of the Chaillot Palace outside Paris, though it was dependent on a similar large-scale vocal

91 *Richard II* 1953 Avignon. D: Jean Vilar. S: Camille Demangeat. C: Léon
Gischia. P: Agnès Varda. Bare stage values, outdoors and on a huge scale. The
curtain call, showing the lower section of the audience and the monumental wall
of the Papal Palace. The production played every summer from 1947 to 1953.

delivery and upon a sense of ritual that resembled High Mass. If its gigantic
simplicity achieved Vilar's purpose of uniting all classes in the mystery of
ceremonial performance, it united them for the performative moment only;
nothing about this "popular" Shakespeare would have caused the members
of the audience to question the social environment of their daily lives.

One of the most inventive of the European productions of Shakespeare
in this period used filmic devices in a thoroughly theatrical way. Erwin
Piscator, architect of epic theatre, who had first integrated film with the

stage in the 1920s, had spent his exile years in New York. He was put in charge of the Freie Volksbühne in West Berlin in 1962, where he directed an impressive *Merchant of Venice* the following year. The play was obviously a sensitive one in postwar Germany. The fate of the Jews under Hitler, and our almost continual subsequent awareness of the horrors of the death camps, have completely transformed our ability to read it anywhere. The external events of the Second World War have affected *Merchant* so thoroughly that it is fair to say that since 1945 we have been in possession of a new text of the play, one which bears relationships to the earlier text but is also significantly different from it. Piscator dealt with the intensive complications of German responsibility and guilt forthrightly, by presenting what he called in the program note a "basically philo-semitic understanding of Shakespeare's play," the only one which could be correct "in the face of historical events."[10] (The social theme was investigated more thoroughly in *The Deputy* – called *The Representative* in Britain – Rolf Hochhuth's play

92 *The Merchant of Venice* 1963 Berlin. D: Erwin Piscator. Des: Hans-Ulrich Schmückle. P: Heinrich Fürtinger. Shylock (Ernst Deutsch) on the bridge separating the palace from the walls of the Ghetto. The decorative motifs, even the medallions and the bricks on the face of the bridge, were created by black and white projections. The boat with two actors rested on a polished mirror floor. This set at the Freie Volksbühne revolved to create other configurations for Belmont and the courtroom.

93 *The Merchant of Venice* 1963 Berlin. P: Heinrich Fürtinger. Bassanio (Günther Tabor) reads the message from the casket in 3.2, as Portia (Hilda Krahl) waits. The costumes here mixed periods but emphasized the wealth and sensuality of Belmont.

about the responsibility of Pope Pius XII for the Holocaust, which Piscator directed at the same theatre, earlier in the same year.)

Ernst Deutsch, himself a Jew, had played Shylock in 1957 under a similar sympathetic conception, and now gave a performance that emphasized Shylock's humanity amid a corrupt and commercially antagonistic world, abandoning entirely the German tradition of Jewish caricature. His alien status was underscored by projected titles: "The Jewish residents of Venice were excluded from commercial shipping activity," read one caption projected onto a brick ghetto wall during intermission, while another gave statistics about the vast extent of the Venetian shipping industry. At the end of the evening a projection of Shylock's "anguished face" filled the sky of Belmont behind Jessica, interjecting his loss and her treachery into the festive conclusion of the play.

Projections formed the heart of Hans-Ulrich Schmückle's design. Both Venice and Belmont were formed by black and white "photogravure settings," in Ossia Trilling's phrase, which were photographic renderings of actual buildings or of baroque engravings. Venice was divided "into two irreconcilable halves," the Rialto and the Ghetto (illus. 92). A practical bridge connected them center stage, above a reflecting floor that represented the canal; at one revealing moment, Launcelot Gobbo spoke the soliloquy about his conscience and the fiend (2.2) standing between the two worlds, "undecided which way to jump."[11] Shylock's house, carved out of a corner of the Ghetto walls and approached by a spiral staircase, was pilfered and ransacked in dumbshow. Belmont displayed the decadent elegance of "these Christians," backed by projections of erotic scenes (illus. 93); Portia often spread herself languorously on a full-length couch downstage. The courtroom, a square platform raised above the mirrored floor, was as brightly lit as a boxing-ring, the dark walls of the Ghetto enclosing it. In a newspaper review Irma Reblitz, perhaps thinking of Piscator's work on *The Deputy*, called this scenography "documentary," and the term is helpful. Using pictures of real places which were then denatured by the theatrical projection process, Schmückle combined the authenticity of photographs with a disturbing or surreal presence: the result was a Venice and a Belmont that seemed to be projections (in the metaphoric sense) of the characters' minds.   Like Meyerhold, Piscator was only tangentially interested in Shakespeare; yet this timely *Merchant* was made thematically authoritative by its visual approach, and anticipated other photo-sets for Shakespeare by some twenty years.

BRECHTIAN SCENOGRAPHY IN BERLIN

Ich denke, wir können Shakespeare ändern, wenn wir ihn ändern können, Bertolt Brecht wrote,[12] "I think we can change Shakespeare, if we can change him": that is, if we are equal to the task. His annexation of the classics and of history to serve the political uses of the present had large implications for the visual aspects of performance in the second half of the century. Roland Barthes summarized that importance when he described Brecht as "a Marxist who has reflected upon the effects of the sign: a rare thing." Some obviously visual facets of the *Verfremdungseffekt* – the placards and projections to counter or control spectators' empathy, the reliance upon masks for characterization, the half-curtain to call attention to the mechanics of scene-shifting by hiding a portion of them – were used by Piscator and Brecht early in the Weimar period. The more substantial visual policies of epic theatre, however, developed over a longer time. These included the subtle effects of costuming on character, the degree of collusion between the setting and the stage fiction, and the relationship between the actors and the physical props required to tell the story, all of which needed the intervention of sophisticated designers to achieve their purposes. It was not until the creation of the Berliner Ensemble in 1949 that these strategies of performance were consolidated, and not until the first tours of the company in the mid-fifties that they were widely disseminated, especially as a result of Brecht's own production of *Mother Courage*. A number of important directors and designers in western Europe recognized that the Ensemble's methods had broad application for the classics and rapidly adapted them to Shakespearean use, as John Bury did at Stratford East and Stratford-upon-Avon.

Caspar Neher originated much of the visual method of the Berliner Ensemble. As John Willett has shown,[13] Neher was actually responsible for the creation of many of scenographic features we now think of as Brechtian, particularly the technique of "selective realism," in which fragmentary or metonymic objects represent objects or circumstances in the real world and yet, because of their deliberate incompleteness, invoke the artifice of the stage and invite the intellectual attendance of the spectator. Though Neher and Brecht were school chums in Augsburg and had been thoroughly associated since the first sketches for *Baal* in 1919, Neher managed to remain in the German-speaking countries in the thirties and forties and even worked with Heinz Hilpert, Goebbels' replacement for Reinhardt at the Deutsches Theater, on a number of Shakespeare plays throughout the war. (Indeed as the Brechts were escaping to Prague after the Reichstag fire in 1933, Neher drove Kurt Weill and Lotte Lenya to Paris, then returned home. Designers, the Nazis apparently thought, were men and women of less conviction than the playwrights and directors they served.) During his exile Brecht turned to Teo Otto, whose designs for the premieres in Zurich of *Mother Courage* in 1941, and for *Galileo* and *The Good Person of Setzuan* in 1943, extended and refined Neher's methods. After the war Neher became head of design at the Berliner Ensemble until 1954, when Karl von Appen succeeded him.

Despite their individual styles, Brecht's scenographers shared important traits that greatly influenced international practice. Chief among them was the sophisticated technique of showing (or allowing the actor to show) a social attitude to the story or to the character at almost every moment. The purpose of the design was not to create beautiful or evocative environments but to anatomize the action: to strip it to the bone and then provide only the optical details necessary for the story. The proper starting-point for the designer, Brecht was fond of saying, is point zero. But the designer must not assume a neutral disposition to objects and colors; Brecht thought that Neher inscribed a moral stance into the visual, "a lovely mixture of his own handwriting and that of the playwright":

His sets are significant statements about reality. He takes a bold sweep, never letting inessential detail or decoration distract from the statement, which is an artistic and an intellectual one.... One chair will have short legs, and the height of the accompanying table will also be calculated, so that whoever eats at it has to take up a quite specific attitude, and the conversation of these people as they bend more than usual when eating takes on a particular character, which makes the episode clearer.[14]

Lighting, central to emotional expression in the modern theatre, assumed a special place for the Brechtians because they denied its empathetic role. The spectator should be able to follow the story "without impediments," Appen wrote (quoted in Bablet 1977: 317). "Therefore, there is no need for darkness, chiaroscuro effects to create atmosphere, or partly illuminated actors. For us light is ... an objective means of clarification. A cold, even and clear lighting is our goal." As Brecht wrote of the spectators in his poem on theatre lighting, "Let them / Do their dreaming in the light."

The careful selection of stage objects and the use of non-illusionist light recall the procedures of the Elizabethans. Brecht's episodic playwriting was heavily influenced by the Elizabethan chronicle play, of course; from his adaptation of Marlowe's *Edward II*, which Neher designed for the Munich Kammerspiele in 1924, Brecht frequently turned to the Elizabethans for material. The most obvious case, that of *Coriolanus*, was something of an obsession. The two friends worked on Erich Engel's production in Berlin in 1925, with Fritz Kortner in the title role, and Neher redesigned it for Engel in 1937 at the Deutsches Theater, in both cases relying on the contrast between white marble and dark rough wood to exhibit the dialectic of patrician and proletarian. Brecht started his adaptation of the text in 1951; Neher made sketches for the Ensemble but the project was abandoned. The script was later completed by Manfred Wekwerth and Joachim Tenschert, who directed it in 1964 in a production designed by Appen. Though it traveled to London and Prague the following year, the production postdated the major influence of the company in Europe; yet in many ways it was a compendium of the Brechtian use of Shakespeare.

Brecht's *Coriolan* turns Shakespeare's tragedy of pride into a tragedy of the specialist: Caius Marcius is a highly skilled warrior, needed by Rome when under threat from the Volces, but obsolete in peace, who is unsentimentally rejected by the populace when he cannot adapt to a society

94 *Coriolanus* 1964 Berlin. D: Manfred Wekwerth and Joachim Tenschert. Des:
Karl von Appen. P: Vera Tenschert. The triumphal return of Caius Marcius
(Ekkehard Schall) to Rome, in the Berliner Ensemble production of *Coriolan*,
Brecht's adaptation of Shakespeare. Helene Weigel as Volumnia leads, holding her
son's knife aloft; Wolf Kaiser as Menenius is in the white gown.

in the process of change. Heroes can be useful but ultimately, like Hitler or
Stalin, they become too expensive to maintain. When the people recognize
that wars are made by human action, they realize that they can be ended by
human action, and thus a fighting machine like Coriolanus becomes
irrelevant. To establish this visually, Appen paid extraordinary attention to
the status signification of the costumes. He marked the differences between
groups clearly – soldiers, noblemen, workers – but also made distinctions
regarding types of worker that cut across the Roman period to the present.[15]
The set showed a parallel tension: it was a monumental city gate on a
revolve, stone-white on one side for Rome (illus. 94), covered with rough
timber on the other for the Corioli scenes (illus. 95), a set that turned its back

95 *Coriolanus* 1964 Berlin. P: Vera Tenschert. The other side of the revolving set, with Schall in the battle scene before Corioli. The revolving gate provided the major signifier of the dialectic of the production.

like Coriolanus. Wekwerth and Tenschert's main concept, what Brecht called the *Grundgestus* or basic signal of the production, was clearly supported by the two-faced setting. Caught between his specialist skill in slaughter on the one side and his utter ruin as a social creature on the other, the hero had in the end no place to be.

Because *Coriolanus* had been rewritten, the production achieved a visual and thematic unity far greater than that of most engaged performances of "untouched" texts, especially in English: Shakespeare's play was hammered until its new shape conveyed a new meaning, a meaning that is at best recessive in the original. Yet Brecht's process, as I suggested at the beginning of this book, differs from the usual methods of the Shakespearean theatre in degree rather than in kind. Granville Barker's clarion call of 1912, "there is no Shakespearean tradition," was a challenge to the director and designer to abandon Victorian conventions by seeking visual freedom founded on a renewed responsibility to the text. But directors and designers, no matter how historically based, can read the text only with their own eyes. To seek fidelity to Shakespeare's "intentions," with regard to meaning or to performance style, is to ignore the vast distance the text has traveled to reach us, and to become, at least in one sense, traitors to our own time. The Brechtian scenographers, admitting to a socially committed view of the theatre, provided for it a new concept of the beautiful. Their redefinition was based not on aesthetic considerations of what is pleasing, which were inherited from the aristocratic and bourgeois traditions of Europe, but rather on materialist theories of what is socially useful.

It was a powerful new concept to apply to Shakespeare. His classic status made his work, especially in England, a repository of the dominant values that maintained the political plays as costume dramas, seeking safety in productions that invoked Rome or medieval England with details of period that delighted the eye. This is why Peter Hall's production of *Coriolanus* with Aronson's city of metal jaws (illus. 81), and of *The Wars of the Roses* with Bury's steel cage of war (illus. 82, 83, and color pl. 8), were visually radical: they applied furnishings and devices that did not deny historical period but did deny the pleasant dimension of historical beauty. The harsh settings and costumes, favoring dramatic utility over comeliness and clarity of character over grace, showed that Bury particularly had learned the major lesson taught by Neher and Appen, that audience attention can be focused onto the social overtones of the action by optical means. But the scenography of the Berliner Ensemble, like most visual codes, proved to be detachable from its specific political origin. At the RSC and at other theatres in the western democracies, the term "Brechtian" soon began to imply a style rather than a social cause.

Not so at home. While the best theatres in the Soviet Union and the socialist countries of eastern Europe were often centers of careful dissent, those in East Berlin remained Marxist both intellectually and politically, perhaps because of Brecht's presence. It's a short walk from the Berliner Ensemble to the Deutsches Theater, and if you strolled from one to the other anytime from 1960 to 1990 – passing the Zirkus Schumann, which Reinhardt used as his Grosses Schauspielhaus – you would not have been surprised at the treatment of Shakespeare on the main classical stage in the German Democratic Republic. Not everything was Brechtian, of course. A 1964 *Hamlet* presented an internalized, psychological prince acting out his fate in front of a world clearly out of joint: a series of bare platforms supported by the nightmares of Bosch and Breughel (illus. 96). It was an overbearing pictorial backdrop; unlike the Russian versions it did not evoke Denmark as prison, constructed by the human actions of a dictator-king, so much as suggest the world as hell. Interestingly, the performance prompted a debate among the East Berlin critics over the play's adaptability to socialist understanding (Leiter 138).

A second production from the Deutsches Theater can show why the Marxist interpretation of Shakespeare continued to suggest a fertile line of thought for theatres further west, just as Robert Weimann's work provided an important alternative to the apolitical criticism that once dominated Shakespeare studies.[16] Friedo Solter directed *The Tempest* in 1974 as a political play with parallels to *Richard III*, stressing the ambivalence and inner contradictions of Prospero as a colonizer. Dietrich Körner played him as a man who had to use force to maintain his dominance but was racked with doubt: middle-aged, strong, reliant upon action, he was far from the wise magus who implied Shakespeare as ethereal poet, transfigured and apotheosized. The island was a rough and alien place, with massive tree trunks padded with cloth and a grass carpet on the stage floor (illus. 97). No one was wise, in fact; Gonzalo came closest, but was merely an astute opportunist, thriving by tactical maneuvers. Dieter Mann's Ariel was rough and athletic rather than spiritual; Alexander Lang, himself an important

96 *Hamlet* 1964 Berlin. D: Wolfgang Heinz. Des: Henrich Kilger. P: Dietlind Krönig. Hamlet's mind reflected in Bosch's visions of hell, at the Deutsches Theater.

97 *The Tempest* 1974 Berlin. D: Friedo Solter. S: Eva-Maria Vieberg and Heinz Wenzel. C: Christine Stromberg. Ferdinand (Roman Kaminski) is tortured by Ariel's music (1.2) as Prospero (Dietrich Körner) and Miranda (Simone von Zglinicki) observe, at the Deutsches Theater. A Brechtian half-cyclorama encircles the upstage area.

director, showed a Caliban who was neither fish nor fowl but an oppressed human being (illus. 98). His white short trousers, black belt, and topnot suggested an Asian identity, though what mattered was his appearance as a man being treated as the manifest Other.

In this microcosmos, Prospero could never be free: the conquerer is perpetually bound by the indigenes. The program notes made this theme clear; Marx was quoted to the effect that any revolution about private ownership must first occur in the mind before it can occur in the land, Lenin quoted to the effect that a new class cannot appear in history without major "battles and tempests" and formidable uncertainty as the old way falls. But Shakespeare anticipated Lenin in this regard, for the final movement of the play relies as much on the freeing of the oppressed as it does on restitution and sexual union, and the production supported this theme by underscoring the human dimension of Prospero's universe visually. Since Ariel and Caliban were represented as fleshly mortal men, controlled by another mortal man, their struggle for freedom became paramount and their

98 *The Tempest* 1974 Berlin. Ariel (Dieter Mann) makes an interpolated appearance on a flying rock, accompanying the thunder of 2.3. Caliban (Alexander Lang) has just dropped his load of enormous logs in fear.

liberation became the rightful conclusion to a comic action. If *The Tempest* can be read as an incipient plea for the rights of the other, the production simply read that text with Marxist eyes.

When Brecht returned from exile in 1948 he concluded that German audiences had been thoroughly corrupted by years of what he called *Göringtheater*, the official Nazi method that deployed music and spectacle to anesthetize thought, a theatre that reproduced the classics in order to maintain social order. To develop a new democratized audience, and to retrain its members to see the material truth of the world rather than its idealized illusions, designers sought a disengagement from the Romantic emotion, the *Weltschmerz*, characteristic of the Wagnerian and Craigian traditions. The unfinished surfaces, the rough but honest treatment of stage mechanics, the pointing out of class distinctions, these were fitting policies not just because they looked more proletarian – that would have been nothing but a different pretense, a new type of visual illusion – but because they corresponded to the truth of the world as perceived by international socialism. Shakespeare's plays, so often concerned with political upheaval and realignment, provided rich raw material for *revolutionäre Praxis*, as Marx called it. The theatres in the eastern region of Germany continued to appropriate the texts for contemporary use, as they had done since the time of Goethe and Schiller, dressing them now not in Romantic silks but in the distressed costumes of *Mother Courage*.

BRECHTIANS ABROAD

The Berliner Ensemble was in Paris in 1954, the company's first visit to the west; ironically the most important of the French Brechtian directors missed *Mother Courage* because he was too busy with his own production of *The Good Person of Setzuan*. The next year, however, Roger Planchon saw the return engagement and arranged a lengthy meeting with Brecht. The encounter was decisive, especially for subsequent French productions of the classics; though he followed Vilar's populist lead, Planchon succeeded by breaking away entirely from the classical restraint and rhetorical grandeur charac-teristic of his countryman. He learned from Brecht, he said, that "a performance combines both dramatic writing and scenic writing," and that this *écriture scénique*, by which he meant the contributions of the director and designer, has an importance equal to the work of the dramatist, and an equal responsibility.[17] Whereas Brecht had to make an audience, Planchon took the Brechtian postulates directly to the workers of Villeurbanne, a blue-collar district of Lyon, and used Shakespeare as a major part of an extended project to provide the highest quality theatre for the proletarian audience. For the inaugural production at his Théâtre de la Cité in 1957 he chose the two parts of *Henry IV*, which he called *Le Prince* and *Falstaff*; the script choice was significant, according to Jean Jacquot (127), "confirming the importance of the history plays in the creation of a new popular dramaturgy." Thus Planchon established the political relevance of the histories for Europe six years prior to Peter Hall's rediscovery of them. Indeed, Planchon's scenographer, René Allio, designed *Cymbeline* at the RSC for the British Brechtian director, William Gaskill, a year before *The Wars of the Roses*.

Kenneth Tynan succinctly summarized Planchon's method, catching both the political and the aesthetic qualities:

The plays were boiled down to the bare social bones; each point was made, coolly and pungently, on a rostrum backed by a map of medieval England, and each scene was prefaced by a caption, projected onto a screen, that summed up the import of what we were about to see. Individual characterization was subjected to the larger image of declining feudalism. The result was not Shakespeare; it was abundance reduced to relevance, riches cut down to a living wage.[18]

Robert Speaight (263), with his conservative social opinions showing as usual, was nonetheless enthusiastic: "Visually, the production was a creative achievement of the first order; and its political intention was readily acceptable to the industrial audience of Villeurbanne." Allio's basic design (color pl. 11) created an overtly fictional space, with the upstage end of the thrust backed by flats painted with large medieval maps, set like a triptych in a frame. Toy models of the City of London or of a street were witty reductions of period sets, used to establish place, just as the printed projections established Planchon's proposition for each scene.

The main object was to clarify how the events of the mighty affect the lives of the many. Using Brecht's process of textual appropriation, Planchon interpolated silent scenes about the "sufferings of the common man or the harshness of the ruling classes," as Jacquot put it.[19] He applied Marxist theory to acting, encouraging his players to stress discontinuities in their characters, which highlighted, in David Bradby's view (111), "the social conditions governing the characters' behaviour." Allio's costumes signified the status of the wearers, making instantly recognizable distinctions between classes: dull colors and distressed materials for the common people, leather and metal for soldiers, rich and warm elegance for the nobles (illus. 99). This

99 *Henry IV* 1957 Lyon. D: Roger Planchon. Des: René Allio. P: René Basset. A play about power performed in front of the symbol of ownership, a huge map of England. Class distinctions by costuming.

may sound obvious, but the traditions of costuming the histories prior to Brecht and the Brecht-influenced RSC laid much more emphasis on clarifying the political allegiances of an entire group (similar colors and patterns for all the royalists, different colors and patterns for all the rebels) than on the class distinctions inside a group.

Planchon's sympathies were those of his audience, and aristocratic characters were generally treated as representatives of a decaying feudal order. Hotspur, for example, who administered his wife as chattel, was himself stabbed in the back while Hal duelled with him in the front; and Hal was utterly callous in his rejection of Falstaff. Actors often played against the text, speaking the most elegant verse with their mouths full of food, or countering the sense of a speech with a violent or vulgar gesture. Allio has said that the purpose of a stage designer is "to invent a sort of visual language for each play, that within a chosen expressive style, underscores its various meanings, extending and echoing them" (in Bablet 1977: 308). Interested in the collective destiny rather than individual psychologies, this *Henry IV* showed the workers of Lyon a Shakespeare who seemed to judge the events of history rather than to present them neutrally. The audience got the point, it seems; Planchon reports that at a public forum a worker, attending any theatre for the first time in his life, summed up the plot this way:

The boss's son has broken with his family, knocks about the night-clubs a bit, then joins the army to go and fight in Indo-China; he comes back and takes over the factory where, his dad having died, he proves a rather stricter master, not scrupling to have his own friends put in prison.[20]

A second Planchon production, designed by André Acquart, extended one of the meanings of *Troilus and Cressida* into 1964, containing hints of modern troop formations and modern battle dress. The set was a large folding screen that pivoted on a center hinge; frequently shifted by the actors, it conveyed the Greek encampment as well as the walls of Troy. Its numerous positions made the production optically dynamic, at times incorporating posts and timbers, tent canopies, and half-curtains; yet the chief visual feature was the highly physical staging of the battle scenes (illus. 100). What appealed to Planchon about the play, Bradby notes (125), was "its fierce demystification of the twin myths of the glory of war and the power of love." Though the translation (by Planchon and his assistants) was

100   *Troilus and Cressida* 1964 Lyon. D: Roger Planchon. Des: André Acquart. P: Roger Pic. A battle scene using the folding screen.

harshly criticized for its linguistic clumsiness, the major point was to demonstrate that high-sounding phrases associated with love and war "serve only to mask the unacceptable aspects of their reality." Ulysses' speech on order, which E. M. W. Tillyard's influence had made into a set-piece on "the Elizabethan world picture" for the English stage, was delivered as a partisan harangue at a contentious political meeting. Planchon's method sought to reveal the discontinuities of the text by showing the backside of the military and amorous virtues; Acquart's setting, with its constantly changing façade, was a particularly appropriate visualization for disorder, treachery, and fragmentation. It was a more protean counterpart to Appen's design for *Coriolanus* of the same year. Turning under the actors' hands to reveal the inside of Troy at the rear of Agamemnon's tent, "its dislocations corresponded to the break-up of a world falling victim to the frenzy of war" (Jacquot 130).

Peter Hall's use of postwar *Realpolitik* as a backdrop for Shakespeare's quadricentennial was anticipated by a similar plan in Vienna, where new productions of the histories were mounted between 1960 and 1964. The Burgtheater, still evoking in its architecture and audience behavior the ornate opulence of the Habsburgs, is the opposite of a proletarian house, and the Viennese traditions of Shakespeare representation tended to emphasize vocal eloquence and period detail, like those of the old SMT. The production of the two history cycles, directed by Leopold Lindtberg and designed by Teo Otto, sought a middle road between the bourgeois elegance of the Burgtheater and the revolutionary passion of the Berliner Ensemble. Oskar Werner's Henry V, for example, was dignified and controlled, an authentic personality convinced of the righteousness of his cause. Yet the general view of war was "decidedly muted and realistic" (Leiter 222), allowing the Chorus to suggest a skeptical attitude to battle and glorious death.

Otto's design enabled this compromise vision; relying on Brechtian methods but stopping short of an insistent political message, it confronted visual plenty with its own contradictions. The basic set for *Henry IV* (1960) was a series of freestanding Gothic screens, a little like the interior of Westminster Hall, which integrated scene location titles.[21] *Henry V* (1961) used a brown-timbered back wall with brightly colored canvas banners stretched above the stage as a canopy; but the banners were in tatters and the soldiers beneath them in dark capes (color pl. 12). Otto provided scenes that were striking in the aesthetic sense, yet used metonymic visuals to signify the devastation of war: the Viennese were allowed to have it both ways.

"It is essential to know *why* we make theatre. And following that, it is essential to know *for whom.*" Jean Vilar's charge,[22] still heard in the drama schools and greenrooms of Europe and America, already implies a socially oriented response. Brecht's international importance was founded on his uncompromising desire to use the theatre to reveal the underlying truth of the world, in order to show this truth to audiences who have never seen it before. One of the most complex European directors, Giorgio Strehler, has provided an arresting visual response to Shakespeare by applying the principle. With Paolo Grassi he founded the Piccolo Teatro of Milan in 1947, the first *teatro stabile* or permanent company in Italy, which subsequently became the model for other municipal and state-supported theatres. His initial productions reflected the uncertain direction of Italian theatre immediately after the war; in June 1948, for example, he directed a spectacular *Tempest* outdoors at the Boboli Gardens in Florence, complete with lavish aquatic displays. He then turned to the English histories, mounting quasi-Elizabethan productions of *Richard II* and *Richard III*. After seeing the Berliner Ensemble, however, Strehler – like Hall and Bury, like Planchon and Allio – realized that Brecht had worked out a new and fully practical method of conveying sophisticated ideas that could be applied to the new Italian working-class audience. Brecht then watched rehearsals for Strehler's production of *The Threepenny Opera* in 1956, with set designs by Teo Otto; "he is probably the greatest director in Europe," Brecht concluded, and gave Strehler European artistic control of all his plays.[23]

Strehler's reformed interest was applied to Shakespeare in 1957 in a powerful version of *Coriolanus*, with sets by Luciano Damiani and costumes by Ezio Frigerio, who had both worked on *Threepenny* and who became Italy's leading Brechtian designers. The production adapted major visual techniques of the Berliner Ensemble outright: bright, steady light; scene titles to establish the dialectical nature of the encounters; simplified, partial set units that stood out severely from a bare plank floor and from a white cyclorama. But despite his acknowledged influence, Strehler did not remain orthodox in his ideas or his methods. An impressive actor himself, he has the extrovert personality of a performer and an adamantine optimism about the future. As Jan Kott said, "In Giorgio's vision, the paradise still exists, at least as a promise";[24] his social philosophy has been infused with a belief in the power of theatre to advance human life. In 1974 he suggested as much to Ralph Berry (126), discussing Shakespeare's own view of history:

Myself, I'm a socialist, with a materialistic view of history: I'm a Marxist; so I believe personally in developing the dialectic in a positive sense. ... I happen to believe in a positive development in the movement of human thought. He [Shakespeare] did not, surely, believe in a blind movement of history, a process where one murder succeeded another. I think that Shakespeare always let it be understood in his tragedies that man himself had his rights even against history, or in dialectic with history. All the great personages of Shakespeare are in dialectic with history, with fetishes of power.

Strehler saw that the early history plays, where the fetishes of power seem most raw, presented an important opportunity for contemporary social comment. Like John Barton, he freely adapted the three *Henry VI* plays himself in 1965, and staged them over two evenings under the title of *Il gioco dei potenti*: the Play of the Powerful, it might be translated, or better, the Game of the Mighty. Heavily affected by Kott's notion of the Grand Mechanism, the director, who also provided the ideas for the design, went well beyond standard Brechtian devices. His context was the common thread he found in Kott and in the avant-garde drama of the fifties and sixties, that "the anguish, the void, the nothingness surrounding man" could be overcome through an act of artistic affirmation. "So *Il gioco dei*

101 *King Lear* 1972 Milan. D: Giorgio Strehler. Des: Ezio Frigerio. P: Luigi Ciminaghi. The revels of Lear's "motorcyclist" knights at Goneril's castle (1.4), showing the rough boards placed over the sand pit. Tino Carraro as Lear faces upstage. Piccolo Teatro.

102 *King Lear* 1972 Milan. P: Luigi Ciminaghi. The blinded Gloucester (Renato De Carmine) and mad Lear (Tino Carraro), in royal rags and paper crown (4.6), recalling Brook's scene ten years earlier (illus. 79).

potenti," he wrote, "was born as a drama of rupture, modern, contemporary."[25]

For Strehler's *King Lear* in 1972, which stayed in repertory for five years and toured much of Europe, Ezio Frigerio expanded this method into a scenographic principle. "The stage for *Lear* was based on Eliot's *The Waste Land*," Strehler said (Berry 124):

It was an empty plain which could be the terrestrial planet, or a cosmic circus, where this event, at once very ancient and close to us, took place. The actors were clad in the manner of the Italian Renaissance, but all in black leather. In my imagination they were personages of Shakespeare's time, but transposed with people who could have been motor-cyclists of today.

The stage floor was covered with sand and surrounded by a cyclorama tied down like a tent at the bottom; with the exception of a few props and a causeway of jagged boards, it was otherwise bare (illus. 101). The royal characters, in long theatrical robes and carnival crowns, seemed to be playing the game of the mighty through the second act, after which they played the game of the clowns. Lear and Gloucester were then in rags, stumbling and twisting in a metaphysical circus of sand (illus. 102). The acting stressed tortured essence, as it did in Brook's production, especially in the Lear of Tino Carraro, Strehler's regular collaborator. To one Italian critic it seemed as if two naked old men were being tamed in a circus ring by animal trainers, or that a motorcycle gang was taunting and torturing them (Leiter 322). "To my mind the most faithful to my book," said Kott of the production: "extremely cruel." But it was also faithful to Strehler's own indelible sense of life. The doubled roles of the Fool and Cordelia, played by Ottavia Piccolo, stressed tenderness in the middle of chaos and indomitable father–daughter love in the middle of all-destroying hatred. Presenting the circus as a metaphor for *Lear* proved a brilliant visual evocation, pitiless and profound, that enhanced Elizabethan cruelty with postwar gestures (illus. 103). Strehler's success in uniting performance style with post-Brechtian scenography was indicative of the European treatment of Shakespeare, and would become even more notable in his production of *The Tempest* (discussed in the final chapter) six years later.

103 *King Lear* 1972 Milan. P: Luigi Ciminaghi. Lear and the Fool (Ottavia Piccolo, who doubled as Cordelia) in a circus image of filial tenderness.

JOSEF SVOBODA

Brecht disliked calling Neher by the standard term *Bühnenbilder*, which can be rendered literally as "maker of stage pictures" (or scene designer, in its usual translation), and preferred instead *Bühnenbauer*, "stage builder" or "stage constructor," in order to emphasize the roundness and dimensionality of his contributions.[26] Josef Svoboda, probably the most influential designer of the postwar period, positively rankles at the suggestion that his theatre work can be equated with that of a painter or adequately suggested by flat drawings on paper:

> What irritates me most are such terms as "Bühnenbilder" or "décorateur" because they imply two-dimensional pictures or superficial decoration, which is exactly what I don't want. Theatre is mainly in the performance… True scenography is what happens when the curtain opens and can't be judged in any other way. (Burian 19)

This is no mere semantic distinction; for Svoboda, the scenographer is at least equal to the director in enabling performance, for the scenographer's job is to render in spatial terms the emotional and narrative essence of the play. His work has been based in experimentation with new materials and new technologies, drawing directly upon the advances in light and the application of levels pioneered by Appia and Craig. It has taken many forms, from an almost magical control of light and projections to the development of new machinery for scene shifting. One of the most fruitful of his experiments has been the molding of "psycho-plastic space," a kinesthetic theatre of three dimensions that responds to the dynamics of the play's action by flexible changes in the setting. It has proved particularly well suited for the frequent locale changes in Shakespeare.

An important school of Shakespearean scenography in the century has been officially antagonistic to theatre technology. From Poel and Barker to Guthrie and Hall, a number of directors (and many scholars) have asked for a simplicity and directness removed from modern stagecraft, returning to the conditions of Shakespeare's theatre by divesting themselves, like Luddites, of subsequent mechanical and illuminant inventions. But despite a public dismissal of technology, Elizabethanist directors and designers often relied on it to carry out their reforms, especially those determined by the practice of playing indoors and at night. Barker needed the new electric "torpedo" lamps and bright light bouncing off a white set to evoke the daylight of the Globe and to make Wilkinson's post-impressionist colors adequately visible; even Poel used a type of horizontal illumination in 1910;

and the open staging of Guthrie and his followers in Ontario has been supported by highly sophisticated lighting systems to suggest mood and locale changes. In proscenium theatres, where most Shakespearean productions occur in Europe, the use of the latest inventions has often meant increased stylistic freedom. The danger of technology is that it achieves a prestige of its own, so tempting that it is used simply because it is installed; more than a few directors and designers have been seduced by expensive toys into creating unnecessary or questionable effects. Svoboda, though he has been at the forefront of developing applications for new technologies, has always understood their place. "It all depends on how you use technology," he said; "an electric current can kill a man or cure him. It's the same in a theatre production: the technical element can harm it or be used to help prepare a masterpiece" (Burian 23).

Svoboda's design for *Romeo and Juliet* at the National Theatre in Prague in 1963, directed by Otomar Krejča, was a major demonstration of psycho-plastic space, and brilliantly solved the challenges of the play for the representation of locale. Composed of a number of architectural units that were visually unified by a stone-like surface, the design sought to evoke the humanistic proportions of Renaissance buildings. Steps, platforms, and walls were arranged in twenty different configurations, determined as much by the mood of a scene as by its setting; yet the total time required for all the changes was only four and half minutes. The major set unit was a delicate, arcaded gallery that appeared to float in the air, an illusion created by mounting it on a black pillar that moved in a track up and down the stage (illus. 104). It could be an upper level in a house, a non-specific space, or, when it glided into a forward position, the balcony itself (illus. 105).

Much of the visual power came from an acute combination of these swift changes with Svoboda's equally dynamic lighting, often directed from a restricted source high above the stage. The lighting gave a dreamlike impulse to the performance, similar to the *Traumtheater* of some of his productions for opera and for Laterna Magika. In general the designer established the mood of Verona by establishing a mood for the actors, relying on advanced technology to achieve quite simple results. An elevator platform, for example, served as a table, a fountain, the bed, and the tomb. When the gallery was rotated it formed a suggestive backdrop for Juliet's bedroom, which was otherwise bare (illus. 106). Despite the high-tech methods, Svoboda's scenography was responsive to the needs of actors and eminently attuned to the human dimension. The production stayed in repertory for five seasons and attracted a large number of youthful spectators

104 *Romeo and Juliet* 1963 Prague. D: Otomar Krejča. S and L: Josef Svoboda. C: Zdenka Kadrnozková. P: Jaromír Svoboda. A street scene in act 1, showing step units and the floating gallery placed in its upstage location. National Theatre.

105 *Romeo and Juliet* 1963 Prague. P: Jaromír Svoboda. Marie Tomášova and Jan
Triska in the balcony scene. The gallery has been brought downstage, while Romeo
kneels on a platform raised to the same height.

(Burian 111), not because of design but because of the integration of the
design with Shakespeare's fable about the destruction of young love.

Three productions of *Hamlet* over a quarter of a century show another
side of Svoboda's contribution to the visual. The first, directed by Jaromir
Pleskot in 1959, treated the play as a new work, with a commissioned
translation by Zdenek Urbanek that reduced the language to "a bare
statement of facts voiced in modern, colloquial phrases," and put the actors
in modern clothes with "the rudiments of traditional dress."[27] The setting
relied on step units on an empty stage, surrounded by movable slabs of an
artificial material that reflected light like a black mirror and showed the
actors in disintegrated images of themselves. A second version, directed by
Krejča and seen in Brussels in 1965, was based on the idea that the Ghost is
Hamlet's alter ego, a fiction he creates to gain sympathy in his cause against
the usurper Claudius. Reflection was again central, this time through a
mirror mounted above the stage that allowed Hamlet to encounter himself:
"two great birds confronting each other in space," said Svoboda. The set

was much more complicated, consisting of a huge vertical structure of geometric shapes, steps, and platforms which could slide into many configurations, continuing the motif of dynamic fragmentation.

The last *Hamlet* used Krejča's theme but returned to a simpler form. Directed by Miroslav Macháček, it played in Prague from 1982 to 1988; Svoboda designed the set and his daughter, Šárka Hejnová, designed the period costumes. Both the interpretation and the stage image appeared rather conventional, even a little old fashioned. František Němec's Hamlet was not indecisive but vigorous and quick, if a little out of his depth among the slippery political machinations at court, more of a warrior than a dreamy intellectual; his Hotspur (1987) was not dissimilar. The setting made the

106 *Romeo and Juliet* 1963 Prague. P: Jaromír Svoboda. The gallery serving as Renaissance windows, having been turned to face the audience; the platform is Juliet's bed, as she prepares to take the potion in 4.3.

107 *Hamlet* 1982 Prague. D: Miroslav Macháček. S and L: Josef Svoboda. C: Šárka Hejnová. P: Jaromír Svoboda. Hamlet's body is carried up the great steps, in Svoboda's homage to Appia and Craig.

proscenium stage of the historic National Theatre into a large square pit surrounded on three sides by stepped platforms and blocked vertically by nothing but heavy, black theatre drapes. The action occurred on an extended forestage as close to the audience as possible, and almost all of the visual changes were evoked by light. Not until the end did Svoboda reveal the purpose behind this austerity. The dying Claudius, avoiding Hamlet's fury, grabbed at the upstage curtain in two or three swipes and pulled it apart. It revealed a gigantic flight of steps receding upstage, lit in a ghastly blue fog. Hamlet died in Horatio's arms, and Fortinbras and his army descended the steps, filling the space vertically with their intrusive bodies. Horatio, waving a piece of paper that contained Hamlet's "prophesy," raised his arms in a gesture that seemed to say, "Look at all this destruction. What can it possibly mean?"

The final moment was unparalleled in Shakespearean staging. Four captains carried Hamlet's body up the steps, accompanied by music and rhythmic cannon shots, moving slowly into the mist and the distance, the wreckage of the action left behind (illus. 107). Svoboda had created a scenography of deferral, deliberately restraining the visual experience for most of the play in order to achieve a magnificent dead march. The bare stage with velvet drops, used for almost all of the production, was Elizabethan in its simplicity; but the final moment changed the condition of everything that went before. Invoking the inventions of Appia, Craig, and Pirchan, the steps seemed to be nothing but gradients of light, while Hamlet seemed a tortured soul now elevated to the heavens. Svoboda had actually tricked the eyes of the spectators, conditioning them for over three hours to expect nothing remarkable, then astonishing them for ten minutes. Like Chris Dyer's Serlio-like setting for *The Taming of the Shrew* in 1978, created only to be demolished at the start of the performance, Svoboda's tactic invited the spectators to deconstruct visually, seeing the set as if drawing it.

Svoboda's work reminds us that while Shakespeare has been extremely important in Europe, he has also been much more a part of general performance trends than in the Anglophone theatre; European designers and directors after the war have used the plays as one segment of a larger social project. Especially under the influence of Brecht, much of the best theatre in Europe has overtly acknowledged that the classics are deep mines of material: we dig up the traces of an earlier culture and remanufacture them. There is a Shakespeare who comes to us encrusted with the loam of the past, but there is also a Shakespeare we forge in the process of staging him. Reworkings of the plays on the European continent have been encouraged by two conditions not present in Great Britain or North America or Australia: high financial subsidy, which regularly supports avant-garde work at levels undreamt of further west, detaching it from the direct influence of the marketplace; and great political instability, which tends to make theatres into crucibles for testing new social ideas rather than into sanctuaries of the status quo. The visual adventurism of European Shakespeare results from taking the theatre more seriously than in English-speaking lands and, at the same time, taking Shakespeare himself a little less seriously.

8 | *New spaces, new audiences*

After the success of the Ontario stage, it was only a matter of time before the growing festival movement in the United States would find its own Stratford. The town that resistantly accepted the mantle, just a few years after Guthrie's tent theatre, seemed to have the right features. It was in Connecticut, close enough to New York to attract actors and large audiences, in a pleasant riverside setting, and was urged on by Lawrence Langer, for years an important force in the Theatre Guild. The enterprise followed the procedure established in Canada, gathering money, obtaining an English director (Denis Carey from the Old Vic), building a theatre. It opened its doors in 1955 to an enthusiastic audience. But its purpose was unclear, its policies shifting, its personnel migratory. The hybrid building, intended to support both proscenium and thrust configurations, was actually suited for neither: it resembled Shakespeare's Globe outside and a New England barn inside. Most of all, its energies were blunted by two insidious factors that have affected much American theatre in the twentieth century, an uncritical acceptance of the star system and an administrative model influenced by the commercial conditions of Broadway. The American Shakespeare Festival called itself the "third Stratford" but had neither the acting traditions of the SMT nor the open stage of Ontario to define it.

John Houseman became artistic director in 1956, and his four years proved the potential of the venture. An early decision suggested an efficient approach to the visual. Rouben Ter-Arutunian, an Armenian designer born in Russia and trained in Berlin, built a series of vertical drops out of wooden slats that were retained for all six productions over two summer seasons. The setting softened the architecture with natural materials and reduced the intimidating size of the upstage playing space. It readily supported atmospheric light and shadow; since the mechanism for the slats was like that of Venetian blinds, the device also provided a straightforward means of

227

108 *Measure for Measure* 1956 Stratford, Connecticut. D: John Houseman and Jack Landau. Des: Rouben Ter-Arutunian. L: Jean Rosenthal. P: Eileen Darby. The "Venetian blind" setting at the American Shakespeare Festival, used for two seasons. The ducal palace (1.1) was suggested by flown-in drapes and lamps. (Despite its poor quality, this photo, reproduced from a program, shows the setting more clearly than any other.)

creating doors, balconies, or windows. A production of *Measure for Measure*, set in nineteenth-century Vienna, showed the suppleness of the idea. In the opening scene a draped velvet curtain and two crystal chandeliers were enough to indicate locale, while three rows of the slats were raised about 3 meters to make a large central entrance (illus. 108). The slats might have been an intriguing realization of the prison motif of the play, but the directors (Houseman and Jack Landau) were more concerned with farce than with metaphor. This was not the Vienna of Freud and Wittgenstein, so profitably used by both Jonathan Miller and Robin Phillips in 1975, but the Vienna of Franz Lehar, with waltzes, Chinese lanterns, and Ruritanian uniforms. The Duke was played as a practical joker, and Morris Carnovsky as the Provost carried Ragozine's head in a leather hatbox.

Some of the future course of the American Shakespeare Festival was already implicit in the light treatment of the darker aspects of this play, and soon the third Stratford became known as the producer of "Shakespeare for those who don't like Shakespeare." Big stars, imported for the sake of the box-office, proved their worth there rather than in their roles. With Katherine Hepburn as Viola, Cleopatra, and Beatrice, or with Alfred Drake as Benedick and Othello, it seemed that the Festival's eye was more on future transfers to New York than on its present purpose in Connecticut. The visual concepts continued to be forceful but too often they were ends in themselves, or served as substitutes for fruitful analysis of the texts. The productions became known by their gimmicks: the Rio Grande *Much Ado* (1957), the Tarot card *Winter's Tale* (1958), the Civil War *Troilus and Cressida* (1961). The Festival sought to make its work accessible; Houseman noted that "fifty percent of our audiences have never seen Shakespeare before."[1] But it is a fine line that divides accessible theatre from culinary theatre, and since its chief rationale seemed to be to maintain operations, this Stratford actually differed little in purpose from Broadway. Houseman left in 1959, with some rancor, and the theatre went through a difficult readjustment.

In 1967 its integrity and fortunes were improved by the arrival of Michael Kahn, who eventually became artistic director and stayed for ten years. An innovative Off-Broadway director familiar with Kott and Brecht, Kahn was dedicated to transforming the Festival into the non-profit status shared by new companies in the burgeoning American regional theatre movement. Kahn's work had Guthrie's irreverence though not his authority, so that the productions often looked faddish and derivative even when they strove for sincere interpretation, as with the "hippie" *Love's Labour's Lost*, complete with a sitar and a guru, in the youth-year of 1968. A more effective result was

109 *Henry V* 1969 Stratford, Connecticut. D: Michael Kahn. S: Karl Eigsti. C: Jeanne Button. L: Thomas Skelton. P: Martha Swope. The French army as ice hockey players in oversized outfits, standing in the jungle-gym. American Shakespeare Festival.

achieved in the "jungle-gym" *Henry V*, at the height of the protests against United States involvement in Southeast Asia; set in a playground, and using Brechtian devices and costumes that ranged from the Vikings to Vietnam, Kahn suggested that all wars are games, that violence is a pastime (illus. 109). It would be simplistic to blame the failure of the Festival on its visual premises, but its frequent inability to go beneath the scenographic surface was a token of its uncertainty about *why* Shakespeare should be the centerpiece of a major theatrical organization. The American Shakespeare Festival did not succeed in justifying the necessity of its playwright in

America, even though that was its intention, and when its insolvency became official in 1985 there were claims that it had been artistically bankrupt years before.

In New York itself Joseph Papp established a major undertaking a year prior to the Connecticut venture. Papp had a clear social goal for the New York Shakespeare Festival, and knew that the methods of commercial theatre were not likely to achieve it. Though he displayed the entrepreneurial instincts of a Broadway producer, Papp's ambition was to bring the highest quality presentations to a broadly based audience, using Shakespeare as a starting-point, much as Roger Planchon intended in Lyon. In 1962 the city built the open-air Delacorte Theatre in Central Park for Papp's use, and he began the tradition of staging two or three productions there every summer, free to anyone willing to wait in line for a ticket. Relying on subsidies of various origin, as well as upon the profits generated by commercially successful productions like *A Chorus Line*, Papp offered over time a democratic Shakespeare, spoken with a distinctly American voice. Relying on an adventurous and multiracial casting policy that reflects the varied cultural landscape of New York, he also brought to Shakespeare both actors and spectators normally excluded by the traditions of Anglophilic high culture.

If the scenographic limits of the Ontario festival are determined by the architecture of its open stage and fan-shaped auditorium, those of the Delacorte Theatre are determined by the open stage and its unusual outdoor site. The view includes a lake and pseudo-Romanesque castle just beyond the upstage boundary, and the skyline of Fifth Avenue in the middle distance. The theatre was designed by Eldon Elder, who left for Connecticut a few years after its construction; by a stroke of good fortune its subsequent direction was established by one of America's greatest contemporary designers, Ming Cho Lee. Born in Shanghai in 1930, Lee had studied in California and was at the beginning of his career when he became resident designer for Papp in 1962. He discovered that the natural background of the Delacorte, unblocked by a permanent wall, was a major distraction for spectators. Normally open-air productions of Shakespeare wish to take advantage of their leafy environments, as those in Regent's Park in London have done for much of the century. But in Central Park, Lee thought, a tall structure was needed to control the action:

When people sitting in the front row look up at an actor, if they see the park, Fifth Avenue and the sky, they lose all interest. But if they look at the actors' faces and there is some surface or line or whatever that belongs to the environment of the show – through which you see the sky – then you feel the performers are acting within something.   (in Aronson 92)

A stage that blends into the cityscape, in other words, is of use only to the extent that the designer can control how much of the city is seen. An unframed action loses intensity in the general ocular field.

To solve the problem of the backdrop, Lee began experimenting with the structures of pipe scaffolding that became his signature. His method has been adapted so frequently that it has become an American design cliché, but in the early 1960s its novelty and flexibility were admirably suited to the kind of Shakespeare Papp envisaged for New York. Though its origins may be traced to Russian Constructivism, Lee's use of industrial materials was closer in intent to the Brechtians like Allio and Bury. On an outdoor open stage, with pictorial illusion impossible, scaffolding provided a distanced attitude to the theatrical event, and at the same time fulfilled the practical needs for a visual frame and for a variety of acting levels. Though Lee admits to a general fascination with "lines cutting across planes," the chief virtue of his scaffolding was that a single unit could acquire different looks through coverage with different materials. A medieval appearance was achieved by placing rough timbered material over the pipes, for example, and an entirely new backdrop could be presented during the same performance by hanging panels or banners from them. Just as spectators at the Delacorte never lose awareness of the city beyond the stage lights, so they also have, in Lee's settings, a double vision of the performance: of the fictive environment, and of the functional scaffolding which supports it.

The possibilities for scaffolding were rapidly deployed and established the chief visual aesthetic of Papp's festival. *Measure for Measure* in July 1966, for example, directed by Michael Kahn and with costumes by Theoni V. Aldredge, was influenced by Brook's production of *Marat/Sade*, which had played in New York in December of the previous year. Kahn's *Measure* opened with a parade of cripples, beggars, and whores; while Brook's version of the play at Stratford in 1950 had used a similar device in the third act, the set at the Delacorte was itself an extension of this grotesquery, composed of metal fire escapes integrated into the scaffolding, and a rough white wall. The effect was a prison environment made of harshly clanging contemporary materials.

One of the most popular of the productions from this period was a *Much Ado* of 1972, designed by the same team. Directed by A. J. Antoon, it revealed a tendency of the New York Shakespeare Festival, still occasionally apparent, to trivialize the plays when faced with elements in the scripts that the director thinks the audience will not understand or accept. Indeed the production, which later moved to Broadway and was broadcast on commercial television for an audience of 27 million, demonstrates how complicated the question of Shakespearean accessibility can become. Placed in the American heartland about 1905, Claudio and Benedick, in white suits and straw hats, were presented as returning from the Spanish–American War, escorted by a brass band playing Scott Joplin tunes. Antoon's idea was based on the premise that old photographs carry an inveterate nostalgia. Wishing to recapture the lost life recorded in photo albums, he studied a number from the period just before the First World War, including the New England family albums of Sam Waterston, who played Benedick.[2] Lee's setting was a major transformation of his scaffolding that drew on two divergent sources: Victorian wrought-iron industrial construction, and the permanent architectural stage in Ontario. The design supported a joyful performance, filled with the celebration of an earlier time, which was uncritically assumed to be a simpler time. A flat backdrop of period posters and tintypes framed the structure, which added American flags, the Watch treated in the manner of the Keystone Kops, and carousel horses in the finale: a Shakespearean Fourth of July.

In itself this performance notion is unobjectionable, even unremarkable. In fact, a number of recent productions had used various nineteenth-century nostalgic allusions for the play, including Michael Langham's 1958 Ruritanian version in Ontario, Douglas Seale's Risorgiamento setting in the same year at the SMT, and Zeffirelli's Sicilian carnival at the Old Vic in 1965. What is disturbing in retrospect about the New York *Much Ado* was that it attempted to relate the fantasy of an heroic reception of war veterans to the present, when the United States was ending its involvement in Vietnam. In interviews[3] the artists spoke of using the warm glow of the production as a preparation for the audience for the homecoming of American troops, which President Nixon was promising. The ironies here are so large that it is difficult to credit that Papp and Antoon could have thought that the public reception of the two wars was somehow parallel; it is more likely that *Much Ado* was being used as a retreat from the dangers and discontents of the present, as a pleasant piece of escapism, since by 1972 the Vietnam War and the soldiers who fought in it were becoming an embarrassment even on the conservative side of American culture. Thus, though it had the appearance of progressive innovation, the production papered over the contradictions in the text and in the social context of the moment to create

110 *King John* 1967 New York. D: Joseph Papp. S: Douglas Schmidt. C: Theoni V. Aldredge. P: George E. Joseph. A high scaffolding with a swinging ladder, the lake of Central Park, and the skyline of Fifth Avenue visible beyond. Here the visual frame has been violated, inviting the natural and urban landscape into the fiction of the play.

111 *Richard III* 1983 New York. D: Jane Howell. Des: Santo Loquasto. L: Pat
Collins. P: Susan Cook for Martha Swope. Rough scaffolding used in a Brechtian
fashion; note the visible lights, the light operator at the top left, and the drummer on
the upper right. The various recessed stages could be closed off with crude curtains.
A portrait of the king in power was illuminated by fluorescent tubes at the top of the
set, clarifying the plot and emphasizing the rapid rise and fall of princes.

a smooth surface of visual reminiscence. The contributions of the designer
in the modern theatre are double-edged, since they are ultimately controlled
by other hands.

Despite the inclination to reductionism at the New York Shakespeare
Festival, Ming Cho Lee's influence has been an extremely positive force. The
roofless stage of the Delacorte has meant that a much greater height can be
achieved in the settings than indoors; Lee's scaffolding has been particularly
useful for the early history plays which rely upon emblematic verticality.
Douglas Schmidt's design for *King John* in 1967, for example, used only a
rough-timbered tower in the center of the stage and left the backdrop open

to show the lake and trees (illus. 110), calling to mind the medieval design for *The Castle of Perseverance*. The scaffold created a daring sense of danger when actors climbed on high, teetering in front of the Fifth Avenue skyline. Some years later a similar effect was achieved by Santo Loquasto, whose pipe scaffolding for *Richard III* incorporated many acting areas above the floor level, and even platforms for follow-spot operators at the very top (illus. 111). This design relied on what Loquasto calls "skewed space" – misaligning the set just enough so that it irritates the spectator – to create "an improvised theatricality" (Aronson 107), similar to the unstudied look of a fairground booth or an impromptu circus. In settings like this Papp's festival achieved its finest results, at least partly because the visual corresponded to the somewhat anarchical mood of the Delacorte audience.

The regional theatre movement in the United States, which flowered after 1960, has encouraged many productions of Shakespeare in cities and festivals far removed from the traditional centers, often in untraditional spaces demanding new scenic approaches. Some of this development was predictably influenced by Guthrie and Moiseiwitsch; the Guthrie Theatre in Minneapolis (1963) is of course the chief realization of the Ontario model in the United States, but the influence extended widely, from the construction of the Vivian Beaumont Theatre at Lincoln Center in New York (1965) to the Mark Taper Forum in Los Angeles (1967). The open stage idea also gave new life to the Elizabethanist movement, most apparent in the outdoor "Old Globe" stages in San Diego and Ashland, which presented inconsistent amateur productions until they were gradually transformed into professional companies with the rise of the regional movement. The smaller non-profit theatres, however, have frequently found classic plays impossible to afford; Actors Equity rules and insufficient subsidies have combined to keep large Shakespearean casts off their stages.

This illogical but characteristically American economy has encouraged a new type of Shakespearean theatre, in status halfway between the professional regional theatres and the conservatory outlets of the drama schools: the numerous summer festivals with connections to theatre departments of universities. These festivals, which have spread all over the United States and have greatly expanded the audience for Shakespeare, usually survive by hiring younger professionals for major roles while relying on students in training to fill out the casts. Some of the productions are of interest in the general ecology of contemporary Shakespeare, some are not. Scenographically, much of the work is derivative; even when distinguished, the productions rarely achieve the prominence or notice needed to make them widely influential. It would be unprofitable (and impossible) to survey this loosely defined movement here. With regret, I must leave it to another historian.

But the major regional theatres and festivals, large enough to afford considerable production budgets, have made some unusual contributions to the visual. One of the most consequential American productions of this period, a "Bismarkian" *Hamlet* at the Arena Stage in Washington in 1978, had an international bent; designed by Ming Cho Lee for the Romanian director Liviu Ciulei, it integrated scenography with the architecture of the theatre and a cogent reading of the text. Ciulei presented Denmark as a Prussian militaristic state, run by the strictest form, with spies and whispers everywhere. The conspiratorial courtiers were in frock-coats, Rosencrantz

112 *Hamlet* 1978 Washington. D: Liviu Ciulei. S: Ming Cho Lee. C: Marjorie Slaimon. L: Hugh Lester. P: George de Vincent. The regular playing floor of the Arena Stage was removed for Lee's set, with its polished raised floor; underneath the elegant surface, out of the "sewers" of Elsinore, death and destruction made their entrances. Kristofer Tabori as Hamlet, facing the camera, with Rosencrantz and Guildenstern (Christopher Allport and George Clark Hosmer) in 2.2.

and Guildenstern were secret policemen, and Ophelia went mad at the dinner table. The Arena Stage is a large in-the-round theatre with no opportunity for pictorial backdrop or proscenium images. Taking a cue from the numerous underground references in the text, and taking advantage of a large trap space, Lee built a visual metaphor of great power: the well-lighted and well-disciplined world of the court was mined by underground tunnels and corridors, imperfectly seen at a lower level. Under the raised stage, through archways and crevices, the audience would now and again have glimpses of catacombs or sewers out of which horrors emerged (illus. 112). The Ghost rose from this cellarage, and so did Hamlet as he approached Claudius in the chapel. Polonius was killed there, and later Laertes erupted from the same place shouting for vengeance. Ophelia's body was sent down through a small hole to her grave.

Sometimes the lower space was visible, sometimes not; but it was always a threat to the order of the upper world, the world of the living.[4] Most of us, like Claudius, think the dead stay dead when they are buried, but the play implies that ghosts walk the night when our minds wake them. Ciulei and Lee created a visual rendering of that theme. Some Washington commentators, attuned to political overtones, noted a similarity to Richard Nixon's Bismarkian presidency, itself filled with spies and an erupting underworld, done in at last by ghosts on tape.

RITUAL AT THE RSC

The momentous changes that occurred at Shakespeare's birthplace during the 1960s continued forcefully when Trevor Nunn assumed charge of the Royal Shakespeare Company in 1968. Firmly established both artistically and socially, the RSC under his guidance went through a dizzying period of growth; though its financial fortunes were at their lowest in early 1970, a decade later, after Brook's *Dream* initiated a series of internationally successful productions culminating with *Nicholas Nickleby*, it had become the largest and most active theatre company in the world, operating four theatres, numerous tours, and extremely profitable transfers to the commercial stage. Artistically these years were marked by a shift away from the Brechtian extractions of Peter Hall and John Bury, towards a new type of theatricalism and a brighter acting style. Hall, despite his radical treatment of text and message, actually remained rather conservative about setting and costume; he has said recently that "unless what's on the stage looks like the language, I simply don't believe it" (Berry 209). But the

113 *Troilus and Cressida* 1968 Stratford. D: John Barton. Des: Timothy O'Brien.
L: John Bradley. Alan Howard as Achilles mocks Helen and the Trojans.

younger directors who came to be associated with Nunn felt little of that
reservation, especially about period allusion; even Hall's cohort John
Barton regularly extended his visual reference far beyond the literal or
historical limits of the plays. (Barton's importance for contemporary
Shakespeare is immense. As the only member of the original company still
directing regularly with the RSC, he has probably staged more Shakespeare
plays than any person in history: well over fifty separate productions
between 1960 and 1990.)[5]

But again it was new designers who empowered a change in method.
Conceptually, the most important may have been Timothy O'Brien, whose
work – unlike that of many other British designers of the period – showed
a cosmopolitan awareness of visual trends. He has said that he is not
interested in the "totally prosaic, very representational set," nor in the set
that is "a quite obvious art object," but rather in "something that lies
between them [and makes] the stage space in some way numinous."[6] For
Barton's production of *Troilus and Cressida* in 1968, the cue was Thersites'
line "nothing but wars and lechery"; the Trojan War became an erotic

114   *Troilus and Cressida* 1968 Stratford. P: Zoë Dominic. Achilles with the Mirmidons. The confusion of battle was signified by fog, and the sensuality of the production by the oiled bodies of warriors.

experience on the battlefield as well in the camps. Achilles was a parody of a transvestite in his impersonation of Helen (illus. 113); Thersites wore a codpiece which had a long serpent-like penis attached, which he would swing like a rope or use to beat time. Cressida's nudity in one scene was matched by glistening, nearly nude warriors on a bare stage saturated with rolling fog in another (illus. 114). For Terry Hands' production of *Pericles* the following year, O'Brien (working now in collaboration with Tanzeena Firth) again costumed the actors in primitive undress, but this time made the stage into a spare white space, filled with mysterious blue light, ceremony, and totemic devices; "ritualized nakedness" was O'Brien's comment on the overall design (illus. 115). Ronald Bryden called it "a Yeatsian voyage to Byzantium" (*Observer* 6 April 1969), a "bare and ritualistic staging." The front cloth held a painting of Leonardo's nude man inside a compass, and the souvenir program emphasized Renaissance iconography of pilgrimage and regeneration.

Ritual motifs were central to *Richard II* in 1973, again designed by

O'Brien and Firth, though the ceremonies were more heavily clothed and bolder in their combination of periods. Barton had Ian Richardson and Richard Pasco rotate the parts of Richard and Bolingbroke, subtly suggesting that the characters are interchangeable, both victims of an inhuman power game, both playing roles assigned them arbitrarily by fate. Of course this suggestion was evoked only on a spectator's repeat visit, or when a spectator was aware of the plan through other means; press coverage and the souvenir program were once more important in establishing the intellectual context, a strategy now used regularly in classical theatres. The interpretation was greatly influenced by Anne Righter's book on Shakespearean metadrama, *Shakespeare and the Idea of the Play*, published in 1962; Righter – who now signs herself Anne Barton – was the director's wife at the time of the production and wrote the program note that outlined the concept, entitled "The King's Two Bodies." Probably never has the

115 *Pericles* 1969 Stratford. D: Terry Hands. Des: Timothy O'Brien and Tanzeena Firth. L: Christopher Morley. P: Thomas F. Holte. Derek Smith as Simonides, Ian Richardson as Pericles (wearing crown), Susan Fleetwood as Thaisa, in an interpolated ceremony in act 2. The white floor and gold idols contrasted to the bare bodies of the dancing attendants.

connection between the academic and theatrical Shakespeare establishments been closer.

The set, fundamental to the director's view, consisted of two giant escalators at the right and left of the stage. Across them a bridge carrying the king silently traveled, making visual the rise and fall imagery of the text (illus. 116). A machine was in control, not Richard or his antagonist:

> Down, down I come, like glist'ring Phaethon,
> Wanting the manage of unruly jades,

said the king (3.3), wearing a metallic robe and illuminated by bright follow-spots, as the bridge descended. These "sky-seeking staircases framing the acting area," as Michael Billington called them, were tokens of an implacable universe, and were strangely appropriate for Shakespeare's picture of the middle ages.

O'Brien has written that the designers felt "that the play was like a bad dream with its central figure wandering without remedy towards certain

116   *Richard II* 1973 Stratford. D: John Barton. Des: Timothy O'Brien and Tanzeena Firth. P: Donald Cooper. Twentieth-century escalators and medieval hobby-horses, signaling period and non-period, theatricalizing the event.

destruction."[7] Their nightmare symbols were thus intended to emphasize the artifice of a histrionic king and a highly theatrical play. A melting snowman, gold masks occasionally worn by both Richard and Bolingbroke, Northumberland and Exton on stilts, a repeated vision of cowled monks, an interpolated prologue in which the figure of Shakespeare ritually handed the crown to Richardson or Pasco, determining which would play the king that night – all were visual devices that embellished metatheatrical facets of the text, outlined in Anne Barton's note. The jousting scene (color pl. 13) provided an excellent example of self-reflexive commentary, with Bolingbroke and Mowbray on medieval hobby-horses and the court precisely, ritualistically arrayed: a cold, mechanical universe of ceremonies and forms.

Trevor Nunn's production of *The Winter's Tale* in 1969, designed by Christopher Morley, used the same basic "modular panels of white"[8] as *Pericles*. In fact it was Morley who designed this unit configuration, used in some manner for all the plays of the season. Nunn added contemporary and

117 *The Winter's Tale* 1969 Stratford. D: Trevor Nunn. Des: Christopher Morley. L: John Bradley. P: Thomas F. Holte. Judi Dench as Hermione (she doubled as Perdita), Jeremy Richardson as Mamillius, Barrie Ingham as Leontes, in the nursery in act 1.

118 *Twelfth Night* 1969 Stratford. D: John Barton. Des: Christopher Morley. C: Stephanie Howard. L: John Bradley. P: Morris Newcombe. Judi Dench as Viola, Don Henderson as the Captain in the wicker cage, entering the dreamworld of Illyria in 1.2.

realistic dimensions to Shakespeare's fantasia on spiritual renewal, most notoriously in Bohemia. Autolycus sang rock songs through a hand-held mike, accompanied by electric guitars, and the dance of the satyrs looked as if it had come from the stage of *Hair*, then playing in London. The servant's description of the satyrs as "all men of hair" (4.4) never had a closer reference for the audience, though Nunn claimed he did not see the rock musical until two or three months after *Winter's Tale* opened. The play began, however, with a more considered and abstract ritual, as Leontes appeared in a tall, mirrored box, arms outstretched like Leonardo's figure of man inside a compass, turning slowly in stroboscopic light. Halfway through, Time would speak from this box, and the statue of Hermione was in it at the end; the first scene opened with a toy version of the box on the floor of Mamillius' nursery, spinning in clockwork time. The royal characters of the romance, especially the King of Sicilia, were trapped in psychological boxes of behavior and form; Leontes' winter-white world was drained of life. The simplicity of the set and the costumes, a cross between Regency styles and the contemporary (illus. 117), made singular visual motifs all the more effective.

Morley designed Barton's famous *Twelfth Night* that same year, a production that encouraged a change in the critical perception of the play by stressing melancholy and fear. The icon of Barton's theme was a long gallery or cage of latticed wicker, with insinuating light (illus. 118). The warmth of the material, associated with gardens and the tropics, was here ambiguously turned to darker uses, suggesting a nightmare prison; Viola's entrance amid fog and mist alluded to a private vision, or a universal womb. Sheila Bannock (*Stratford Herald*, 29 Aug. 1969) called it "a dream tunnel, a journeying place of the mind."

Morley also supervised the design team for Nunn's ambitious mounting of the four Roman plays in 1972. The staging took full advantage of a new hydraulic system in the Stratford theatre which permitted rapid restruc-

119 *Coriolanus* 1972 Stratford. D: Trevor Nunn with Buzz Goodbody and Euan Smith. Des: Christopher Morley and Ann Curtis. L: John Bradley. P: Joe Cocks Studio. Ian Hogg as Coriolanus kneels in triumph before Margaret Tyzack as Volumnia, circled by his prisoners on the wide forestage extension and by the Roman army and Roman wolf on the hydraulic platform upstage. Note the marble treatment of the white panels, which framed the stage in the manner used by Bridges-Adams in the 1930s (see illus. 53).

turing of the floor: level to rake, to steps, to platforms at odd angles, and even to a pyramid.[9] While *Titus* was lined in rich black draperies, exhibiting the decadence of empire, the other plays were cast in Roman marble, accenting the ceremonial and the primitive. Each began with an invented ritual calling to mind the ancient human order: Caesar walked on a blazing red carpet under a huge bronze statue of the Roman wolf, for example, and Antony and Cleopatra performed a frolicsome pageant dressed as pharaonic gods. Though the ambience of period was essential to the treatment, it was achieved by extreme visual metonymy rather than by pictorial detail. The triumphal return of Coriolanus exemplified Morley's method well (illus. 119). The rough yokes on the backs of the captives, evoking crucifixion as well as imprisonment, drew the harshness of conquest with a minimum of strokes, while on the receding platform upstage the glory of Rome was summoned by totemic imagery. The main action – visually reduced but staged emblematically, the triumphant son on his knees before his patrician mother – occurred between compressed and compelling emblems of early Rome.

The ritualistic styles of O'Brien and Morley were vivid aids to revised interpretations, and it's worth noting that Barton's *Troilus*, *Twelfth Night*, and *Richard II*, as well as Hands' *Pericles*, prompted new critical and public attention to those texts. The search for the new, of course, does not insure artistic success; as we have noted before, originality in thought and design has been an ambiguous passion for classical theatres in the twentieth century. The RSC has assumed the singular responsibility of working through a canon of thirty-seven plays by a single author on a regular cycle, playing for audiences who can easily recall the last mounting and for critics who are likely to compare versions in print; even a relatively neglected script like *Pericles* has appeared at Stratford every ten or eleven years since the war. Within the organization itself the pressure for innovation is very strong, leading to an occasional production that is clearly a reaction to the last staging of the same play. In this period the unprecedented response to Brook's *Dream*, and the powerful utility of Sally Jacobs' design, seemed to place an extra burden on scenic innovation; in his article on company scenography O'Brien confessed that only in that case had a director or designer "actually made any worthwhile discovery," though "mandarin discussions of the ingredients of style have seemed a necessary, if daunting, preamble to every production."[10] Despite O'Brien's disavowal, the cumulative work of designers in the early 1970s evolved a new platform for performance at the RSC.

This was most apparent in 1975, when Terry Hands directed a season of the history plays to celebrate the centenary of the founding of the SMT. He started with *Henry V* in March, then added the two parts of *Henry IV* in April and June, and finally remounted his 1968 *Merry Wives of Windsor* in August. By opening the units of the cycle out of sequence, and by omitting *Richard II* from the season entirely (Barton's production had been in repertory for the two previous years), Hands wished to give privileged place to *Henry V* and to counter its conventional reading as chauvinist propaganda (Beauman 326). Further, he believed that the opening speech of the Chorus, stressing the primacy of the audience's imagination in the theatre event, could provide a new performance "dictionary" for the season and for the future.[11]

The Henriad was designed by Farrah (Abd' Elkander Farrah, an Algerian-born protégé of Michel Saint-Denis), who made the visual life of the cycle most simple and plain, a clear departure from the epic realism of *The Wars of the Roses*. The cast size of *Henry V*, for example, was half that of the 1964 version, so that the English army consisted only of the seven men who have speaking parts, and many other roles were doubled. In place of Bury's ironclad floor and walls, Farrah stripped the stage back to bare wood and bricks. The signification, however, was not simple, and operated at levels beyond the ocular. This was an instance where scenography was intended both as an aesthetic and a political statement, and the politics were much more immediate than those of the play's themes. In 1975 the RSC and the nation were going through an extreme financial crisis; because of major cutbacks in public funding a real threat existed that the company would not survive. The connection was made plain by – of all people – Prince Philip, who implicitly equated the RSC with the endangered animal species so dear to his heart; "it is unthinkable," he wrote in the foreword to a book on the production, "that the present and future generations should lose what has become a national institution." And Trevor Nunn, speaking as a responsible fiscal administrator, could exult that "one of the cheapest seasons we'd mounted in recent years [was] hailed as one of the most spectacular."[12] What was seen on stage, therefore, was a message to the government. More precisely, what was *not* seen on stage was the message.

After the prologue, the opening visuals of *Henry V* were certainly a shock: actors on a bare stage, in jeans and miscellaneous dress, casually discussing great matters of state and the Salic Law as if at rehearsal, the King in a new track suit and running shoes. The French Ambassador, arriving in full panoply and graceful voice, established an early contrast between the

120 *Henry V* 1975 Stratford. D: Terry Hands. Des: Farrah. L: Stewart Leviton. P: Nobby Clark. The informal English court in the tennis balls scene (1.2). Alan Howard as Henry V in track suit, Philip Brack as Exeter, Oliver Ford-Davies as the French Ambassador.

down-to-earth English – costumed to signal "like us" – and an alien tribe (illus. 120). Only gradually did the English assume the costumes and manners of the fifteenth century, as they dressed for war from costumes rolled out on a cannon mount, though the Chorus (Emrys James, who acted Henry IV in the other plays) remained in modern dress throughout.

Farrah's solution to the scenic demands of pageantry and battle was equally simple. A billowing canopy emblazoned with the English coat of arms was suspended above the stage in the second act (color pl. 14). Framed by its regal patterns and by the upstage brick wall of the theatre, the action was focused and intensified. In act 3 the canopy dropped to the floor, its gray side now representing the mud of battle, blending with the cloaks of the King and his army (color pl. 15). Raised again for the conclusion, the fleurs-de-lis in the English colors acquired new meaning at the French court. The concentration of visual resources was essentially Brechtian, similar to Teo Otto's design for the same play in Vienna in 1961 (see color pl. 12). In

121 *2 Henry IV* 1975 Stratford. D: Terry Hands. Des: Farrah. L: Stewart Leviton.
P: Joe Cocks Studio. "I know thee not, old man": a golden Hal (Alan Howard),
brilliantly lit and treading on rushes, mechanically and ritualistically turns away from
Falstaff (Brewster Mason), dead branches in the background.

abandoning Bury's low-key selective realism of *The Wars of the Roses*, Farrah
was abandoning a British adaptation of the Berliner Ensemble method, not
the method itself. This was perhaps clearer in *Henry IV*, *Part 2*, where a
clutch of bare branches on a tree trunk, derived literally from the scenes in
Shallow's garden, stood throughout as a symbol of rebellion, decay, and the
death of Hal's former life. In the rejection scene the new King was encased
in gold armor, cap-à-pie, moving like a machine, visually a stranger to an old
man's merry love (illus. 121). Hal was presented like the new Pope in scene
12 of Brecht's *Galileo*, so heavily attired that nothing human remained inside
the symbols of responsibility and the garments of office.

A complex of rationales, then, lay behind Terry Hands' artistic choices.
Some of the rationales were not immediately apparent from an ordinary or
naïve viewer's perspective, requiring commentary or conditioning to be
effective. This was readily provided, within and without the theatre, since
part of the object was to gain public support for increased funding. The RSC
budget deficit was widely reported, and most reviewers commented on the

attendant austerity of the scenography. (The summary essay on the season in *Shakespeare Survey* was titled "Towards a Poor Shakespeare.") Even so, not everyone buys souvenir programs or reads notices; some spectators were bound to miss the unseen ramifications of *Henry V*, and to struggle with its visual contradictions. I remember that my own responses had been conditioned by the press so that I read the production predisposed to its intentions, while a playgoer seated next to me quietly admitted her confusion during the interval; she felt left out of the specially coded meaning and – since I was a stranger and foreigner explaining it – embarrassed over her "ignorance." Though this is merely anecdotal evidence, the complexity of the signifiers on stage was so great that misreadings were probably frequent. On one level the scenography was in key with the interpretation, yet on another level it was heavily burdened with extra-textual meaning. Aside from the potential for bewilderment, this was a dangerous political game for the company to play. Since the results of your adversity are so effective dramatically, a hard-pressed government might ask, why do you need more money?

CHAMBER SHAKESPEARE

The search for the right performance space for Shakespeare has been one of the continuing stories of production in the twentieth century. At Stratford the search has a burdensome history, since the building has been so restrictive. Every artistic director since Bridges-Adams has spent inordinate time and money attempting to lessen the rigidity of the proscenium in what remains – despite architectural and scenic alterations – an adamantly proscenium house. This pattern reached its apogee in 1976, when John Napier designed a unit set along Elizabethan lines for the entire season, very loosely based on the de Witt drawing of the Swan Theatre. Napier thrust a temporary stage well into the house, forcing the front seats into a new configuration, extended galleries around the outer walls, and even provided seats for about eighty spectators inside the visual frame of the ludic space. The productions, most of which were directed by Nunn and Barton, emphasized costume and made full use of numerous discovery spaces. Barton's *Much Ado about Nothing*, set in a nineteenth-century officers' mess during the Raj, reveled in the open stage; there was no scenery, said B. A. Young,[13] only some "cheesecloth curtains" for actors to hide behind (illus. 122). The Elizabethan season was a highly successful visual and spatial experiment that, for the first time, changed the audience–actor relationship

122 *Much Ado about Nothing* 1976 Stratford. D: John Barton. Des: John Napier. L: Clive Morris. P: Joe Cocks Studio. The unified Elizabethan design for the 1976 RSC season. The reshaped stage and seats in the RST were used for all productions; props and furniture for the Indian setting of *Much Ado* are seen here. Spectators were seated in some of the wooden upper galleries. (This photo was taken from the regular house balcony.)

of the theatre in any significant way. But its survival depended on the artistic plans of directors; when Terry Hands found it inhibiting for *Henry VI* the following year, out it went.

Meanwhile, another type of spatial experiment had been gaining advocates inside the company, one that deliberately turned away from the relatively conservative traditions and passive audiences of the main house. Since the rise of the avant-garde in the late nineteenth century, a good deal of renovative theatre work has been done in small spaces, where costs can be contained and where intimacy of playing can have a potent effect, especially in prompting a more active engagement between spectators and actors. It is now regular policy for established theatres to have second or even third stages for laboratory work, a practice begun in 1905 when Stanislavsky created the Studio of the Moscow Art Theatre. Shakespeare has not often been a part of this movement, for obvious reasons: the large casts of the plays, the high production expense, the persistent claim on his work by advocates of high culture. But by 1974 the growing fringe theatre movement in England, firmly committed to social change, reached into the heart of Stratford. A storage shed near the RST, converted to a tiny theatre and called The Other Place, opened its doors in April of that year; made of corrugated iron and seating about 140 people, its rough, jerry-built look was in remarkable contrast to the traditions of the main house.

The opening production was directed by Buzz Goodbody, who had been put in charge of the new venture. Brought into the company as John Barton's assistant, she was the first woman to direct for the RSC. Her own background, a combination of leftist politics and radical theatre work, led her to attempt a change in attitude at Stratford that was realized in the drastically remodeled style imposed by the small space.[14] The production, a version of *King Lear* that treated the play as a domestic tragedy, called attention to the value of small-scale Shakespeare, and led directly to Goodbody's *Hamlet* the following year, with Ben Kingsley in the title role.

123   *Hamlet* 1975 Stratford. D: Buzz Goodbody. Des: Chris Dyer. L: Leo Leibovici. P: Joe Cocks Studio. The Murder of Gonzago in a village hall setting at The Other Place, the sliding screens upstage. The Players (from left to right) were Bob Peck, Stuart Wilson, Terrence Wilton, and Charles Dance (with guitar).

Chris Dyer designed it as a "village hall" performance (illus. 123): the stage was a raised, shallow platform at one end of the space, and the simple set, consisting of "sliding white paper screens on stage" and white cloth dropped at edges of the auditorium, focused attention on inner character, according to Nicholas de Jongh. A Kabuki-style bridge ran through the audience to the rear of the house, continually enforcing intimacy with the spectators. Fashionable modern dress and subtle, psychological acting increased the immediacy of the story – Claudius (George Baker) seemed like a director of a commercial company at an annual shareholders' meeting, said Irving Wardle, and Kingsley's playing invited the audience to make decisions about the correctness of events as they unfolded. The egalitarian style of acting proceeded from the space itself, where the audience had all paid the same admission price (70 pence) and all sat on backless benches.

Buzz Goodbody killed herself in London in April, three days after the first preview. The reasons for her suicide were as complex as her personality, but it is clear that among the contributing factors were a nagging sense of inadequacy and a desperate fear of failure that derived from being the only female director in the male-dominated world of the RSC. This unfortunate story is connected to my subject because more attention was paid to her last production as a result of her death. Trevor Nunn himself took charge of the final rehearsals; while he had supported Goodbody's project from the start, his close involvement with the results of her *Hamlet* made him see more clearly the power of small-scale production for Shakespeare and for contemporary drama. Following a successful run at Stratford, *Hamlet* transferred to the Roundhouse in London, and thereafter studio work became a policy of the RSC. The Donmar Warehouse was acquired in 1977 as a regular outlet in the capital, a flexible small space was integrated into the plans for the RSC's permanent home in the Barbican (the Pit, opened in 1982), and a third Stratford theatre, the Swan, was eventually built in 1986 to experiment further with a non-proscenium space and relatively intimate surroundings.

Goodbody's legacy for Shakespeare was best exemplified in Nunn's production of *Macbeth* in 1976 at The Other Place, with the main house stars Ian McKellen and Judi Dench in the leading roles. Nunn had directed the play at the RST in 1974 with a different cast, in a church setting by John Napier. It was restaged at the Aldwych the next year, but only when completely reworked in the small space did the implications of the interpretation, based on the simplest contrast between good and evil, achieve full strength. Though it had more gloss than Goodbody's productions, *Macbeth* nonetheless worked chiefly by minimizing the visual field and emphasizing actor proximity to the audience. There was no raised stage and there were no raised voices; everything, as John Barber put it, was "plain, quiet, austere."[15] A bare wood floor in the middle of the space, outlined with a circle of black paint, was the chief scenographic device, supplemented by a few packing crates for actors to sit on, and by minimal emblematic props like a kingly robe and a thunder sheet (color pl. 16). The audience sat on three sides around the circle, only a few rows deep, and elevated above the floor on scaffolding. Some of the cast of fourteen would stay on stage to watch scenes with particular relevance to their characters, to which they were not party; Robert Cushman noted that it was the witches who observed Macbeth as he damned himself, and Macduff who looked on as his family was murdered. The sense of peering in at a corrupting ritual was thus strengthened by a double spectatorship, and became central to the emotional quality of the production.

Equally central, and actually part of the same aesthetic, was McKellen's extrovert and coldly murderous performance. With slicked-back hair, jack boots, and a tendency to spin around quickly, he seemed like an intense 1930s fascist, but still likeable and compelling: "the company commander whose men would gladly follow him through hell and high water," wrote Richard David (95). McKellen was particularly well suited to the close-up style of a production which drew much of its power from the intense but restrained acting associated with cinema, where an empty stare or a slight facial gesture are used to convey plot as well as character. No doubt the familiarity of audiences with psychological-realist film acting made this, and other chamber productions of Shakespeare, more accessible. Already short by Shakespearean standards, *Macbeth* was cut down to two and a quarter hours and played without interval, like a film. Some of the visuals also came from filmic sources, like the thin line of red blood on her skin as a murderer slashed Lady Macduff's throat just before a blackout. Generally, however, the intimate power was theatrical rather than cinematic, intensified by highly metaphoric scenography. The best example occurred after Lady Macbeth's death (5.5), when McKellen was standing under a single lightbulb. He shoved it, setting it swinging; as he spoke the words of despair, his face was alternately in darkness and light during the rhythm of its arc:

> I 'gin to be aweary of the sun,
> And wish th'estate o'th' world were now undone.

It was natural that the production be televised, but the TV version, I think, is less moving than the original precisely because the cinematic effects of close-up and intimate intensity seem rather ordinary on the small screen.

The homespun virtues of the early productions at The Other Place, emphasizing that the tragedies of *Lear*, *Hamlet*, and *Macbeth* are deeply rooted in family matters, continued to prove a fruitful area for performance investigation, especially with John Barton's staging of *The Merchant of Venice* in 1978. Domesticity was magnificently exploited in the visual presentation of *Othello*, directed by Nunn and designed by Bob Crowley, seen in limited runs at Stratford and at the Young Vic Theatre in London in 1989. (It was the final production in The Other Place before the theatre was closed for major renovations mandated by new local safety regulations.) McKellen's Iago, a rigidly disciplined non-commissioned officer obsessed with order and tidiness, was like cold steel in the marriage bed. The set, a bleached wooden back wall with a double door but without an upper level, was a variation of an Elizabethan configuration that emphasized imprisonment. In the first act the floor was covered with Persian carpets thrown on top of each other; Iago established his military precision by frequently straightening them and the furniture. The costumes seemed generalized from mid-nineteenth-century wear, and were particularly successful in the Senate scene: a few actors in cutaways, Othello (Willard White, a black opera singer from Jamaica, acting Shakespeare for the first time) in blue uniform at a small table with a brandy decanter, quietly narrating the story of his love.

In Cyprus the carpets were removed to reveal a canvas-covered square floor in the center of the thrust, with a light layer of sand on it. This sandpit, or desert, which sounded like sandpaper as the actors' shoes scraped across it, forcefully suggested the aridity of the locale and the nerve-wracking, hopeless energy of someone endlessly pacing a room. After intermission the costumes became more specific, subtly indicating the military uniforms of the American Civil War. No political statement was intended, Crowley said; "I tried rather to elicit key objects from the period that would have a huge resonance in a small space. This was Shakespeare under the microscope."[16] The general effect remained metaphoric rather than realist, though the barracks setting used for some scenes, constructed out of two iron beds and washstands, made Iago's familiarity frighteningly claustrophobic (illus. 124). Using such a period setting in England, the designer was effectively relying upon the audience's collective experience of Hollywood films: men going to a distant outpost for war, the women tagging along, always out of place. "It's hard to do that with doublets and hose," Crowley noted,

124   *Othello* 1989 Stratford. D: Trevor Nunn. Des: Bob Crowley. L: Chris Parry.
P: Richard Mildenhall. Willard White as Othello and Ian McKellen as Iago in an
American Civil War barracks (2.3), at The Other Place.

whereas uniforms from more recent periods can instantly establish character
hierarchies as well as significant emotional overtones.

The chamber Shakespeare movement, which has spread worldwide, may
be the most consequential development for classic plays in recent time. It
gathers together a hundred years of Shakespearean concerns about intimacy
of playing, the importance of non-illusionist setting, and the shape of the
performance space. By stressing low budgets, and by putting the play in the
lap of the audience, small-scale productions have forced designers to seek
reduced visual essences for work that has frequently been treated with
extravagance. It's interesting that the RSC's first experiments at The Other
Place occurred at the moment of publication of John Russell Brown's *Free
Shakespeare* (1974), a book that roundly attacked the lavish principles behind
dominant Shakespearean representation, and called for a small group of
actors to operate as a public laboratory for exploring new methods of
performance.[17] In Brown's model, the director and the designer would

recede as the actor achieved more authority. In practice this has only partly been true; certainly Ian McKellen dominated *Macbeth* and *Othello*, for example, but Trevor Nunn set the outlines and the intellectual context. At first glance scenography also seems less important in a tiny theatre, but actually the designer's job becomes more difficult: an inappropriate visual concept or inessential detail or even the wrong color will be harshly magnified and will likely ruin the total performance. Chamber Shakespeare, which has restored the elementary relationship between player and spectator, is another reminder of the irreducible importance of the eye.

WELL, THIS IS THE FOREST OF ARDEN

Certain plays of Shakespeare have been used in the century to challenge the scenographic and performance assumptions of the time, their directors and designers finding perplexity or encumbrances in material that earlier periods had found unequivocal and comforting. *The Winter's Tale* was such a document for Reinhardt and Granville Barker at the beginning of the century, *Romeo and Juliet* a similar case for Tairov, Terence Gray, and John Gielgud between the wars, the history plays for the Brechtians in the 1960s. *As You Like It* became a problematic text in the next decade, chiefly because the distinction between the court and the forest offers an opportunity to stress how "civilization" and "nature" are ambiguous partitions: the ancient longing for escape to a pastoral haven has been significantly qualified by the extreme urbanization of contemporary culture. Arden already had an intriguing visual history, dating back to the abstract forests of Claud Lovat Frazer for Nigel Playfair's production at the SMT in 1919, and of Wincenty Drabik for Schiller's version in Warsaw in 1925. But most of the earlier designs, whether symbolic or pictorial, tried to suggest that for all its adversity the forest was a beautiful place, archaic, pre-civilized, Edenic.

The seminal adjustment occurred in Clifford Williams' all-male production in 1967 for the National Theatre at the Old Vic. The director's idea, much debated and much misunderstood, was to investigate love "in an atmosphere of spiritual purity that transcends sexuality. It is for this reason that I employ a male cast," he wrote; "so that we shall not – entranced by the surface reality – miss the interior truth."[18] The teasing sexuality of a beautiful actress in a part written for a boy disturbed Granville Barker as well, who went to great lengths in his 1912 production of *Twelfth Night* to attenuate the woman behind Viola-Cesario, though he used his wife in the role (see Kennedy 1985 : 136–40). Harold Hobson seemed to get Williams' point, and thought the performance put "eroticism, whether ambiguous or straightforward, out of the theatre altogether"; most critics, however, could not accept this slant on the play and were confused by the device, some even accusing the director of a homosexual approach. It's doubtful whether Ronald Pickup as Rosalind succeeded entirely in transcending sexuality, but the transgendered casting certainly underlined sexual confusion and questions of personal identity, implying a darker, Kottian view of human relationships, despite Williams' announced intention. Indeed Kott's essay on the play, "Bitter Arcadia," was quoted in the program.

More significantly, the absence of women on the stage impelled a renewed attention to the power of convention in the theatre. Shakespeare's use of boy actors for female roles derived from cultural, social, and religious circumstances deeply rooted in his age, just as our use of actresses for those same roles is rooted in many unexamined contemporary assumptions about realism. Forcing the issue, Williams risked making the all-male casting a mere gimmick; it succeeded partly because of subtle acting in the female roles, but chiefly because of Ralph Koltai's design, which transformed Arden into a manmade forest, a dreamspace of modern art. As Rosenfeld said (195), it was "a dream in which there was no reality – only a hint of timeless trees." On a burnished, raked stage, mostly empty for the court scenes, the forest descended in the form of hanging Plexiglas tubes and abstract shapes cut out of a metal screen (illus. 125). White light, and black and white Carnaby Street costumes (often in plastics), underscored the artificiality of a psychedelic reverie, an airy contrast to the heavy actuality of John Bury's metal for *The Wars of the Roses*, seen just four years earlier. It was an Arden detached from nature and detached from the comforts of the natural, a space-age Arden, like a Calder mobile; "so different, so strange, so visually and aurally hypnotic," wrote Peter Lewis, "that the fact that all the girls are really men takes its place as merely one of the elements in a dream-like total experience."[19]

An all-male production of one of the few Shakespearean plays normally owned by actresses was bound to prompt a reaction. It came in the next RSC staging of *As You Like It*, directed by Buzz Goodbody in 1973. As Colin Chambers (33) wrote, this was an attempt "to win the play back for women"; but it seemed at odds with itself, succeeding neither as a feminist rebuttal nor as a more conventional reading. Christopher's Morley's set, hundreds of metal tubes hanging from the flies, was an obvious allusion to

Koltai's design, an example on the visual level of how self-reflexive British Shakespearean production can be.

Four years later, however, Trevor Nunn took a completely different tack by reinstituting the Restoration mode of Shakespearean representation, infused with some glimmerings of postmodern sensibility. Taking a cue from the masque of the last act, Nunn offered a baroque spectacle in the form of a pastiche Stuart opera, with a Purcell-like prologue, arias for Celia and Orlando (Judith Paris and Peter McEnery), and much of the fifth act set to music, composed by Stephen Oliver. John Napier's design stressed artificiality in the first part of the play, which was set in front of monochrome drop-flats; too refined for its own good, Duke Frederick's court seemed already about to disintegrate in a swirl of Cavalier flounce and feather. The forest was in marked distinction, harsh, wintry, and rather ugly; nonetheless

125 *As You Like It* 1967 London. D: Clifford Williams. Des: Ralph Koltai. L: Robert Orubo and John B. Read. P: Zoë Dominic. Jeremy Brett as Orlando, Ronald Pickup as Rosalind, Charles Kay as Celia, in a "contempo" Forest of Arden. National Theatre at the Old Vic.

it remained inside the strict artifice of seventeenth-century opera, heightening Shakespeare's contrived plot and the unreality of his ending. Spring arrived, paper petals supplanting paper snowflakes, and the masque of Hymen was framed by visual allusions to Italian baroque staging (color pl. 17).

It was a bold attempt, thought Noel Witts,[20] to unify the play's heterogeneous elements of pastoral, masque, and morality through visual means. The program notes made clear that Nunn's intention was to use music in a Renaissance manner, to symbolize the movement to universal harmony. But a harmony so allusively signalled would suggest to an audience that the escape to Arden was not an authentic possibility outside the realm of art. The fabled psychological reality of Shakespeare's characters was undercut by an artifice so profound that even sexuality seemed at times to be detached from human agency. By reconstituting the text as a self-conscious imitation of early opera, Nunn had transgressed the performance principles he and Peter Hall had made central for the RSC, moving Shakespeare out of the logocentric tradition and into the precinct occupied earlier in the century by Craig, Jessner, Gray, Welles, and Komisarjevsky.

This other realm, where the visual stands almost separate from interpretation of the text, or where visual readings are freed from verbal determinants, was again becoming a major alternative for Shakespeare in Europe. As if to make the point, a production of *As You Like It* that magnified the trend opened in West Berlin in September 1977, just two weeks after Nunn's. Peter Stein, the director of the Schaubühne since 1970, had become internationally noted for a series of remarkable deconstructive and Marxist stagings of the classics, but he and his participatory company had put off Shakespeare because they felt unready for the challenge. In 1976 they provided themselves with the necessary study in an unprecedented two-part production called *Shakespeare's Memory* (the title was given in English), which was an amalgamation of dramatic and non-dramatic texts relevant to the Elizabethan period. Performed for a promenade audience in an open space at a film studio in Spandau, often with two or more events occurring simultaneously, the purpose was to prepare the ensemble and its audience for a Shakespeare play by recreating some of the material held in the playwright's "memory." The design by Karl-Ernst Hermann was framed by an enormous wooden scaffold, and included huge objects like a multi-layered, gyroscopic zodiac (with a nude actor standing inside), a pageant wagon, and the keel of an Elizabethan ship under construction.[21] For the 360 wandering spectators who could be accommodated each evening, the experience was a disturbing cross between a series of dramatized lectures (much of the information was factual and rather dryly presented) and a trip in a time machine. Visually the primary achievement was the creation of a sensuous environment for an imaginative journey.

This became the central object of Hermann's settings for *As You Like It* the following year, performed in the same location with many of the same objects. One of Stein's greatest productions, it went to extraordinary lengths to investigate the dream of escape visually. In the first part of the play the audience was required to stand in a long, narrow hall with light blue walls, brightly lit from below, which looked like an empty art gallery. The text was rearranged so that all the scenes in the court and near Oliver's house were played here, on various shallow acting spaces in front of doors or archways along two sides (illus. 126). The action was not presented as written, however; a few lines from one scene would be followed by a short burst from another in a different location, rapidly intercut in montage fashion, so that the audience had to turn about to follow the story. As in *Shakespeare's Memory*, the spectators were partially free to construct the play

126   *As You Like It* 1977 Berlin. D: Peter Stein. S: Karl-Ernst Hermann. C: Moidele Bickel. P: Ruth Walz. Orlando (Michael König) throws Charles (Günter Nordhoff, actually a professional wrestler) before the Duke's court, as the audience stands in the narrow hall. Schaubühne, at CCC Film Studio.

in their heads. The costumes were Elizabethan but in the darkest of colors, so that characters appeared harsh and artificial against the cold light of the room, a quality that was conveyed by the formal style of the acting as well.

The audience, having shared the confinement of the court, shared the journey to the forest. As Oliver escaped his brother's wrath through a door at one end of the hall, the spectators were invited to follow, single-file, through a tunnel of marvels:

We found ourselves in a dimly lit, green labyrinth, artificial creepers hanging from above, water dripping down the walls. As we followed the twists and turns of this passage, we passed curious collages pasted on the walls, small booth-like openings containing, for example, an Elizabethan workshop or, more strikingly, the androgynous man from *Shakespeare's Memory* ... The conception was brilliant: to pass from the formality and brutality of the court through an underground labyrinth to the freedom and innocence of the forest was like being born anew.[22]

As the audience emerged at the other end, they took their places (some 300 seats on risers in a U-shape) in the middle of a scenographic sensurround, both inviting and threatening, containing, it seemed, all the world, all weather (illus. 127). They moved, in other words, from a black and white metaphor of the court to a full-color metonymy of Arden. Tall trees, green grasses, a real pond, sheaves of wheat growing in a field, sand, Orlando's fight with a wild beast enacted on stage – this Arden was an equivocal landscape of delights and fears. Henning Rischbieter called it a "monster Disneyland," and many commentators recalled Reinhardt's desire to realize the natural world on stage in an earlier Berlin.

But Stein's purpose was essentially different. While spectators might focus momentarily on the scenic illusion of a single area (a tactic used by some production photos which framed a sectional locale like a movie, cutting off the larger view), it was clearly not possible to ignore the full picture for long. As the text was deconstructed, so was the scene: to see all of an expansive Arden around you is to see an obviously created set of objects that have been reassembled. When the dramatic travelers arrived, they were out of their elegant Elizabethan dress and in clothing crossed between the nineteenth and twentieth centuries (illus. 128). Similarly when Hymen entered all in gold (on the pageant wagon from *Shakespeare's Memory*), the forest-dwellers threw off their rough cloaks to reveal their Elizabethan garments underneath, as if they had been playing at exile all along. In Hermann's rendering, the artificiality of Arden lay not in a formal

127 *As You Like It* 1977 Berlin. P: Ruth Walz. The forest of Arden setting with the audience in place. The wooden scaffolding was from *Shakespeare's Memory*; the suspended round object is a model of the Ptolemaic universe. Orlando is seen writing "Rosalind" on the ground.

128 *As You Like It* 1977 Berlin. P: Ruth Walz. Touchstone (Werner Rehm), Celia
(Tina Engel), and Rosalind (Jutta Lampe) arrive in Arden in updated dress.

stylistic distancing, of the type John Napier provided for the RSC operatic version, but rather in an agglutination of discordant elements.

When the messenger entered to relate the conversion of Duke Frederick, he left the door to the court open so that the audience saw again that cold blue light beckoning in the distance. The wedding dance continued on the wagon as it rolled off toward the light. But the wagon wouldn't fit through the door, stopped with a bump and knocked off the actors, who stumbled back on foot to the world of politics and intrigue. Meanwhile Duke Frederick had actually appeared in Arden, choosing, like Jaques, hermitage rather than society. Rosalind was not present to speak the epilogue. In her place Frederick recited a poem on autumn by Francis Ponge that emphasized the independence of nature from human life, and Corin began to clean up the mess left by these over-civilized *pastores*: a powerful memorandum that the work of the working class goes on.

Shakespeare's text, far from sacrosanct, had been rewritten by the visual. Though the production shared with the chamber movement an interest in the arrangement of the playing space, the visual means were in notable contrast to the poor Shakespeare of The Other Place; the Schaubühne is one of the mostly highly subsidized theatres in the world, and the combined design costs for *Shakespeare's Memory* and *As You Like It* were over DM 700,000.[23] The extravagance of Hermann's scenography, however, was clearly related to Stein's theme. Arden, a beautiful falsehood, was seen as an illusory escape; ideal nature is a dream of the city-dweller, at best a temporary respite from the concerns of society left behind. As Patterson notes, this thought had particular resonance in West Berlin, a city surrounded by a hostile country. To escape urban life, to frolic in the forest like Rosalind and Orlando, its residents in 1977 had to drive hundreds of kilometers nonstop to the West German border. By using an environmental setting that required the spectator's participation, Stein made the spectator part of the court, part of the forest, and part of the journey between them. In this light the production was distinctly opposite to the naturalistic displays of Reinhardt, which depended upon audience passivity. In the final analysis the most disturbing aspect of Stein's visual approach was not that it rewrote Shakespeare but that it did so with the active collaboration of its viewers.

9 | *Imaging Shakespeare*

Post-Christian, post-industrial, post-structuralist, post-Marxist, post-civilized, post-nuclear, *post-histoire*: we seem to know what our age comes after, not what it is. In their attempts to historicize contemporary aesthetics, commentators have failed to uncover a convincing paradigm – indeed, have concluded that the lack of a paradigm or "totalizing narrative" is a key feature of postmodernism. One of the most notable characteristics of the postmodern sensibility, however, from pop art to music videos, has been an obsessive attention to the singular or detachable image. This obsession, driven by commercial interests and encouraged by visual advertising, has affected high art as well as popular entertainment. In the theatre the postmodern has chiefly involved a reconsideration of the purpose of scenography; as Brecht's designers redefined the nature of the beautiful, so postmodern designers have been redefining the relationship of the ocular to the action. The visuals achieved by the New York school of performance art, by *Tanztheater*, and by designer-directors like Tadeusz Kantor, Richard Foreman, and Robert Wilson, have often carried the burden of the event, or have been detached from verbal meaning in order to encourage active self-consciousness, extreme alienation, hallucinatory fantasy, or intellectual destabilization in the audience. This scenography stands in marked distinction to that of the Brechtians and of the modernists, who relied on design to assist interpreted meaning or to reinforce character and fable. (Though the work of Wilson, with its emphasis on dreamlike inner states, can be seen as the logical conclusion of Craig's modernism.)[1]

It's impossible to define what postmodern Shakespeare means, or even if such a thing exists; indeed, Shakespeare's verbal text and psychological interest in character resist a thoroughly imagistic presentation. Yet certain international trends unmistakably tie contemporary Shakespeare production to postmodern approaches, and two distinctive properties are prominent. The first is a clear preference for the metaphoric over the metonymic, which parallels the movement away from Brechtian or other political uses of the

266

texts. The second is a trans-historical or anti-historical use of eclectic costuming and displaced scenery, creating, through irony, a disjunction between the pastness of Shakespeare's plays and the ways we now receive them.

TROUSERS DOWN: ZADEK AND TRAVESTY

The beginnings of a postmodern scenography for Shakespeare are most apparent in the productions of Peter Zadek, who excessively rejected postwar standards of interpretation, whether Brechtian or British. The son of a Jewish merchant who escaped Germany in 1933, Zadek was raised in England, attended Oxford at the same time as Peter Brook, was expelled from the Old Vic Theatre School, and had a minor career as an avant-garde director in London in the 1950s. He began directing Shakespeare soon after his return to Germany in 1958, though it wasn't until his adaptation of *Measure for Measure* at Bremen in 1967 that his method clarified. The production was essentially an attempt to confront subjectively the ideas that the text evoked in the director's mind. Wilfred Minks' design used lightbulbs placed around the proscenium arch, modern hippie dress, and the bare brick walls of the stage to suggest the new approach. The actors, relying on body language rather than Shakespeare's language, substituted a contemporary spirit of anarchy for the play's consideration of justice. Instead of the discussion of the uses of power in act 1, for example, Angelo and Escalus physically fought over the Duke's chair. In the end the Duke was murdered by the citizens of Vienna and Mistress Overdone was installed in his place. Her justice proved merciless: she had Angelo and Mariana executed and, measure still for measure, Isabella confined to a brothel. As Zadek wrote in the program note, he had discarded any responsibility to an objective analysis of the text, and decided "at all costs only to stage the images arising in my imagination from reading the play."[2]

As artistic director of the Schauspielhaus at Bochum, Zadek presented a series of travesty versions of Shakespeare that were chiefly interested in provoking German audiences out of their respectful lethargy to the classics by outlandish means. His *Merchant of Venice* in 1972, with a set of winding causeways by René Allio, offended conventional opinion and reproached the collective German "loss of memory" by presenting Shylock as a *Jud Süss*, the snarling, spitting, Nazi stereotype of the German Jew, done in by the hegemonic culture. *King Lear* in 1974, performed in a cinema building, sought to recapture "the other 90%" to the theatre by using *Volkstheater* or

129 *Othello* 1976 Hamburg. D: Peter Zadek. S: Zadek and Peter Pabst. C: Pabst. P: Roswitha Hecke. Travesty of stereotypes: Ulrich Wildgruber as Othello, Eva Mattes as Desdemona, for the arrival in Cyprus (2.1). As in a number of his productions, Zadek followed here the long history of men making theatre out of the bodies of women, catering to the male gaze.

carnival techniques (see Leiter 323–4). It was a vaudeville sketch of Shakespeare: Gloucester spoke to Kent through a megaphone, Goneril wore cardboard breasts, Gloucester's blinding was signalled by ramming his top hat over his eyes.

An *Othello* at Hamburg in 1976 made typological mockery into the central issue. Ulrich Wildgruber, his white face obviously blackened in Negro Minstrel fashion, wearing a parody of an Emperor Jones jacket, deliberately played Othello on the surface, underscoring the cliché and therefore deconstructing it (illus. 129). When Cassio took Desdemona's handkerchief to Bianca (3.4), Zadek had Othello observe the scene, irrationally contradicting the plot which demands that he remain ignorant of the encounter. Wildgruber, dressed in an absurd King Kong costume, his uniform jacket inside out, carrying a mandolin, put on a carnival papier-mâché mask of a stereotyped African over his already blackened face: "the theatrical figure is overtheatricalized," as Volker Canaris wrote.[3] The method, intended to affront and shock, also proved a supple means of connecting the audience to the "hidden" play, going beyond traditional psychology into the realm of cultural myth and cultural fear. "All I'm interested in is trying to find out what is *behind* what the author wanted," Zadek has said, "what was at the back of his mind."

The director was most outrageous at the end, treating the last scenes in an overtly sexual manner. After undressing her mistress, Emilia, herself in a glittering sequined dress, sat on the lap of the innocently naked Desdemona for the "husbands' faults" speech and toyed with her nipple. In the same key, the murder became a parody of a sex crime. Othello straddled his wife on the bed as he throttled her, her naked legs kicking high in the air. Demented, embracing her body, he then threw it over a curtain rod, deliberately pulling up her nightgown to expose her nude posterior to the audience. When the audience laughed and shouted at him, Wildgruber shouted back, then recovered enough to continue the scene – five minutes or so of pandemonium, a pandemonium of comic terror. Ridiculously, and yet most movingly, as Wildgruber kissed and hugged her dead body, his black makeup smeared more and more on his cheeks, rubbing off onto Desdemona's white face.

Zadek frankly turns the high public subsidy of German theatre back on itself to condemn public German values. Reason, logic, reverence for the past, those eminently bourgeois virtues so characteristic of West German society, are theatrically demolished. The connections he seeks with the audience are not refined or interpretive; the stage events do not mediate between Shakespeare and the present, in the manner of Peter Brook or Peter Stein, so much as proffer a dismantled, visceral replacement for Shakespeare. Shakespeare is treated as an equal, his plays providing an arsenal of indelible images for exploitation. For Stein there is no room for the arbitrary; the Schaubühne is a political but highly intellectual company, precise, careful, under extreme control. Zadek, on the other hand, thinks Stein's work is brilliant and boring; he has said that the Schaubühne actors are like overcooked vegetables that have lost their flavor, that he would rather watch second-rate amateurs who are at least interesting because unpredictable.[4] Stein has returned the compliment: what Zadek produces, he is reported to have said, is "Shakespeare with his trousers down."

The intellectual rivalry between the two directors reached a grand climax when Zadek, just ten days after the opening of Stein's *As You Like It* in a film studio outside Berlin in 1977, presented *Hamlet* in an abandoned factory in an industrial suburb of Bochum. Whereas Stein and Karl-Ernst Hermann used an environmental staging to bring the audience on the journey from court to forest (see chapter 8), Zadek and his designer Peter Pabst used the open space to parody the play, the theatre, and its audience. Wildgruber was a Hamlet no German Romantic of any century would recognize (illus. 130). "Fat, zestful, versatile, he upstaged everybody," wrote Wilhelm Hortmann, "drowned the audience in his idiosyncratic cascading declamation and reveled in mad action such as cutting up Polonius's corpse and throwing the dismembered carcass out of the window."[5] In keeping with this iconoclasm, Zadek (with Gottfried Greiffenhagen) made a colloquial and often vulgar translation; avoiding the "classical" and familiar qualities of the Schlegel–Tieck edition, it was based on an earlier version by Schlegel and J. J. Eschenburg, well suited to Wildgruber's ranting delivery. "My Hamlet," wrote Zadek, "lives in a chaotic world, a world of appearances, and he plays roles while watching others play roles."

The production exhibited Zadek's usual interest in scenic dislocation and visual anarchy. Gray and black gym mats were placed in the center of the ludic space, and around the walls of the factory were various useful objects and disturbing signifiers: a sofa, a tailor's dummy, a stuffed bird, a skeleton. The lighting came from standard factory fluorescent lamps, which remained unchanged for the five and a half hours of the performance. Thus atmospheric effects were ruled out entirely; indeed stage illusions and conventions were often caricatured, as when the Ghost, played by a woman, appeared in the bright light attended by busy stagehands working a fog machine. Costumes were selected from onstage racks, and were changed to

130 *Hamlet* 1977 Bochum. D: Peter Zadek. S: Zadek and Peter Pabst. C: Pabst.
P: Gisela Scheidler. Ulrich Wildgruber as Hamlet the iconoclast.

suit the circumstances of inner character rather than to accent the circumstances of the fable. The most notorious example occurred in the second scene when Gertrude, much younger than her son, signified the underlining obscenity of the new power alignment of Denmark. Paraded by Claudius in front of his court, she suddenly exposed her breasts, which were painted bright red like bullseyes (color pl. 18).

In this case, at least, Zadek's staging of what was "at the back of" Shakespeare's mind, though abstract and anti-realistic, was rooted in an easily accessible psychology. Eva Mattes was showing Gertrude's situation by scenic simile, using actor gesture and visual expression to suggest hidden meaning: to her son, Gertrude is like a whore. Her painted breasts emphasized her double position as sex object and mother. When an actress reveals her breasts on stage, especially in a classic play at an illogical moment, she can become an ambiguous symbol of brazen sexuality and haunting vulnerability, and Zadek often made powerful use of the tactic. The nunnery scene was a parallel example. Ophelia, dressed in a gorgeous brocade gown and holding her prayerbook, was sent to Hamlet "as a political call girl," Canaris wrote.[6] As Hamlet entered, Polonius (also played by a woman) ripped a fur stole from Ophelia's dress, exposing her breasts, and shoved her toward the prince, who stood at a distance, meditating on death: "Sein oder nicht sein, das ist die Frage." The first part of their scene together was quiet and erotic, until Hamlet asked after her father. Polonius suddenly came on in a huge pig mask, dragging his (her) feet, while Claudius appeared in a monstrous horse's head, prompting a wild outburst from Hamlet. Thus the scene showed the King and his counselor metaphorically, rendering a complicated situation (they are in hiding from Hamlet, they are voyeurs, they are behaving like beasts) by visual signifiers.

Metaphoric visuals became paramount in *The Winter's Tale*, staged in 1978 at the Deutsches Schauspielhaus in Hamburg. Again Zadek collaborated with designers (Daniel Spoerri and Lioba Winterhalder) to evoke the hidden play, disregarding some matters that are normally considered essential to the work; Shakespeare's mixing of genres provided latitude for Zadek's mixing of disjunctive scenography. The costumes were exceedingly eclectic, ranging from the classical to the present and the future, and included the usual seminudity: Perdita was clothed only in forsythia branches, and Paulina's Renaissance armor gave new meaning to the word breastplate. Continuing his portrayal of obsessive Shakespearean tragic characters, Wildgruber acted a Leontes eaten alive by patriarchal possessiveness. Even his speech was affected by cancerous jealousy, as he accented the words strangely, making them difficult to follow. In the second act, as Ann Fridén notes, he "stormed into Hermione's room with a horde of half-animal, half-transvestite figures who performed a macabre mummery that included rape" (Leiter 830). The judgment scene was a medieval witch trial; as Leontes' destructiveness reached its climax the scenography corresponded to his inner state, for the entire set fell apart, collapsing on stage into "a heap of rubble."

Rubble was a visual clue for the transference to Bohemia, where the most remarkable device was a stage floor covered with two tons of plastic green slime – the ooze of life, I suppose, the primal, vernal state, slippery, amphibious, and fecund. Dominating the scene was a large torso of Flora (illus. 131). This section of the play was treated with vaudeville impudence, some of which is apparent in the composite visuals of the photograph. The rough disorder of cross-dressing, of bare breasts, and of the Vetruvian drawings improperly placed, was echoed by actors from Sicilia invading the Bohemian pastoral: Wildgruber and Rosel Zech (Hermione) doubled as

131 *The Winter's Tale* 1978 Hamburg. D: Peter Zadek. S: Daniel Spoerri.
C: Spoerri and Lioba Winterhalder. P: Gisela Scheidler. Flora watches over the sheepshearing on a floor of green slime. Note the parody panels of Renaissance perspective in the background. Perdita (Ilse Ritter) is clothed in forsythia, and her infant-image hangs above.

shepherd and shepherdess, Christa Berndl (Paulina) doubled as the Clown: Shakespeare's contrary locales were really the same, character integrity just another delusion. The recognition scene was out-and-out burlesque; the main characters took the roles of the three Gentlemen and jostled each other at the edge of the stage to spit out their own stories. As usual Zadek polarized his audiences. Traditionally-minded critics, naturally enough, found much of this offensive, self-indulgent, chaotic without reason or rationale.[7] Pushing the play to the far metaphoric pole, Zadek had deliberately interposed a major cryptographic task between the production and its reception, denying in some cases the stability and value of signs.

In Germany, famous stage directors have a status analogous to football players, admired for their ability to bring a higher cultural shine to the municipal authorities who hire them. They are not judged by the commercial or artistic standards of Great Britain or North America, and are not always judged by their ability to communicate with audiences either. That an iconoclastic and avant-garde director like Zadek could receive a high level of state subsidy, and be sought after by the competing industrial cities of the north, suggests how detached theatre in Germany can become from market factors. Yet Zadek, for all his idiosyncrasy, actually managed powerful connections with his spectators, deliberately seeking out working-class audiences and moving outside the deadly traditions of *Stadttheater* that he loathes. Canaris notes that Zadek's deep knowledge of English is behind much of his effrontery. Recognizing that no translation can hope to indicate the full value of Shakespeare's language, Zadek has created a "scenic stage language" to reveal "Shakespeare's nonverbal dramatic potential."[8]

His method, though original to the extreme, is reminiscent of the collage Shakespeare of Charles Marowitz at the Open Space Theatre in London, on the one hand, and of the full-throated absurdity of Charles Ludlam of the Ridiculous Theatre in New York, on the other: a cross between psychological *assemblage* and hysterical poses. In the postmodern view unified and consistent personality, whether in life or art, is an illusion; a dramatic character like Othello or Hamlet consists exclusively of deceptions and role-playing. There is no "inner self" for the actor to reveal, only a sequence of more or less self-conscious masquerades. For Zadek this awareness led to a strategy of theatrical deconstruction in which the director chose the plays of Shakespeare because of their mythic resonance and cultural status, then cut them open to find the exotic characters and fables that familiarity has made tame.

Visually Zadek has elevated scenography above a subservient or interpretative role. In a Zadek production, anarchical design substitutes for plot, creating through aberrant emblems not a rational picture of the world, or a readable portion of the world, but something crazy, frightening, and destructive like the world. Thus his metaphors are closest to the visuals suggested by the absurdist playwrights, especially those in the early plays of Ionesco and in the late plays of Beckett, where intensified abstractions convey the illogical universe we feel around us but normally do not see. Zadek has rejected what Hortmann calls "the two prevailing modes" of postwar German theatre, the political and the spiritual, looking instead for a Shakespeare that encompasses the chaos, obscenity, and joy of contemporary life.

Though Zadek has supplied some of the most challenging revisions of Shakespeare in our time, he has never interested English-speaking theatres in his work, and even in Germany his case remains anomalous. It has been more characteristic of contemporary German-speaking theatre to relate scenography to a coherent intellectual content, as the designer Jürgen Rose has done in Munich with the director Dieter Dorn, and as Karl-Ernst Hermann has done in collaboration with both Peter Stein and Claus Peymann. Hermann's setting for Peymann's *Richard II* in Braunschweig in 1969 made the semicircular arena look like a cut-away barrel, with wooden slats curving upwards from the sawdust floor to the flies, making a graphic metaphor of claustrophobic space. More recently Hermann's designs for Peymann at the Burgtheater in Vienna have used visuals in the Zadek manner, but much more restricted in implication. *Richard III* in 1987, for example, had an upstage wall upon which a mechanical raven sat (and flew from), and a man-sized drain center stage down which Richard's body was tossed at the end (illus. 132). *The Tempest* in 1989 placed giant egg shapes, huge seashells, and a pond of water on stage, a more abstract variation of Hermann's design for *As You Like It* in Berlin. Caliban, in blackface and heavy clothing, and Ariel, played by an older woman with white hair and bare breasts, gave a further sense of mysterious dislocation. To frighten the Spaniards, Prospero materialized a full-size replica of a crocodile, which crawled slowly across the floor (illus. 133). These remarkable photos suggest how Hermann's precise scenography has made a commanding, and even disturbingly beautiful, ocular revision of the two plays.

One of the most intellectually adventurous of the German iconoclastic productions, however, was Hansgünter Heyme's "electronic" *Hamlet* in 1979, probably one of the most startling Shakespearean representations of the century. Heyme used the play to evoke the extreme personal and cultural

132 *Richard III* 1987 Vienna. D: Claus Peymann. Des: Karl-Ernst Hermann.
P: Abisag Tüllmann. Gert Voss as Richard (left) confronts Richmond in front of a
row of upright spears, which dangerously dropped from the flies and stuck in the
floor, observed by the raven of death. Burgtheater.

schizophrenia of the late twentieth century, reflected in our over-dependence
on intrusive technology. Wolf Vostell, a well-known arranger of "hap-
penings" in the 1960s, designed a world where nothing could be experienced
or seen directly, but only through electronic mediation. The iron safety
curtain of the Cologne Municipal Theatre, lowered almost to the stage floor,
had eighteen television monitors attached to it; on the narrow playing space
in front was a video camera which the actors turned on themselves or each
other, reproducing their images eighteen times on the monitors. Stage left,
the stuffed carcass of a horse hung upside down, blood dripping from its
mouth into a glass chalice, the amplified drips echoing through the
auditorium. The costumes, exorbitant indicators of temporal displacement,
had bizarre items attached to them: herrings on Laertes' uniform, for
example, a weasel on Claudius' top hat, kitchenware on the clothing of the
minor characters. Many of these details remained inscrutable, but the overall

133 *The Tempest* 1989 Vienna. D: Claus Peymann. Des: Karl-Ernst Hermann.
P: Abisag Tüllmann. Ariel (Therese Affolter) helps push a crocodile, as Prospero
(Gert Voss) watches from behind his cell.

idea was clear enough, and was realized best in the figure of Hamlet, split
into two actors. The first, onstage and physical, was completely aphasic,
"lost in the crude sexual fantasies of his subconscious," as Hortmann said,
"and reduced largely to gestures and to a wondering preoccupation with his
own body, which he studied in poses and grimaces in front of the video
camera."[9] The second was nothing but an amplified voice in the house,
played by the director, who spoke much of Hamlet's verse disconnected
from the visible body.

Individual tragedy, the production suggested, is no longer possible in a
world where electronic phantasms are more compelling than human life.
Thus the production centered on the conflict between the gracious and
familiar language of Schlegel heard through the speaker system and the
disconnected, random, and pictorially fractured images on stage, "the

visible performance working in direct opposition to the text," in Hortmann's phrase. This was manifest in the final scene; since Hamlet was in no physical state for a fight, the duel was canceled and all the characters killed at the end were immediately laid out on death trolleys, their entrails piled on top of them, a Zadek-like ploy to accent the strangeness of the story. The safety curtain rose about 3 meters to reveal a hundred additional TV sets on tables, each showing the current evening's news (illus. 134). Ophelia, dressed as a beautiful racing driver or a pilot, came forward as Fortinbras to claim what was left of this kingdom of lost souls, a sensual rather than a political figure. We know *Hamlet* so well, and are so detached from its Reformation humanism, that all we can do is comment ironically on the inappropriateness of its themes.

The audience, it seems, was prepared to go along with some of this but not with all, and took an opportunity or two to react. The best instance occurred during Hamlet's advice to the players; it was delivered by Horatio,

134   *Hamlet* 1979 Cologne. D: Hansgünter Heyme. S: Wolf Vostell. C: Vostell and Helen Fabricus. P: Hannes Kilian. The ending of the electronic *Hamlet*, showing the iron safety curtain and the TV monitors, along with a video camera and the horse carcass. (This photo is from the revival of the production at the Württembergisches Staatstheater in Stuttgart later the same year.)

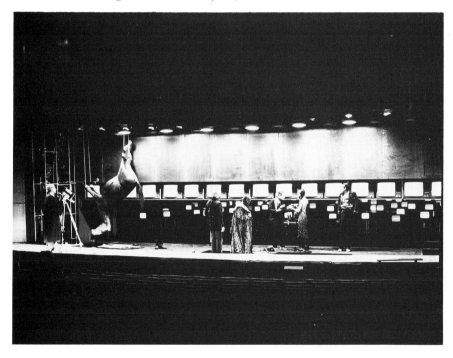

who found a slip of paper in his incapacitated friend's pocket and read it out loud, not understanding a word of it. When he reached the lines exhorting the players to suit the action to the word, and not to overstep "the modesty of nature," the audience spontaneously applauded – as if to say, this is counsel those of you on stage might have heeded.

INTERCULTURAL SHAKESPEARE

When Peter Brook reappears in this history, as the director of the International Center for Theatre Research in Paris, his visual approach has undergone another sea-change. This company, composed of actors from many lands, defines itself by exploration into the essences of dramatic signification, based on research into theatrical and paratheatrical conditions in nonwestern societies. It has become highly visible in global tours of performances adapted from Third World cultures, especially with *The Ik* of 1975, *The Conference of the Birds* of 1979 and *The Mahabharata* of 1985. Brook's Shakespeare work with the troupe differs sharply from his earlier productions at Stratford, with regard to actors and mise en scène. RSC actors, grounded in verse-speaking and the traditions of Shakespearean performance, often have serious inhibitions about improvisation and rarely are trained in nonrealistic physical movement; the ICTR actors are, in a word, the opposite. And whereas Brook's productions in Stratford were rooted in a compelling visual image or a consistent visual concept that emphasized the dramatist's uniqueness, the Paris performances have stressed how Shakespeare's plays are related to multiple theatrical experiences.

Brook had been much impressed by Akira Kurosawa's film *Throne of Blood* (1957), a cross-cultural retelling of the *Macbeth* story in cinematic pictures of the samurai period. From Kurosawa, Brook learned to disarm the archaism of the text by concentrating on fable and theme.[10] For his first presentation in Paris he chose *Timon of Athens*, which, being unfamiliar (and apparently incomplete), permitted a looser approach. A new translation by Jean-Claude Carrière sought to make the language accessible, while Brook's thematic approach stressed connections to the present. Timon faces the "profound liberal dilemma," Brook said, and fails at it; Pierre Schneider wrote (*New York Times* 3 Dec. 1974) that the production was "a living emblem of the West brutally awakened from its paradisial consumer's dreams by the oil crisis." Apemantus, played in an army surplus greatcoat by the African actor Malik Bagayogo, seemed a Third World prophet denouncing western decadence; Alcibiades (Bruce Myers), dressed like a South American general or a Greek admiral with sash, epaulets, and oversized medals, forced the Athenians into submission by a military coup. The costumes were transtemporal as well as transcultural, ranging from Middle Eastern capes to European opera hats; Timon's wealth, signalled at the start by a modern white suit and gold lamé shirt, gave way to a simple and timeless white robe at the final banquet.

But Brook's new path was most marked by the fact that the performance context was not established by performance scenography. It was the theatre building itself that controlled the visual experience and conditioned audience reception – not as Moiseiwitsch did in Ontario, by a unified and modernist application of the Elizabethan architectural stage, but by the deliberate modeling of an old theatre into a complicated signifier of the continued stress of history. Les Bouffes du Nord, a nineteenth-century variety playhouse hidden behind the Gare du Nord, was discovered in a state of near collapse: "wrecked, charred, streaked by rain, pockmarked, yet noble, human, glowing-red and breathtaking," Brook said (1987: 151). Preserving its antique and crumbling look, he made it into a relic with its traces visible, a signifier of how history is an artifact of the present. Classic plays would be contained by an edifice that exposed its own framework, its own record: an architectural and theatrical palimpsest. The director thus had a double task for the opening production, reconstructing a demolished theatre and staging a play that is not really finished. "That's why a study of the space of *Timon* cannot be separated from an analysis of the reinvention of les Bouffes," Georges Banu wrote; the architectural refitting was "an action inscribed into the thinking that governed the whole performance." Or, as David Williams put it, the building mirrored "the leprous state of society and the decay of human relationships within the play." Perhaps more importantly, it implied a similar comment on contemporary society.[11]

How this was accomplished is difficult to articulate, since the unusual quality of Les Bouffes du Nord comes from the physical reality of its materials and configuration and is not fully conveyed by either pictures or words. The general effect on a spectator is a little like sitting in an antique armchair in the middle of a junk yard – comfortable yet musty, dislocated, and with a slight sense of danger. Indeed Brook relates that a big ovation on opening night "literally brought the house down, as large lumps of plaster decoration were dislodged by the vibration and fell, just missing the heads of the audience" (Brook 1987: 152). Simple benches are arranged on the main floor in a full horseshoe shape, enclosing the playing space, and on the same level (illus. 135). Above them three steep balconies echo this figure. The upstage wall is

135 *Timon of Athens* 1974 Paris. D: Peter Brook. Des: Michel Launay. P: Avraham Dana. Les Bouffes du Nord, showing the horseshoe shape of the balconies and floor seating, and the decaying walls. This snapshot (taken from the top balcony by a student) depicts the arrival of Timon, greeted by his friends. The cushions on the floor were used by the actors, and marked the limits of the playing space. Metal catwalks in front of the back wall provided an upper acting level.

the most prominent architectural feature, towering some 16 meters above the stage; scarred and pitted by fire and age, it was a metaphoric backdrop for *Timon* and part of the larger signifying system of the building.

The deliberate denial of a unified style in the renovation of the building extended to Brook's treatment of the play. Eclectic costumes were paralleled by an eclectic cultural reference that had nothing to do with Shakespeare's Jacobean conception of Athens, but that drew heavily on the ICTR experience in Third World villages. The first banquet, for example, ended in a dance of whirling dervishes, Arabic capes flying over gold cloth on the floor. The interculturalism of the production, however, was not a style so much as an actor attitude. Visually this quality was most apparent in the blocking, where repeated patterns of circles invoked the story-telling traditions of Africa (illus. 136). Aside from the actors, there was very little to see on stage, which remained an empty space. The bitter tale of philanthropist become misanthrope, so resonant amid the materialism of the late twentieth century, gained additional force from its conveyance through

136 *Timon of Athens* 1974 Paris. P: Nicholas Treatt. A story-teller's circle for the first banquet (1.2). Apemantus (Malik Bagayogo, the black actor in the center) scorns luxury, as Alcibiades (Bruce Myers, to the right) listens with the rest. Timon (François Marthouret) is slightly elevated.

the methods of "rough" or poor theatre. Another of the actors, Malik Bowens, has said that after the company's experiences in Africa Brook sought to replace "scenographic hardware" with "a human décor." Abandoning his modernist ideal of visual unity, Brook created, David Williams notes, "an impression of a non-homogeneous, discontinuous montage."[12]

Exactly how the spectator fits into this social, architectural, and mental complex is problematic. While the theatre is located in a working-class district, and further suggests by its multiracial troupe that it solicits a pluralistic population, in fact its audience tends to be young professionals and intellectuals, like Peter Stein's audience in Berlin – the "emergent bourgeoisie," in Wolfgang Sohlich's analysis. Though the hierarchical structures of the original theatre (Italian stage, *parterre*, balconies, loges) have been redefined, they are calculatedly visible; though everyone pays the same price for admission, not everyone has an equally good place. "It is as if the spectator is invited to rediscover a state of naturalness," comments Sohlich, "by consciously playing a role of his own choosing in a scenario signified as *passé*."[13] We can see in Les Bouffes, and in the Shakespeare presented there, some of the ascendant features of postmodernism: the present consciously overlaying the past so that both are observable, the eclectic accumulation of cultural quotations, the ironic detachment from the unified style of the modernists. Most of all we can see how a spectator, in order to connect with the representation, must become a transcultural time-traveler, aloof from the scene. Aware of the impossibility of recapturing the past (whether in Shakespeare or in the nineteenth-century playhouse), the spectator must always stand partially outside the event: coolly engaged, moved and unmoved, fascinated by the past and fascinated by that fascination.

Brook's *Measure for Measure* of 1978 relied on many of the same mentalities as the *Timon*, though with less general success. (Also less successful than usual, though more interesting from a visual standpoint, was his production of *Antony and Cleopatra* for the RSC that same year.) It wasn't until 1990 that he returned to Shakespeare, with a version of *The Tempest* that used intercultural strategies more deliberately. By then the scenic and spatial implications of Les Bouffes had been thoroughly studied, and the performance modalities of the company widely disseminated (and the institution itself renamed as the International Center for Theatrical Creations). Some of the distinguished international actors from *The Mahabharata* took major roles here: the West African Sotigui Kouyate, who played Bishma, was Prospero; the Japanese Yoshi Oïda (Drona and Kitchaka) was Gonzalo; and the Englishman Bruce Myers (Ganesha and Krishna) was Trinculo. Marvin Carlson noted the "very close scenographic relationship" to *The Mahabharata*, especially the sand on the floor of the stage, the African and Asian instrumentalists in full view, the flowing robes of the actors, and the extreme visual simplicity.[14] A few bamboo sticks became the sinking ship (illus. 137), the surface of the water for a drowning sailor, and a cage for Ferdinand. This essentially metaphoric design was joined by occasional witty metonyms, like the model of a ship worn as a headpiece by Ariel in the opening, or the scene in which Gonzalo, sitting on the floor, was surrounded by miniature castles, created by green-clad stagehands who inverted flowerpots filled with sand. In its rough and

137 *The Tempest* 1990 Paris. D: Peter Brook. Des: Chloé Obolensky. L: Jean Kalman. P: Gilles Abegg. The nobles in the first scene, bamboo poles representing the ship and the waves. Left to right, the intercultural actors shown are Ken Higelin, Georges Corraface, Yoshi Oïda, Mamadou Dioume.

improvised way the moment recalled Rolf Gérard's sandcastle set for Brook's *Romeo and Juliet* of 1947 (illus. 75), which seemed a world away.

Having a large number of Third World actors available might tempt a director to stress *The Tempest* as a representation of imperialism, but Brook took trouble to upset this reading, as Dominique Goy-Blanquet noted. A dark-skinned Prospero, with "an exquisite Indian miniature of a daughter" and an African Ariel, threw off any easy view of European domination of the magic isle. Casting David Bennent as Caliban, who appeared to be "the degenerate offspring of white colonials," deliberately upset the standard political interpretation; even Antonio and Sebastian were racially mixed, "a black-and-white pair of scoundrels."

The point was underlined by Carrière in a program note, which reminded the audience that the last word of the play – which may be the last dramatic word that Shakespeare wrote – is "free." Politically speaking, the actors in *The Mahabharata*, who came from at least twenty different countries, signified as a group a United Nations of drama. There is something a little naïve about this, even sentimental, a bit like the famous Coca Cola

138 *The Tempest* 1990 Paris. P: Gilles Abegg. The wedding masque, combining multicultural and multiracial elements. Ken Higelin and Shantala Malhar-Shivalvingappa (Ferdinand and Miranda, at left) watch the goddesses; Sotigui Kouyate (Prospero) at right. Note the sand on the floor, and the pockmarked walls of the theatre.

commercial of multiracial young people on a hilltop singing "I'd like to teach the world to sing, in perfect harmony." Whatever harmony is possible in the Paris company, under the unique conditions of a well-funded artistic enterprise, might stand as an idealized model but does not indicate that the world's dissensions are illusory. Interculturalism in the theatre, by underplaying the very real differences that exist among peoples, can dangerously underplay the social principles at work in drama and in life. Yet Brook's *Tempest*, using multiracial and multinational casting detached from specific racial or political conditions, perhaps came closer than most productions of the play to realizing on stage the theme of freedom as a universal desire. This was often evident scenographically, and particularly so in the wedding masque. There, Asian and African visuals blended with Asian and African actors, presenting a new image of intercultural concord (illus. 138).

The second major example of intercultural Shakespeare also comes from a Parisian experimental company. The Théâtre du Soleil was founded in 1968 as a democratic or communal alternative to the French theatrical system. Though it has undergone many changes of personnel and stylistic objectives, both its director, Ariane Mnouchkine, and the ideal of "collective creation" have remained central to its life. The company became established with revisionist pieces on the French Revolution, called *1789* and *1793*, which were theatrically and politically radical, as was *L'âge d'or* a few years later; all of these works of the early 1970s were true group creations. The stress of this work led to a number of resignations and some questioning of the value of collective responsibility, both inside and outside the group. A period devoted to more scripted material followed, which produced a remarkable film on the life of Molière and a stage adaptation of Klaus Mann's novel *Mephisto*. Both, David Bradby says (210), were meditations "on the life of a theatre company and its political role" that showed how commercial and social pressures affect artistic integrity.

For these projects Mnouchkine found herself in an unwonted position of total control as writer and director. She next tried an original play on the tragedy of Southeast Asia in our time but seemed to get nowhere, and the very principles of the Théâtre du Soleil seemed under attack by exhaustion and changes in the political climate. Shakespeare became the way out. Most curiously, considering Mnouchkine's own political commitment and the history of Shakespearean representation in our time, she turned to Shakespeare because of what she called his ideological neutrality; "Shakespeare is not our contemporary and must not be treated as such," she said in an interview; "he is distant from us, as distant as our own profoundest depths." She introduced a number of young actors into the company, and announced a program of six plays (the *Richard II* tetralogy, *Twelfth Night*, and *Love's Labour's Lost*), "hoping to learn how to represent the world in a theatre," as she wrote in the note for the opening production.[15] Thus her notion of Shakespeare's utility was grounded in his timelessness, which she thought required an abstract style, one that evoked images rather than messages. Already thinking about the east, and steeped in Asian theatre from her studies in the 1960s, Mnouchkine manufactured an eclectic orientalism to uncover the mythic dimensions she sensed in the text.

Kicking high and chanting in elevated speech, accompanied by cymbals and gongs, her actors burst through the accepted conventions of Shakespearean playing like Kabuki players through a paper screen (color pl. 19). *Richard II*, in 1981, was a self-consciously mixed metaphor in which French actors borrowed elements from Asian performance to create a vision of the

English medieval court. As Felicia Londré put it, the director "super-imposed the stylized vocal effects and precisely patterned movements of Japanese theatre forms on the ritualized fourteenth-century English codes of behavior" (Leiter 589). Character was established by mask or mask-like makeup, and by individual (but non-psychological) patterns of gesture and movement; emotion was signified through formalized song and dance; the tragic dimension was conveyed through ritual conjurations like those in Noh and Kabuki, with some additions from Kathakali and Peking Opera. To appropriate Shakespeare, Mnouchkine first appropriated the cultural details of the east, transforming both in the process. Her scenic means were simple, like Brook's, but Mnouchkine struck images of more deliberate precision and formality. The upper level of Flint Castle (3.3), for example, was represented by the King standing on the poles of a scaffolding tower; for the prison scene the same scaffold poles became Richard's cage (color pl. 20). Here, as in many moments of great intensity, the production tended to signify meaning through tableaux.

The visual methods of the Théâtre du Soleil are controlled by its performing space, the Cartoucherie, a disused cartridge factory in the district of Vincennes. The main building is a large, hangar-like warehouse – an open space capable of many configurations. For Shakespeare a square platform stage was placed at one end, roofed and backed by colorful billowing cloths that were oriental in their appearance and in their use. Actors become visually more prominent when set pieces are minimized, as on the Ontario Festival stage, but here the scenography emphasized the exoticism of the characters rather than their humanity. Hieratic costumes and poses, even in the midst of battle, ritualized these wars of the roses in a manner quite opposite to the methods of Tanya Moiseiwitsch or John Bury, and suggested that Shakespeare's historical figures were nothing less than demigods (color pl. 21). This was certainly an innovative and promising approach to the monarchical theme, though it also encouraged a nostalgia for regal feudalism at odds with the frame of mind of the audience and with the company's earlier critique of kingship in *1789*. Some observers perceived a parallel stylistic problem: the monotonous declamatory mode, which "ironed out differences between characters," also blunted some important dramatic or plot issues, "both political and erotic," as Bradby and Williams note (104).

Twelfth Night relaxed the oriental formality of the history plays, adapting an Indian look but not an Indian performance style. Whereas the male-dominated world of the English court sanctioned the extreme stylization of

Japanese theatre, the romance spirit of Illyria was given the flavor of *The Arabian Nights*. Mnouchkine originally intended to use an all-woman cast to compensate for the masculinity of *Richard II*; in the end, however, only the male roles of Andrew and Curio were played by actresses. The confusions wrought by love were nonetheless emphasized, especially those with homosexual implications, and none of the characters seemed happy about the ambiguous pairings of Shakespeare's ending. The generality of setting, which had removed the history plays from some of their political meanings, seemed wonderfully appropriate to romantic fantasy. When a great billowing pink cloth swallowed the cast at the end, the actors seemed to disappear into their visual images.

The Shakespeare cycle was abandoned when the Falstaff, Phillipe Hottier, left the company in 1984. (Some of the theatrical discoveries have since been adapted for a play on Norodom Sihanouk in 1985, and in a brilliant Kathakali version of *The Oresteia*, prefaced by *Iphigenia in Aulis*, which opened between 1990 and 1992 under the title of *Les Atrides*.) Yet the international effect of Mnouchkine's Shakespeare has been very great, and was consolidated in Los Angeles when two of the plays were seen at the Olympic Arts Festival in 1984. The sensory power of these productions was overwhelming – perhaps especially in a foreign country, where the French language was not well understood – and the boldness of the scenographic and performance methods without rival in contemporary Shakespearean representation. Some spectators, of course, noted with melancholy the losses in the verbal and intellectual dimensions, and there can be no doubt that such an insistently metaphoric approach could easily become routine, a clichéd replacement for the human virtues of Shakespeare's drama; perhaps it was a good thing that the Théâtre du Soleil stopped after three plays. It is undeniable, however, that Mnouchkine's intercultural tactics, alongside those of Peter Brook, have vastly expanded the visual reference available for Shakespeare in our time. The reference has been further extended in recent Japanese productions, especially those by Yukio Ninagawa,[16] which have reclaimed the value of native theatre forms for Shakespeare.

NEO-PICTORIALISM

The movements to deconstruct Shakespeare's plays, or to revise their representation by radical visual methods, have been located chiefly in Europe. The traditions of performance in English, dominated and continually reinforced by the two Stratfords, have normally maintained that

Shakespearean interpretation and Shakespearean acting should be centered in textual analysis and linguistic appreciation. In English the open stage movement has been particularly influential; though the RSC has never had a permanent Elizabethan stage, its general performance tendencies, as we have seen, were greatly affected by Guthrie's remaking of the stage space. Thus it is surprising to note a new kind of pictorialism developing after 1975 on the very boards that Guthrie and Moiseiwitsch laid, both in Canada and in Minneapolis.

Robin Phillips, an English director who had worked at the RSC and at the Chichester Festival, took over in Ontario that year, and made it immediately apparent that the pictorial would be important to his approach. His *Measure for Measure*, set in Vienna in 1912, established the world of Freud and Wittgenstein by costumes indicating repressed sexuality and by dominating, realist set pieces, including a caged unit installed under the upper stage. Angelo's office was conveyed by a large polished desk that covered much of the open platform, effectively denying the Elizabethanist condition of the stage. In subsequent productions Phillips moved further away from Guthrie's postulates. In 1976 he made the permanent stage balcony of the Festival Theatre removable so that a simpler architectural façade, more neutral in its visual coding, became an alternative to the original configuration. For *Antony and Cleopatra* that year the balcony was replaced by a canopy hanging over the stage, a design tactic essentially the same as that used in proscenium theatres.

The majority of the Phillips productions, especially those designed by Daphne Dare, were set in the extended Victorian period, ranging from an 1850s *King Lear* to a 1913 *Love's Labour's Lost*. The settings were established by pictorial means familiar enough to Charles Kean. Though the effects were metaphoric, the methods depended upon the audience's ability to read explicit historical details – mid-Victorian crinolines, for instance, or Edwardian cigarette cases – and intellectualize some connection between the original text and its enforced relocation. In such a situation the signifiers on stage make sense only to the degree that the audience holds a visual knowledge in common with the designer. Spectators in England, living among the architecture and artifacts of the past, often can read the distinctions between, say, Queen Anne and Georgian styles, and Shakespearean settings can profit from the political and social overtones of that historical knowledge. But such subtle discriminations are not part of the culture of North America, where collective memory sometimes seems to extend only to last Tuesday, and the same strategy leads to a perplexing semiosis. Nevertheless, Phillips and Dare achieved reasonable success by choosing periods and details readily accessible to their audiences – especially details reinforced by other media like films or photographs. Thus the Chekhovian *Winter's Tale* (1978), set in Russia about 1910, relied more on the visuals of the film of *Doctor Zhivago* than on direct knowledge of the Winter Palace. Daphne Dare herself pointed out that her chosen periods were of use because they coincided with the early development of photography.[17]

As Phillips was leaving his post in 1980, Liviu Ciulei was assuming his at Guthrie's second theatre, where Moiseiwitsch had rebuilt the basic Ontario model without the permanent upper stage. The repertory in Minneapolis was to be based on classic plays in general, not primarily on Shakespeare, and the material result was an uncompromising bare thrust, with no architectural additions, backed only by an accordion fire door that permitted rolling sets to pass (see Leacroft 179–80). Ciulei, trained as an architect in Bucharest before becoming a director, made an architect's decision immediately: he enlarged and squared off the asymmetrical platform, eliminated the steps surrounding it, and broke through the fire door and back wall. There he built a 9-meter proscenium, opening onto the backstage area originally designed for set storage. The area of the thrust was thus increased by 30 percent without reducing the size of the house, and the addition of the new stage behind the proscenium more than doubled the total performing space.

Suddenly the Guthrie had become a hybrid theatre, its main acting area still an open platform in the middle of a semicircular auditorium, but behind it a perspective or Italian stage had been created which could be used for pictorial scenery or closed off entirely. The physical alterations left little doubt that Ciulei wished to reanalyze the values and capacities of the pictorial stage. For Shakespeare and for many earlier dramatists, he said, the actor was "the universe in microcosm. Now the stage is the universe of which the actor is a single component." Scenography, in other words, precedes acting. "I must first know where I am," he said, "and then I know how to behave. And the actors need that, too. They must know what universe they populate, what their surroundings are."[18]

His experiments with neo-pictorial Shakespeare occurred in four productions of the comedies between 1981 and 1985. Designed by a mixture of Americans and Europeans, they had a distinctly postmodern look and often offended conservative tastes. The most important of them was the first, a version of *The Tempest* that flaunted the alterations Ciulei had made to the theatre. In a program note he made his visual premises clear:

In our time, more than ever before, the traditional and the new coexist, creating an eclectic landscape of forms. Our own style has not yet crystallized, but is rather an in-gathering of a variety of styles. Thus the setting, costumes and acting styles of this production are deliberately eclectic.

In key with this notion, Ciulei, who designed the set himself, made the stage into a metaphoric landscape of the twentieth-century mind. Both the scenic stage beyond the proscenium and the open acting area were used to refine and highlight the meaning of the action visually. Most prominent was the treatment of the thrust, which was propped up by books and surrounded by a moat or sea of red liquid. In the moat and on the stage were a large number of objects from the past and present, from a clock without hands to the Mona Lisa and a battered typewriter. As Ciulei's note explained, the moat was "red blood filled with the half-submerged relics and debris of our cultural heritage and our wars." Also tipping out of drawers at the edges of the stage, the objects included a suit of medieval armor face down in the blood, a vintage cash register, a headless and armless Greek statue, a stone horse's head, an antique sewing machine, a modern rifle, a stuffed chicken, a chair, an old helmet, a lute, a hunting horn, a globe, a floating violin. "The detritus of the history of creative man," one critic wrote.[19] On the stage the skeleton of a rowboat reminded the audience of Prospero's enforced exile.

In a play very much about the effects of time, Ciulei presented an image of time's paradox: instruments of art, mercantilism, and violence confused and simultaneous, all of equal value, all of equal meaning. The perspective stage behind the proscenium was used for larger scenic effects: a projection of the opening storm, or views of a seascape through a suspended doorway and factory window in the back wall, done in Magritte fashion at impossible angles. Art and nature thus became overt subjects and their "inter-textualities" (Ciulei's word) were investigated visually. The banquet scene, for example, was augmented by de Chirico mannequins, frightening but prominently artificial presences. In the wedding masque the three goddesses, framed like giant Gainsborough portraits in a triptych of high niches beyond the proscenium, "tended to totter or lose their microphones," wrote Thomas Clayton.[20] (See illus. 139.) Prospero, with white hair like Einstein, was usually in a white lab coat; both Miranda and Ariel were saucy modern teenagers, contrasting markedly with the rather stiff courtiers in black Napoleonic suits. Caliban was a Man Friday figure with strangely feathered skullcap; Jan Triska's Czech accent added a further exoticism, but his switchblade made him incongruously contemporary and dangerous. And when Trinculo and Stephano, dressed in early American homespun, sang Rossini's "Figaro" together, and "O sole mio" while trying to file Caliban's nails, the audience was presented with an aural equivalent of the trans-temporality of the design.

The type of postmodern pictorialism that Ciulei forced into Moisei-witsch's architecture fits naturally and almost automatically in proscenium houses. Indeed postmodern performance, in opera, dance, theatre, and in the hybrid forms, has a strong inclination to the distance, coolness, and irony of proscenium images. The confrontational tactics of the avant-garde of the 1960s, and the experiments of the chamber and open stage movements

139   *The Tempest* 1981 Minneapolis. D and S: Liviu Ciulei. C: Jack Edwards. L: Duane Schuler. P: Bruce Goldstein. The wedding masque on Ciulei's remodeled Guthrie Theatre, with three giant goddesses in niches on the scenic stage beyond the proscenium. Ken Ruta as Prospero sits in reflection at the right of the picture. Note the abandoned rowboat on the platform, and the suit of armor falling off the downstage edge.

that sought to include spectators in a collective experience with the performers, have been rejected by postmodernists as naïve or primitivist. Like the post-structuralist commentary essential to its understanding, postmodern art emphasizes not the independence and perfection of the object, but rather the object's relationship to its subjective reception. Arnold Aronson maintains that non-proscenium design "implies continuity and sameness between image and viewer," whereas postmodern design "is discontinuous and requires a perceptual interruption." Thus postmodern design is apt to rely on visual quotation and dislocation, methods that ask the spectator to assume a skeptical or even sardonic relationship to the ocular: the signifier is drained of its conventional signification. At the same time postmodern performance has often been tantalized by spectacle and lavish representation, situating on stage a glorious commodification of the image. It is this characteristic that has led Marxist critics like Fredric Jameson to call the movement "the cultural logic of late capitalism," seeing it as an aesthetic extension of the unbridled consumerism of western society at the end of the century, fueled by multinational capital.[21]

A number of Shakespeare productions in England exploited the new methods in the 1980s, often relying on ocular luxury and expensive "high concept" design. As Jan Kott has noted, the contemporary distrust of politics in the theatre in the west has meant that artists have looked to a "new visual expression" for Shakespeare as a replacement for the rough-edged emphasis on intellectual meaning of the postwar avant-garde, whose workers were, in any event, "restricted to the limited resources of the small stage."[22] Trevor Nunn's production of both parts of *Henry IV*, which inaugurated the Barbican Theatre in 1982, encouraged John Napier to exploit the huge stage – a symbolic gesture marking the RSC's turn toward the proscenium in its new (and rather uncomfortable) London home. William Dudley designed a Gothic *Richard III* for Bill Alexander in 1984, with a remarkable performance by Antony Sher. Here the pictorial was more old than new: four massive white tombs strongly inclined the stage toward the metonymic, and a coronation scene with massed extras and musicians ended the first half; some commentators noted the similarity to nineteenth-century historicism.[23]

The lavish connotations of the decade were continued in Adrian Noble's *Henry V* in 1984, with Kenneth Branagh in the lead; in 1988–9 the earlier history cycle, also designed by Bob Crowley in a neo-pictorial manner, was performed in a three-part adaptation under the general title *The Plantagenets* (illus. 140). Though most of these productions appeared first at Stratford,

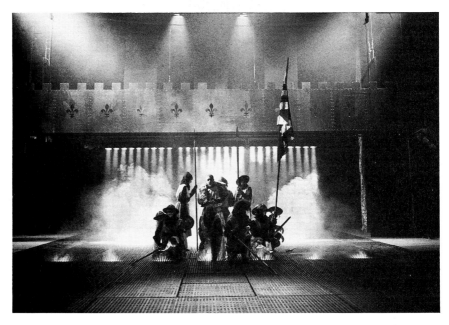

140   *1 Henry VI* 1988 Stratford. D: Adrian Noble. Des: Bob Crowley. L: Chris
Parry. P: Richard Mildenhall. The siege of Orleans from *The Plantagenets*,
demonstrating the frontal design and high chiaroscuro lighting characteristic
of the neo-pictorial. Robert Demeger as Lord Talbot in the center (act 4).

they seemed intended for the vast space of the Barbican. Back-lit and down-
lit, often by high-powered halogen lamps, the stage pictures sometimes
appeared to levitate from their solid surroundings: images literally detaching
themselves from both historical and human contexts. Emphasizing the
pageantry of the histories rather than their politics, the company departed
further from the roughness of the Brechtian mode towards a scenography
that filled the stage with opulence.

The tendency to historical eclecticism was most apparent in the
productions designed by Maria Bjornson for Ron Daniels, which regularly
combined lavish visuals with disjunctive temporality. For Roger Rees'
performance in *Hamlet* in 1984, Bjornson's set looked like a postmodern
fashion statement: "black marble staircases, plain black walls, silver
chandeliers," a Jacobean film noir; the costumes were called everything
from "academic" to "Rosenkavalier"[24] (see illus. 141). Even Peter Hall and
John Bury, normally conservative about costume and time period, presented
a *Coriolanus* on the open stage of the National Theatre that mixed the Roman
with the contemporary, togas with three-piece suits (illus. 142). It seemed

141 *Hamlet* 1984 Stratford. D: Ron Daniels. Des: Maria Bjornson. L: Chris Ellis.
P: Joe Cocks Studio. The set for the second scene. The floating platform and the
formal chairs emphasized the theatricality of the court; the projections, the staircases,
and the perspective ironically quoted the Italian stagecraft of the seventeenth
century. Similarly the rigid false proscenium was both reinforced and violated by
the platform and chandeliers.

"in a time warp between ancient and modern worlds," Jack Kroll wrote.
Michael Bogdanov's double cycle of the history plays for the English
Shakespeare Company accented this method, though much less lavishly
since it was staged for touring. A metal unit set was the framework for
costumes that generally advanced from the Regency dress of *Richard II* to
the contemporary clothes of *Richard III* (illus. 143). In a wonderfully
disturbing moment, Richard and Richmond, seen for most of the play in
dark business suits, fought the final duel with broadswords, in fog and in
slow motion, dressed in full medieval armor made of plastic.

More characteristic of Bogdanov's work with Chris Dyer, however, were
modern dress versions of Italian plays that substituted our contemporary
image of stylish and wealthy northern Italy for Shakespeare's land of
treachery and romance. The series began with Jonathan Pryce tearing down

the pastiche Serlio set for *The Taming of the Shrew* at Stratford in 1978, erasing the play's *commedia* inscriptions and rewriting it with a darker, unsentimental view of the condition of women. (This is the production discussed at the start of the book; see illus. 1 and 2.) *Measure for Measure* – an Italianate play, if not literally Italian – converted the open stage in Ontario into Mistress Overdone's orgiastic jazz club, with a half-hour prelude of drinking, dancing, and erotic incidentals (illus. 144). Contemporary culture frequently reasserted itself in the text proper: the club reappeared, and the petitioners in the final scene appealed to the Duke through microphones. Amplified public address thereafter became a signature device, effectively used in a brilliant production of *Julius Caesar* in German at the Deutsches Schauspielhaus in Hamburg in 1986, where Bogdanov staged the assassination and the funeral as media events, complete with paparazzi and intrusive TV coverage. (The English Shakespeare Company *Richard III* also relied on electronic media, ending in a modern television studio. Richmond, wearing a business suit with a red rose and a white rose together on his lapel, spoke "England hath long been mad" into an amplified mike, his face multiplied on TV monitors.)

These Foucauldian visions of the complicity of knowledge and power

142   *Coriolanus* 1984 London. D: Peter Hall. Des: John Bury. P: John Haynes. Ian McKellen as Coriolanus amid costume signifiers of the present and the past. National Theatre, Olivier stage.

143   *Henry VI* 1987–8 world tour. D: Michael Bogdanov. S: Chris Dyer.
C: Stephanie Howard. L: Mark Henderson. P: Laurence Burns. The Jack Cade
rebellion from the English Shakespeare Company's *The Wars of the Roses*, text
adapted by Bogdanov. Michael Pennington as Cade sits on the cart in Union Jack
T-shirt and Victorian helmet.

were most effectively realized in *Romeo and Juliet* at the RSC in 1986. Played
on and around a giant marble revolving staircase, in a Verona highly
conscious of Giorgio Armani, the production received attention chiefly for
methods borrowed from *West Side Story*, including a rock band, choreo-
graphed street fights with flick knives and bicycle chains, and a bright red
roadster – an Alfa Romeo, no less. While this was energetic and highly
successful with young audiences it was also relatively habitual, both
thematically and visually, little different from the method of Barry Jackson
in 1925. More distinctly contemporary was Bogdanov's tendency to force
the present and the past to exist simultaneously; Romeo committed suicide
by lethal injection, for example, yet Juliet's "O churl, drunk all, and left no
friendly drop / To help me after" was retained.

   The most disturbing revision of the play, equivalent to the demolition of
the Renaissance view of Padua in *Shrew*, occurred at the end, where realistic

144   *Measure for Measure* 1985 Stratford, Ontario. D: Michael Bogdanov. Des: Chris
Dyer. L: Harry Frehner. P: David Cooper. Erotic characters for "The Club," an
atmospheric prologue that invited the audience to join in dancing and revelry on
stage.

metonyms enlarged to a grim metaphor about the politics of post-
civilization. After Juliet's death there was a long blackout with loud music;
no more of Shakespeare's scene was heard. When the lights came up the
audience saw a public square, with a gold statue of the lovers mounted on
a pedestal, and TV cameramen and technicians milling about (illus. 145).
Montague and Capulet arrived and stood apart. The Prince entered, a man
of power dressed to kill, and TV lights flared as microphones were stuck in
his face. What he spoke, astoundingly, were the opening eight lines of the
prologue – the Chorus' lines, which had been omitted – but placed into the
past tense, and read from a notecard. He forced Montague and Capulet to

shake hands, and left. When the cameras stopped, the two fathers glared at one another and departed separately. The scene broke up informally, the play was over. Thoroughly manipulated, the media gave the illusion of peace, but it was only an illusion; suffering had accomplished nothing; except for the politician's image, nothing had changed; the tragedy of the young lovers had been reduced to a photo-op.

A century earlier Henry Irving cut all but four lines of the last scene after Juliet's death for the sake of a magnificent stage picture of destruction and reconciliation. Irving recognized that in the image-conscious world of his audience a sentimental visual sign held more power than the formal rhetorical system Shakespeare had provided. The picture on Bogdanov and Dyer's stage, of course, was not so simple: it relied on the same method and yet offered a critique of it. Calling attention to the misuse of images in our

145 *Romeo and Juliet* 1986 Stratford. D: Michael Bogdanov. S: Chris Dyer. C: Dyer and Ginny Humphreys. P: Laurence Burns. A slick, present-day Verona became the background for an ironic investigation of power. Here the two families await the arrival of the Duke in an interpolated final scene, as a TV camera crew sets up shots in front of a golden statue of Romeo and Juliet. The brooding projected face upstage belongs to Capulet (Richard Moore).

world, ironically emphasizing the complicity between mediated news-pictures and politics, at the same time the director and designer presented a revisionist meaning for the play in visual terms. Like much of postmodern art, in the end the production questioned the value of images while capitulating to their power.

Because of their modern dress these Bogdanov–Dyer productions achieved a degree of visual unity that postmodernism normally avoids. The calculated anachronisms, historical overlays, and illustrative quotations from divergent periods that Bogdanov preferred for the history plays were mostly absent in the Italian plays, making them more accessible to the regular Shakespeare audience. In this regard it's important to acknowledge that the standard acting style of the RSC, which is still a cross between Brechtian realism and rhetorical "good" speech, actually runs counter to postmodern methods, so that the visuals of deconstructive productions at Stratford often seem at odds with the moment-by-moment treatment of scenes contained within them. Rarely do any of the major Anglophone companies hazard the transgressive Shakespearean acting of Ulrich Wild-gruber or Gert Voss or Jutta Lampe in German; in many cases what looks postmodern in Britain or North America is nothing more than a look, an innovative visual frame for rather traditional performances. The Bogdanov productions, and the more recent ones by Deborah Warner, are departures from the dominant observance, offering a looser, more informal approach to acting and to speech, delighting in diversity and incongruity. This approach shares qualities with the democratization of Shakespearean acting seen in some provincial and smaller companies in Britain, notably in the work directed by Declan Donnellan for Cheek by Jowl, and by Giles Havergal and Philip Prowse for the Citizens' Theatre in Glasgow.[25]

One of the most remarkable of the new approaches to Shakespeare in English integrated a multiracial cast, diverse styles of acting, an uncommonly effective design, and music by a leading postmodern composer, Philip Glass. The result of JoAnne Akalaitis' production of *Cymbeline* at the New York Shakespeare Festival in 1989, produced indoors at the Public Theatre, was a measured and comprehensive rethinking of the play. Despite its careful presentation, however, it offended conservative critics so strongly that it can stand as a icon of the problematics of postmodern Shakespeare. The basic performance idea was indebted to a Brechtian estrangement of the fable; Akalaitis reconsidered its Renaissance romance features in terms of the nineteenth-century melodramatic imagination, heightening the anach-ronism and dislocation already present in the text. Instead of the unified

146 *Cymbeline* 1989 New York. D: JoAnne Akalaitis. S: George Tsypin. C: Ann
Hould-Ward. L: Pat Collins. P: Martha Swope. Belarius (Frederick Neumann, lower
right) leads on the British army against the Romans. Aviragus and Guiderius (Don
Cheadle and Jesse Borrego, upper left) appeared as Native Americans. Note the
projections on the walls of the Public Theatre.

transference of the Robin Phillips' productions, Victorian romance was
framed by visual patterns that were ironically eclectic: Guiderius and
Aviragus were seen as North American Indians, for example; the British
army wore kilts and pith helmets, while the Romans wore Victorian military
tunics and ancient helmets; Imogen's bedchamber was a silk-draped room
cut out of a corner of a rock cave; the performance sometimes seemed
filtered through water or moonbeams.

George Tsypin's setting was disconcertingly fluid, relying on mobile
solid pieces and light to transform the shallow depth of the Newman
Theatre (illus. 146). Tsypin, born in the Soviet Union and, like Ciulei,
trained as an architect, used space provocatively, often with rapidly changing
photo-projections of nineteenth-century buildings or etchings, to create
what he calls "an architecture of the mind" (Smith 160). His method moved
the disjunctive or anti-realistic elements of the text to the foreground, and
this is what unsettled the New York critics. Most of them assumed the play
to be a wistful romance, and then objected to the production's resistance to

a unified style supporting that view ("there is a gorgeously autumnal mood to *Cymbeline*," wrote Clive Barnes; "one scarcely knows how to discuss a misreading so ignorant as to be effectively beneath consideration"). The reactions of Barnes, Frank Rich, John Simon, and other established critics were noteworthy examples of powerful judgments about Shakespeare – powerful in that they had severe implications for ticket sales – based on intentional hermeneutics.[26]

The audiences at the Public Theatre, much more adventurous than the official arbiters, generally seemed delighted by the unexpected treatment of a little-known text that itself seems to anticipate some of the qualities of postmodernism. But the extremely metaphoric nature of the scenography and the staging, which required Shakespearean spectators to think in unaccustomed ways in order to decode the signifiers, and then questioned the results of that decoding, clearly perplexed some viewers. It's highly disturbing to watch Shakespeare, even the Shakespeare of a disjointed play like *Cymbeline*, laid open to a detotalizing instability.

THE MAGIC OF VISION

The distinctive strain of Shakespearean representation in our time, a tension between a decentering aesthetic and the desire to retain the plays as touchstones of traditional western culture, has produced uneven results. There has been no clear resolution of this tension, not in European and not in English-language productions; as Shakespeare has become more popular than ever before the expression of his plays has become more complex, and old-fashioned historicism often exists next door to forms of postmodernism. Further visual adventures have ranged from an operatic yet political *Titus* by Fabià Puigserver in Catalan (Teatre Lliure, Barcelona, 1977), to a nightmare *Dream* by Alexander Lang at the Deutsches Theater (East Berlin, 1980); from a disturbingly elegant *Julius Caesar* by Maurizio Scaparro that ironized the scenic facilities of the Teatro Olimpico (Vicenza, 1978), to the series of challenging productions by Daniel Mesguich in Paris (1977 to present) which trespass many boundaries of Anglo-American interpretation.[27] The productions that have most effectively reanalyzed scenography, however, have been less self-conscious than those about postmodernity and have extended postwar Shakespeare practice by overlaying a new temperament onto the methods and ideas of Brecht and Kott.

The postmodern suspension of the past inside the present can actually be traced to Brecht, as Aronson notes,[28] particularly to his realization that the rapidity of change and the increase in knowledge in the modern world have forced us to see history in a new light: not as a finalized past but as a process in which the new continuously transfigures the old. Though many recent British and American Shakespeare productions have slighted public themes, social issues have remained vital to Shakespeare in Europe, east and west. This development could be demonstrated with a number of important productions of the 1980s; as a simple index I will look at three versions of *King Lear* that span the decade.

Hungary was the location for a number of innovative scenographic departures that enlarged Kottian cruelty. Imre Csiszár, who presented *Macbeth* on a dunghill in 1979, staged *Lear* on a unit set that signified a decaying factory (illus. 147). Performed in a large industrial town in the north, with the great socialist actor Tomas Major in the lead, the politics of the play became proletarian and contemporary: Lear was an industrial despot made into an industrial outcast, just as the heath was seen as an

147 *King Lear* 1981 Miskolci. D: Imre Csiszár. S: István Szlávik. C: György Szakács. An abandoned factory as the location for a political parable about authority, complete with a railway car in the storm scenes and at the end. Note the prominent loudspeakers.

industrial wasteland. He and his daughters, speaking through microphones in the first scene, wore contemporary costumes cut in futuristic silhouettes, while others seemed dressed in parodies of nineteenth-century clothes in plastics and other artificial materials, so that past, present, and future persisted visually. In the storm scenes a railway freight car screeched on the tracks which are visible in the picture, and came on again at the end of the play, crashing into the downstage barrier, suggesting an apocalypse thoroughly removed from nature.

Ingmar Bergman's production, designed by Gunilla Palmstierna-Weiss (Stockholm, 1984), was a highly visual account of an abhorrent world. The seventy cast members remained on throughout, their bodies becoming stage implements like Kent's stocks or Cornwall's bier, their costumes in conflict between the medieval and the Renaissance. On the heath a writhing line of "naked wretches" became the storm itself. At the close the set and cyclorama collapsed: the "promised end" appeared as a blinding light in the audience's eyes. Robert Sturua's version, designed by Mirian Shvelidze (Tbilisi, 1987), which seemed to take place in a police state, ended with the set flying apart to the sound of thunder or of a nuclear explosion.[29] Shakespeare's doomsday, which is an intellectual occurrence or a literary trope, was considered in these cases insufficient – the horror of *King Lear* needed the self-reflexive, physical dismantling of the very materials used to establish the fictive world. It's doomsday for most sets at the end of a run, of course; but, in keeping with the discovery of the Bogdanov–Dyer *Shrew*, to show that demolition to the audience is a powerful violation of convention and confers added conceptual weight to scenography.

Despite contemporary inclinations towards artistic pluralism and the decentering of authority, directors and designers in the theatre have become more important than ever. It's a rich paradox that the instability expressed in postmodern performance appears to require even greater artistic management. This is a notable tendency in Shakespeare; most of the productions discussed in this chapter would have been impossible without firm directorial control. Giorgio Strehler's *Tempest*, my final example, displayed this control as an element of its meaning, and at the same time established through radical scenography a renewed urgency for Shakespeare in a world that sees too much Shakespeare. First seen in Milan in 1978, and continued in repertory for about ten years, it may have been the most important Shakespearean production since Brook's *Dream*.

Its premise was disarmingly simple: Prospero's magic is the magic of the theatre, and is subject to the same illusive limitations. It has been commonplace for some time to read *The Tempest* as a play about art, but traditionally its magic has been equated with poetry, the magus equated with Shakespeare. Strehler offered instead a Prospero who could accomplish only what a theatre director can accomplish, and noted in particular that neither can do anything without the active accord of their actors and spectators. To convey its theme, the production emphasized that Prospero's magic is almost entirely visual, visions in the literal sense: the magus creates unrealities which are nonetheless seen, like stage effects.

The opening storm lasted five full minutes: the shadow of a ship loomed behind transparent and billowing cloth, itself looking like a sail; sailors were thrown about, climbing and falling from rigging; lighting and thunder flashed and echoed in the house; huge waves rolled and crested downstage (illus. 148). It was spectacular, overwhelming, a powerfully physical tempest which took advantage of the large stage of the Teatro Lirico. Yet it was contextualized by a conspicuous theatricality, for the blue sea lay quietly on the floor as silk cloth before it began, the sailors were "drowned" its folds,

148 *The Tempest* 1978 Milan. D: Giorgio Strehler. Des: Luciano Damiani. P: Luigi Ciminaghi. The opening scene, with the ship created by a projection against billowing cloth. Piccolo Teatro di Milano, at Teatro Lirico.

149 *The Tempest* 1978 Milan. P: Luigi Ciminaghi. Ariel (Giulia Lazzarini), conspicuously supported by a wire, flies above Prospero (Tino Carraro). Their hieratic gestures also suggest an intimate relationship. Note the treatment of the stage floor, and the white cloth backdrop.

and at the end of the tempest Prospero and Miranda calmly folded up a large section of cloth like a sheet and put away the magic in a stage trap. The waves were created by silk manipulated by sixteen hidden operators in transverse grooves or furrows built into the orchestra pit. The stage floor, which could be raked on the diagonal, was made of simple boards with a magician's circle painted on them. Backed by white sheeting and with most costumes in white tones, the island was a bleached world of milky light; far from cinematically realistic, however, it depended on a contemporary and self-reflexive review of seventeenth-century scenography.

Strehler gave much of the burden of the theme to Ariel. Played by a woman (Giulia Lazzarini) as a white-faced Pierrot, dressed in a billowing white clown suit and skullcap, the character entered through the air at the master's call. But this Ariel flew on an obvious theatrical wire, hooked to a harness on the actress's body, a vivid signifier of her peculiar slavery; she could fly but not fly away, and tugged and pulled at the cable when Prospero denied her freedom. As David Hirst notes (62), Strehler converted "their relationship into a metaphor for the interaction of director and actor." Ariel, longing for personal liberation, nonetheless submitted to the mind of the controller, willingly performing balletic turns on the wire as signifiers of active submission. Their rapport, colored by a subtle eroticism, was perversely intensified by its parallel to the Prospero–Miranda relationship. Intellectually there was never a question about who was in charge; visually there was an insidious ambiguity to the characters' status that complemented Strehler's investigation of magic as willed pretense, like acting itself (illus. 149). This was also apparent in the banquet scene, when the wind rose in the sheets as food appeared for the courtiers. Suddenly the tempest erupted again as Ariel, a screeching harpy, descended from the flies like a giant black bat against a blue sky, accompanied by flashes of lightning. All the while Prospero stood by, controlling and approving his eerie actor.

Luciano Damiani's counterfeit baroque stagecraft, filled with quaint devices, supported the thematic atmosphere particularly well in act 4. For the wedding Prospero carried a torch and sheaf of wheat – the simplest of symbols – and the great opportunity for spectacle, the wedding masque, was cut entirely. The curious omission gave further emphasis to the moment when Prospero recalls Caliban's plot against him: the sky was darkened and the silk clouds were lowered to create a powerful stage image filled with artifice (illus. 150). Here the techniques, based in Brechtian scenography, combined postmodern irony with profound emotion. In a similar way Strehler combined acting styles. The Trinculo subplot was performed as a *commedia* sketch, the actors in half-masks and clown costumes; the seventeenth-century Italian reference brought it more into the spirit of the main plot than usual in productions of the play, without forcing a unified style.

To perform *The Tempest* in Malta or in Bermuda would, by the incontestable power of location, insist on the play as a depiction of European colonialism and on the equivocal nature of Prospero's power over others; in such a case the ending emphasizes liberation. To perform it in Milan, on the other hand, makes it a play about indemnity and restoration, and the ending looks toward return. It was this unspoken, underlying motif that Strehler managed to emphasize in the figure of his magus, indirectly equating Prospero to himself, suggesting the limits of art and also its danger. As Hirst puts it (65), "the theatrical artist cannot commit himself too deeply; he must, however, realise when to stop"; Ariel's repeated claim for freedom was also a warning to the director "that he was using his

150   *The Tempest* 1978 Milan. P: Luigi Ciminaghi. Baroque stage techniques used ironically, as Miranda and Ferdinand (Fabiana Udenio and Massimo Bonetti) seem about to be swallowed up by descending artificial clouds (4.1). Prospero's arms and head are just visible in the foreground, directing the effect.

'meaner ministers' (his actors) thoughtlessly." The most powerful emotional moment of the production therefore came when Tino Carraro released Giulia Lazzarini. This Prospero did so literally, by unhooking her from the aerial wire, which snapped away into the flies. She stood surprised a moment, experimented with walking, then slowly and gleefully danced up the aisle of the auditorium, exiting through a spectators' door.

Prospero removed his crown and cape for the epilogue, drowned his book in the artificial waves, and broke his staff in two. On this cue the magic of the set fell apart: all the sheets and curtains crashed down on the stage, the tracks holding the waves were released, the floor rocked a moment, and the waves extended in a distorted position. "Now my charms are all o'erthrown," Carraro said quietly, standing in the house. But unlike the demolition in Bergman's or Sturua's *Lear*, representing the end of the world, Strehler's metatheatrical moment stressed the limitations of the theatre. Thus the epilogue became a plea to recognize that the rough magic of the stage, which cannot change Caliban or insure that the rightful Duke of Milan will govern properly, requires a reciprocal benediction:

> As you from crimes would pardoned be,
> Let your indulgence set me free.

Shakespeare's *plaudite*, couching a conventional appeal for approbation in the terms of Christian redemption, was here a request for audience complicity. And as the audience began to applaud, the magic was complicitously restored. The liberated Lazzarini returned, like any actor in the curtain call, to stand next to her former master; Carraro bowed, as himself, as Prospero, and as Strehler's deputy; in the tradition of Italian theatre, Strehler himself bowed on opening night. Even the stagehands operating the sea bowed, dressed in blue, standing waist-high in the tracks of the waves. Most notable of all, the spectators' indulgence caused the set to be reassembled: the sails, sheets, and stage floor were righted. Scenography itself – like Prospero's vision of a fairer world, the cloud-capped towers, the gorgeous palaces – is held in place by the pulleys and wires of our collective will.

So Strehler and Damiani suggested. Acknowledging that Shakespeare's play is assertively visual, they offered a reminder that the fundamental simplicity of the theatre lies in a productive rupture between the artificial visions it displays and the semiotic dreams we assign. It's intriguing that the three productions of *The Tempest* discussed in this chapter, directed by Strehler, Ciulei, and Brook, all emphasized the centrality of the visual to the theme of power, and were ultimately more interested in the effect of power on Prospero than on his former enemies or slaves. Strehler's Prospero was often violent and angry, especially with Caliban, yet the ending, so thoroughly concerned with absolution, felt a little soft compared with some directly political interpretations. Jan Kott, invited to the final dress rehearsal, thought that a debilitating characteristic, as if there were too much life and liking on stage and not enough anxiety and despair. "The Milan version of *The Tempest*," he wrote, "despite all its beauty, has no Shakespearean bitterness nor any of Shakespeare's renouncements."[30]

Kott's disappointment with a director he had earlier admired is easy enough to understand; Kott's reading of Shakespeare, which affected international performance for a generation, has not changed much since the 1950s, whereas Strehler's practice has developed in unpredictable ways. Indeed one wonders if Brecht, who in 1956 thought Strehler the greatest director in Europe (see chapter 7), would have approved twenty and more years later. Not that it matters. What matters is that Strehler and Damiani had forged an approach for *The Tempest* that built on Brechtian principles and went beyond them, finding in Shakespeare a source for renewed visual inventiveness. The approach shared much with the postmodern attraction to the emphatic image; some moments in the production, especially in the later years of its life, were so visually beautiful that they threatened to separate themselves as isolated tableaux, as they do in the photographs. On the whole, however, the visuals were anchored in thought and integrated with an interpretation as compelling as it was contemporary. They were often best when at their simplest. The meeting of Ferdinand and Miranda, for example, took place without effects, in white light on the unadorned white stage. Centered on a human drama, we watched two young people fall in love, heedless of the political and historical forces that had brought them together: a vision close to what Shakespeare's audience probably saw.

Fitting a stage with striking images is, in an age that is overwhelmed by the ocular, a relatively easy matter. The success Strehler and Damiani achieved comes not from finding potent images but from finding images that resonate across time, that seem to participate in two worlds at once: the inscribed (but lost) world of Shakespeare's text, and the mightily confusing world we are daily caught in. Perhaps that is the true work of designers, to create visual environments that make the strangeness of the plays seem right or comfortable or arresting in the present. Indeed one way to imagine the scenographic history of the century for Shakespeare is to see it as a series of attempts to make a home for the otherness of the texts. "Somewhere in there," Bob Crowley said – somewhere among the prodigious variety of visual choices – "is that world where Shakespeare wants to be."[31] Since the designer and director get to decide where Shakespeare wants to be, and since audiences must ultimately sanction their decisions, the nature and appearance of that world will continue to change.

I can't pretend to know what those changes will be, or which current trends are most important: this chapter is longer than the others because I can't sort out contemporary movements with the same conviction. Shakespeare's plays are not inexhaustible, as some critics in the past have implied; they do not encompass the entire universe or anticipate all time. Even with brilliant productions they will not settle refugees, solve overpopulation, or reverse the decay of the biosphere. Confounded by the obstructions of our difficult age, our reading of the texts may in fact turn more limited and more perverse as we move farther and farther from their language and from the Renaissance humanism that formed them. But it seems reasonably certain that visual solutions will continue to surprise us, and that some Shakespearean visions we look at on stage will strike our eyes with wonder. Like Prospero's magic, those insinuating visions, incontrovertible and artificial, sure signs and sham signs, will be torn between the deception of sight and its mysterious truth.

Table of productions

This is a chronological list of the chief productions discussed in the text, with their directors, designers, producing organizations, and original venues.

D = director, Des = designer (sets and costumes by same person or team), S = set designer, C = costume designer, L = lighting designer. Th = Theatre, SMT = Shakespeare Memorial Theatre, RSC = Royal Shakespeare Company, RST = Royal Shakespeare Theatre, NYSF = New York Shakespeare Festival.

Twelfth Night 1840 Düsseldorf.
D and Des: Karl Immermann.
Düsseldorfer Künstler, 29 Feb.

The Winter's Tale 1856 London.
D: Charles Kean. Des: Thomas Grieve *et al.* Princess's Th, 28 April.

Julius Caesar 1874 Berlin.
D: Georg II of Saxe-Meiningen and Ludwig Chronegk. Des: Georg. Friedrich Wilhelmstädtisches Th, 1 May.

Romeo and Juliet 1882 London.
D and L: Henry Irving. Des: Hawes Craven. Lyceum Th, 8 March.

King Lear 1889 Munich.
D: Jocza Savits. Des: Karl Lautenschläger. Shakespeare-Bühne, Residenztheater, 1 June.

Measure for Measure 1893 London.
D and S: William Poel. C: Jennie Moore. Shakespeare Reading Society at Royalty Th, 9 Nov.

Twelfth Night 1895 London.
D and Des: William Poel. Elizabethan Stage Society at Burlington Hall, 21 June.

Measure for Measure 1898 Paris.
D: Aurélien Lugné-Poe. Des: R. Hista. Cirque d'Eté, 10 Dec.

Twelfth Night 1901 London.
D: Herbert Beerbohm Tree. Des: Hawes Craven. Her Majesty's Th, 5 Feb.

Much Ado About Nothing 1903 London.
D and Des: Edward Gordon Craig. Imperial Th, 23 May.

A Midsummer Night's Dream 1905 Berlin.
D: Max Reinhardt. S: Gustav Knina. C: Karl Walser. Neues Th, 31 Jan.

The Winter's Tale 1906 Berlin.
D: Max Reinhardt. Des: Emil Orlik. Deutsches Th, Kammerspiele, 15 Sept.

King Lear 1908 Berlin.
D: Max Reinhardt. Des: Carl
Czeschka. Deutsches Th,
Kammerspiele, 16 Sept.

Hamlet 1909 Berlin.
D: Max Reinhardt. Des: Fritz Erler.
Deutsches Th, 16 Oct. (first seen at
Künstlertheater in Munich in June).

Hamlet 1911/12 Moscow.
D: E. G. Craig and K. S. Stanislavsky.
S: Craig. C: Craig and K. N. Sapunov.
Moscow Art Th, 23 Dec. O. S./5 Jan.
N. S.

The Winter's Tale 1912 London.
D: Harley Granville Barker. S:
Norman Wilkinson. C: Albert
Rothenstein. Savoy Th, 21 Sept.

Twelfth Night 1912 London.
D: Harley Granville Barker. Des:
Norman Wilkinson. Savoy Th,
15 Nov.

A Midsummer Night's Dream 1914
London.
D: Harley Granville Barker. Des:
Norman Wilkinson. Savoy Th, 16 Feb.

Twelfth Night 1914 Paris.
D: Jacques Copeau. S and L: Louis
Jouvet. C: Duncan Grant. Th de
Vieux-Colombier, 15 May.

The Tempest 1915 Berlin.
D: Max Reinhardt. Des: Ernst Stern.
Volksbühne, 8 Oct.

As You Like It 1919 Stratford.
D: Nigel Playfair. Des: Claud
Lovat Fraser. SMT, 22 April.

Richard III 1920 New York.
D: Arthur Hopkins. Des: Robert
Edmond Jones. Plymouth Th,
6 March.

Richard III 1920 Berlin.
D: Leopold Jessner. Des: Emil
Pirchan. Staatstheater, 5 Nov.

Macbeth 1921 New York.
D: Arthur Hopkins. Des: R. E. Jones.
Apollo Th, 17 Feb.

Othello 1921 Berlin.
D: Leopold Jessner. Des: Emil
Pirchan. Staatstheater, 11 Nov.

Romeo and Juliet 1921 Moscow.
D: Alexander Tairov. Des: Alexandra
Exter. Kamerny Th, 17 May.

Hamlet 1922 New York (1925
London).
D: Arthur Hopkins. Des: R. E. Jones.
Sam H. Harris Th, 16 Nov.

The Winter's Tale 1924 Warsaw.
D: Leon Schiller. Des: Andrzej
Pronaszko. Th Boguslawski, 23 Oct.

Hamlet 1925 London.
D: H. J. Ayliff. Des: Paul Shelving.
Kingsway Th, 25 Aug.

Hamlet 1926 Prague.
D: Karel Hugo Hilar. Des: Vlastislav
Hofman. National Th, 24 Nov.

Hamlet 1926 Berlin.
D: Leopold Jessner. Des: Caspar
Neher. Staatstheater, 3 Dec.

Julius Caesar 1928 Warsaw.
D: Leon Schiller. Des: Andrzej and
Zbigniew Pronaszko. Polish Th,
21 Jan.

Macbeth 1928 London.
D: H. J. Ayliff. Des: Paul Shelving.
Court Th, 6 Feb.

Richard III 1928 Cambridge.
D and Des: Terence Gray. L:
C. Harold Ridge. Cambridge Festival
Th, 20 Feb.

Romeo and Juliet 1929 Cambridge.
D: Terence Gray. Des: Doria Paston.
L: C. Harold Ridge. Cambridge
Festival Th, 18 Feb.

King John 1929 Berlin.
D: Leopold Jessner. Des: Caspar
Neher. Staatstheater, 24 May.

Romeo and Juliet 1931 Warsaw.
D: Arnold Szyfman. Des: Karol
Frycz. Polish Th, 29 Oct.

A Midsummer Night's Dream 1932
Stratford.
D and L: William Bridges-Adams.
Des: Norman Wilkinson. SMT,
27 April.

The Merchant of Venice 1932 Stratford.
D: Theodore Komisarjevsky. S:
Komisarjevsky and Lesley Blanch. C:
Lesley Blanch. SMT, 25 July.

The Merchant of Venice 1932
Cambridge.
D: Terence Gray. Des: Doria Paston.
L: C. Harold Ridge. Cambridge
Festival Th, 14 Nov.

Macbeth 1933 Stratford.
D and Des: Theodore Komisarjevsky.
SMT, 18 April.

Coriolanus 1933 Stratford.
D, Des, and L: William Bridges-
Adams. SMT, 24 April.

Romeo and Juliet 1935 London.
D: John Gielgud. Des: Motley. Old
Vic at New Th, 17 Oct.

King Lear 1936 Stratford.
D and Des: Theodore Komisarjevsky.
SMT, 20 April.

Julius Caesar 1936 Prague.
D: Jirí Frejka. Des: František Tröster.
National Th, 9 June.

Macbeth 1936 New York.
D: Orson Welles. Des: Nat Karson.
L: Abe Feder. WPA Negro Th Project
at Lafayette Th, 14 April.

Julius Caesar 1937 New York.
D: Orson Welles. Des: Samuel Leve.
L: Jean Rosenthal. Mercury Th,
6 Nov.

The Comedy of Errors 1938 Stratford.
D and Des: Theodore Komisarjevsky.
SMT, 12 April.

Twelfth Night 1939 Stratford.
D: Irene Hentschel. Des: Motley.
SMT, 13 April.

Love's Labour's Lost 1946 Stratford.
D: Peter Brook. Des: Reginald Leefe.
SMT, 26 April.

Romeo and Juliet 1947 Stratford.
D: Peter Brook. Des: Rolf Gérard.
SMT, 5 April.

The Tempest 1947 Łódź.
D: Leon Schiller. Des: Władysław
Daszewski. Shakespeare Festival at
Wojska Polskiego Th, 19 July.

Richard II 1947 Avignon.
D: Jean Vilar. S: Camille Demangeat.
C: Léon Gischia. Papal Palace, 4 Sept.

Macbeth 1948 Gothenburg.
D: Ingmar Bergman. Des: Carl-Johan
Ström. Gothenburg City Th,
12 March.

As You Like It 1948 Rome.
D: Luchino Visconti. Des: Salvador
Dali. Teatro Eliseo, 26 Nov.

Troilus and Cressida 1949 Florence.
D: Luchino Visconti. Des: Franco
Zeffirelli. Maggio Musicale at Boboli
Gardens, 21 June.

Henry VIII 1949 Stratford.
D: Tyrone Guthrie. Des: Tanya Moiseiwitsch. SMT, 23 July.

Richard II 1951 Stratford.
D: Anthony Quayle. Des: Tanya Moiseiwitsch (assisted by Alix Stone). SMT, 24 March.

The Tempest 1951 Stratford.
D: Michael Benthall. Des: Loundon Sainthill. SMT, 26 June.

Richard III 1953 Stratford, Ontario.
D: Tyrone Guthrie. Des: Tanya Moiseiwitsch. Festival Th, 13 July.

All's Well That Ends Well 1953 Stratford, Ontario.
D: Tyrone Guthrie. Des: Tanya Moiseiwitsch. Festival Th, 13 July.

Romeo and Juliet 1954 Stratford.
D: Glen Byam Shaw. Des: Motley. SMT, 27 April.

The Taming of the Shrew 1954 Stratford, Ontario.
D: Tyrone Guthrie. Des: Tanya Moiseiwitsch. Festival Th, 29 June.

Hamlet 1954 Moscow.
D: Nikolai Okhlopkov. Des: V. F. Ryndin. Mayakovsky Th, 16 Dec.

Titus Andronicus 1955 Stratford.
D: Peter Brook. Des: Brook with Michael Northen, Desmond Heeley, and William Blezard. SMT, 16 Aug.

Measure for Measure 1956 Stratford, Connecticut.
D: John Houseman and Jack Landau. Des: Rouben Ter-Arutunian. L: Jean Rosenthal. American Shakespeare Festival, 27 June.

Henry IV 1957 Lyon.
D: Roger Planchon. Des: René Allio. Th de la Cité, Villeurbanne, 31 Oct.

Coriolanus 1957 Milan.
D: Giorgio Strehler. S: Luciano Damiani. C: Ezio Frigerio. Piccolo Teatro, 9 Nov.

A Midsummer Night's Dream 1959 Stratford.
D: Peter Hall. Des: Lila de Nobili with Jean Marie Simon. L: Michael Northen. SMT, 2 June.

Coriolanus 1959 Stratford.
D: Peter Hall. Des: Boris Aronson. SMT, 7 Aug.

Henry V 1961 Vienna.
D: Leopold Lindtberg. S: Teo Otto. C: Ploberger. Burgtheater, 7 Feb.

King Lear 1962 Stratford.
D and Des: Peter Brook (C in collaboration with Kegan Smith). RSC at RST, 6 Nov.

The Wars of the Roses (Henry VI plays and Richard III) 1963 Stratford.
D: Peter Hall with John Barton and Frank Evans. Des: John Bury with Ann Curtis. RSC at RST, 17 July–20 Aug.

Romeo and Juliet 1963 Prague.
D: Otomar Krejča. S and L: Josef Svoboda. C: Zdenka Kadrnozková. National Th, 25 Oct.

The Merchant of Venice 1963 Berlin.
D: Erwin Piscator. Des: Hans-Ulrich Schmückle. Freie Volksbühne, 1 Dec.

Troilus and Cressida 1964 Lyon.
D: Roger Planchon. Des: André Acquart. Th de la Cité, Villeurbanne, 10 Jan.

The Wars of the Roses (Richard II, 1 and 2 Henry IV and Henry V) 1964 Stratford.
D: Peter Hall with John Barton and Clifford Williams. Des: John Bury

with Ann Curtis. RSC at RST,
15 April – 3 June.

Hamlet 1964 Berlin.
D: Wolfgang Heinz. Des: Heinrich
Kilger. Deutsches Th, 17 April.

Romeo and Juliet 1964 Verona.
D and S: Franco Zeffirelli. C: Peter
D. Hall. Teatro Romano, 4 July.

Coriolanus 1964 Berlin.
D: Manfred Wekwerth and Joachim
Tenschert. Des: Karl von Appen.
Berliner Ensemble, 25 Sept.

Henry VI 1965 Milan (*Il gioco dei
potenti*).
D: Giorgio Strehler. Des: Strehler,
Carlo Tomassi, Enrico Job. Piccolo
Teatro at Teatro Lirico, 19–20 June.

Measure for Measure 1966 New York.
D: Michael Kahn. S: Ming Cho Lee.
C: Theoni V. Aldredge. NYSF at
Delacorte Th, 12 July.

King John 1967 New York.
D: Joseph Papp. S: Douglas Schmidt.
C: Theoni V. Aldredge. NYSF at
Delacorte Th, 5 July.

Measure for Measure 1967 Bremen.
D: Peter Zadek. Des: Wilfred Minks.
Th am Goetheplatz, 16 Sept.

As You Like It 1967 London.
D: Clifford Williams. Des: Ralph
Koltai. L: Robert Orubo and John B.
Read. National Th at Old Vic, 3 Oct.

Troilus and Cressida 1968 Stratford.
D: John Barton. Des: Timothy
O'Brien. L: John Bradley. RSC at
RST, 8 Aug.

Pericles 1969 Stratford.
D: Terry Hands. Des: Timothy
O'Brien and Tanzeena Firth. L:
Christopher Morley. RSC at RST,
2 April.

The Winter's Tale 1969 Stratford.
D: Trevor Nunn. Des: Christopher
Morley. L: John Bradley. RSC at
RST, 15 May.

Henry V 1969 Stratford, Connecticut.
D: Michael Kahn. S: Karl Eigsti. C:
Jeanne Button. L: Thomas Skelton.
American Shakespeare Festival, 8 Aug.

Twelfth Night 1969 Stratford.
D: John Barton. Des: Christopher
Morley. C: Stephanie Howard. RSC at
RST, 21 Aug.

A Midsummer Night's Dream 1970
Stratford.
D: Peter Brook. Des: Sally Jacobs.
RSC at RST, 27 Aug.

Hamlet 1971 Moscow.
D: Yuri Lyubimov. Des: David
Borovsky. L: K. Panshin. Taganka
Th, 29 Nov.

Coriolanus 1972 Stratford.
D: Trevor Nunn with Buzz
Goodbody and Euan Smith. Des:
Christopher Morley and Ann Curtis.
L: John Bradley. RSC at RST,
11 April.

King Lear 1972 Milan.
D: Giorgio Strehler. Des: Ezio
Frigerio. Piccolo Teatro, 11 June.

Much Ado About Nothing 1972 New
York.
D: A. J. Antoon. S: Ming Cho Lee. C:
Theoni V. Aldredge. NYSF at
Delacorte Th, 10 Aug.

Richard II 1973 Stratford.
D: John Barton. Des: Timothy
O'Brien and Tanzeena Firth. RSC at
RST, 10 April.

Timon of Athens 1974 Paris.
D: Peter Brook. Des: Michel Launay.
CIRT at Th des Bouffes du Nord,
15 Oct.

The Tempest 1974 Berlin.
D: Friedo Solter. S: Eva-Maria Vieberg and Heinz Wenzel. C: Christine Stromberg. Deutsches Th, 5 Dec.

Henry V 1975 Stratford.
D: Terry Hands. Des: Farrah. L: Stewart Leviton. RSC at RST, 31 March.

Hamlet 1975 Stratford.
D: Buzz Goodbody. Des: Chris Dyer. L: Leo Leibovici. RSC at The Other Place, 8 April.

1 and *2 Henry IV* 1975 Stratford.
D: Terry Hands. Des: Farrah. L: Stewart Leviton. RSC at RST, 24 April and 17 June.

Othello 1976 Hamburg.
D: Peter Zadek. S: Zadek and Peter Pabst. C: Pabst. Deutsches Schauspielhaus, 7 May.

Macbeth 1976 Stratford.
D: Trevor Nunn. Des: John Napier. L: Leo Leibovici. RSC at The Other Place, 4 Aug.

As You Like It 1977 Stratford.
D: Trevor Nunn. Des: John Napier. L: John Watts. RSC at RST, 6 Sept.

As You Like It 1977 Berlin.
D: Peter Stein. S: Karl-Ernst Hermann. C: Moidele Bickel. Schaubühne at CCC Film Studios in Spandau, 20 Sept.

Hamlet 1977 Bochum.
D: Peter Zadek. S: Zadek and Peter Pabst. C: Pabst. Bochum Schauspielhaus at a factory in Hamm, 30 Sep.

Hamlet 1978 Washington.
D: Liviu Ciulei. S: Ming Cho Lee. C: Marjorie Slaimon. L: Hugh Lester. Arena Stage, 29 March.

The Taming of the Shrew 1978 Stratford.
D: Michael Bogdanov. Des: Chris Dyer. L: Chris Ellis. RSC at RST, 19 April.

The Tempest 1978 Milan.
D: Giorgio Strehler. Des: Luciano Damiani. Piccolo Teatro at Teatro Lirico, 28 June.

The Winter's Tale 1978 Hamburg.
D: Peter Zadek. S: Daniel Spoerri. C: Spoerri and Lioba Winterhalder. Deutsches Schauspielhaus, 16 Sept.

Hamlet 1979 Cologne.
D: Hansgünter Heyme. S: Wolf Vostell. C: Vostell and Helen Fabricus. Bühnen der Stadt Köln at Schauspielhaus, 17 Feb.

King Lear 1981 Miskolci.
D: Imre Csiszár. S: István Szlávik. C: György Szakács. National Th, 6 March.

The Tempest 1981 Minneapolis.
D and S: Liviu Ciulei. C: Jack Edwards. L: Duane Schuler. Guthrie Th, 8 June.

Richard II 1981 Paris.
D: Ariane Mnouchkine. S: Guy-Claude François. C: Jean-Claude Barriera and Nathalie Thomas. L: Jean-Noël Cordier. Th du Soleil at the Cartoucherie, Vincennes, 10 Dec.

Twelfth Night 1982 Paris.
D: Ariane Mnouchkine. S: Guy-Claude François. C: Jean-Claude Barriera and Nathalie Thomas. L: Jean-Noël Cordier. Th du Soleil at Avignon Festival, 10 July; then at the Cartoucherie, Vincennes.

Hamlet 1982 Prague.
D: Miroslav Macháček. S and L: Josef Svoboda. C: Šárka Hejnová. National Th, 13 April.

Richard III 1983 New York.
D: Jane Howell. Des: Santo Loquasto. L: Pat Collins. NYSF at Delacorte Th, 13 Aug.

King Lear 1984 Stockholm.
D: Ingmar Bergman. Des: Gunilla Palmstierna-Weiss. L: Klas Möller. Royal Dramatic Th, 9 March.

Richard III 1984 Stratford.
D: Bill Alexander. Des: William Dudley. L: Leo Leibovici. RSC at RST, 14 June.

Hamlet 1984 Stratford.
D: Ron Daniels. Des: Maria Bjornson. L: Chris Ellis. RSC at RST, 9 Aug.

Coriolanus 1984 London.
D: Peter Hall. Des: John Bury. National Th, Olivier Stage, 15 Dec.

1 Henry IV 1984 Paris.
D: Ariane Mnouchkine. S: Guy-Claude François. C: Jean-Claude Barriera and Nathalie Thomas. L: Jean-Noël Cordier. Th du Soleil at the Cartoucherie, Vincennes, 18 Jan.

Measure for Measure 1985 Stratford, Ontario.
D: Michael Bogdanov. Des: Chris Dyer. L: Harry Frehner. Festival Th, 29 May.

Romeo and Juliet 1986 Stratford.
D: Michael Bogdanov. S: Chris Dyer. C: Dyer and Ginny Humphreys. RSC at RST, 31 March.

Wars of the Roses (history play cycles) 1987–8 world tour.
D: Michael Bogdanov. S: Chris Dyer. C: Stephanie Howard. L: Mark Henderson. English Shakespeare Company; first cycle opened 3 Nov. 1986, second cycle 8 Dec. 1987.

Richard III 1987 Vienna.
D: Claus Peymann. Des: Karl-Ernst Hermann. Burgtheater, 15 Feb.

King Lear 1987 Tbilisi.
D: Robert Sturua. Des: Mirian Shvelidze. Rustaveli Th, 11 May.

1 Henry VI 1988 Stratford.
D: Adrian Noble. Des: Bob Crowley. L: Chris Parry. RSC at RST, 29 Sep.

The Tempest 1989 Vienna.
D: Claus Peymann. Des: Karl-Ernst Hermann. Burgtheater, 6 Feb.

Cymbeline 1989 New York.
D: JoAnne Akalaitis. S: George Tsypin. C: Ann Hould-Ward. L: Pat Collins. NYSF at Public Th, Newman stage, 7 May.

Othello 1989 Stratford.
D: Trevor Nunn. Des: Bob Crowley. L: Chris Parry. RSC at The Other Place, 9 Aug.

The Tempest 1990 Paris.
D: Peter Brook. Des: Chloé Obolensky. L: Jean Kalman. CICT at Th des Bouffes du Nord, 27 Sept. (opened in Zurich, 14 Sept.).

Notes

Sources frequently cited are listed in the Selected References and are evoked
here by author's last name only. Other sources are cited in full in the notes.
SQ = *Shakespeare Quarterly*. *SS* = *Shakespeare Survey*

1 Shakespeare and the visual

1 Michael Billington, *Guardian* 5 May 1978. Some of my comments on audience
   reactions rely on an interview with Chris Dyer in London in Oct. 1989.
   Graham Holderness discusses the production well in *The Taming of the Shrew*,
   Shakespeare in Performance series (Manchester, 1989), 73–94.
2 Aristotle, *Poetics*, trans. Gerald F. Else (Ann Arbor, 1967), 29. The
   implication of Aristotle's word *skeuopoios* (property man, costumer, or stage
   carpenter) has been much debated; see Else, *Aristotle's Poetics: The Argument*
   (Cambridge, Mass., 1957), 280.
3 Peter Hall, in a review of Strong and Orgel's *Inigo Jones*, quoted in Hirst 66.
   Hall has repeated the thought recently in his foreword to Goodwin 14–16.
4 Marvin and Ruth Thompson, "Performance Criticism: From Granville-
   Barker to Bernard Beckerman and Beyond," *Shakespeare and the Sense of
   Performance: Essays in the Tradition of Performance Criticism in Honor of Bernard
   Beckerman*, ed. M. and R. Thompson (Newark, 1989), 13. Two different
   critiques of the traditions of Shakespearean literary criticism, both with
   implicit application to performance critics, are the books by Gary Taylor and
   by Michael Bristol. More recently both Hugh Grady and Margreta de Grazia
   have placed Shakespearean commentary in large cultural and historical
   contexts.
5 W. B. Worthen, "Deeper Meanings and Theatrical Technique: The Rhetoric
   of Performance Criticism," *SQ* 40 (1989): 455.
6 It has most recently been attacked by revisionist textual editors and
   commentators as well, who recognize that a final or "ideal" authorial text is
   impossible to establish because the playwright privileged the actor above the
   printer. Bristol discusses the history of Shakespearean editing, 91–119.
   Stephen Orgel's "The Authentic Shakespeare," *Representations* 21 (1988):

1–25, is important and coincidentally has valuable comments about the relationship of the text to eighteenth-century Shakespeare iconography. The best general account of the adversarial relationship between script and production is Patrice Pavis' essay "From Page to Stage: A Difficult Birth" (in Pavis 1992): "Mise en scène is reading actualized: the dramatic text does not have an individual reader, but a possible collective reading, proposed by the mise en scène. Philology and literary criticism use words to explain texts, whereas mise en scène uses stage actions to 'question' the dramatic text" (31).

7 Marco de Marinis, "Lo spettacolo come testo 1," *Versus* 21 (Sept.–Dec. 1978): 57. Marvin Carlson's two recent books introduce the "European" school of theatre semiotics well. Keir Elam outlined the field in English, and my own thinking has been influenced by Patrice Pavis. Susan Bennett combines a semiotic approach with attention to the cultural and ideological inscriptions of the performance event. Surprisingly little work has been done directly on the semiosis of set or costume design since the original contributions of the Prague School; a useful starting point is Freddie Rokem's "A Semiotic Definition of Scenography," *Semiotics 1982*, ed. John Deely and Jonathan Evans (New York, 1987), 449–58. Martin Esslin (72–8) makes some basic comments on visual signification.

8 Handke, *Offending the Audience*, in *Kaspar and Other Plays*, trans. Michael Roloff (New York, 1969), 10; see Carlson 1990: 75. In using the terms *metonymic* and *metaphoric* for scenography, I am of course relying on the two master linguistic tropes as outlined by Roman Jakobson; see Jakobson and Halle. David Lodge's *The Modes of Modern Writing* (London, 1977) is a useful explication of the subject for literature; even more useful is his essay on the relationship of narration to the visual, "Narration with Words," in *Images and Understanding*, ed. Horace Barlow *et al.* (Cambridge, 1990). Jakobson's terms seem to me better for scenography than the more common semiotic terms *icon*, *index*, and *symbol* established by C. S. Peirce; the two-term dichotomy is clearer, and a little less tied to methods of linguistic analysis. (Although semiotic philosophy is based in linguistics, it's worth noting that the terms used by both Peirce and Jakobson are essentially visual in nature.)

9 Fredric Jameson, *Postmodernism, or, the Cultural Logic of Late Capitalism* (Durham, North Carolina, 1991), 10. I discuss the implications of postmodernism for Shakespeare performance in the final chapter. Kaja Silverman's "short history" of semiotics is useful here, especially her treatment of the relationship between structuralist and post-structuralist thought; see chapter 1 of *The Subject of Semiotics* (New York, 1983).

10 Donald Oenslager is representative of this approach: an important designer and collector himself, Oenslager's influential book uses a biographical method for the history of scenography and reproduces designs only, not

production photographs. On the other hand, René Hainaux's four-volume work, covering the period from 1935 to 1975, relies almost entirely upon photos; but since there is no written text other than identifying captions, this can hardly be called a history. As usual Denis Bablet provides a balance, particularly his seminal book *Esthétique générale du décor de théâtre du 1870 à 1914* (1965), which has not been translated. Also essential is Bablet's *The Revolutions in Stage Design in the Twentieth Century* (1977), though it doesn't have the theoretical precision of his earlier volume. Douglas Russell has been influential, and the relationship between theatre and general visual artists is addressed by Henning Rischbieter.

11 Nicoll's treatment of pictorial evidence, one of few discussions of the subject, is from *The Garrick Stage: Theatres and Audience in the Eighteenth Century* (Athens, Georgia, 1980), 102–43.

12 R. A. Foakes, *Illustrations of the English Stage, 1580–1642* (Stanford, 1985), 50.

13 See Adrian Woodhouse, *Angus McBean* (London, 1982), 5, and McBean's *Vivien: A Love Affair with the Camera* (Oxford, 1989). The McBean theatre photographs and glass negatives are at Harvard.

14 See Marco de Marinis, "'A Faithful Betrayal of Performance': Notes on the Use of Video in Theatre," *New Theatre Quarterly* 1 (1985): 383–9.

2 Victorian pictures

1 Some of these matters are addressed by Bernard Beckerman in "Shakespearean Playgoing Then and Now," in *Shakespeare's More Than Words Can Witness: Essays on Visual and Nonverbal Enactment in the Plays*, ed. Sidney Homan (Lewisburg, 1980).

2 Schivelbusch, *Disenchanted Night: The Industrialization of Light in the Nineteenth Century* (Berkeley, 1988). Martin Meisel's *Realizations: Narrative, Pictorial, and Theatrical Arts in Nineteenth Century England* (Princeton, 1983) is relevant to Kean's pictorial representations of historical painting.

3 The cathedral scene is recorded in a famous painting by Johnston Forbes-Robertson in the Players Club in New York, reproduced in color in Speaight 54–5. Contemporary comments on the production are quoted in Odell 11:428–31.

4 Granville Barker, "Repertory Theatres," *The New Quarterly* 2 (1909): 493–4.

5 A valuable European treatment is Christopher Smith's "Shakespeare on French Stages in the Nineteenth Century," in Foulkes; for America see the standard work by Shattuck.

6 DeHart, *The Meininger Theater, 1776–1926* (Ann Arbor, 1981), 65. John Osborne (ed.), *Die Meininger: Texte zur Rezeption* (Tübingen, 1980), collects the most important documents relating to the troupe; Ludwig Speidel's

review appeared in *Neue Freie Presse* (Vienna), 4 Nov. 1875, and is reprinted in Osborne, 82–90. See Williams 164.

7 Savits' *Lear* is discussed by Hans Durian, *Jocza Savits und die Münchener Shakespeare-Bühne* (Emsdetten, 1937), 59–61. Williams (187–8) summarizes the first scenes.

8 The three quotations in this paragraph are taken from Poel, *Monthly Letters* (London, 1929), 92; Poel, *Shakespeare in the Theatre* (London, 1913), 177; and 204.

9 See Arthur J. Harris, "William Poel's Elizabethan Stage: The First Experiment," *Theatre Notebook* 17 (1963): 113. Poel's letters to W. J. Lawrence about gallants on the stage suggest that he considered them integral to the Elizabethan mode of performance; they are quoted in Robert Speaight's *William Poel and the Elizabethan Revival* (London, 1954), 85–6.

10 Speaight, *William Poel*, 102–11.

11 Borsa, *The English Theatre of Today*, trans. Selwyn Brinton (London, 1908), 185–6. Barker's comment on Poel is from an interview in the *Evening News* 3 Dec. 1912; see Kennedy 1985: 150–1.

3   The scenographic revolution

1 Quoted in Richard C. Beacham, *Adolphe Appia, Theatre Artist* (Cambridge, 1987), 42.

2 Yeats, *Saturday Review*, 8 March 1902, quoted in Innes 41–2; Barker, letter to the *Daily Mail*, 26 Sept. 1912, included in *Granville Barker and His Correspondents*, ed. Eric Salmon (Detroit, 1986), 527–9.

3 Max Beerbohm, *More Theatres* (New York, 1969), 574; Shaw's letter is from Christopher St. John (ed.), *Ellen Terry and Bernard Shaw: A Correspondence* (London, 1949), 369–70.

4 Quoted in Janet Leeper, *Edward Gordon Craig: Designs for the Theatre* (Harmondsworth, 1948), 8.

5 Bablet (1965: 90–1) discusses the scenographic implications of Cubism, though not its relationship to Craig. The date of the Moscow *Hamlet* is recorded variously as 1911 or 1912 because it opened on 23 Dec. 1911, Old Style, which is 5 Jan. 1912, New Style.

6 Kozintsev, *King Lear: The Space of Tragedy*, trans. Mary Mackintosh (Berkeley, 1976), 156. I have borrowed the phrase "the scenic actor" from my student Jay Scott Chipman.

7 See L. M. Newman, "Reinhardt and Craig?" in Jacobs and Warren 6–7.

8 By 1930 he had produced 2,527 performances of Shakespeare, according to Franz Horch's accounting in Hans Roth's *Max Reinhardt: 25 Jahre Deutsches Theater* (Munich, 1930), 73.

9 Kraus' comment from 1935 ("das ... Gras echt und die Schauspieler aus

Pappe") is quoted by Michael Patterson, "Reinhardt and Theatrical
Expressionism," in Jacobs and Warren 51. Patterson argues that the visible
turning of the stage undercut the reality of the forest so that a "productive
tension between realistic illusion and awareness of artifice" was created in
the audience. Williams (213) discusses the Munich version. "Little kiddie
coffin" is quoted in Peter Jellavich, *Munich and Theatrical Modernism*
(Cambridge, Mass., 1985), 211. On the 1913 setting see Ernst Stern and
Heinz Herald, *Reinhardt und seine Bühne* (Berlin, 1918), 38. My commentary is
based on a review of designs in Munich and Cologne.

10 Ernst Stern, *My Life, My Stage*, trans. Edward Fitzgerald (London, 1951), 76;
Stern worked in England in the latter part of his career and this translation
appeared prior to the German edition, entitled *Bühnenbilder bei Max Reinhardt*
(Berlin, 1955), which differs in minor ways from the English version. In fact
Reinhardt gave much more freedom to Stern than to most of his designers.
As Director of Costumes and Scenery until 1921 he designed more than 200
productions for Reinhardt's theatres, including almost all of the plays in the
1913–14 Shakespeare cycle. See Hugh Rorrison's paper "Max Reinhardt and
Ernst Stern" in Jacobs and Warren; and Rorrison's "Designing for
Reinhardt: The Work of Ernst Stern," *New Theatre Quarterly* 7 (1986):
217–32.

11 According to the records in Heinrich Huesmann, *Welttheater Reinhardt*
(Munich, 1983), a massive production calendar. It was of course common in
the beginning of the century for a director or manager to order sets from a
scenery firm, or to rely upon his theatre's stock of wings and drops, or to use
a combination of stock and newly made pieces.

12 Sheldon Cheney, *Stage Decoration* (New York, 1928), caption to pl. 46. Arthur
Hopkins' comment in the previous paragraph is from *Max Reinhardt and His
Theatre*, ed. Oliver M. Sayler (New York, 1924), 339.

13 Newman, in Jacobs and Warren 12–13. Craig's designs for *Lear* are in Paris.

14 Stern, *My Life, My Stage*, 150–1. The drawing I discuss is in Cologne, along
with most of Stern's Shakespeare designs; it is reproduced in Speaight 206.

15 Reinhardt's letters, speeches, interviews, and occasional pieces have been
collected in Max Reinhardt, *Schriften*, ed. Hugo Fetting (Berlin, 1974). The
"magical, complete world," from a 1930 speech on Shakespeare, is on p.
324. The 1916 interview is on p. 265, as translated by Williams (212).
Newman's comment is from Jacobs and Warren 14.

16 J. L. Styan discusses the *Macbeth* in *Max Reinhardt* (Cambridge, 1982), 64.
The Stern designs for the production are in Cologne and in Vienna.

17 Berry, "The Aesthetics of Beerbohm Tree's Shakespeare Festivals,"
Nineteenth Century Theatre Research 9 (1981): 44.

18 Woolf's famous phrase comes from a 1924 lecture "Mr. Bennett and Mrs.
Brown," published in *The Captain's Death Bed and Other Essays* (London,

1950), 91. The general question of artistic and social change is discussed especially well by Samuel Hynes in *The Edwardian Turn of Mind* (Princeton, 1968), who catalogues the two post-impressionist exhibitions in an appendix.

19 *Athenaeum* 4431 (28 Sept. 1912): 351. Grein in *The Sunday Times*, 22 Sept. 1912. *Daily Mail*, 23 Sept. 1912.

20 P. G. Konody, *Observer*, 29 Sept. 1912. The *Times* review appeared on 23 Sept. Barker's notes on the three productions were printed as prefaces to the playtexts on sale at the theatre (published by Heinemann in 1912 and 1914); they are reprinted in *More Prefaces to Shakespeare*, ed. Edward M. Moore (Princeton, 1974). Barker's Shakespeare is treated in more detail in Kennedy 1985; see also Christine Dymkowski, *Harley Granville Barker: A Preface to Modern Shakespeare* (Washington, 1986). Albert Rothenstein changed his name to Rutherston during the war; his costume designs are at Harvard, and some are beautifully reproduced in his *Sixteen Designs for the Theatre* (London, 1928).

21 They are listed in Account Book for Barker's productions at the Savoy and St. James's Theatres, 1912–14, in the Theatre Museum, London. The listing does not make clear when each of the curtains was used, and the promptbook is lost.

22 *Daily Mail* 26 Sept. 1912, reprinted in *Granville Barker and His Correspondents*, 527–9.

23 Letter to *Play Pictorial* 21.126 (Nov. 1912): iv, in *Granville Barker and His Correspondents*, 530; Barker's letter to Reinhardt about Poel is on p. 482 of the same volume. The *Referee*'s review quoted below is from 17 Nov. 1912.

24 Preface to the acting edition, reprinted in *More Prefaces to Shakespeare* 35, 38. For identification of the reviewers' comments, see Kennedy 1985: 160; color studio photos of Oberon and Titania are reproduced there as a frontispiece to the clothbound edition.

25 Barker, *Prefaces to Shakespeare* (Princeton, 1946–7), 1: 407.

4 Styles of politics

1 I rely here on the standard account by Jacquot (38–62) and on the more detailed consideration in Bablet (1965: 348–52, 370–4); both include photos of Antoine, Gémier, and Copeau productions. Speaight (182–93) provides some photos and cursory attention. Jean Chothia's *André Antoine* (Cambridge, 1991), 134–54, is a recent valuable treatment.

2 Copeau's reminiscences are contained in *Souvenirs du Vieux-Colombier* (Paris, 1931), and are summarized in John Rudlin, *Jacques Copeau* (Cambridge, 1986), 16–18. Barker's review of *Twelfth Night* was published in *The Observer*, 1 Jan. 1922: 10.

3 Jessner's comments on the job of the director are from his article "Der

Regisseur," in *Der Neue Weg* 16 April 1929: 149–50; the quotation about classic writers is from his "Das Theater, ein Vortrag," in *Die Szene* March 1928: 70. His writings have been conveniently collected in Jessner, *Schriften: Theater der zwanziger Jahre*, ed. Hugo Fetting (Berlin, 1979). Günter Rühle's *Theater für die Republik, 1917–1933, im Spiegel der Kritik* (Frankfurt am Main, 1967) collects some important general documents, including selected reviews of the Shakespeare productions. In English, Willett provides an overview of the period and a handy production list, and Patterson is the most lucid account of theatrical Expressionism. Julius Bab's 1937 essay "The Theatre in the German Language Area Since the World War" (in Dickinson) is an intriguing report of the period by one of its most important contemporary critics. See also Andreas Höfele, "Leopold Jessner's Shakespeare Productions, 1920–1930," *Theatre History Studies* 12 (1992): 139–55.

4 Bablet, "L'Expressionisme à la scène," in *L'Expressionisme dans le théâtre Européen*, ed. Bablet and Jean Jacquot (Paris, 1977), 206–8. See also Bablet's "Leopold Jessner et Shakespeare," *Revue d'histoire du théâtre* 1 (1965): 58–68.

5 Patterson 93. Polgar's article "Shakespeare, Jessner und Kortner," appeared in *Die Weltbühne* 3 (1922): 69–71. Jessner's phrase below is from "Das Theater, ein Vortrag," 67. Pirchan's designs for *Richard* and *Othello* are in Cologne; some smaller copies and many photos are in Vienna. Some of Neher's designs discussed below are also in Vienna.

6 Kerr's 1920 review is reprinted in Rühle's *Theater für die Republik* 257–60. I am indebted here to my student David Kuhns, whose dissertation "The Synthetic Actor: A Theoretical Approach to German Expressionist Performance, 1916–21" (University of Pittsburgh, 1988) treats the production in detail; "staircase directing" is his phrase. See Kuhns' "Expressionism, Monumentalism, Politics: Emblematic Acting in Jessner's *Wilhelm Tell* and *Richard III*," *New Theatre Quarterly* 7 (1991): 35–48. Kortner's claim to have suggested the steps is in his (not altogether reliable) autobiography, *Aller Tage Abend* (Munich, 1959), 369.

7 Ihering, *Regisseure und Bühnenmaler* (Berlin, 1921), 64.

8 "The Theatre in Berlin," *The Times* 19 Nov. 1910: 6.

9 See Edward Braun, *The Theatre of Meyerhold* (New York, 1979), 153–4. Meyerhold had directed an unimportant *Dream* in 1904 and acted in a number of Shakespeare plays; in 1937 he had plans for *Othello* and *Hamlet* which were cut short by his official disgrace.

10 Tairov, *Notes of a Director*, trans. William Kuhlke (Coral Gables, 1969), 97, 52 [emphasis is Tairov's]. The work of his designer, Alexandra Exter, is discussed well in a recent exhibition catalogue, *Theatre in Revolution: Russian Avant-Garde Stage Design, 1913–1935*, ed. Nancy Van Norman Baer (New York, 1991).

11 A. M. Píša, "Czech Actors and Producers," in Jindřich Honzl (ed.), *The*

Czechoslovak Theatre: A Collection of Informative Material on Theatrical Activities in Czechoslovakia (Prague, 1948), 78. See also Jarka M. Burian, "*Hamlet* in Postwar Czech Theatre," in Kennedy 1993.

12 The designs of Hofman (and of many others) are in the National Library in Prague. The ITI Centre in Prague has an excellent general photo collection, and the archive of the National Theatre is well-organized and complete. The standard illustrated study of twentieth-century design is Věra Ptáčková, *Česká Scénografie XX. Století* (Prague, 1982). Jiří Hilmera's *František Tröster* (Prague, 1989) is a pictorial record of Tröster's career. Unfortunately little material on this crucial period has been published in languages other than Czech.

13 Władysław Zawistowski, "The Polish Theatre After the War" in Dickinson 379. See also August Grodzicki and Roman Szydłowsi, *The Theatre in Modern Poland* (Warsaw, 1963), 10–11. Edward Csató's *The Polish Theatre*, trans. Christina Cenkalska (Warsaw, 1963), is useful, and a number of articles in French and English relating to the period have appeared in the journal *Le théâtre en Pologne*.

14 Designs and photographs of the Szyfman and Schiller productions are in Warsaw. I am much in debt here, and in chapter 7, to Krystyna Duniec for information and pictorial research; her thesis on Schiller's productions of Shakespeare (Institute of the Arts, 1990) treats this material in detail, and her article on *As You Like It*, with scenographic documentation, appeared in *Pamiętnika Teatralnego* (1981): 296–316. Edward Csató's *Leon Schiller: twórca monumentalnego teatru polskiego* (Warsaw, 1966) is a survey treatment.

15 Quoted in Csató, *The Polish Theatre* 107.

16 Promptbooks, programs, photos, and clippings are in Birmingham. *The Observer* of 30 Aug. 1925 printed Jackson's interview along with Hubert Griffith's review and other articles on the production; the *Illustrated London News* of 29 Aug. contains a portfolio of photographs, and others were included in *The Sketch* of 2 Sept. The *Times* review quoted below appeared on 26 Aug.

17 Tori Haring-Smith, *From Farce to Metadrama: A Stage History of The Taming of the Shrew, 1594–1983* (Westport, Conn., 1985), 113.

18 See Claire Cochrane, "Paul Shelving and Modern-Dress Shakespeare," in *Paul Shelving (1888–1968), Stage Designer*, exhibition catalogue, ed. Tessa Sidey (Birmingham, 1986), 26.

19 Barker, "*Hamlet* in Plus Fours," *Yale Review* 16 (1926): 205.

20 *The Festival Theatre Review* 54 (16 Feb. 1929): 3. Similar proclamations often appeared in this elegantly prepared newsletter; the encouragement to smoke (below) is from number 73 (25 April 1931): 2. The earlier quotation is from Rosenfeld 182–3. A complete run of the *Review*, photographs, and other materials are in Cambridge. Richard Cave's *Terence Gray and the Cambridge*

Festival Theatre (Cambridge, 1980), is a valuable short monograph in the Theatre in Focus series, accompanied by a slide set.

21 Ridge, *Stage Lighting* (Cambridge, 1928), 170. I also rely here on Graham Woodruff, "Terence Gray and Theatre Design," *Theatre Research* 11 (1971): 114–32.

22 Marshall, *The Other Theatre* (London, 1947), 57.

5   The stuffed stag and the new look

1 Nigel Playfair, *The Story of the Lyric Theatre Hammersmith* (London, 1925), 55.

2 Letter to J. C. Trewin, 1932, in *A Bridges-Adams Letter Book*, ed. Robert Speaight (London, 1971), 29.

3 Harcourt Williams, *Old Vic Saga* (London, 1949), 20. Other treatments of the theatre between the wars include his *Four Years at the Old Vic* (London, 1935), Audrey Williamson's *Old Vic Drama, 1934–1947* (London, 1948), and a celebratory history by Peter Roberts, *The Old Vic Story: A Nation's Theatre, 1818–1976* (London, 1976).

4 Bridges-Adams, *Looking at a Play* (London, 1947), 25. On the question of the rise of Shakespeare's literary status, see Hawkes. Other works dealing with relevant aspects of bardolatry include Holderness; Taylor; and Ivor Brown and George Fearon, *Amazing Monument: A Short History of the Shakespeare Industry* (London, 1939).

5 Fabia Drake, *Blind Fortune* (London, 1978), 100–1. Bridges-Adams' comments on Barker's lighting effects are from "Granville Barker and the Savoy," *Drama* NS 52 (1959): 30. The archival photos and some designs for SMT productions are housed at Stratford. Useful general treatments include Brock and Pringle; and T. C. Kemp and J. C. Trewin, *The Stratford Festival: A History of the Shakespeare Memorial Theatre* (Birmingham, 1953).

6 Bridges-Adams, *Looking at a Play* 32. He set forth his intentions in an interview in the *Birmingham Mail*, 25 April 1933. Brock and Pringle discuss the production, 49–50.

7 Richard E. Mennen, "Theodore Komisarjevsky's Production of *The Merchant of Venice*," *Theatre Journal* 31 (1979): 396.

8 See Ralph Berry, "Komisarjevsky at Stratford-upon-Avon," *SS* 36 (1983): 73–84. Komisarjevsky's books include *Myself and the Theatre* (London, 1929), *Costume of the Theatre* (London, 1931), and *Settings and Costumes of the Modern Stage* (with Lee Simonson, London, 1933, where his designs for *Lohengrin* and *Macbeth* are reproduced on p. 29).

9 13 June 1936, quoted in Berry, "Komisarjevsky" 79. Trewin (169) reports that the production had only six rehearsals; though this seems incredible, it was in keeping with the usual SMT policy.

10 *The Times*, 21 April 1936; Kemp, *Birmingham Post*, same date.

11 Berry ("Komisarjevsky" 81) is referring to a well-known photograph of the final scene (contained in Trewin 37 and in Crosse 97). I have reproduced a different picture because it shows the general scenography more clearly, even though it has fewer examples of the range of costumes. Strangely not many photos of the Komisarjevsky productions have survived.

12 Gielgud discusses *Romeo* in *Early Stages*, rev. edn. (New York, 1976), 159–60. Many Motley designs and costumes are housed at the University of Illinois at Champaign-Urbana. The Motley team wrote two books: *Designing and Making Stage Costumes* (New York, 1965) and *Theatre Props* (New York, 1975); significantly, both are practical manuals with no interest in the theory of theatre design.

13 Stark Young, "Robert Edmond Jones: A Note," in *The Theatre of Robert Edmond Jones*, ed. Ralph Pendleton (Middletown, Conn., 1958), 5. Many of Jones' early designs are reproduced in his *Drawings for the Theatre* (New York, 1925). Jones' comments on light below are from *The Dramatic Imagination* (New York, 1941), 114, a book that had wide influence on subsequent design thinking. Larson treats the Jones Shakespeare productions well, and has an extended portfolio of drawings and photos from *Macbeth*.

14 Richard France, *The Theatre of Orson Welles* (Lewisburg, 1977), 55.

15 Houseman, *Run-Through* (New York, 1972), 190, a primary source for the Welles Shakespeare productions. Other treatments include Charles Higham's *Orson Welles: The Rise and Fall of an American Genius* (New York, 1985); and Hallie Flanagan's *Arena: A History of the Federal Theatre* (New York, 1940).

16 Roi Otley in the *Amsterdam News*, 18 April 1936, quoted in France 70. The story of Percy Hammond is from Houseman 202–3. Ruby Cohn provides an interesting slant in *Modern Shakespeare Offshoots* (Princeton, 1976), 69–73.

17 Quoted in Ripley 223. The promptbook and other materials are in New York; Ripley's quotation comes from a Mercury Theatre press release in these files.

18 Jean Rosenthal, *The Magic of Light* (New York, 1972), 22. My references to the press, including the unidentified newspaper quotations in the next paragraph, come from clippings in the New York files.

19 New York *World-Telegram*, 15 Nov. 1937, quoted in Ripley 229, where a photo of the scene is reproduced. France discusses the production particularly well, pp. 106–23. Another book, *Orson Welles on Shakespeare*, ed. Richard France (Westport, Conn., 1990), contains annotated scripts of Welles' Shakespeare productions.

6 Reinventing the stage

1 Tyrone Guthrie, "Theatre at Minneapolis," in *Actor and Architect*, ed. Stephen Joseph (Toronto, 1964), 37.

2 Granville Barker, *The Exemplary Theatre* (London, 1922), 204–6; see Kennedy 1985: 200ff. On Monck see Franklin J. Hildy, *Shakespeare at the Maddermarket: Nugent Monck and the Norwich Players* (Ann Arbor, 1986).

3 Langham, interview in *Astonish Us in the Morning: Tyrone Guthrie Remembered*, ed. Alfred Rossi (London, 1977), 284.

4 Guthrie 319. The genesis of the Festival is also discussed in Rossi's collection of interviews and in James Forsyth's biography *Tyrone Guthrie* (London, 1976). The first seasons at Stratford are recorded in *The Stratford Festival, 1953–1957*, ed. Herbert Whittaker (Toronto, 1958), and in three Festival books written by Guthrie with Robertson Davies and Grant MacDonald: *Renown at Stratford* (1953), *Twice Have the Trumpets Sounded* (1954), and *Thrice the Brinded Cat Hath Mew'd* (1955), all published in Toronto. See also *The Stratford Scene, 1958–1968*, ed. Peter Raby (Toronto, 1968), and John Pettigrew and Jamie Portman's *Stratford: The First Thirty Years*, 2 vols. (Toronto, 1985). The archives at the Festival Theatre are complete and well organized; they include photos, press cuttings, some designs, and selected costumes. Archival videotapes exist from 1968 onwards.

5 Berners A. W. Jackson, "The Shakespeare Festival: Stratford, Ontario, 1953–1977," *SQ* 29 (1978): 181.

6 Brook's essay appeared in the first volume of *Orpheus* (1948), and has been reprinted in *The Modern Theatre: Readings and Documents*, ed. Daniel Seltzer (Boston, 1967), where this passage appears on p. 256. Brook's comment about Watteau's dresses, quoted below, is on p. 254. Photos and promptbooks are at Stratford.

7 H. S. Bennett and George Rylands, *SS* 1 (1948): 110. The production is treated in detail by Levenson (64–81), who sees it as a turning-point in Shakespeare performance.

8 Foreword to Michael Warre's *Designing and Making Stage Scenery* (London, 1966), 7.

9 Foreword to Warre, 7. The long quote from *The Shifting Point* (Brook 1987) is a slightly revised form of an interview conducted by Ralph Berry in 1974 (see Berry 135–6).

10 Reprinted in Kenneth Tynan, *Profiles*, ed. Kathleen Tynan and Ernie Eban (New York, 1990), 78.

11 Kott 353. Martin Esslin's introduction to this Anchor Books edition discusses the resonance of *Lear* for eastern Europe. The French translation, by Anna Posner, was published in Paris in 1962, the year of the initial publication in Warsaw; Taborski's English translation first appeared in 1964.

12 See Dennis Kennedy, "*King Lear* and the Theatre," *Educational Theatre Journal* 28 (1976): 35–44.

13 J.C. Trewin, *Peter Brook: A Biography* (London, 1971), 128. Charles Marowitz's description in the next paragraph comes from his rehearsal journal, published as "Lear Log" in *Theatre at Work*, ed. Marowitz and Simon Trussler (New York, 1967), 134.

14 Interview with Kott, "Directors, Dramaturgs and War in Poland," *Theater* 14 (Spring 1983): 27; Kott's comment on the stage plateau is from the same source.

15 See Roy Strong, "The Years Before" in Goodwin 17. Quayle tells of the need to secure "Great Big Names" to Stratford to excite the press and public in his uncompleted autobiography, *A Time to Speak* (London, 1990), 323. Lila de Nobili's color sketch for Orsino's palace in *Twelfth Night* (mentioned below) is at Harvard, and is reproduced in Speaight 261.

16 See Frank Rich and Lisa Aronson, *The Theatre of Boris Aronson* (New York, 1987), 7. Pryce-Jones' review is from *The Observer*, 12 July 1959.

17 Howard Goorney, *The Theatre Workshop Story* (London, 1981), 101.

18 See the published text by John Barton, *The Wars of the Roses* (London, 1970). Bury's "great steel cage of war," quoted below, is from p. 237.

19 Hall, Foreword to Goodwin 13. See also Jarka M. Burian, "Contemporary British Scenography," *Theatre Design and Technology* (Fall 1983): 6.

20 Robert Potter, "The Rediscovery of Queen Margaret: 'The Wars of the Roses,' 1963," *New Theatre Quarterly* 4 (1988): 106. Bury's lecture "Against Falsehood" is reprinted in Payne 31–3.

21 See Addenbrooke 26–9; Beauman 268; and Christopher J. McCullough, "The Cambridge Connection: Towards a Materialist Theatre Practice," in Holderness.

22 Interview with Brook in *The Daily Telegraph* (14 Sept. 1970), quoted in Roger Warren, *A Midsummer Night's Dream: Text and Performance* (London, 1983), 55. Other important discussions of the production include Styan (223–31) and Beauman (301–8). Glen Loney's *Peter Brook's Production of William Shakespeare's A Midsummer Night's Dream* (Stratford, 1974) is an authorized version of the acting script that includes interviews with Brook, Jacobs, and the cast.

23 John Kane, "When My Cue Comes Call Me," in *Peter Brook: A Theatrical Casebook*, ed. David Williams (London, 1988), 150. In fact the basic set and production concepts were established in advance, but they were broad enough to permit changes and actor development. David Selbourne's *The Making of A Midsummer Night's Dream* (London, 1982) is an eyewitness journal that chronicles the production from first rehearsal to opening, by a writer almost wholly out of sympathy with Brook's methods.

24 Brook had been preceded by Ariane Mnouchkine, who mounted a full circus

setting of the same play at the Cirque Montmartre in Paris in 1968, which forcefully emphasized its dark undertones as seen by Jan Kott. See Leiter 482–3, and Edward Trostle Jones, *Following Directions*: *A Study of Peter Brook* (New York, 1985), 113. The objections to Brook's *Dream* are summarized in Warren 57–61.

7   The liberation of Europe

1   A. Grodzicki and R. Szydłowsi, *Theatre in Modern Poland* (Warsaw, 1963), 50.

2   Edward Csató, *Leon Schiller*: *twórca monumentalnego teatru polskiego* (Warsaw, 1966), 85–6.

3   Okhlopkov, writing in *Teatr* in January 1955, quoted in R. M. Samarin, *SS* 9 (1956): 118. Norris Houghton's comment below is from *Return Engagement* (New York, 1962), 100. Worrall treats Okhlopkov's career in detail and discusses *Hamlet* (181–4).

4   Trilling, "How Different Can One Be," *World Theatre* 13.1–2 (1964): 96; Bowers, *Broadway*, *U.S.S.R.*: *Ballet, Theatre, and Entertainment in Russia Today* (New York, 1959), 101. Felicia Londré's entries on the Okhlopkov and Lyubimov productions (in Leiter 131–2 and 144–5) are useful, and I am grateful for a copy of her unpublished paper "*Hamlet* as Political Allegory on the Soviet Stage."

5   Hedrick Smith, *The Russians* (New York, 1976), 388. "Broken montage" is the phrase of Alexander Gershkovich in *The Theatre of Yuri Lyubimov*: *Art and Politics at the Taganka Theater in Moscow*, trans. Michael Yurieff (New York, 1989), 124. See Spencer Golub, "Between the Curtain and the Grave: The Taganka in the *Hamlet* Gulag," in Kennedy 1993. See also Micky Levy, "David Borovsky Designs for Lyubimov," *Theatre Crafts* 12 (Nov.–Dec. 1978): 32–7, 57–8.

6   Praz, *SS* 3 (1950): 118, where a picture of the design is reproduced (plate VIIB). His report also includes a comment on Visconti's *Troilus*. A souvenir program published by Dali's Roman gallery contains the color designs as well as ink sketches (copy seen in Washington); Isidre Bravo's *L'escenografia catalana* (Barcelona, 1986) reproduces some of them. The three Zeffirelli versions of *Romeo and Juliet* (Old Vic, Verona, and the film) are discussed in detail by Levenson.

7   See Ann Fridén, *Macbeth in the Swedish Theatre, 1838–1986* (Malmö, 1986), 171–226; and Lise-Lone Marker and Frederick J. Marker, *Ingmar Bergman*: *Four Decades in the Theater* (Cambridge, 1982), 32–7. Both contain illustrations.

8   A lecture given at the Edinburgh Festival in 1948, prior to Barrault's performance in *Hamlet*, contained in his collection *The Theatre of Jean-Louis Barrault*, trans. Joseph Chiari (New York, 1961), 89. The quotation from

Pitoëff below is from Gilles Quéant, *Encyclopédie du théâtre contemporain* (Paris, 1957–9), II:61.

9   The production photographs are in Paris. Jacquot (104) discusses the visual aspects of *Richard II*. Vilar's *Le théâtre, service public*, ed. Armand Delcampe (Paris, 1975), is a useful collection of his essays and occasional pieces.

10   Materials from the production, including photos, clippings, and designs, are housed in Berlin (Academy of Arts) and in Cologne. I am indebted to Elmar Goerden of the University of Cologne, whose unpublished thesis on Shylock on the German stage has been very useful. Piscator's career is well documented in German and English, though little attention has been paid to his *Merchant*; see John Willett's *The Theatre of Erwin Piscator* (London, 1978) for a good general bibliography. Design records for *Merchant* have been published in Hans-Ulrich Schmückle and Sylta Busse, *Theaterarbeit: Eine Dokumentation*, ed. Eckehart Nölle (Munich, 1975), 75–95.

11   Trilling, *World Theatre* 13.2 (1964): 101, a review previously printed in *The Times*, 30 Dec. 1963; "anguished face" is her phrase as well. Reblitz's commentary appeared in *Allgemeine Zeitung* (Mannheim), 13 Dec. 1963.

12   Brecht, "Die Dialektik auf dem Theater," *Gesammelte Werke* (Frankfurt am Main, 1967), XVI:879. Barthes' phrase on Brecht comes from "Réponses," *Tel Quel* 47 (1971): 95.

13   The best introduction to this question in English is the essay "Brecht and the Visual Arts" in Willett's *Brecht in Context* (London, 1983). Willett's exhibition catalogue *Caspar Neher, Brecht's Designer* (London, 1986) is illustrated and very useful. The standard work on Neher is Gottfried von Einem and Siegfried Melchinger, *Caspar Neher* (Hanover, 1966), which is profusely illustrated. Neher (like Brecht) took Austrian citizenship after the war, and in 1956 succeeded Emil Pirchan as professor of stage design at the Vienna Academy of Fine Arts; many of his designs, including watercolor sketches for the two productions of *Coriolanus* discussed below, are in Vienna.

14   Brecht, "Stage Design for the Epic Theatre" (1951), in Willett (ed.), *Brecht on Theatre* (New York, 1966), 231. Brecht's poem "The Lighting" is from *Poems*, ed. Willett and Ralph Manheim (London, 1976), 426.

15   Crucial pictorial evidence is reproduced in Friedrich Dieckmann's documentary study, *Karl von Appens Bühnenbilder am Berliner Ensemble* (Berlin, 1971). See Lawrence Guntner's "Brecht and Beyond: Shakespeare on the East German Stage" in Kennedy 1993. Wekwerth and Tenschert staged a similar conception of Shakespeare's original, in English, at the National Theatre at the Old Vic in 1971, the design modified by Manfred Grund and Anna Kashdan-Clarke, with Anthony Hopkins in the lead.

16   Weimann's *Shakespeare and the Popular Tradition in the Theatre*, ed. Robert

Schwartz (Baltimore, 1978), was published in the GDR in 1967 as *Shakespeare und die Tradition des Volkstheaters*. Photos and other materials for these productions are in the archives of the Deutsches Theater in Berlin. I also rely on a published collection of sketches, photographs, interviews, and commentary: *Friedo Solters Inszenierung 'Der Sturm' am Deutschen Theater Berlin 1974*, ed. Regine Herrmann (Berlin, 1977), Workbook 25 from the Academy of Arts of the GDR, which includes the complete production text of the play in Maik Hamburger's translation. Brecht's general importance to postwar theatre is treated with great sensitivity by John Rouse, *Brecht and the West German Theatre: The Practice and Politics of Interpretation* (Ann Arbor, 1989). See also *Re-interpreting Brecht: His Influence on Contemporary Drama and Film*, ed. Pia Kleber and Colin Visser (Cambridge, 1990).

17 Bradby 107. See also Yvette Daoust, *Roger Planchon: Director and Playwright* (Cambridge, 1981); and chapter 3 in Bradby and Williams. A brief summary is provided in Bradby's *The Theatre of Roger Planchon* in the Theatre in Focus series (Cambridge, 1984), which is accompanied by useful slides. The most complete treatment in French is Emile Copfermann, *Théâtres de Roger Planchon* (Paris, 1977).

18 Tynan, *The New Yorker* 35 (1 Aug. 1959): 51.

19 Jean Jacquot, *SS* 13 (1960): 127.

20 Planchon has related this story in many places; I have taken it from his introduction (in English) to the Folio Society edition of *Henry IV, Part I* (London, 1965), 7, which contains color reproductions of Allio's costume designs. Some of my comments on Planchon rely upon archive photographs in Paris.

21 Otto's designs are in Vienna and in Cologne. An exhibition catalogue of his Austrian work reproduces many of the Shakespeare designs, along with a collection of essays: *Der Bühnenbilder Teo Otto: Inszenierungen in Österreich* (Salzburg, 1977). Otto wrote about his work in a number of books, the best known of which is *Meine Szene* (Cologne, 1965).

22 Vilar, *Le théâtre, service public*, 81.

23 Richard Trousdell, "Giorgio Strehler in Rehearsal," *The Drama Review* 30.4 (1986): 65.

24 Interview with Kott, "Directors, Dramaturgs and War in Poland," *Theater* 14 (Spring 1983): 28. For details of the Strehler productions I rely on Battistini, which contains selections from the critics and many photos.

25 Quoted in Battistini 196. Strehler has frequently written of his intentions and his desires for a social theatre; Battistini includes a lengthy bibliography. His major collection is *Per un teatro umano* (Milan, 1974). The production of *King Lear* is well treated by Stéphan de Lannoy and by Jean Jacquot in *Les Voies de la création théâtrale* (Paris, 1978), VI:399–503.

26 Brecht's poem "Die Freunde" (*Gesammelte Werke* X:953), uses the term
Bühnenbauer to describe Neher, though it is translated in the English edition
as "stage designer" (*Poems* 415). See Willett, *Brecht in Context* 132.

27 Bretislav Hodek, *SS* 14 (1961): 118. Burian discusses the 1959 and 1965
versions on pp. 123–7 (the quotation about two birds is from p. 124); and
the 1982 production in "Shakespeare on Today's Prague (and Other)
Stages," *Cross Currents* 8 (1989): 172–83. See also Denis Bablet, *Josef Svoboda*
(Lausanne, 1970). My general commentary relies on the scenographic library
of ITI in Prague, including a film of the 1963 *Romeo and Juliet* and a
videotape of the 1982 *Hamlet*, and on the archives of the National Theatre.

8   New spaces, new audiences

1 Quoted in Roberta Krensky Cooper, *The American Shakespeare Theatre,
Stratford, 1955–1985* (Washington, 1986), 61, which treats the history of the
enterprise in detail. See also John Houseman and Jack Landau, *The American
Shakespeare Festival: The Birth of a Theatre* (New York, 1959).

2 Stuart W. Little, *Enter Joseph Papp: In Search of a New American Theater* (New
York, 1974), 47. For further information on Lee, see Patricia MacKay,
"Designers on Designing: Ming Cho Lee," *Theatre Crafts* 18.2 (Feb. 1984):
14–21, 68–75.

3 Conducted by Margorie J. Oberlander in 1981, and reported in an
unpublished paper delivered at the Shakespeare Association of America
meeting in Boston in 1988.

4 See Jeanne Addison Roberts, *SQ* 30 (1979): 193–4; and Dennis Kennedy,
"The Director as Scenographer: Ciulei's Shakespeare at the Guthrie,"
Theatre Three 7 (Fall 1989): 37.

5 On Barton's career see Greenwald, which contains a complete production
calendar to 1984. Beauman (288–312) discusses the organizational impact of
the Nunn years.

6 Quoted in Jarka Burian, "Contemporary British Scenography," *Theatre
Design and Technology* (Fall 1983): 9. O'Brien used the term "ritual nakedness"
in an interview with me in London in Oct. 1989.

7 Timothy O'Brien, "Designing a Shakespeare Play: *Richard II*," *Shakespeare
Jahrbuch/West* (1974): 113. Billington's reviews of the two opening nights
appeared in the *Guardian*, 11 and 12 April 1973 (the quotation is from the
second). Greenwald discusses the production in detail, 115–27. *Staging
Shakespeare: Seminars on Production Problems*, ed. Glenn Loney (New York,
1990), offers – sixteen years after the fact – transcripts of formal discussions
that occurred in conjunction with the tour of the production to the Brooklyn
Academy of Music in 1974.

8 O'Brien 112. Bartholomeusz (213–21) discusses this production at length, and quotes Nunn about *Hair* (218).

9 Morley, who was Head of Design at the RSC at the time, designed the new stage and the alterations to the auditorium made in the winter of 1971–2. Ripley discusses the hydraulic stage, 270–4.

10 O'Brien, 112.

11 Terry Hands, "An Introduction to the Play," in *The RSC's Production of Henry V for the Centenary Season*, ed. Sally Beauman (Oxford, 1976), 16.

12 Philip, Duke of Edinburgh, foreword to *Henry V for the Centenary Season* 3; Nunn, introduction to same source, 8.

13 Young, *Financial Times* 9 April 1976. John Barton related the fate of the permanent Elizabethan setting to me in an interview in London in Aug. 1986.

14 Goodbody's story, and the history of the chamber Shakespeare movement in the company, is detailed in a short book by Chambers; Beauman discusses the issues intermittently in her final chapter. A recent essay by Dympna Callaghan places Goodbody's work in a larger feminist and political context: "Buzz Goodbody: Directing for Change," in *The Appropriation of Shakespeare: Post-Renaissance Reconstructions of the Works and the Myth*, ed. Jean I. Marsden (New York, 1991). De Jongh's review of *Hamlet* from the *Guardian*, and Wardle's from *The Times*, appeared on 17 May 1975.

15 Barber, *Daily Telegraph* 11 Sept. 1976. Robert Cushman's review is from *The Observer* of 12 Sept.

16 Crowley, in an interview with me in London, Oct. 1989.

17 The connection between J. R. Brown's *Free Shakespeare* and Goodbody's *Hamlet* was noticed by Peter Thomson in his review of the 1975 RSC season, "Towards a Poor Shakespeare," *SS* 29 (1976): 153.

18 Clifford Williams' program note, in the Theatre Museum, London. Simon Williams' entry on the production in Leiter (53–4) is a useful summary of the critical reaction. Hobson's review is from *The Sunday Times*, 8 Oct. 1967.

19 Peter Lewis, *Daily Mail* 4 Oct. 1967.

20 Noel Witts, *Plays and Players* 25 (Nov. 1977): 22.

21 Peter Lackner's "Stein's Path to Shakespeare," *TDR* 21.2 (1977): 80–102, discusses *Shakespeare's Memory*. The best study of Stein's early work is fortunately in English: Michael Patterson, *Peter Stein: Germany's Leading Theatre Director* (Cambridge, 1981). In German see Peter Iden's *Die Schaubühne am Halleschen Ufer, 1970–1979* (Munich, 1979); and an anniversary documentary volume, *Schaubühne am Halleschen Ufer/am Lehniner Platz, 1962–1987* (Berlin, 1987), which contains production details and excellent photographs. Michael Raab treats Stein in the context of postwar trends in *Des Widerspenstigen Zähmung: Moderne Shakespeare-Inszenierungen in Deutschland*

und England (Rheinfelden, 1985), and a recent interview with reference to Shakespeare is in Herbert Mainusch, *Regie und Interpretation* (Munich, 1989). Video versions of both *Shakespeare's Memory* and *As You Like It* were broadcast by the West German network ZDF.

22 Patterson, *Peter Stein* 137–8. Henning Rischbieter's phrase is from a review article with pictures in *Theater heute* 18.11 (1977): 11–16. Also see Leiter 59–60.

23 Patterson 153; the costs were for sets, costumes, and props alone, excluding salaries and other expenses. Patterson quotes the Francis Ponge poem in part on p. 149, and the point about the absence of woodland for the West Berlin audience is made on pp. 132–3. For a general treatment of environmental staging (though without reference to Stein), see Arnold Aronson, *The History and Theory of Environmental Scenography* (Ann Arbor, 1981).

9   Imaging Shakespeare

1 See Arnold Aronson, "Postmodern Design," *Theatre Journal* 43 (1991): 6. In the vast literature on postmodernism, almost none speaks of Shakespeare performance. My own thinking has been influenced by Wilhelm Hortmann, especially his "Word into Image: Notes on the Scenography of Recent German Productions," in Kennedy 1993.

2 Quoted in an interview by Roy Kift, "Hoping for the Unexpected: The Theatre of Peter Zadek," *New Theatre Quarterly* 1 (1985): 329. A recent short article by Andreas Höfele is useful: "The Erotic Theatre of Peter Zadek," *New Theatre Quarterly* 7 (1991): 229–37. Though little is published in English on Zadek, he has been much discussed in German. See especially Volker Canaris, *Peter Zadek: der Theatermann und Filmemacher* (Munich, 1979), which treats the Shakespeare productions in detail. Mechthild Lange's *Peter Zadek* (Frankfurt am Main, 1989) is a collection of interviews with Zadek and his collaborators; another interview is contained in Jörg W. Gronius and Wend Kässens, *Theatermacher* (Frankfurt am Main, 1987); a miscellaneous collection, *Peter Zadek, das wilde Ufer, ein Theaterbuch* was published in Cologne in 1990.

3 Volker Canaris, "Peter Zadek and Hamlet," *The Drama Review* 24.1 (1980): 54. The quotation from Zadek is from Kift, "Hoping," 334–6. See also Ron Engle, "Audience, Style, and Language in the Shakespeare of Peter Zadek," in Kennedy 1993.

4 See Michael Patterson, *Peter Stein* 168, and an interview with Zadek in *Theater heute* 20.1 (1979): 15. Stein's supposed comment is reported in Kift, "Hoping," 323. Michael Raab compares Zadek and Stein as "antipodes of Shakespeare reception" in *Des Widerspenstigen Zähmung* 7–61.

5 Wilhelm Hortmann, "Changing Modes in *Hamlet* Production: Rediscovering

Shakespeare after the Iconoclasts," in *Images of Shakespeare*, ed. Werner Habicht, *et al.* (Newark, 1988), 224. The production is pictorially documented in a book of photos by Gisela Scheidler, *Zadeks Hamlet in Hamme* (Bochum, 1977), which also contains the performance text (the book originally served as the production program); the quotation from Zadek ("My Hamlet...") is from p. 56. A review article by Peter von Becker contains some good pictures, *Theater heute* 18.11 (1977): 6–10.

6 Canaris, "Peter Zadek and Hamlet" 60–1.

7 Selections from the critics are given in Canaris, *Peter Zadek: Der Theatermann* 205–16.

8 Canaris, "Peter Zadek and Hamlet" 56. Hortmann (in next paragraph), "Changing Modes" 222.

9 Wilhelm Hortmann, *SQ* 31 (1980): 411, who also reports on the audience reaction cited below.

10 See David Williams, "'A Place Marked by Life': Brook at the Bouffes du Nord," *New Theatre Quarterly* 1 (1985): 42. Brook and Schneider, in the following quotations, are from p. 43.

11 Georges Banu, "L'écriture spatiale de la mise en scène," in *Les Voies de la création théâtrale*, ed. Denis Bablet and Jean Jacquot (Paris, 1977), V:61; this lengthy and well-illustrated essay is the major critical account of the *Timon* production. Williams, "A Place" 40.

12 Williams, "A Place" 41, where Bowens is also quoted.

13 Wolfgang Sohlich, "Prolegomenon for a Theory of Drama Reception: Peter Brook's *Measure for Measure* and the Emergent Bourgeoisie," *Comparative Drama* 18 (1984): 63. The *Measure* of 1978 is discussed in two essays by Martine Millon in *Les Voies de la création théâtrale*, ed. Georges Banu (Paris, 1985), XIII:82–118, which volume is devoted entirely to Brook. My own comments on the RSC *Antony and Cleopatra* can be found in *Theatre Journal* 31 (1979): 420–3.

14 Marvin Carlson, "Peter Brook's *The Tempest*," *Western European Stages* 2 (1990): 19–20. Dominique Goy-Blanquet's review appeared in *TLS* 19 Oct. 1990: 1129. Carrière's translation, with a short essay by Brook, was published with a portfolio of color photos by Gilles Abegg: *La Tempête* (Paris, 1990). Also see Patrice Pavis, "Wilson, Brook, Zadek: An Intercultural Encounter?" in Kennedy 1993.

15 Quoted in Bradby and Williams 100, 98. Two articles by Adrian Kiernander on Théâtre du Soleil are in *New Theatre Quarterly* 7 (1986): 195–211; another, "The Role of Ariane Mnouchkine at the Théâtre du Soleil," appeared in *Modern Drama* 33 (1990): 322–31. Anne Neuschäfer and Frédéric Serror, *Le Théâtre du Soleil: Shakespeare*, ed. J. M. Armand (Cologne, 1984) is a picture book with French and German text. Two issues of the French pictorial magazine *Double Page* contain the remarkable photos by Martine Franck of

the Shakespeare productions: no. 21 (1982), and no. 32 (1984). See also Jean-Jacques Roubine, "The Théâtre du Soleil: A French Postmodernist Itinerary," in *The Dramatic Touch of Difference*, ed. Erika Fischer-Lichte, *et al.* (Tübingen, 1990).

16 On the productions of the 1970s and 1980s by Ninagawa, Terence Knapp, and Tadashi Suzuki, see Andrea J. Nouryeh, "Shakespeare and the Japanese Stage," in Kennedy 1993.

17 Cited in R. B. Knowles, "History as Metaphor: Daphne Dare's Late 19th- and Early 20th-Century Settings," *Theatre History Studies* 5 (1985): 25.

18 Quoted in Susan Lieberman, "Style on the Stage – Liviu Ciulei Reshapes the Guthrie," *Theatre Crafts* 17 (Aug.–Sept. 1983): 46; and in Thomas Clayton, *SQ* 36 (1985): 355.

19 Peter Vaughan, *Minneapolis Star*, 12 June 1981. For a more complete treatment, see Dennis Kennedy, "The Director as Scenographer: Ciulei's Shakespeare at the Guthrie," *Theatre Three* 7 (Fall 1989): 35–47.

20 Clayton, *SQ* 33 (1982): 368. See also Gitta Honegger, "How German Is It," *Performing Arts Journal* 16 (1981): 10.

21 Aronson, "Postmodern Design" 13. See Jameson, *Postmodernism, or, the Cultural Logic of Late Capitalism* (Durham, 1991).

22 Quoted in Charles Marowitz, "Kott, Our Contemporary," *American Theatre*, Oct. 1988: 100.

23 See, for example, Nicholas Shrimpton in *SS* 38 (1985): 207. Lois Potter notes how the luxurious scenography of *The Plantagenets* undercut political themes in an essay comparing the RSC's cycle to the English Shakespeare Company's, "Recycling the Early Histories," *SS* 43 (1991): 171–81.

24 Michael Ratcliff, *Observer*, 9 Sep. 1984; Victoria Radin, *New Statesman*, 14 Sep. 1984; Sheridan Morley, *Punch*, 19 Sep. 1984. Kroll (below), *Newsweek*, 15 Jan. 1985. Bogdanov's history cycle is documented in a book by Bogdanov and Michael Pennington, *The English Shakespeare Company: The Story of "The Wars of the Roses" 1986–1989* (London, 1990), which contains a number of Laurence Burns' photos of the productions.

25 Ralph Berry has an interview with Donnellan (190–207), and recent interviews with Noble, Alexander, and Bogdanov. Rowell and Jackson (139–46) discuss the Citizens' Theatre. Interestingly Bogdanov replaced Zadek as artistic director in Hamburg in 1989, where he used some of the same actors that his predecessor relied on. (Bogdanov resigned the position in 1991.) Contemporary RSC acting has been chiefly influenced by the textually based work of John Barton and of the company's voice coach, Cicely Berry. Both Barton's *Playing Shakespeare* (London, 1984) and Berry's *The Actor and His Text* (London, 1987) insist that Shakespeare's text is a combination of rhetorical principles and psychological clues for the actor – methods based in rationality, personality logic, and Stanislavskian

assumptions about the integrity of character that postmodernism normally denies.

26 The production became a *cause célèbre* and a special section of *American Theatre* (Dec. 1989: 24–31, 63–5) was devoted to the critical controversy, from which I quote Barnes' review. Elinor Fuchs' article there, "Misunderstanding Postmodernism," is worth especial attention.

27 On Puigserver, see Isidre Bravo, *L'escenografia catalana* (Barcelona, 1986), 296–7; and Migel Martí i Pol, *et al.*, *Teatre Lliure, 1976–1987* (Barcelona, 1987), 74–9. On Lang, see Maik Hamburger, "New Concepts of Staging *A Midsummer Night's Dream*," *SS* 40 (1987): 51–6. Paolo Emilio Poesio's *Maurizio Scaparro: l'utopia teatrale* (Venice, 1987) is valuable. On Mesguich, see essays by Dominique Goy-Blanquet and by Marvin Carlson in Kennedy 1993. All contain illustrations.

28 Aronson, "Postmodern Design" 9.

29 My comments on Csiszár's production are based on the records in Budapest, including a videotape. On Bergman see Ishrat Lindblad, *SQ* 36 (1985): 458–60; and Ann Fridén, "'Is This the Promis'd End?': Bergman's *King Lear*," in *40 Years of Mise en Scène, 1945–1985*, ed. Claude Schumacher (Dundee, 1986). On Sturua see Alma Law, "Georgia Variations," *American Theatre*, Oct. 1988: 24–6, 104–5.

30 Kott, "Prospero or the Director," *Theater* 10 (Spring 1979): 22. The issue is treated at greater length by Pia Kleber, "Theatrical Continuities in Giorgio Strehler's *The Tempest*," in Kennedy 1993, which contains further illustrations. For visual records of this production I rely on Battistini 266–9, a portfolio of Luigi Ciminaghi's photos in Girault, and the video version broadcast by the Italian network RAI in 1987. A number of set and costume designs for forty years of Strehler productions are reproduced in Fabio Battistini and Caterina Pirina (eds.), *Gli spazi dell'incanto: Bozzetti e figurini del Piccolo Teatro, 1947–1987* (Milan, 1987).

31 Crowley, in an interview with me in London, Oct. 1989.

Selected references

Collections of documents and other archival material relating to Shakespeare scenography (designs, photographs, promptbooks, videotapes, etc.) are listed in the first section, and are referred to in the text and notes by city. Major published sources are listed in the second section, which includes only those works cited frequently or those of general importance to the subject. Other references are given in full in the notes.

Scenographic archives

Berlin
Academy of the Arts (formerly West Berlin)
Deutsches Theater archive (formerly East Berlin)

Birmingham
Birmingham Shakespeare Library

Budapest
Hungarian Theatre Institute

Cambridge
Cambridgeshire Collection, Cambridge Public Library

Cologne
Theatre Museum, University of Cologne (Institut für Theaterwissenschaft, at Schloss-Wahn)

Harvard
Harvard Theatre Collection, Harvard College Library

London
National Theatre press archive
British Theatre Museum, Covent Garden

Munich
Deutsches Theater Museum

New York
Lincoln Center Library of the Performing Arts, New York Public Library

Paris

 Bibliothèque de l'Arsenal, of the Bibliothèque Nationale

Prague

 International Theatre Institute scenography collection

 National Theatre archive

Stratford, Ontario (Canada)

 Stratford Festival archive

Stratford-upon-Avon, Warwickshire (England)

 Shakespeare Centre Library

Vienna

 Austrian National Library Theatre Collection

Warsaw

 Polish Theatre Museum

 Institute of the Arts, National Academy of the Sciences

Washington, D. C.

 Folger Shakespeare Library

Published sources

Addenbrooke, David. *The Royal Shakespeare Company: The Peter Hall Years.* London, 1974

Aronson, Arnold. *American Set Design.* New York, 1985

Bablet, Denis. *Esthétique générale du décor de théâtre de 1870 à 1914.* Paris, 1965. [A 1989 reprint contains better-quality reproduction of illustrations]

 The Revolutions of Stage Design in the Twentieth Century. New York, 1977

Bartholomeusz, Dennis. *The Winter's Tale in Performance in England and America, 1611–1976.* Cambridge, 1982

Battistini, Fabio. *Giorgio Strehler.* Rome, 1980

Beauman, Sally. *The Royal Shakespeare Company: A History of Ten Decades.* Oxford, 1982

Bennett, Susan. *Theatre Audiences: A Theory of Production and Reception.* London, 1990

Berry, Ralph. *On Directing Shakespeare: Interviews with Contemporary Directors.* 2nd edn. London, 1989. [Expanded edition of 1977 collection, containing six additional interviews. A German version, *Shakespeare Inszenieren*, ed. Berry and Christian Jauslin (Basel, 1978), adds interviews with Peter Palitzsch, Peter Zadek, Wilfred Minks, and Hans Hollmann to the 1977 English contents]

Bradby, David. *Modern French Drama, 1940–1990.* 2nd edn. Cambridge, 1991

Bradby, David, and David Williams. *Directors' Theatre.* New York, 1988

Bristol, Michael D. *Shakespeare's America, America's Shakespeare.* London, 1990

Brock, Susan, and Marian J. Pringle. *The Shakespeare Memorial Theatre, 1919–1945* (Theatre in Focus). Cambridge, 1984

Brook, Peter. *The Empty Space*. New York, 1968
  The Shifting Point, 1946–1987. New York, 1987
Brown, John Russell. *Shakespeare in Performance*. London, 1966
  Free Shakespeare. London, 1974
Burian, Jarka. *The Scenography of Josef Svoboda*. Middletown, Conn., 1971
Carlson, Marvin. *Places of Performance: The Semiotics of Theatre Architecture*. Ithaca,
  1989
  Theatre Semiotics: Signs of Life. Bloomington, 1990
Chambers, Colin. *Other Spaces: New Theatre and the RSC*. London, 1980
Craig, Edward Gordon. *On the Art of the Theatre*. London, 1911
  Towards a New Theatre. London, 1913
  Scene. New York, 1968 [1923]
Crosse, Gordon. *Shakespearean Playgoing, 1890–1952*. London, 1953
David, Richard. *Shakespeare in the Theatre*. Cambridge, 1978
de Grazia, Margreta. *Shakespeare Verbatim: The Reproduction of Authenticity and the
  1790 Apparatus*. Oxford, 1991
Dickinson, Thomas H., ed. *The Theatre in a Changing Europe*. New York, 1937
Elam, Keir. *The Semiotics of Theatre and Drama*. London, 1980
Esslin, Martin. *The Field of Drama: How the Signs of Drama Create Meaning on Stage and
  Screen*. London, 1987
Foulkes, Richard, ed. *Shakespeare and the Victorian Stage*. Cambridge, 1986
Fuerst, Walter René, and Samuel J. Hume. *Twentieth-Century Stage Decoration*. 2 vols.
  New York, 1929
Girault, Alain, ed. *Photographier le théâtre*. Avignon, 1982
Goodwin, John, ed. *British Theatre Design: The Modern Age*. London, 1989
Grady, Hugh. *The Modernist Shakespeare: Critical Texts in a Material World*. Oxford,
  1991
Greenwald, Michael L. *Directions by Indirections: John Barton of the Royal Shakespeare
  Company*. Newark, 1985
Guthrie, Tyrone. *A Life in the Theatre*. New York, 1959
Hainaux, René, ed. *Stage Design Throughout the World*. 4 vols. New York, 1956–76
Hawkes, Terence. *That Shakespeherian Rag: Essays on a Critical Process*. London,
  1986
Hirst, David L. *The Tempest: Text and Performance*. London, 1984
Holderness, Graham, ed. *The Shakespeare Myth*. Manchester, 1988
Hughes, Alan. *Henry Irving, Shakespearean*. Cambridge. 1981
Innes, Christopher. *Edward Gordon Craig*. Cambridge, 1983
Jacobs, Margaret, and John Warren, eds. *Max Reinhardt: The Oxford Symposium*.
  Oxford, 1986
Jacquot, Jean. *Shakespeare en France: mises en scène d'hier et d'aujourd'hui*. Paris, 1964
Jakobson, Roman, and Morris Halle. *Fundamentals of Language*. 2nd edn. The
  Hague, 1975
Kennedy, Dennis. *Granville Barker and the Dream of Theatre*. Cambridge, 1985
  (ed.). *Foreign Shakespeare: Contemporary Performance*. Cambridge, 1993
Kott, Jan. *Shakespeare Our Contemporary*. Trans. Boleslaw Taborski. New York,
  1966

Larson, Orville K. *Scene Design in the American Theatre from 1915 to 1960*. Fayetteville, Ark., 1989

Leacroft, Richard and Helen. *Theatre and Playhouse*. London, 1984

Leiter, Samuel L., ed. *Shakespeare Around the Globe*: *A Guide to Notable Postwar Revivals*. New York, 1986

Levenson, Jill L. *Romeo and Juliet* (Shakespeare in Performance). Manchester, 1987

MacGowan, Kenneth, and Robert Edmond Jones. *Continental Stagecraft*. New York, 1922

Mazer, Cary M. *Shakespeare Refashioned*: *Elizabethan Plays on Edwardian Stages*. Ann Arbor, 1981

Merchant, W. Moelwyn. *Shakespeare and the Artist*. London, 1959

Mikotowicz, Thomas J. *Theatrical Designers*: *An International Biographical Dictionary*. New York, 1992

Mullin, Michael, with Karen Morris Muriello, ed. *Theatre at Stratford-upon-Avon*: *A Catalogue-Index to Productions of the Shakespeare Memorial/Royal Shakespeare Theatre, 1879–1978*. 2 vols. Westport, Conn., 1980. [A supplement covering 1978–1990 is due in 1993.]

Odell, G. C. D. *Shakespeare from Betterton to Irving*. 2 vols. New York, 1920

Oenslager, Donald. *Stage Design*: *Four Centuries of Scenic Innovation*. New York, 1975

Osborne, John. *The Meiningen Court Theatre, 1866–1890*. Cambridge, 1988

Patterson, Michael. *The Revolution in German Theatre, 1900–1933*. London, 1981

Pavis, Patrice. *Dictionnaire du théâtre*: *termes et concepts de l'analyse théâtrale*. Paris, 1980
Languages of the Stage: *Essays in the Semiology of the Theatre*. New York, 1982
Theatre at the Crossroads of Culture. London, 1992

Payne, Darwin Reid. *The Scenographic Imagination*. Carbondale, 1981

Ripley, John. *Julius Caesar on Stage in England and America, 1599–1973*. Cambridge, 1980

Rischbieter, Henning, ed. *Art and the Stage in the Twentieth Century*. Greenwich, Conn., 1970

Rosenfeld, Sybil. *A Short History of Scene Design in Great Britain*. Oxford, 1973

Rowell, George, and Anthony Jackson. *The Repertory Movement*: *A History of Regional Theatre in Britain*. Cambridge, 1984

Russell, Douglas A. *Theatrical Style*: *A Visual Approach to the Theatre*. Palo Alto, 1976

Senelick, Laurence. *Gordon Craig's Moscow Hamlet*: *A Reconstruction*. Westport, Conn., 1982

Shattuck, Charles H. *Shakespeare on the American Stage*. 2 vols. Washington, 1976–90

Simonson, Lee. *The Stage Is Set*. New York, 1932

Smith, Ronn. *American Set Design 2*. New York, 1991

Sontag, Susan. *On Photography*. New York, 1977

Speaight, Robert. *Shakespeare on the Stage*. Boston, 1973

Stanislavsky, Konstantin. *My Life in Art*. Trans. J. J. Robbins. New York, 1956 [1924]

Styan, J. L. *The Shakespeare Revolution*. Cambridge, 1977

Taylor, Gary. *Reinventing Shakespeare*: *A Cultural History, from the Restoration to the Present*. New York, 1989

Trewin, J. C. *Shakespeare on the English Stage, 1900–1964.* London, 1964

Wells, Stanley. *Royal Shakespeare: Four Major Productions at Stratford-upon-Avon.* Manchester, 1977

Willett, John. *The Theatre of the Weimar Republic.* New York, 1988

Williams, Simon. *Shakespeare on the German Stage, 1586–1914.* Cambridge, 1990

Worrall, Nick. *Modernism to Realism on the Soviet Stage: Tairov – Vakhtangov – Okhlopkov.* Cambridge, 1989

Index

Shakespeare's plays are listed by title; the major productions discussed are further identified by directors and dates. Page numbers in **bold** type refer to illustrations. Elementary biographical information is given in the entries for the chief designers and directors treated in the text.